Clinical Supervision in Latin America

Maria del Pilar Grazioso • Rodney K. Goodyear
Maritza Gallardo-Cooper
Hector Fernandez-Alvarez • Carol A. Falender
Ana Alicia Cobar
Editors

Clinical Supervision in Latin America

Springer

Editors
Maria del Pilar Grazioso
Asociación Proyecto Aiglé Guatemala
Universidad del Valle de Guatemala
Guatemala City, Guatemala

Maritza Gallardo-Cooper
Clinical and School Psychology
Nova Southeastern University
Fort Lauderdale, FL, USA

Carol A. Falender
Department of Psychology
Pepperdine University
Malibu, CA, USA

Rodney K. Goodyear
North University Hall
University of Redlands
Redlands, CA, USA

Hector Fernandez-Alvarez
Fundación Aiglé, Buenos Aires
Argentina

Ana Alicia Cobar
Department of Psychology
Universidad del Valle de Guatemala
Guatemala City, Guatemala

ISBN 978-3-031-82372-5 ISBN 978-3-031-82373-2 (eBook)
https://doi.org/10.1007/978-3-031-82373-2

This Springer imprint is published by the registered company Springer Nature Switzerland AG
The registered company address is: Gewerbestrasse 11, 6330 Cham, Switzerland

The original version of the book has been revised. A correction to this book can be found at https://doi.org/10.1007/978-3-031-82373-2_14

This book is dedicated to all of those who have contributed to the development of clinical supervision practices in Latin America; particularly to the memory of our dear Dr. Hector Fernandez-Alvarez who left us a legacy full of wisdom, hope, and encouragement. Through his integrative spirit may clinical supervision continue to develop throughout our worldwide community.

Acknowledgments

Although clinical supervision is more similar than different across the world, there are regional and country-specific differences that arise from culture, law, and policy. International conferences such as the International Interdisciplinary Conference on Clinical Supervision (IICCS) and the Society for Psychotherapy Research provide opportunities to understand and discuss these similarities and differences. As well, those opportunities are occurring in the literature, which has featured internationally focused works, including supervision books like those of Cutcliffe, Sloan, & Barshaw (2018); Watkins (1997); and Watkins and Milne (2014). Largely absent from these international conversations, though, has been a comprehensive examination of clinical supervision in Latin America.

This is a large region comprised of a number of countries that are bound by similar yet diverse nuances of language and culture. The exciting developments in supervision concepts and practices that are occurring in those countries have been largely unacknowledged. We were motivated to develop this volume in order to give voice to supervision scholars who have been largely overlooked in the mainstream literature, both to present their ideas and provide opportunities for the possible synergies that can result.

We editors faithfully believed in the power of genuine collaboration, respect for cultural and linguistic diversity, value to differential thinking, and commitment for the advancement of clinical supervision in the helping professions. We are thankful to the authors who made such rich contributions to this volume. Consequently, these voices resulted in rich chorus of creative and unique ideas, scientific knowledge, and clinical practices that supported the pedagogy of professional formation and bridged the sometimes-vast geographical and cultural differences among us.

Challenged by the aspiration of expanding the audience to Spanish and English speaking professionals, we relied on bilingual school psychology doctoral students from Nova Southeastern University who assisted with Spanish to English chapter translations during the preliminary stages of this volume. Our heartfelt thanks for the hard work and enthusiasm consistently evident with the following graduate students: Daniela Constanza Torres, Angélica Rodríguez, María Alejandra Chávez, María Gabriela Rangel Salcedo, Ricardo Antonio Mogo, Verónica L. Marí Álvarez, and Daniela Di Carlo. Our appreciation to Angelly González from Proyecto Aiglé Guatemala who devoted her technical expertise to enhance our final manuscript.

None of this could have been possible without all the learnings from mentors, colleagues, supervisors, supervisees, and clients who during many hours of clinical supervision have taught us and continue to teach us to be reflective and open to the meaningful practices that can enhance the services we offer.

Thank you to our families, who during many days and hours have seen us devote our work toward completion aiming at contributing with a broader perspective of what Latin American clinical supervision can share.

About this Book

The edited book, Clinical Supervision in Latin America: Voices from the Field, addresses the current realities of clinical supervision in Argentina, Brazil, Chile, Colombia, Cuba, Guatemala, Mexico, Puerto Rico, and the United States. Each chapter is structured to include relevant content about the formation of psychotherapists and clinicians through training and supervision. Authors examine the focus of programs that support advanced university training of psychologists, code of ethics that govern such practice, regulatory professional bodies established, and training formats. Through the lenses of culture and diversity, the authors analyze how these factors influence practice as they shape training, confront professional challenges, and create solutions in their communities. Attention is given to the modalities used to provide supervision in both individual and group formats; face-to-face and/or virtual; and other technologies that allow supervision to be offered remotely. The various chapters share the mechanisms used to ensure the well-being of clients, the opportunities available to supervisors who wish to receive ongoing training, as well as the state of the art of supervision and supervisory research that have been conducted and/or are in process. The models of supervision utilized in these different countries are explained, emphasizing the characteristics of each one, such as issues of origin, dynamics in the development of the supervisory alliance, and the repair to ruptures in the supervisory relationship. These frameworks include the type and quality of feedback provided to those being supervised and the resources they rely on to support it, contextualized to the needs of each country, so that they are culturally relevant while aligning with the knowledge, expertise, and experience of the authors. In this manner, supervisors from these countries rely on professional resources based on evaluation instruments, for both the supervisor and supervisee, the self-report, the verification scale, and direct observation. This book is unique in that it is the first attempt to explore the field of clinical supervision and professional formation in the psychological field from the perspective of several Latin America countries. The book reflects, therefore, an appreciation of the current state of clinical supervision in each participating country, where strengths, challenges, problems, achievements, and processes are candidly revealed. Authors capture the value and implications of going against culture by daring to continue blazing a trail. The resulting exploration leads to a look into the future and some of the actions considered to continue the growth and development of clinical supervision in Latin America.

Contents

Editors and Contributors

About the Editors

Ana Alicia Cobar holds a PhD in Applied Psychology, a master's degree in Psychological Counseling and Mental Health, and a bachelor's degree in psychology from the Universidad del Valle de Guatemala. Specialization in Family and Couple Psychotherapy with Cognitive Behavioral Orientation from Fundación Aiglé, Argentina and Universidad de Maimonides, Argentina. Internships at the Ackerman Family Institute in New York. Director, teacher, and supervisor in the Department of Psychological Counseling and Mental Health. Professor in the Department of Applied Neuropsychology and in the master's degree in Community Counseling at the Universidad del Valle de Guatemala. She is a member of the Aiglé Guatemala Project Association where she conducts her private practice as a psychotherapist and counselor for adults, couples, families, as well as providing clinical supervision. Areas of interest in research and publication are counseling, well-being and quality of life, self-management competencies, clinical supervision, crisis care, and expressive arts interventions. Member of the College of Psychologists of Guatemala, Inter-American Society of Psychology, Guatemala Chapter and American Psychological Association. Emails: aacoma@proyectoaigle.org.gt aacobar@uvg.edu.gt

Carol A. Falender has co-authored/edited seven books on clinical supervision and consultation and has presented workshops on clinical supervision, consultation, multicultural supervision, and decolonizing supervision. She led APA-accredited internship programs for more than 20 years and was chair of the American Psychological Association's (APA) Supervisory Guidelines Working Group. She received an APA Presidential Citation for his groundbreaking contributions to the theory and practice of clinical supervision, nationally and internationally, and received the APA's 2018 Distinguished Professional Contributions to Psychology Education and Training Award, and in 2023, the 29 Division Distinguished Award, Society for the Advancement of Psychotherapy, the Distinguished Award for the International Advancement of Psychotherapy. Dr. Falender is an adjunct professor at Pepperdine University; Clinical Professor, University of California, Los Angeles, Department of Psychology. Email: cfalender@gmail.com

Hector Fernandez-Alvarez (1944–2023) obtained a PhD in Psychology, and was a psychotherapist, founder, and president of the Aiglé Foundation; since 1977 dedicated his work on education and training, research, and mental health assistance programs. He directed the Foundation's Center for Research in Psychotherapy and developed a Supervision Program based on his experience as a therapist and supervisor, the Specialization Career in Cognitive Psychotherapy of the Aiglé Foundation and at the National University of Mar del Plata and was a postgraduate professor at Argentine and foreign universities. He wrote, among others, the books Fundamentals of an Integrative Model in Psychotherapy; Intervention Guide in Personality Disorders; Integration in psychotherapy and social anxiety, conceptualization, and treatment. Among the many recognitions, he received the 2022 Distinguished Award for the International Advancement of Psychotherapy from Division 29 of the American Psychological Association (APA) and the International Sigmund Freud Award for Psychotherapy 2002 of the City of Vienna from the World Council for Psychotherapy (WCP). He chaired the Inter-American Society of Psychology (IAPA) and the Latin American chapter of the Society for Psychotherapy Research (SPR).

Maritza Gallardo-Cooper is a faculty member in the Department of Clinical and School Psychology at Nova Southeastern University, Florida. She has an extensive professional career working in the public and private sectors as a practitioner, supervisor, and administrator. Her professional experience includes the development of outpatient and residential clinics, school psychological services, prevention programs, clinical supervision, and internship programs. She has published several articles/chapters as well as co-authored two books on counseling Latinx populations in the USA. She has received recognition from the professional community for her leadership, innovation, and clinical performance. Dr. Gallardo-Cooper is a graduate from the University of Puerto Rico, received her master's degree from the University of Houston and her doctorate from the University of Florida. Her professional interests include therapeutic assessments, psychocultural factors in prevention and intervention, crisis intervention in schools, and bilingual practice and supervision. Email: mg1011@nova.edu

Rodney K. Goodyear is a professor emeritus at the University of Southern California, where he directed the APA-accredited doctoral program in counseling psychology for two decades, and at the University of Redlands. He has been a member of the American Psychological Association's Commission on Accreditation, past president of the Society for the Advancement of Psychotherapy, APA Division 29, and served on the APA's Board of Educational Affairs (BEA) Oversight Guidelines Working Group. In 2015 he received the APA Distinguished Professional Contributions to Psychology Education and Training Award, and in 2018 the Distinguished Award for the International Advancement of Psychotherapy, Society for the Advancement of Psychotherapy, APA Division 29. He is co-author of Fundamentals of Clinical Supervision (2019), now in its sixth edition, and author of numerous chapters and articles on supervision. His work is increasingly focused on the international arena. Email: rodk.goodyear@gmail.com

Maria del Pilar Grazioso has expertise in pediatric development and learning, community mental health, prevention, gender, multiculturalism, higher education, psychotherapy, counseling, and supervision. She has held administrative, research, teaching, and clinical positions, as well as professional duties in higher education and private practice. She developed graduate programs and began formal training in supervision at the university level in Guatemala. She has publications and recognition for her leadership and contributions to the development of Psychology having leadership positions at the international level. She is currently co-coordinator of the Aiglé Guatemala Project Association and is a researcher affiliated with the Universidad del Valle de Guatemala and Maya Health Alliance/Wuqukawoc. Email: mpgrazioso@proyectoaigle.org.gt

Contributors

Maira Anaya-López The Building Bridges Collective, University of California, Santa Barbara, CA, USA

Patricia Arredondo Arredondo Advisory Group, Phoenix, AZ, USA

María Alejandra Auyón Asociación Proyecto Aigle Guatemala, Universidad del Valle de Guatemala, Guatemala City, Guatemala

Janaína Bianca Barletta University of São Paulo, São Paulo, Brazil

Carmem Beatriz Neufeld University of São Paulo, São Paulo, Brazil

Ana Alicia Cobar Asociación Proyecto Aigle Guatemala, Universidad del Valle de Guatemala, Guatemala City, Guatemala

María Antonia Carbajal Godínez Universidad Nacional Autónoma de México, Mexico City, Mexico

Andrés J. Consoli The Building Bridges Collective, University of California, Santa Barbara, CA, USA

Carol A. Falender Pepperdine University, Malibu, CA, USA

University of California, Los Angeles, Los Angeles, CA, USA

Hector Fernandez-Alvarez Fundación Aiglé, Buenos Aires, Argentina

Iliana Flores The Building Bridges Collective, University of California, Santa Barbara, CA, USA

Maritza Gallardo-Cooper Department of Clinical and School Psychology, Nova Southeastern University, Ft. Lauderdale, Florica, USA

Keishalee Gómez Arroyo Institute of Psychological Research, University of Puerto Rico, Río Piedras Campus, San Juan, Puerto Rico

Verónica Ruiz González Universidad Nacional Autónoma de México, Mexico City, Mexico

Marielly González Chardón Ponce Health Sciences University, Ponce, Puerto Rico

Rodney K. Goodyear University of Southern California, Los Angeles, CA, USA

School of Education, University of Redlands, Redlands, CA, USA

Maria del Pilar Grazioso Asociación Proyecto Aigle Guatemala, Universidad del Valle de Guatemala, Guatemala City, Guatemala

Diana Kirszman Fundación Aiglé, Buenos Aires, Argentina

Isabel López The Building Bridges Collective, University of California, Santa Barbara, CA, USA

Yaritza López Robledo Ponce Health Sciences University, Ponce, Puerto Rico

Meri Lubina Asociación Proyecto Aigle Guatemala, Universidad del Valle de Guatemala, Guatemala City, Guatemala

Mariana Maristany Fundación Aiglé, Buenos Aires, Argentina

Fundación Aiglé, CIUDAD DE BUENOS AIR, Argentina

Evelyn A. Melendez The Building Bridges Collective, University of California, Santa Barbara, CA, USA

Hiradith Menéndez Ponce Health Sciences University, Ponce, Puerto Rico

Mónica Novoa Gómez Fundación Universitaria Konrad Lorenz, Bogotá, Colombia

María Inés Pesqueira Banderas Centro MIP, Santiago, Chile

Norka Polanco Frontera Ponce Health Sciences University, Ponce, Puerto Rico

Ivonne Ramírez Clavería Centro MIP, Santiago, Chile

Yvette Ramírez-Gutiérrez The Building Bridges Collective, University of California, Santa Barbara, CA, USA

Marcos Reyes Estrada Albizu University San Juan Campus, San Juan, Puerto Rico

José Domingo Salvo Rivera Centro MIP, Santiago, Chile

Himadhari Sharma The Building Bridges Collective, University of California, Santa Barbara, CA, USA

Antonio Tena-Suck Universidad Iberoamericana, Mexico City, Mexico

Bárbara Zas Ros Center for Psychological and Sociological Research and University of Havana, Havana, Cuba

Part I
Outlining Clinical Supervision in Latin America

Introduction: Supervision in Latin America

Patricia Arredondo

To begin with, I would like to congratulate all of the contributors who have opened up a discussion of a topic of immense importance in the practice, training, and education of psychotherapy in Latin America and worldwide. Based on what has been written, it can be said that there is a broad space to create extensive discourse for the recognition of supervision in clinical psychology. It is essential to recognize the potential and the emanating benefits of preparing this book. For each chapter, approaches, models, and structures for the practice of supervision are described. Instruction or training is addressing ethics, evaluation, regulations, practice, and the formalization of supervision as a field. With each of the narratives prepared, we become aware of the many possibilities for the development of supervision in each country.

The authors (primarily women), comment on the context in which supervision takes place. These include the cultural, sociohistorical, and professional, and how these affect and/or influence, different forms of preparation for clinical practice, in particular. There are references to different types of training programs, from undergraduate to postgraduate and continuing education. All of the chapter authors make reference to the cultures and diversity of their respective countries because of historical facts that have left imprints throughout. All countries have people from diverse heritages including European, Indigenous, African, Asian, and so forth. I will also comment on the particulars and perspectives of supervision that are described for the various countries. I will point to the similarities and differences. As is noted, there are different resources and support in each country as well as intentionality to regulate the preparation and practices of psychotherapists. Not all is uniform. The "licenciatura", equivalent to a bachelor's degree although a five-year program of study, does not signal that an individual is prepared to be a clinician, much less a supervisor. But at the same time, there is a great need to have a

P. Arredondo (✉)
Arredondo Advisory Group, Phoenix, AZ, USA

M. P. Grazioso et al. (eds.), *Clinical Supervision in Latin America*,
https://doi.org/10.1007/978-3-031-82373-2_1

profession of supervision to ensure that supervisors are well-prepared to benefit from the work they undertake with clients.

At the end of my introduction to the various chapters, I shall also discuss in brief, the multicultural models of supervision that have been recognized in the United States. These models were informed by the Multicultural Counseling Competencies (Arredondo et al., 1996; Sue et al., 1992) based on the premises that all cultures have considerable variability that needs to be considered, although the therapist may think she is like her client. I believe there are some learnings from the multicultural competencies that can inform psychotherapy and supervision practices in Latin America. In my Spanish narrative I used feminine terms in relation to the supervisors because most of the authors for this book are women. In the various chapters, there is no mention of the percentage of men and women who are clinicians and/or supervisors. This is an important point, because in the U.S.A., there are many more women preparing at the master's and doctoral levels in clinical psychology and psychoanalysis. In this last section, I will write about the benefits and challenges for women as supervisees and supervisors.

There are eight country-specific chapters, I will comment about each country and their approaches to supervision and clinical psychology. There are challenges in each country at various levels, university, political, and more as the authors indicate. These too will be discussed.

The Countries

Argentina We begin with the country with a long history of teaching and practice of psychotherapy, and as mentioned by the authors, *Argentina has had a culture of psychotherapy, very broad and significant* (Maristany & Kirszman, 2024, p. 2). In terms of supervision, they comment on the cultural context and diversity, the practice of supervision, and looking toward the future. They also comment on investigations that have been carried out in order to learn more about the functions of supervision in various contexts. What we learn is that supervision is embedded and thus advanced in different aspects of preparation for trainees, to advanced levels in undergraduate and postgraduate phases. Specifically, in psychoanalysis, the analysts play two roles, that of analyst and supervisor. This perhaps is an exception from other applications of psychotherapy because supervision is administered didactically and through actual treatment or practice. The Aiglé Foundation began a systematic program with four guiding principles (p. 12):

- The importance of providing information, support, and orientation as well as guidance for assessment.
- The weight of the relationship between the supervisor and supervisees.
- The benefits and values provide not only the generic principles for the application not only to personal and individual aspects not only for the supervisor but also the supervisee

- Consideration of the sociocultural context and elements.

In 2023, the formation of the university's Clinical Supervision program was formalized.

Brazil Supervision in Brazil has roots in the formation of clinical psychologists, but at the same time, it does not have a particular approach; preparation is manifested in different ways. Neufeld et al. (2021) present facts from various studies about the practice of psychotherapy. In one survey, it was found that therapist's value being emphatic instead of resolving issues. This attitude likely extends to supervision as well. As it relates to these comments, Bakos and Kristensen (2013) state that the Brazilian culture is pragmatic and that the cultural context has an influence on supervision practices.

The chapter authors comment about the development and practice of supervision. As for the developmental process, several surveys were undertaken to learn about how supervisors had been prepared. In one national survey to which there were 180 respondents, 27.8% indicated that they had received "some type of preparation in order to function as a supervisor" (p. 11). In Brazil, there is no certification for supervisors.

Similar to the other chapters about supervision in Latin America, Neufield and Barletta describe examples of supervision at the graduate and postgraduate levels. Again, these approaches can be individual, group, and at times, the training follows the training of clinical psychologists. In a country as vast as Brazil, with different regions and cultures in the different regions, there is great variability to the practice of supervision. The authors comment about the challenges that exist in terms of the practice of supervision. First, as has been mentioned, there are few training programs and few institutions where one can study. Another challenge mentioned is the perspective at the national level about psychotherapy and supervision. What happens is that there is a disagreement about the importance about the need to prepare people professionally, not only for the experience of therapist and supervisor alike. Although there is great interest in the preparation of supervisors, there are insufficient opportunities.

Colombia Dr. Monica Novoa Gómez describes the current state of affairs for clinical supervision in the context of clinical psychology in Colombia. She comments on the formation or development of psychologists, the situation regarding supervision, and the challenges faced by the profession. In terms of psychological theories, she indicates that these are applied in practice and that there are various forms of applications as this relates to the relationship between the supervisor and supervisee. She states that supervision provides support, evaluation, and instruction in the competencies necessary regarding supervision, knowledge about what it means to be a supervisor, and the attitudes necessary to be open to the differences that patients/clients bring based on their heritages, lived experiences, and unique situations. In short, the supervisor is a guide and also a collaborator. Supposedly, she (the supervisor), has the experience and knowledge, that can be transmitted to the trainee who sees her supervisor as a model. She describes the theme regarding the relationship as “a relationship between colleagues” (p. 12).

Colombia, like the other countries, has practices for supervision on an individual basis, in a group format, in-person, and virtual. Particular to Colombia, Dr. Novoa Gomez states that the development of regulations for supervision are just beginning to evolve in the country and indicates that it is not at the level of attention that it deserves to have. In Colombia, there is also a requirement for social service for students.

Dr. Novoa Gomez also conducted an investigations involving supervisors in 24 programs. Her findings indicate that (a) There is preparation for supervisors but perhaps not full preparation; (b) Only 48.9% have knowledge of the law; and (c) There is a need to disseminate the competencies for supervision. There is no accreditation for clinical supervisors, “leaving criteria at the individual program level” (p. 4). At the same time, there is no evaluation of competencies in the process of supervision (p. 19).

Chile The chapter about Chile describes the cultural, professional, and regulatory context for the practice of supervision. It needs to be mentioned that Chile was the first country in Latin America to establish the profession of psychology in 1946. With respect to clinical supervision, the author offers particulars related to this theme. First, she states that supervision is required in the preparation of psychotherapists at the postgraduate level and when it comes to specialty preparation, and that it is highly valued throughout the country. This commitment is not the same in all of the other countries. The second point is that clinical supervision is optional “beyond one’s preparation” (p. 1). In terms of culture and diversity, there are several points to take into account that demonstrate the inequities in the county, particularly as it relates to access to services as well as the study of psychology. Contributing to these inequities is the geography of the country. There are regions throughout the country where there are differences in languages spoken, climate, and cultures within cultures that are often isolated. The social, historical, geographical, and political context affect people and their well-being, and of course their access to healthcare services.

It is also mentioned that there is dissonance because Chile is ranked 24th of 159 countries based on available data, with great inequities (Lambeth et al., 2019). In general, there is little contact among people from different socioeconomic levels and when it comes to psychotherapy and supervision, this is noteworthy. Although there is a recognition of the multiple aspects of human diversity, not all identities that are “different” are accepted. There are laws in place to protect persons with disabilities since 2015, and these are estimated to be about 13% of the population. According to the authors of this chapter, there are public policies “designed to advance inclusion and there has been an increase in the approval of laws that protect the rights of people with disabilities and favor inclusion”. For example, public law 21.015 (Bibliotca del Congreso Nacional de Chile, 2017) established set-aside positions for persons with disabilities and has sanctions for employers who do not fulfill this obligation (p. 9). With respect to the LGBTQ+ population, private organizations have demonstrated their support and have prepared cultural competencies applicable in psychotherapy. Another positive condition is that "there are supervision-related initiatives and study groups that have been established specifically to address cultural diversity and sexual orientation" (p. 10).

In terms of the development of supervisors, there are provisions for preparation. Preparation may be either direct or indirect. In terms of direct supervision, this means that psychotherapy can be observed through a two-way mirror and immediate feedback be provided. The clinical applications are adapted for the context and objectives of the supervision and the supervisor takes the role of guide for the process.

The preparation of supervisors has three approaches that have become formalized over time. The first is called self-learning and applies to the first supervisors in Chile. "The self-taught supervisors have a particular academic and clinical trajectory in addition to validation and approval of colleagues who vouch for them" (p. 13). The second approach is called tutorial development and takes place under the supervision of two or more supervisors. In these situations, there is trust among the professionals, the supervisors and the supervisees alike. The third format refers to the formal training programs. These are structured programs and include theoretical foundations, supervisory practices, ethics, and meta-supervision. With these forms of development, supervisors are best prepared for contemporary needs and situations.

Cuba Supervision in Cuba is discussed by Barbara Zas Ros with attention to the cultural, professional, and regulatory context. She states that currently there is not a formal recognition of psychological supervision in professional practices and that the practice of supervision is isolated and rarely practiced. When it takes place at an institutional level, it is free. Because the practice of supervision is not systematized or structured, how often it takes place cannot be reported. In terms of supervisory preparation, Zas Roa reports that at the pre-graduate level, the introduction of supervision is taught in the course, Introduction to Psychology for students in the psychology department at the Universidad de la Habana. Additionally, during the time at the undergraduate or pre-graduate level, students can contract for four supervision sessions as part of an assignment. It is also possible through an optional course to have ten supervisory sessions. In terms of postgraduate experiences, Zas Roa states that there is a proposal to have a course for the development of supervisors, but there is not a high demand.

Similar to other countries, there are models and approaches to psychological supervision. In Cuba, an operative model has been rolled out based on a 10-year study. At the same time, it is necessary to have a developmental process for supervision in the country and the preparation of accredited supervisors. If these premises are accepted, Zas Roa indicates this will be a contribution for "the betterment of the quality of available and free services that will be a positive experience in the country" (p. 2).

Guatemala With academic initiatives and with the practice of psychotherapy in Guatemala, Guatemalan psychologists have taken their country to be a center in the development and practice of supervision for clinical psychology. The authors (Lubina et al., 2024), from the Asociación Proyecto Aigle and Universidad del Valle, Guatemala, provide us with "An approximation of clinical supervision in the social justice context in Guatemala". Here I cite the themes of social justice and multiculturalism that are prevalent in the foundation of psychology in the country. The authors indicate that there is an integrated focus including "liberating practices and self-determination" and the development of intersectionality of supervision. In this chapter, in particular, there is mention of intersectionality and multiculturalism. The vignettes in this chapter introduce different contexts and perspectives that are part of a process of development of trainees or the person being supervised. The role that is taken by the supervisor to guide the discussion, attending to the emotions and the case or situation being discussed.

The themes of culture and diversity are very present in Guatemala. For within this country of 17.4 million persons, there are more women, younger people and socioeconomic diversity, access to formal public education, opportunities for employment, and of course different ways of living in rural and urban environments. Within the population there are many languages spoken and situations and locations where people cannot be cared for in their primary language. This is to say that there are barriers to psychotherapy and supervision in terms of the different languages, policies in place, and ways of living.

In Guatemala, as in other countries, there are various approaches to the practice of supervision and to training. For supervision, there are different formats—group, hybrid, and in-person. At the same time there are challenges that may affect the confidentiality and type of care, and the relationships among individuals. But it is the supervisors that carry the primary responsibility to "take care of and monitor the well-being of clients and the competency development of those receiving supervision" (p. 15). In this sense, the authors indicate that the supervisors have the role of "guardians of the profession" (p. 15).

Mexico To begin with, it is necessary to speak of the culture, diversity, size, history, and position of Mexico on the global stage. In the era of the Spanish conquest, Mexico played a large role in the development of all Latin America, as we know it today. Perhaps the footprints and fingerprints of the Virreinato (monarchy) persist with the visible challenges and inequalities that are found in this country of 132 million persons. The majority are women and persons speaking 55 distinct Indigenous languages in addition to Spanish. It is observed that although some of the richest men in the world are found in Mexico, the World Bank (2023) states that 43.9% of Mexican people live in poverty and 8.5% in extreme poverty. These data points, with their diversity and inequalities, demonstrate how barriers to education and access to social and health services affect mental health. Additionally, violence against women and feminicide are forms of violence that affect everyone.

Psychology is viewed like other health sciences. The difficulties for people in general to have a professional career—educational at the postgraduate level, in particular—affect those who become clinical psychologists. According to the authors, "There are 12 psychologists for every 1000 persons" (p. 2). In terms of psychotherapists, it is fewer because professionals have to complete a postgraduate specialty in order to earn their credentials for professional practice.

There has been an interest in supervision in Mexico since 1980, and research regarding the development or formation of clinical psychologists and psychotherapists. Attention was given to the curriculum or program of studies and changes were made to add the process of supervision in order to heighten the responsibility for communities.

Nowadays, two models of practice are followed; one is called the "First Generation" and the other, the "Second Generation". According to Consolí and colleagues (2017), the "Second Generation" is broader and perhaps more relevant because in addition to attention to theories of supervision, the practical skills, and the roles of the therapist and client, the model of contextual psychotherapy is applied. Additionally, models of the "Second Generation" emphasize competencies that give importance to values, strengths, challenges, attitudes, and knowledge in order to develop clinical skills. These models are based on ones applied in the United States and are called Multicultural Counseling Competencies (Sue et al., 1992).

In Mexico, there are many professional associations and universities that represent the particular interests of these organizations and these relate to psychology. In other countries, professional associations are not mentioned so frequently, although there probably exist similar ones. In Mexico there is (all translated from Spanish names and titles), the Society of Mexican Psychology, the National College/University of Psychology, the National Federation of Colleges/Universities, Societies and Associations of Mexican Psychologists, the Mexican Association of Alternative Psychology, the Mexican Association of Social Psychology, the Mexican Association of School Psychology/Counseling and Psychotherapy, the Mexican Association of Family Therapy, and many others. There is an irony that there are so many professional associations because of what has been mentioned as the low number of psychologists, and also the "great indifference and shortcomings in terms of the practices of psychotherapy—in terms of the minimal formal preparation" (p. 4). One association in particular, the Association of School Psychology/Counseling and Psychotherapy, has a relationship with the National Board of Certified Counselors (NBCC) in the United States.

At the same time, there is no formal preparation of certification in supervision. The supervisors maintain responsibility to provide the development of others outside of their specialty areas. In academic programs, there is greater hope for the development of processes and training to enhance practices of supervision.

Puerto Rico Of all of the countries presented in this book, Puerto Rico has the most alignment with many of the processes and practices of training, regulations for clinical psychology, and advances with the development and opportunities for supervision similar to those of the U.S.A. The doctoral programs, accredited by the Council of Accreditation aligned with APA, are also evident with the Universidad de Carlos Albízu, founded in Puerto Rico. Also, postgraduate programs have a depth that aligns with the APA Competency-Based model. This model includes the application of theory to practices, integrating the ethical and scientific standards.

In Puerto Rico, the four principal models are recognized, inclusive of the Second-Generation principles and practices (Consolí et al., 2017) (previously mentioned). There are three supervision approaches—individual, group, and distance, adapting the use of the context where the supervision takes place, the resources available, and the specifications of the given program. The techniques and methods of supervision that are used, recommended by APA, include taping of the supervision, live supervision, and observation of the therapy underway through a two-way mirror. Each university has its preferred format. Additionally, the preparation of supervisors, adheres to the APA guidelines, integrating ethics and cultural competencies. Also, there are processes to evaluate the process of supervision itself. The latter take place independent of the program and in a summative format.

In Puerto Rico, the practice of supervision is regulated by the Office of Regulations and Certification of Healthcare Professionals and the Board of Psychology. All of this is supported by the law that requires that it is necessary to be licensed in order to be a practicing professional. Also, the authors of this chapter state that the preparation of supervisors is minimal and offer specific recommendations. For example, they suggest continuing education to reinforce supervisory skills over the lifespan. They also recommend training to address specific populations including the LGBTQI+ persons with disabilities, and also in specific clinical areas. At this time, it is possible to access continuing education through APA coursework but only online.

Supervision Models Outside of Latin America

Taking a quick look to the supervision models and practices in the United States, it occurs to me that the focus on multicultural counseling competencies may be an approach to elevate the context for supervision in Latin America. I would like to comment in brief about supervision models based on research (Falender et al., 2012; Field et al., 2010; Inman & DeBoer Krieder, 2013) that describe criteria and dynamics between the supervisor and supervisee; these deserve attention.

According to the Multicultural Counseling Competencies (Sue et al., 1992; Arredondo et al., 1996), each supervisor and supervisee arrive to the supervision encounter with their own sense of intersecting identities. This signifies that there are similarities and differences between people who will work together in formal groups. Therefore, from the beginning the supervisor has to present this reality in the professional relationship. For example, in Mexico, perhaps the supervisor was born in Mexico City and studied at the National University of Mexico (UNAM) and the person she is supervising is from Tijuana and studied at San Diego State University. Although they share Mexican heritage their worldview is likely to be different. What may be dynamics and other aspects of this professional relationship? In the Critical Events Model, Inman and DeBoer Kreider (2013) indicate that there are three components of importance to the professional relationship of supervisor and supervisee. These are the emotional connection, an agreement about the goals for supervision, and another agreement about the "work" to be carried out and the tasks of supervision. According to the authors and other experts in multicultural supervision, supervisors with multicultural competencies may provide the support necessary for those on the journey to become psychotherapists. If a supervisor is not competent, there are greater chances of damaging the development of a supervisee. The relationship with the supervisee is critical to the development of a relationship of a therapist (supervisee) with her clients.

In research of U.S. Latinas, supervisors and supervises, there were interesting results. Using the proverb, "There are no roses without thorns", five doubled-edged conditions or dynamics resulted. Many times, there is anticipation that because one is going to have a Latina supervisor or vice versa. This raises the expectations and enthusiasm, but there also are challenges. One of the challenges is not maintaining professional boundaries, idealization of the supervisor, and disagreements because of ethnic differences (Field et al., 2010). To the supervisor lies the responsibility to notice these dynamics and not allow herself to be seduced by the admiration of the supervisee. The authors also mention the need to be aware of dynamics of transference and countertransference.

The final article comes from the co-author of this book, Dr. Falender and her colleagues. In the article, she proposes high level competencies that serve as a point of reference in multicultural clinical supervision. She states that these points of reference are guides for the training and practice of supervisors (Falender et al., 2012).

References

Arredondo, P., Toporek, R., Brown, S. P., Jones, J., Locke, D. C., Sanchez, J., & Stadler, H. (1996). Operationalization of the multicultural counseling competencies. *Journal of Multicultural Counseling and Development, 24*, 42–78.

Bakos, D. S., & Kristensen, C. H. (2013). Supervising cognitive behavioral therapy practitioners in urban Brazil. *Journal of Cognitive Psychotherapy, 27*(1), 42–50. https://doi.org/10.1891/0889-8391.27.1.42

Biblioteca del Congreso Nacional de Chile. (2017). *Ley 21.015 INCENTIVA LA INCLUSIÓN DE PERSONAS CON DISCAPACIDAD AL MUNDO LABORAL*. Colección Biblioteca Nacional de Chile, disponible en Biblioteca Nacional Digital de Chile. Available at https://www.bcn.cl/leychile/navegar?idNorma=1103997&idParte=

Consoli, A., Beutler, L., & Bongar, B. (2017). *Unity and diversity among psychotherapies* (pp. 11—30). Oxford, New York: Oxford University Press.

Falender, C. A., Burnes, T., & Ellis, M. V. (2012). Multicultural clinical supervision and benchmarks: Empirical support informing practice and supervisor training. *The Counseling Psychologist, 41*(1), 8–27.

Field, L. D., Chávez-Korell, S., & Domenech Rodriguez, M. M. (2010). No hay rosas sin espinas: Conceptualizing Latina-Latina supervision from a multicultural developmental supervisory model. *Training and Education in Professional Psychology, 4*(1), 47–54.

Inman, A. G., & DeBoer, K. E. (2013). Multicultural competence: Psychotherapy practice and supervisión. *Psychotherapy, 51*(3), 346–350.

Lambeth, G., Otero, C., & Vergara, D. (2019). *La Desigualdad es una decisión política.* CiperAcadémico, available at https://www.ciperchile.cl/2019/12/10/parte-ii-la-desigualdad-es-una-decision-politica/

Lubina, M., Auyón, A., Cóbar, A. A., & Grazioso, M. (2024). *Una aproximación a la supervisión clínica como campo de acción en Guatemala.* Supervisión Latinamericana.

Neufeld, C. B., Barletta, J. B., Scotton, I. L., & Rebessi, I. P. (2021). Distinctive aspects of CBT in Brazil: How cultural aspects affect training and clinical practice. *International Journal of Cognitive Therapy, 14*, 247–261.

Sue, D. W., Arredondo, P., & McDavis, R. (1992). Multicultural competencies and standards: A call to the profession. *Journal of Counseling and Development, 70*, 477–486.

World Bank. (2023). *Poverty & Equity Brief Mexico Latin America & the Caribbean.* World Bank Group poverty and equity. https://databankfiles.worldbank.org/public/ddpext_download/poverty/987B9C90-CB9F-4D93-AE8C-750588BF00QA/current/Global_POVEQ_MEX.pdf

Patricia Arredondo has dedicated her career to advancing social justice, cultural competency, mental health education for immigrants and Latinos, feminist leadership and organizing, Diversity Strategist. She is the co-author of the Core Competencies of Multicultural Counseling. She has authored more than one hundred articles, training videos, and book chapters and authored/co-authored eight books. Her most recent co-authored book is Women in Stem: Thriving in the Chilly Climate. Her next book with ACA is Counseling with Immigrants, Refugees, and Families from Social Justice Perspectives. She held tenured and senior administrative positions at Arizona State University and the University of Wisconsin-Milwaukee. As a servant leader, she served as president of the American Counseling Association (ACA), among other associations, and is the founding president of the National Latino Psychological Association. She is an ACA and APA Fellow (from three divisions). A psychologist, Dr. Arredondo received her master's degree in school counseling from Boston and a doctorate in counseling psychology from Boston University. President of the Arredondo Group Advisory, she leads a team and advises organizations nationally on their diversity, equity, inclusion, belonging, and leadership strategies. She is proud of her Mexican-American heritage and culture, learnings from her grandmother and parents. She lives in Phoenix and Mexico City.

Landscape of Clinical Supervision in Latin America

Hector Fernandez-Alvarez and Maria del Pilar Grazioso

Current Overview

In 2002, we began dreaming of new possibilities to expand training and supervision in psychotherapy (Fernández-Álvarez, 2008). Many years have passed, and it is now that we are able to share this edited book that offers an overview of Clinical Supervision in Latin America with the contributions from seven different regions of our America, i.e., Cuba, Mexico, Colombia, Argentina, Chile, Guatemala, and Puerto Rico. Nonetheless, in lieu of the relevance of an integrative ecological perspective we consider it essential to include Brazil and the perspective of the Latin American populations in the United States. We begin by providing a brief introduction to psychotherapy in the region, largely because even though supervision was not systematized from its beginnings, it has generally been an inherent component of the evolution of psychotherapy in Latin America.

The Framework of the Discipline of Clinical Supervision in Latin America

As a starting point, we provide a sketch of psychotherapy in the region with the intent to frame the context in which clinical supervision is developed. The history of "official" psychotherapy in Latin America has been characterized by having had

H. Fernandez-Alvarez
Fundación Aiglé, Buenos Aires, Argentina

M. P. Grazioso (✉)
Asociación Proyecto Aigle Guatemala, Universidad del Valle de Guatemala, Guatemala City, Guatemala
e-mail: mpgrazioso@proyectoaigle.org.gt

M. P. Grazioso et al. (eds.), *Clinical Supervision in Latin America*,
https://doi.org/10.1007/978-3-031-82373-2_2

early developments in several countries of the continent, which was consonant with its beginnings in Central Europe in the early years of the twentieth century and later in the United States of America.

Taking as a reference that psychotherapy began in Central Europe in the early years of the twentieth century and then, in the United States of America, the first developments in Latin America took place a few years later. Prominent examples are that of Honorio Delgado, a Peruvian psychiatrist who promoted psychoanalysis in Lima, Peru, in the 1920s, after having received training at Freud's circle in Vienna.

During that decade psychoanalysis was introduced in Brazil, particularly in the area of Rio de Janeiro, with Julius Porto-Carrero promoting the use of the psychoanalytic method, especially applied with children.

Psychoanalysis also arrived early in Argentina. In 1930 Jorge Thenon presented his doctoral thesis on "*Comparative Psychotherapy and Psychogenesis*". Freud wrote to him expressing his satisfaction with the treatment of psychoanalysis in Argentina and proposed that he published the summary of his thesis in the *International Journal of Psychoanalysis* (personal communication of August 25, 1930). In the Argentine province of Córdoba a very active movement led by Gregorio Berman promoted the development of the discipline, including the publication of a journal called *Psicoterapia*, which was launched in 1936.

By the early 1940s, psychotherapy had achieved strong momentum in the region. In the south, the creation of the Argentine Psychoanalytic Association in 1942 marked a milestone that had a very important social impact that has endured till the present day. The arrival of European psychoanalysts trained in Freud's environment contributed to this movement.

Around the same time, Ignacio Matte Blanco, who had trained in London with personalities such as Jones, Strachey, and Klein, returned to Chile and in the 1940s promoted the creation of the Chilean Society of Psychoanalysis.

In the north of the region, the arrival of Erich Fromm in Mexico was a trigger that fostered the development of psychotherapy within a post-Freudian current that highlighted the role of social and cultural factors in therapeutic practices, as well as the visits of Viktor Frankl that expanded perspectives on different theoretical orientations. In short, psychotherapy took root strongly from its beginnings, adopting the model of psychoanalysis developed in European countries.

The United States was another important source, especially in the experimental and behavioral therapy aspects. E. Ribes-Iñesta in Mexico took advantage of his studies at several universities in the United States and Canada (Kansas, Toronto, Illinois), as well as Rubén Ardila, in Colombia, who received his training at the University of Nebraska and brought this model of psychotherapy in the region.

All these references testify that "official" psychotherapy in Latin America found a very fertile ground that has remained highly active throughout the history of the discipline. The most relevant and widespread theoretical approaches, such as humanistic-existential psychotherapy and systemic therapy approaches, also spread rapidly throughout the continent.

The Distribution of Psychotherapeutic Practices in the Region

When we say "official" psychotherapy, we refer to the developments and applications that have achieved the most recognition from public health organizations and society in general, especially in the urban areas.

It is important to bear in mind that the population of Latin America is mostly located in urban areas. A significant percentage of people live in cities with at least 20,000 inhabitants and just over 80% live in urban areas. It is estimated that by 2050 that percentage will reach 89%.

This means that the practice of psychotherapy (and, therefore, of supervision) is aimed at providing help to people who live in social environment and are deeply influenced by cultural patterns typical of those environments. However, the needs for mental health care and socio-emotional well-being of rural and Indigenous populations merit considering the urgent need to offer help to people who do not necessarily represent the cultural characteristics of urban populations to provide supervision to those who offer this help (Ussher, 2008).

Psychotherapy practices aimed at providing help to populations that resided in urban areas and belonged, preponderantly, to the most privileged socio-economic sectors. Accordingly, psychotherapy services were private individual psychotherapy. In the last part of the last century and throughout this twenty-first century, these practices have expanded on a large scale, becoming part of public mental health programs, and aimed at low-income socio-economic sectors with greater vulnerability.

Although at the academic level, psychotherapy initially encountered some resistance in the educational field and in health institutions, it gradually gained ground until it achieved widespread social acceptance over the years to such an extent that psychotherapy and psychotherapists in Latin America achieved a certain notoriety in the international context. Many of these psychotherapists (in particular some very prominent ones) migrated and continued their scientific and professional development in European countries and in the U.S.A. Many Latin American psychotherapists also found space and recognition in international organizations such as the International Psychoanalytical Association, the Society for the Exploration of Psychotherapy Integration (SEPI), the Society for Psychotherapy Research (SPR), the International Family Therapy Association, the Latin American Association for Psychotherapy Integration (ALAPSI), the Association of Psychotherapists, and others.

The Place of Supervision

Supervision is a component of clinical practice in general and of psychotherapy in particular that has been developed since the origin of the discipline (Fernández Álvarez, 2008, Villafuerte Montiel, 2020). It is a component that has become widespread and is commonly practiced by therapists around the world. In Latin America it is also a frequent and habitual practice used by therapists in training, interested in achieving skilled professional training. Supervised trainees typically provide favorable opinions of their experiences in clinical supervision, especially when referring to the guidance and support they receive (Falender et al., 2021). Accordingly, it is a widespread practice, both as an institutional prescription and a subjective choice of novice and experienced psychotherapists.

Therefore, it is clear that as the practice of psychotherapy had an early origin and a strong dissemination in Latin America, supervision was also present from the beginning and is very widespread today (Fernández Alvarez, 2016).

Supervision is offered at large in health care facilities and has been regularly included in Latin America as a core foundation for training programs, both at the undergraduate and graduate levels. However, it still has several barriers that must be addressed (Carbajal et al., 2021). Among the most important are the following:

1. The lack of specific training for those who aspire to perform the role of supervisor. The supervisors are usually experienced therapists who have high professional prestige, but the vast majority have not received specific training in supervision due to the lack of academic offerings in this regard.
2. Further, in Latin America there are generally no certified regulatory and accreditation systems for the practice of supervision or the supervisor role, despite the fact that this situation is gradually changing, and various programs are being implemented throughout the region. Therefore, ethical issues and dilemas are not necessarily addressed nor taken into consideration.
3. The lack of empirical evidence that documents that supervision impacts psychotherapeutic interventions impacts on patients' well-being. There is not sufficient evidence of the effects of supervision on patient care, although evidence exists that supervision is viewed as very useful for supervisees.
4. Obstacles exist including intercultural and multicultural identities, potential for misunderstanding and alliance ruptures between the supervisor and supervisee. Also, power may be abused ignoring the relevance of self care.
5. Ethical dilemmas and critical incidents that arise in oversight processes do not necessarily receive appropriate attention or follow-up.
6. The development of evidence-based studies that include cultural and contextual dimensions is scarce and the first evidence-based supervision programs (Milne & Martín, 2018) are relatively recent, and their outcomes are relevant to Latin American countries.

All the vulnerabilities mentioned above are present in multiple countries across the region with variability across venues. In some respects, these weaknesses are even more pronounced.

Formal Aspects of Supervision in Latin America

There are several formal elements of supervisory practices that are implemented in different Latin American countries. For example:

1. The practice of monitoring is quite common, but documentation on such practices is scarce. A good example of this is the scarcity of publications such as texts and articles. In the major manuals of the specialty (Bernard & Goodyear, 2018; Falender & Shafranske, 2020; Watkins & Milne, 2014; Borders & Brown, 2005) there are very few references to Latin America.
2. The accreditation and regulation of the practices is scarce, in accordance with the lack of or weakness of regulation for the practice of psychotherapy.
3. The development of specialized training programs is also emerging and in continuous development. A prominent example is the program of the Pontificia Universidad Católica de Chile, which is carried out in conjunction with the University of Heidelberg (Germany) and the program offered by Fundación Aiglé and Universidad El Salvador in Buenos Aires.

This book is organized in chapters that describe the formal aspects of how supervision is implemented in each of the regions represented, brings us closer to a greater understanding of the fundamental dimensions of our clinical supervision discipline in Latin America.

Strengths of Supervision in Latin America

The growing need to offer evidence-based psychotherapeutic services also increases the need to offer evidence-based supervision processes, which has awakened interest and commitment to identify the characteristics of supervision processes. Deliberate efforts in several countries already reflect sustained steps towards the development of programs entailing processes that take into account empirical evidence as a basis for their implementation (Villafuerte, 2016a, 2016b; Cóbar, 2019).

When reviewing the development of clinical supervision in Latin America, it is essential to highlight, as reflected in the chapters that make up our book, the strength highlighted through recognition that the clinical experience of professionals who, after practicing the profession of psychotherapy or university teaching, are encouraged to initiate clinical supervision processes with students in training programs. Initially, they rely on psychotherapeutic models that gradually include considerations related to developmental models from the perspectives of those who supervise.

Evidence exists that supervisees value the benefits and impact of supervision in support of the development of their competencies such as psychotherapy theories and models, self-care, increased capacity for self-reflection, openness to feedback, and systematization of processes. And by considering supervision as a process, those who participate in it and seek novel training approaches and training in specific topics of supervision are enriched by the supervisor's personal style and with their competencies and individual characteristics (Goodyear & Falender, 2017).

The practice of supervision inevitably includes working with vulnerable groups since, in general, those who are trained in professional settings and university programs undertake their clinical practice in psychological services offered in university clinics or health centers that serve populations with limited socio-economic resources. While this offers the strength of having access to diverse populations, it does not necessarily adequately address the multicultural dimensions of the supervisory relationship.

Clinical Supervision in Mental Health

In 2022, the Pan American Health Organization, PAHO, launched a Self-Learning Program in Supervision, with free and open access, which can be carried out online and is available on the Educational Platform of the organization's Virtual Campus of Public Health for all countries in the Region and for all professionals who want to train as clinical mental health supervisors, thus innovating the training of clinical supervisors. The implications for the recognition of clinical supervision in the professional practice of mental health care at the institutional and international levels by PAHO are a milestone that deserves to be considered a significant advance to legitimize the importance of considering it both in education and training and in professional practice (Resumen de Curso Virtual de Autoaprendizaje: Supervisión Clínica en Inververciones de Salud Mental).

Given the high prevalence rate of mental disorders in the continent and the need to optimize interventions to improve these conditions, the training of supervisors is a fundamental element and PAHO certainly meets this need by recognizing that clinical supervision is "a collaborative and non-hierarchical strategy, focused on supporting staff to carry out quality interventions, through the strengthening of their professional skills, self-care and community participation". It highlights the fundamental role of clinical supervision in addressing the problems that afflict the mental health of the population in the region given the mental health situation and burnout and distress of professionals who work in the area.

According to documents from the organization, the global burden of disability due to mental health-related issues reaches one-third of total disability in the Americas. This has been aggravated in recent years because of the cumulative effects of the Covid-19 epidemic. The HEROES study shows that between 15% and 22% of health personnel developed depressive symptoms and between 5% and 15% showed signs of suicidal behavior, with few receiving the necessary support. In this context, the WHO and PAHO recommended developing programs to strengthen and support the mental health teams. A fundamental principle of such programs is to have trained personnel to carry out clinical mental health supervision that provide support and support to health personnel. "Clinical supervision is conceived as a collaborative and non-hierarchical strategy, focused on supporting staff to carry out quality interventions, by strengthening their professional skills, self-care and community participation" (Campus PAHO).

The course "Clinical Supervision in Mental Health Interventions" prepared by PAHO, available on the educational platform of the PAHO/WHO Virtual Campus of Public Health, can be navigated from a computer, tablet or cell phone. The course is aimed at mental health specialists who are in charge of supervision, monitoring and/or clinical supervision of personnel who care for people with mental health problems. The hourly load is 120 min for each module, with a total time load of 25 h.

The course is developed over 14 modules articulated in five blocks that address the following areas:

1. Keys to clinical supervision: objectives, roles, challenges, and practical aspects.
2. Medical history.
3. Basic communication skills: listening, facilitators of narrative activity, and facilitators of alternative narrative generation.
4. Clinical supervision strategies: direct clinical observation, case discussion, peer supervision, and review of medical records.
5. Self-care.

Fundamentals of Clinical Supervision in Latin America

A. Documentation

The practice of psychotherapy is very prominent in Latin America and the psychotherapist is usually identified with psychology professionals. In regions this extends to the specialization of psychoanalysis and psychiatry. Supervision is incorporated as a necessary component from the final stages of obtaining the psychology "licenciatura" degree and increases at the moment when the student reaches graduation and begins to work as a professional authorized to provide therapeutic help.

The relationship between supervisor and supervisee is closely tied to the dominant model of the psychotherapy, that is, an individual relationship, which is contracted within the rules of private and independent practice. When supervision is carried out in institutional settings, the group arrangement is more frequent. This is particularly prominent in the first years of professional practice (residents or mental health practitioner).

The supervisees usually select their supervisors within the circuit of teachers who have assisted them during undergraduate or graduate training. A high percentage of young therapists spend several hours a month in supervision and the scheme of the supervision activity leans towards free narration that adjusts to the presentation of the main doubts or concerns that the supervisee encounters in their daily work. The format of supervision is generally conducted within the theoretical model held by the supervisor. The degree of formalization depends on the characteristics of the professionals involved, but in all cases, the registration of the processes is not associated with the need to carry out a strict form of documentation.

This conspires, of course, against the formation of databases that can facilitate empirically supported research tasks.

B. Theoretical Models: Integration.

As we know, the different models of supervision are grouped into three categories:

1. Specific models: In them, the format and manner of conducting the process depends on the theoretical model of psychotherapy used by the users (supervisors and supervised). The most frequently used models are: psychodynamic, cognitive-behavioral, humanistic, and systemic, in accordance with the four major theoretical models that make up the discipline.

Those professionals who have a strong adherence to any of these models strongly subscribe to it. The psychodynamic model was subject to very strict supervisory relationship modalities, although this has become more flexible, especially since the transition from classical psychoanalysis to relational psychoanalysis.

A variant that has had a strong presence in many countries of the continent is the Lacanian current that proposed a different variant. In this approach, the emphasis is placed on the fact that the supervisory relationship must avoid any temptation to promote a dominant knowledge on the part of the supervisor. A good description of the supervisory approach from this perspective is expressed in an article in the journal *Freudiana* (Nos. 89/90) from 2020. Gustavo Dassel says:

"Such an experience must have produced a loss: the renunciation of all phantoms of mastery of knowledge." This assumption of the castration of the Other translates into a narcissistic wound. It implies, as Lacan expresses it in his lecture of December 17, 1969 [1], abandoning "… the idea that somehow or at some time, even if it is as a hope for the future, knowledge can constitute a closed totality…".

One of the problems related to supervision is the possibility that the analyst in the position of supervisor tries, unconsciously, to restore that loss, to alleviate that narcissistic wound by occupying the place of master of knowledge, or of a meta-knowledge. **"The position of the supervisor entails the risk of playing the role of being the Other of the Other."**

This text is part of a periodical published in Europe (Spain), but that publication is very illustrative, since the Lacanian movement has expanded to a great extent throughout Latin America. Examples of how supervision is translated from this approach in Latin America are offers such as those of the Tiempo Foundation (Buenos Aires) or the New School of Psychoanalysis (Guayaquil, Ecuador).

1. The cognitive-behavioral model is widely represented throughout the continent. The supervision proposals are focused to a greater extent on guiding and advising the supervised on the quality of the practices that are provided. The emphasis on the procedures and techniques used is the natural passage to develop

evidence-based practices, but this process is still in its infancy, although specialized centers exist including, the Institute of Cognitive Behavioral Therapy (CBT) in Argentina.

In Colombia, Ballesteros de Valderrama et al. (2019) report that for the supervisors who participated in their study, behavioral supervision as a central category of analysis is related to two fundamental aspects: (a) the factors that affect supervision and (b) the supervision process as such. This shows that behavioral supervision is nested in a contextualist vision, understanding it as a process that involves specific actions within the content of the therapist-supervisory interaction, which in turn are influenced by contextual factors.

A very interesting study on the characteristics of cognitive-behavioral guidance supervisors was carried out in Brazil (Neufeld et al., 2022; Barletta et al., 2021a, 2021b). The article begins by pointing out the difference between the requirements for the training of supervisors in Cognitive Behavioral Therapy between Brazil and other countries (especially the United States) and seeks to contribute to having more elements to improve such training. The work includes a qualitative research study carried out based on interviews with ten supervisors in the training stage for the exercise of the role. The framework of the study is inscribed in the need to explore the perceptions of candidates to obtain the title of supervisors.

The humanistic model has placed the emphasis on the person of the supervisee and on promoting the development of the relationship with the supervisor. López Marín (2021) reviews person-centered psychotherapy whose main characteristic is that it is an essentially relational and intersubjective process, and the fundamental thing is the supervisor-supervised interpersonal relationship in which the supervisor seeks to facilitate a climate of empathy, acceptance, and congruence, highlighting that supervision from this approach is integral, and thus seeks to work on theoretical, practical, and experiential aspects.

The systemic model has undergone an important evolution (Hernández, 2007), since supervision has been included as part of the therapeutic intervention itself. Orellana Bahamondes (2019) describes dimensions of the systemic supervision of the Humaniza Institute in Chile, emphasizing the three vertices on which the supervision process is carried out: the person of the therapist, the elements of theory, and clinical practice that is developed in the training from an integration of the systemic perspective—linking and the psycho-corporal approach.

There are, of course, offers of supervision that concern other approaches that arise, in different ways, from these traditional modes. Examples of this can be found in psychodrama and Eye Movement Desensitization and Reprocessing (EMDR).

In the case of psychodrama, we can cite the work of Barros (2017) who refers to the construction of the role of the "psychodramatist" in socio-educational training. Barros (2017) clarifies that the role of the supervisor is to stimulate practice, offering links with theory and reflections for the coherence of the application of the method. Once the difficulties and impasse of the supervisee in the conduct of the sessions have been identified, the supervisor must be cautious in his orientations and behaviors so as not to reinforce blockages and weaknesses, throwing him even more into the abyss or darkness. On this journey he holds in himself, or is supposed to carry, the subtlety of illuminating the way. It helps to build the bridge to the effective learning of the role of the therapist. What is expected of this professional is an attitude of facilitation, helping the supervisee to establish adequate conditions for the management of situations and scenarios that arise in the relationship with the patient (Santiago de Carvalho, 2021). Through dramatic play, personal aspects of the supervisee are recognized that interfere in the psychotherapeutic process and in the spontaneous-creative management of their interventions, integrating knowledge with the experiential dimension. She concludes that the supervisor developed greater security in his professional role, also pointing out the great importance of the supervisor in this process.

Conceptualizing supervision as a process and not as an outcome leads to the activities of supervised supervisory interaction being configured over time, and although its purpose is the training of skilled psychotherapists, the result is not the defining criterion, coinciding with elements that have been developed by the work of Milne (2018). In addition, supervision as a process also implies that it is based on a set of historical and contextual variables, which are related to the previous experience of both the supervisor and the supervisee, and includes the development of personal and therapeutic skills of the supervisee.

Regarding the development of these personal and therapeutic skills, it is necessary to mention three elements: first, training in psychotherapy must focus on technical skills such as the interview, its structure, and self-reflective practice; second, the training must include nontechnical skills among which can be mentioned, the empathy and its influence on the therapist-patient relationship; and third, it must include discrete skills such as facilitating communication, attentive behaviors, and evaluation, as Bootzin and Ruggill (1988) had pointed out, and recently researched by Novoa-Gómez et al. (2019).

C. Lack of Empirical Studies.

The last decade has reflected a greater number of publications that address relevant aspects of clinical supervision in Latin America; for example, the 20th issue of a special edition of the Revista Psicólogos en Guatemala dedicated to clinical supervision (Consoli et al., 2017). However, of these publications, the articles or chapters that reflect empirical studies are significantly limited, highlighting publications in Colombia and Brazil that begin to develop the field of clinical supervision research in Latin America.

A review carried out by Botero García et al. (2022) on empirical studies on supervision in clinical psychology in the period between 2012 and 2021 provides a systematic search, in which they identified 123 empirical studies that met the inclusion requirements. Contents are organized around (a) supervision models, (b) clinical competencies/skills, (c) relationship between supervisory and supervised, (d) techniques, (e) instruments, (f) variation of supervision according to approaches, (g) usefulness, and (h) evaluation, identifying the scarcity of empirical research on the different pedagogical models and practices in supervision, which encourages researchers and professionals to continue bridging this gap.

When considering the empirical studies that contribute to the advance, we cannot ignore the above about all the efforts made to make a scientific transfer of the foundations developed in other contexts, which includes the adaptation and acculturation of instruments. An example of this is the study carried out by Santangelo & Conde (2020) when adapting the Supervisory Relationship Questionnaire (SSQR) to the Argentine context.

D. Undergraduate and Postgraduate Training.

The training of clinical psychology and psychotherapy professionals at both the undergraduate and graduate levels, although it includes exposure to clinical supervision, recently accounts for documentation on models of supervision programs (Gutierrez et al., 2020; Bastidas Bilbao & Velásquez, 2016; Tena Suck, 2021).

E. Specialized Studies and Regulation.

Although in Latin America the practice of supervision is widespread and plays an important role in training therapists, in operating as a system at the service of therapists' care, and also as a tool for evaluating the course of treatments, this practice is generally not regulated by institutionalized agencies.

This lack of regulation has several consequences. On the one hand, the exercise of the profession as a supervisor is not sufficiently endorsed. This is derived, in principle, from the fact that the practice of clinical psychology and psychotherapy, in general, have also suffered long delays in reaching the regulatory systems for their practice (Consoli et al., 2017).

These circumstances have delayed the development of specialized training programs for supervisors. In recent years this situation has been producing favorable changes and various proposals have been developed. One, which has been developed for several years, is the International Diploma in Clinical Supervision developed by the Pontificia Universidad Católica de Chile, in agreement with the University of Heidelberg (Germany), which is structured in three modules: (1) Theoretical aspects, (2) General skills and techniques, and (3) Specific approaches, composed of the four major predominant theoretical models. It began to be implemented in the 2006/2007 school year, lasts 9 months and covers a total of 200 theoretical-practical hours. Each cohort is made up of between 12 and 24 participants and has been approved by the National Commission for the Accreditation of Clinical Psychologists. Graduates are licensed to act as accredited Supervisors.

There are isolated higher education programs at the graduate level like the ones in Mexico, Puerto Rico, and Guatemala (Cóbar Catalan et al., 2019; Grazioso et al., 2021b) that have included clinical supervision training at their masters programs with this, those who aim to be clinical supervisors can receive systematic training so do not have to rely solely on their own accumulated experience.

F. Transculturality.

Despite the richness and cultural diversity of the different Latin American regions, attention and recognition of cultural elements is recent. Although ethnic, linguistic, and cultural groups are multiple, the emphasis on training in multicultural competencies of those who supervise as well as attention to cultural orientation that considers the value of cultural humility, the introduction of these elements in supervision practices and processes is very recent. The movement from Cultural Psychology, Multicultural Competences, Multicultural Orientation, towards a Cultural Humility approach has followed its own path in Latin America. While cultural diversity is clearly evident, discrimination, lack of appreciation for diversity, socio-economic, and educational barriers have influenced the significant disparity existent in access to services and to clinical supervision particularly in those areas working with the underserved and less privileged. Gradually, there is evidence that literature in the field from western regions has been culturally adapted to make it pertinent, so their influence those in training and practice can make into relevant with reflective and critical reflection (Grazioso et al., 2021a).

G. Remote Supervision.

The literature on clinical supervision in Latin America is scarce and in the initial stages of production, more so is the literature on remote supervision. We have witnessed the exponential emphasis on the deliberate use of technologies as a resource to offer both psychotherapy and supervision services, however, we are still in the learning phase. It has been our intention (Fernández Alvarez et al., 2015; Fernández Álvarez et al., 2019) to reduce these shortcomings by offering the perspectives of the practice conducted in our countries, recognizing that in Latin American regions, similar developments have occurred. Acknowledging that the Covid-19 pandemia has helped us identify the weaknesses and strengths, barriers, and opportunities, which are inherent to practicing clinical supervision online, opens a new dimension to rely on technologies in a meaningful way (Galleguillos et al., 2022).

Future Developments

We know that our coverage continues to have limitations (Fernández-Álvarez, 2017), mostly because there is so much evidence from the field of clinical supervision in Latin-American countries that has not been published nor disseminated sufficiently. We are confident that the content of our book will contribute in a meaningful way to further advance our field towards enriched new developments (Fernández-Álvarez, 2022, Valdiviezo-Oña et al., 2022). We find extremely valuable this compilation of interesting chapters and hope they serve as an invitation to continue building bridges in a continuous "dance" that include evidence-based practices, voices from the field, practice-oriented research, culturally relevant and solid theoretical foundation, integrative contextual pertinent practices that will promote advances in training, regulation, and ethical practices. Let us be humble! We cannot move forward in isolation. We welcome new collaborative learnings that invite clinical supervisors, those in training and those who are proficient, to join us in our networks to embrace new opportunities. This is an invitation to our reading audience to share their agreements and disagreements around our clinical supervision discipline that, although it is an inherent practice to the practices of psychotherapy, it is not until recently that it has been enriched with the processes of systematization, training, regulation, and research. Let's continue our narratives, writing the story from our Latin American lens.

References

Ballesteros de Valderrama, B. P., Muñoz-Martínez, A. M., Novoa-Gómez, M., Bazzani-Orrego, D., Brandwayn-Briceño, N. E., Lasso-Báez, R. A., Pachón-Basallo, M., & Restrepo-Vélez, D. (2019). Características de la supervisión clínica en las terapias conductuales: un análisis del proceso de supervisión clínica. *Universitas Psychologica, 18*(4), 1–14.

Barletta, J. B., Rodrigues, C. M. L., & Neufeld, C. B. (2021a). A Formação de Supervisores em Terapia Cognitivo-Comportamental. *Revista Brasileira de Orientação Profissional, 22*(1), 61–72.

Barletta, J. B., Versuti, F. M., & Neufeld, C. B. (2021b). De la enseñanza híbrida a la virtual: relato de experiencia docente con la asignatura de Supervisión Basada en Evidencias en el posgrado stricto sensu brasileño. *Revista Brasileira de Terapias Cognitivas, 17*(2), 79–86.

Barros, L. M. S. (2017). Supervisão socioeducacional: compartilhando a construção do papel de supervisor em Psicodrama. *Revista Brasileira de Psicodrama, 25*(2), 28–36. https://doi.org/10.15329/2318-0498.20170019

Bastidas-Bilbao, H., & Velásquez, A. M. (2016). Modelo lógico de la supervisión como actividad educativa para la formación en psicología clínica: concepciones de supervisores clínicos. *Avances en Psicología Latinoamericana, 34*(2), 293–314. ISSNe2145-4515.

Bernard, J. M., & Goodyear, R. K. (2018). Fundamentals of clinical supervision (6th ed.). Pearson.

Borders, L. D., & Brown, L. L. (2005). *The new handbook of counseling supervision*. Lawrence Erlbaum Associates Publishers.

Bootzin, R. R., & Ruggill, J. S. (1988). Training issues in behavior therapy. Journal of Consulting and Clinical Psychology, 56(5), 703–709. https://doi.org/10.1037/0022-006X.56.5.703

Botero-García, C., Giovanni, I., & Morales Arias, C. (2022). Supervisión en psicología clínica: Una revisión sobre estudios empíricos. *Universitas Psychologica, 21*, 1–19.

Carbajal, M. A., Díaz-Marroquín, N., & Félix, V. (2021). *Modelo de supervisión para la formación en la práctica profesional en psicología. [Supervision model for training in professional practice in psychology]*. Publicaciones y Fomento Editorial. Universidad Nacional Autónoma de México.

Cóbar Catalán, A. A., Cazali, L., Erdmenger de Staebler, I., Grazioso, M. D. P., & Gallardo-Cooper, M. (2019). Modelo de supervisión integrativo: Construyendo una identidad profesionalen el campo de la Consejería Psicológica en. *Revista Brasileira de Psicoterapia, 21*(2), 1–20.

Consoli, A., Grazioso, M., Fernández, M., & Cóbar, A. (2017). La supervisión hoy: Lo que sabemos y lo que nos falta saber. *Revista Psicólogos, 7*(20), 06–19.

Falender, C., Goodyear, R., Duan, C., et al. (2021). Lens on international clinical supervision: Lessons learned from a cross-National Comparison of supervision. *Journal of Contemporary Psychotherapy, 51*, 181–189. https://doi.org/10.1007/s10879-021-09497-5

Falender, C. A., & Shafranske, E. P. (2020). *Fundamentos básicos para la práctica clínica de la supervisión basada en competencias*. Giuntieos.

Fernandez Alvarez, H., del Pilar Grazioso, M., & Kirszman, D. (2019). Distance supervision in the Aiglé Foundation's Latin American psychotherapy training program. *Journal of Clinical Psychology, 75*(2), 282–291.

Fernández-Álvarez, H. (2008). La supervisión en psicoterapia. In H. Fernández-Álvarez (Ed.), *Integración y salud mental. El proyecto AIGLÉ 1977–2008* (pp. 177–199). Desclée de Brouwer.

Fernández-Alvarez, H. (2016). Reflections on supervision in psychotherapy. *Psychotherapy Research, 26*(1), 1–10.
Fernández-Álvarez, H. (2017). El futuro de la supervisión. *Revista Psicólogos, 7*(20), 97–108.
Fernández-Álvarez, H. (2022). Practice oriented research: the case of psychotherapy supervision (Investigación orientada por la práctica: el caso de la supervisión en psicoterapia). *Studies in Psychology, 43*(3), 510–524.
Fernández-Alvarez, H., Pérez, A., & Palavezzatti, C. (2015). Inclusion of the supervisor in the therapeutic setting. *Psychotherapy Bulletin, 49*(4), 21–24.
Galleguillos, S., Sánchez Cea, M., Koetzle, D., Mellow, J., Piñol, D., & Schwalbe, C. (2022). La pandemia COVID-19 y libertad vigilada en Chile: Supervisión remota y diferencias regionales Polít. *Criminalia, 17*(34), 897–924. Doc. 2. http://politcrim.com/wp-content/uploads/2022/12/Vol17N34D2.pdf
Goodyear, R., & Falender, C. (2017). ¿Cómo pueden psicólogos/as maximizar su efectividad como supervisores/as? Ocho condiciones esenciales. *Revista Psicólogos, 7*(20), 83–96.
Grazioso, M. P., Bang, K., Duan, C., Falender, C., & Goodyear, R. (2021a). Toward more differentiated and nuanced understandings of clinical supervision practices and expectations around the world. *Psychoterapy Bulletin, 56*(3), 6–10.
Grazioso, M. P., Lubina, M., & Cóbar, A. A. (2021b). Perspectivas sobre el desarrollo de la supervisión clínica en Guatemala. In A. Tena Suck (Ed.), *Supervisión clínica en psicoterapia: una guía con las mejores prácticas*. Vesalius.
Gutierrez, D., Hiatt, K., & Lee, A. (2020). Spiritually competent orientation in supervision: Application of the Cultural Third. The Clinical Supervisor, 39.
Hernández Córdoba, Á. (2007). Supervisión de psicoterapeutas sistémicos: un crisol para devenir instrumentos de cambio. *Diversitas: Perspectivas en Psicología, 3*(2), 227–238.
López Marín, A. (2021). Supervisión clínica en psicoterapia centrada en la persona. *Enfoque Humanístico, 38*, 1–12.
Milne, D., & Martin, P. (2018). Supportive clinical supervision: Supported at last. *Journal of Advanced Nursing, 75*(2), 264–265. https://doi.org/10.1111/jan.13816
Neufeld, C. B., et al. (2022). Propuestas de intervención y formación de terapeutas y supervisores: Visión general de los programas en línea del LAPICC USP. *Revista Brasileira de Terapias Cognitivas, 18*(2), 79–86. 130–137.
Novoa-Gómez, M., Córdoba-Salgado, O., Rojas, N., Sosa, L., Cifuentes, D., & Robayo, S. (2019). A descriptive analysis of the interactions during clinical supervision. *Frontiers in Psychology, 10*, 669–669. https://doi.org/10.3389/fpsyg.2019.00669
Orellana Bahamondes, F. (2019). Dimensiones significativas de la supervisión clínica en el contexto de formación de terapeutas y supervisores del Instituto Humaniza Santiago. *Vincularte. Revista Clínica y Psicosocial, 4*(4), 49–70.
Resumen de Curso Virtual de Autoaprendizaje: Supervisión Clínica en Intervenciones de Salud Mental | Campus PAHO. (n.d.). https://campus.paho.org/mooc/course/info.php?id=343#:~:text=La%20supervisi%C3%B3n%20cl%C3%ADnica%20es%20una%20estrategia%20colaborativa%20y,habilidades%20profesionales%2C%20del%20autocuidado%20y%20la%20participaci%C3%B3n%20comunitaria
Santangelo, P. R., & Conde, K. (2020). Relación de supervisión: adaptación del S-SRQ en psicoterapeutas argentinos. *CES Psicología, 13*(3), 76–87. https://doi.org/10.21615/cesp.13.3.5
Santiago de Carvalho, M. D. (2021). o jogo dramático em supervisão: do desenvolvimento do papel Do psicoterapeuta ao processo psicoterapêutico do paciente. *Rev. Bras. Psicodrama, São Paulo, 29*(3), 188–197.
Tena Suck, A. (2021). *Supervisión clínica en Psicoterapia*. Vesalius.
Ussher, M. (2008). La supervisión en la psicología social comunitaria. *Psicología Para América Latina, 12*, 1–9. Retrieved from http://pepsic.bvsalud.org/scielo.php?script=sci_arttext&pid=S1870-350X2008000100006 [Google Scholar] [Ref list]
Valdiviezo-Oña, J., Granja, E., Cuadros-López, A., Valdivieso-Meza, G., Evans, C., & Paz, C. (2022). Practice-based research with psychologists-in-training: Presentation of a supervi-

sion model and use of routine outcome monitoring (Investigación basada en la práctica con psicólogos en formación: presentación de un Modelo de supervisión y uso de la monitorización rutinaria de resultados). *Estudios de Psicología, 43*(3), 583–608. https://doi.org/10.1080/02109395.2022.2132749

Villafuerte, A. L. (2016a). La Práctica de la Supervisión Clínica en México: Una Actividad Profesional en Desarrollo. *Multidisciplinary Health Research, 1*(2), 43–46. https://doi.org/10.19136/mhr.a1n2.1560

Villafuerte, A. (2016b). *Dilemas éticos en la supervisión clínica y su resolución (tesis doctoral no publicada).* Universidad de las Américas, Ciudad de México.

Villafuerte Montiel, A. (2020). Modelos contemporáneos de supervisión clínica: nuevas direcciones. *Multidisciplinary Health Research, 5*(1), 3.

Watkins, C. E., Jr., & Milne, D. L. (Eds.). (2014). The Wiley international handbook of clinical supervision. Wiley Blackwell. https://doi.org/10.1002/9781118846360

Hector Fernandez-Alvarez (1944–2023) obtained a PhD in Psychology, and was a psychotherapist, founder, and president of the Aiglé Foundation; since 1977 dedicated his work on education and training, research, and mental health assistance programs. He directed the Foundation's Center for Research in Psychotherapy and developed a Supervision Program based on his experience as a therapist and supervisor, the Specialized Training in Integrative Cognitive Psychotherapy of the Aiglé Foundation and at the National University of Mar del Plata. He was a mentor and professor in Argentina and in foreign universities. He was a prolific author of books and articles, like Fundamentals of an Integrative Model in Psychotherapy; Intervention Guide in Personality Disorders; Integration in Psychotherapy and Social Anxiety, Conceptualization, and Treatment. Among the many recognitions, he received the 2022 Distinguished Award for the International Advancement of Psychotherapy from Division 29 of the American Psychological Association (APA) and the International Sigmund Freud Award for Psychotherapy 2002 of the World Council for Psychotherapy (WCP). He chaired the Inter-American Society of Psychology (IAPA) and the Latin American chapter of the Society for Psychotherapy Research (SPR).

Maria del Pilar Grazioso has expertise in pediatric developmental psychology and learning, community mental health, prevention, gender, multiculturalism, higher education, psychotherapy, counseling, and supervision. She has held administrative, research, teaching, and clinical positions, as well as professional duties in higher education and private practice. She developed graduate programs at the master and doctoral level and began formal training in supervision at the university level in Guatemala. She has publications and recognition for her leadership and contributions to the development of Psychology and fulfilled leadership positions in her country and internationally. She is currently co-coordinator of the Asociación Proyecto Aiglé Guatemala and is a research affiliated with the Universidad del Valle de Guatemala and Maya Health Alliance/Wuqukawoc.

Part II
Clinical Supervision in North America

Clinical Supervision in Psychotherapy in Mexico

María Antonia Carbajal Godínez, Verónica Ruíz González, and Antonio Tena-Suck

Mexico is a country with a territory of almost 2 million km^2 in North America, with a population of more than 126 million inhabitants (INEGI, 2020) of which 51.2% are women and 48.8% men.

Our Latin-American culture has a rich history as the cradle of the Mesoamerican civilization, one of the oldest in the world (Enciclopedia humanidades, 2023). This legacy gives rise to the fact that we have more than 66 indigenous languages, even if our official language is Spanish (Ministry of Foreign Affairs, 2023). On the other hand, we are one of the few megadiverse countries in the world; which, in addition to significant geographical diversity and abundant natural resources, contributes to extensive multiculturalism and social challenges.

In this context, psychology in Mexico seeks, together with other health sciences, to meet the significant challenges of a large population with very diverse requirements and often with few resources.

According to the National Association of Universities and Institutions of Higher Education, higher education in our country is taught by public institutions, either state or autonomous, and private, whether free or incorporated; which are usually divided into two large sectors: the university and the technical. Most offer high school and undergraduate studies, and few offer postgraduate studies (National Association of Universities and Institutions of Higher Education, 2023). In this regard, the Organization for Economic Cooperation and Development (OECD) reports that only 27.1% of Mexicans between 25 and 34 years of age have a professional education, and only 0.7% of professionals in Mexico study a graduate degree (specialty, master's or doctorate). Thus, in our country, there are approximately 12 psychologists per hundred thousand inhabitants (Chamber of Deputies LXV

M. A. Carbajal Godínez (✉) · V. Ruíz González
Universidad Nacional Autónoma de México, Mexico City, Mexico
e-mail: mariaantonia@comunidad.unam.mx

A. Tena-Suck
Universidad Iberoamericana, Mexico City, Mexico
e-mail: antonio.tena@ibero.mx

M. P. Grazioso et al. (eds.), *Clinical Supervision in Latin America*,
https://doi.org/10.1007/978-3-031-82373-2_3

Legislature, 2023), and those who are psychotherapists have had to go through a university education to access a postgraduate degree in which they can comply with a specialized academic program involving hours of clinical supervision to get the credentials that will accredit them to practice professionally.

Given this situation, and taking into account that to date in our country there are no training certifications of clinical supervisors in psychotherapy, the university academic staff responsible for psychotherapists training are the ones who carry out the supervisory functions. As is the case of the authors of this chapter, supervisors lacking training options frequently resort to generating support networks with colleagues at national and international level in order to exchange knowledge and experiences.

In this way, we have managed to have an informed practice in supervision, building what Dr. Grazioso defines as "Clinical Community" (Consoli et al., 2017).

In this chapter we will try to share with the reader a view of the current state of clinical supervision in Mexico in psychotherapy, focusing especially on that which occurs in University Institutions that offer accredited graduate programs for therapists training and contextualizing it in the requirements of Mexican society. Needless to say, this panorama is not intended to be exhaustive but to contribute to what has already been done by other authors on the subject.

The Regulation of Psychotherapy in Mexico

Licensing, Certification, and Professional Membership

The role of a psychologist differs from that of a psychotherapist; since psychotherapy is one of several specialized fields within psychology. Hence the importance of defining the professional activity and delimiting the borders with other professional exercises in the culture of university education.

In Mexico, after studying a degree in psychology between 4 and 5 years long, the psychotherapist requires a particular postgraduate training, understood as a master's or doctoral degree, which will allow him or her to obtain the relevant licenses and certifications to be able to practice the profession; differentiating them from a licensed psychologist, who cannot and should not practice as a psychotherapist.

Therefore, psychotherapists in Mexico have the obligation to be duly accredited to exercise their functions; which includes at least having a professional degree and license (*título y cédula profesional*) and at least one postgraduate certificate issued and registered by the competent educational authorities, this ensures that the users can corroborate that they are attending to a mental health specialist.

Certification serves as official validation that an individual or organization meets professional standards required for a specific field. This document must be issued by an organization of recognized prestige and experience in a particular professional area, in this way in addition to taking care of users, the welfare of the community is promoted through ethical methods and procedures. To regulate this, there are institutions responsible for the psychotherapists certification that seek to regulate the ethical practice of the profession and the fulfillment of specific requirements to each professional field. The certification is granted solely and exclusively to the trained professional who approves the entirety of a course or training program in a particular domain/subject and obtains the minimum passing percentage in the evaluation of competencies; either through a general knowledge test or a portfolio with supporting documents.

It is important to note that in Mexico the document obtained at the end of professional training is a "*cédula profesional*" issued by the Ministry of Public Education which certifies that all the requirements for graduation from a professional level training program with official validity (RVOE) has been obtained and that therefore the professional can practice psychotherapy for life. This implies of course that the educational institutions themselves are exercising the role of guardians of the profession, being responsible for verifying that the programs they teach meet the necessary requirements to issue a valid document of completion. Unfortunately this and other factors may carry a great laxity in the terms and practices of psychotherapy in our context which can lead to the users being exposed to the iatrogenic effects of professionals with little or deficient professional training.

It is at this point that professional *colegios* and associations make their entrance with the main objective of representing the collective interests of the members of these corporations before the State. Some of these are: the Mexican Society of Psychology A.C. (SMP), the National College of Psychologists, A.C. (CONAPSI), the National Federation of Colleges, Societies and Associations of Psychologists of Mexico, A.C. (FENAPSIME), the Mexican Association of Alternatives in Psychology (AMAPSI), the Mexican Association of Social Psychology (AMEPSO), the Mexican Association of Psychological Orientation and Psychotherapy (AMOPP), and the Mexican Association of Family Therapy (AMTF), among many others. In all of them, membership requires periodic renewal and is voluntary; with the lack of representativeness that this may entail. However, some of them have sought international alliances to improve the quality of psychological care provided to patients, such as the collaboration between AMOPP with the National Board for Certified Counselors (NBCC), through which a certification has been achieved. AMOPP has also supported, through legislative efforts and initiatives, the promotion of the practice of psychological counseling and psychotherapy in Mexico.

Codes of Ethics

The purpose of codes of ethics is to establish rules of professional conduct and provide guidance for psychologists within the professional practice of psychology in any of its possible functions.

Currently, in our country there are several codes of ethics of different kinds. These are intended to guide therapists in their daily work and generally belong to different associations, but their scope is limited since they address only those who join the specific association who proposes it.

One of the outstanding exceptions is that of the Psychologist Code of Ethics, of the Mexican Society of Psychology (SMP), which aims to ensure that all those graduates in psychology carry out their professional practice in accordance with its principles without necessarily being ascribed to a particular theoretical school or working with specific populations. Since the ethical standards of the mental health professions are constantly changing, the Code is reviewed every 4 years with the aim of making the work of psychologists and clients the reference for appropriate standards for the profession, as both become aware of their fundamental rights and principles in their professional relationship.

Likewise, in the specific field of Psychotherapy, we have a Code of Ethics for psychotherapists prepared by AMOPP, which contains the desirable guidelines that lead and inspire its readers towards the ethical ideals of the profession.

This code includes a specific section regarding supervision that includes topics such as the power difference inherent to the supervisory relationship, the responsibility to provide up-to- date, balanced, and complete information, to give appropriate recognition to alternative points of view, to prevent multiple relationships, to avoid sexual relations of any kind with supervisees, students and current employees, to not involve in sexual or any other type of harassment, to not supervise cases that are beyond their scope, experience or capacity, to frame supervision and to keep adherence to the rules of the ethical code (Mexican Association of Psychological Orientation and Psychotherapy, A.C., 2011).

Culture and Diversity of the Mexican Context

Mexico ranks among the fifteen largest economies in the world and is the second-largest economy in Latin America (World Bank, 2023), this highlights an enormous cultural diversity and a marked socioeconomic contrast, while some of the richest men in the world live in Mexico, it is estimated that around 43.9% of Mexicans live in poverty and 8.5% of which live in extreme poverty (CONEVAL, 2020).

To this economic reality it must be incorporated the environmental deterioration, the lack of order in the process of growth in cities, the academic and labor overdemands, the risky lifestyles lead by many Mexicans (inadequate nutrition, sedentary life, lack of respect for times to sleep and rest, lack of recreation spaces, inadequate management of stressful situations, etc.), the dominant violence culture, discrimination, and exclusion experienced daily. Deriving from this reality we can understand that despite the increase in the life expectancy of Mexicans, the state of social, physical, and psychological well-being for all Mexicans has not been achieved, and on the contrary the number of suicides and psychological disorders has increased in our population.

According to statistical data from the Mexican Academy of Science (2015), in our country 12% of the population suffers from a mental disorder. This trend, unfortunately, can be related to other health conditions that significantly reduce people's life expectancy (Medina-Mora et al., 2015).

This statistic is particularly concerning given that many of these disorders emerge during early adulthood, as reported by the National Survey of Psychiatric Epidemiology (Medina Mora et al., 2015), which indicates that 50% of mental disorders begin before the age of 21 years old. According to other studies (Benjet et al., 2009), 24.7% of adolescents are affected by one or more mental health problems, with the most recurrent disorders among this population group being learning problems, intellectual disability, anxiety and attention deficit disorders, depression, substance use, and suicide attempts.

Another emerging problem related to the above is violence (Orrego et al., 2019). The increase in its incidence raises the urgent need for psychologists to research and intervene addressing individual factors such as cognitive, behavioral, and socio-affective aspects, as well as to take into account contextual aspects as family, social context, and culture (Amarís Macias et al., 2019).

On the other hand, there is a clear correlation between life stressors, discrimination, oppression, and poverty with mental health problems (Belle & Doucet, 2003; Foss-Kelly et al., 2017). Key issues of injustice, such as racism, sexism, and other forms of oppression have even been found to negatively affect neurogenesis and brain plasticity in minors and adults alike (Zalaquett & Ivey, 2018).

Another relevant data regarding the detection of the needs of vulnerable groups is that referring to the elderly, who require some special educational need and those belonging to the LGBTIQ+ community (lesbian, gay, bisexual, transgender, transsexual, transvestite, intersex, and queer).

By 2020, the National Institute for the Elderly (2019) estimated that individuals aged 60 or older would make up more than 10% of the total population. Additionally, data from INEGI (2010) indicate that over 7.5 million people have at least one disability that limits their ability to integrate into society. Among the reported disabilities, two categories account for 42.4%: difficulty walking and difficulty seeing, even with glasses. Another 36.4% includes challenges related to learning, memory, concentration, hearing, or using arms or hands. The remaining 21.2% comprises difficulties with bathing, dressing, eating, emotional or mental health issues, and communication impairments (INEGI, 2010).

On the other hand, according to INEGI (2021, September 8), in 2020, 7818 suicides were registered in Mexico, representing an average rate of 6.2 suicides per 100,000 inhabitants. By sex, males have a rate of 10.4 deaths per 100,000 (6383) and 2.2 per 100,000 females (1427).

This panorama implies that many of the prevalences in mental health at a national level, those that psychotherapists in Mexico are affected by depend on the greater extent of the context in which they are exposed; each state represents a culture in which we believe that the therapists should be able to contextualize their practice and take into account the specializations that are most necessary for the population that they serve.

The above presents a contrast between how significant the cultural and social context is in our practice and the attention paid to diversity as a transversal axis in our professional practice. In 2021, an exploratory survey was carried out with clinical supervisors in Mexico in which it was found that all of them referred to the importance of questioning and reflecting on social, institutional, and personal values to promote change and advocate for integration of differences and diversity. In fact, when asked about the diversity issues that have had to be taken into consideration, sexual, religious, special educational, cultural, and ethnic needs, among others, are mentioned. However, something that we must work more on is that in general, diversity is still seen mostly as linked to sexuality and the focus is mainly on the characteristics of the client, sometimes on the characteristics of the supervisee and is not done a lot in reference to the characteristics of the supervisor (Carbajal et al., 2019).

Clinical Supervision in Psychotherapy in Mexico

Contexts and Implementation of Clinical Supervision in Psychotherapy

In Mexico, since the 1980s, clinical supervision is proposed as a facilitating instrument of professional training and therefore of a higher quality of professional psychological help services.

Falender and Shafranske (2014) define supervision as a professional activity in which education and training to develop science-informed practices are facilitated through a collaborative interpersonal process. Involving observation, evaluation, feedback, facilitation of the self-assessment of the supervisee, the acquisition of knowledge and skills by instruction, modeling, and mutual problem-solving. That is why, in our country, clinical supervision is an essential part of the practicum of undergraduate and graduate programs, which is defined as "integrated sets of practices to be carried out in university centers or linked to the university by agreements that put students in contact with the problems of professional practice" (Zabalza, 2013, p. 128).

At the national level, some educational institutions such as the University of Baja California (UABC/UNAM, 2013–2015), the National Pedagogical University (UPN, 2012), the University of Colima (CENEDIC, 2012), the Iberoamerican University (Montes de Oca, 2017), and the Faculty of Psychology of the UNAM (Urbina, 1989, Ayala & Vázquez, 2001; Coordination of Educational Psychology, UNAM, 2009; Diaz, 2010; Valenzuela, 2011; Carbajal et al., 2019; Jiménez & Rivera, 2019) have founded, developed, and published schemes of institutional practices that start from the need for students to integrate both curricular content and the needs of the receiving institutions. In such traineeship programs, supervision is a central element.

In Mexico, interest in clinical supervision emerged in the 1980s and some research has been carried out, mainly within the framework of training clinical psychologists and psychotherapists. For example, in the Faculty of Psychology of the National Autonomous University of Mexico, Urbina (1989) analyzed the relevance of the curricular change and proposed a restructuring regarding the insertion of the supervision process in the professional work of the psychologist that would allow him to respond to the needs of society. In the same tone, Ayala and Vázquez (2001) carried out the PAPIME project entitled "The strengthening of Vocational Training, through Practical Training Programs under Undergraduate and Postgraduate Supervision", where it was proposed that supervision was essential for the development of the professional skills of students so that they are better prepared to respond more appropriately to the needs of today's society. From this project, the practical training program under supervision (PEPS) was developed through which it was intended that its students acquire and develop professional skills, ethical behavior, as well as social awareness and an attitude of commitment; all of this expressed through the link between professional actions and health institutions and the community.

Likewise, Díaz (2010) developed a training program for clinical psychologists in the care of gender violence against women in the couple, with a comprehensive model that sought to impact professional work in three axes: theoretical, acquisition of skills, and reflection of beliefs and attitudes. The results obtained show in the evaluation carried out before and after the student program, a significant difference in knowledge, development of diagnostic and treatment skills. In the content analysis of the interviews, it was found that the participants modified those beliefs about gender violence against women in the couple, permeated by myths and cultural stereotypes and that favor revictimization, they understood the complexity of the phenomenon, they reflected about their personal history and achieved the self-perception of an increase in their knowledge and greater prevention and treatment skills for this problem.

Another study is the one carried out by Valenzuela (2011), related to psychotherapeutic supervision and its importance as a fundamental space in the training of the clinical psychologist. In this work, the author analyzes different implications of the term supervision and psychotherapeutic supervision, as well as the main objectives, functions and stages that are part of the process, roles and links that are established between supervisor and supervisee, as well as some models of psychotherapeutic supervision, in the practice of the clinical psychologist. Likewise, a broad review of contributions to psychotherapeutic supervision is carried out from various approaches: psychoanalysis, brief dynamically oriented psychotherapy, psychotherapy and work with groups and systemic therapy. Finally, in this study a proposal is made for a supervision model that is aimed at the training of clinical psychologists in the community and institutional settings.

On the other hand, Villafuerte (2021) completed the doctoral thesis titled "Ethical dilemmas in clinical supervision and their resolution", in which he analyzes the training and specific evaluations for the performance of supervision, codes, and legislation in this regard. However, the author points out that in Mexico, the codes are not very specific "the training for the training of supervisors that is offered is not mandatory to exercise supervision and lack specifications that standardize them, the proposals being very different from each other" (p. 44). Plus there is no formal training. On the other hand, she also points out that in systemic, cognitive behavioral, and psychoanalytic schools there is an active promotion of supervision. Finally, the author highlights that the majority of supervisors replicate the way they were trained, but they are based on their experience (she does not necessarily frame this as negative) but highlights the importance of generating formal training, based on a training model of competencies in clinical supervision.

Finally, we find the publication made by Carbajal and collaborators (2019), who propose the "Supervision model for professional training in psychology." The purpose of this document is to link professional training and the provision of psychological services to various populations.

This supervision model is closely linked to the 2008 Curriculum of the Bachelor's Degree in Psychology, the Unique Program of Specializations in Psychology, Master's and Doctoral Program of the UNAM.

Structure of Supervised Practices

In Mexico, the different universities that offer both bachelors and postgraduate degrees in psychology currently include a period of practical training, with clinical supervision being a central element. However, based on the General Health Law, the psychotherapist must be a psychologist with a professional license and with postgraduate studies in psychotherapy, carried out in institutions that have official validity.

Supervision is understood as a professional training process in which a supervisor offers possibilities of accompaniment, discovery and learning in real-world settings to the supervisees, through the reflective integration of theory with practice, for their autonomous and ethical professional development (Carbajal et al., 2019).

The duty of universities and teaching staff is then to provide quality practices to future mental health professionals and the figure of the supervisor provides a space for teaching and feedback, helping students to grow in self-confidence and self-understanding, while taking care of the maintenance and attention to users (Hackney & Goodyear, 1984 as cited in De Lebl, 2000).

Within the graduate programs in which psychotherapists are trained, about 200–2000 h of clinical supervision are normally covered in an average of 2–3 years for the master's level and 4 or 5 years at the doctoral level. Usually these hours of supervision include a mix of group and individual supervision either live or narrated; with on-site or seconded supervisors to training programs and peer-to-peer or cascade (therapists in more advanced training supervising less experienced therapists). Sometimes video or audio recording is used to review the sessions or written reports depending on the supervisory approach and the psychotherapeutic training model.

Evidence of skill development through supervised practice and teaching opportunities for students is often an accreditation criterion for higher education training

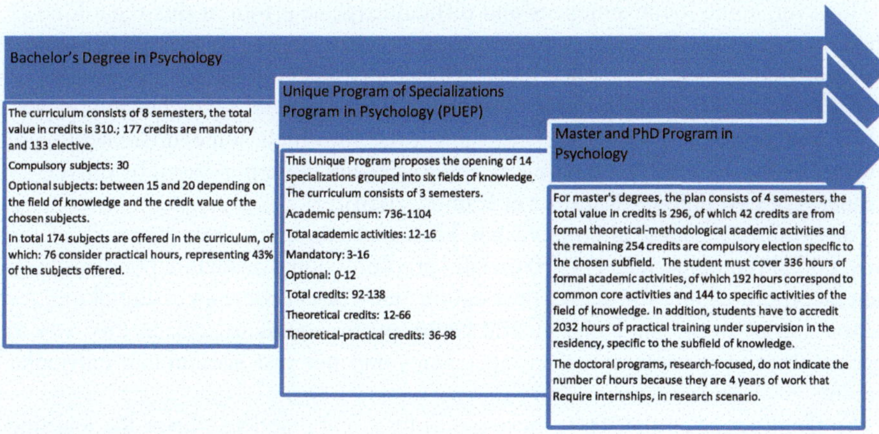

Fig. 1 General characteristics of the curricula. Source: Carbajal et al. (2019). Supervision model for professional training in Psychology. p. 8. UNAM

programs and criteria for obtaining academic degree (Hyson et al., 2009, as cited in Kneppe, 2018; Saiz & Susinos, 2017).

In Mexico, there are differences in credit requirements in undergraduate and graduate study plans in Psychology. In such a way that, to obtain a bachelor's degree, a minimum of between 366 and 400 credits (3–4 years) is required. To obtain the specialty degree, at least 45 credits after the bachelor's degree (1 year) and after the master's degree, 90 post-baccalaureate credits (2 years).

For example, in the current curriculum of the Faculty of Psychology of the National Autonomous University of Mexico (UNAM), both undergraduate and different graduate programs, professional practices are required that respond to the learning of different approaches and theoretical-technical and methodological platforms of psychology, such as the clinical, educational, social, neurophysiological, among others.

With regard to postgraduate studies, the curriculum of the Unique Program of Specializations in Psychology (PUEP) has an internship program that also contemplates the needs of the subjects that make it up and that students can develop in scenarios linked to the Faculty; the same happens with the Master's Program in Psychology, which is made up of different residences in which students develop, in a significant number of hours, professional skills through supervised practice (see Fig. 1).

Supervision in the Bachelor Program

It is desirable that undergraduate students be trained as professionals capable of recognizing the problems of the context in which they operate and seeking answers through the design, application, and evaluation of their interventions.

However, some inconveniences and difficulties have arisen in this regard, since when interviewing graduating students, some perceive themselves as not being professionally competent to practice their profession, especially in the development of internships and not so much in the classrooms. That is, there is a dichotomy in academic and practical training, at the same time in which some mismatches are detected between the skills required by employers and those possessed by university graduates of psychology (Ramirez & Ramos, 2016).

An extremely useful alternative has been that for more than 40 years at the Universidad Iberoamericana (1970 to date) preprofessional academic practices have been incorporated into the degree curriculum and it has become an essential tool for the training of future students, mental health professionals to seek in this way to develop their own professional competencies and not just accumulate curricular content.

For Domínguez et al. (2007) these preprofessional practices "favor the learning of knowing how to do, being able to do, and knowing how to be, it is not only about applying intervention techniques and strategies, but about learning the role of the future psychology professional" (p. 24).

Trying to summarize what has been written about the conception of these preprofessional practices, it can be said (Montes de Oca, 2017):

- They help professional identity.
- Link theory with real scenarios.
- They encourage reflection on professional work.
- They promote self-knowledge.
- They facilitate the development of professional and generic skills.
- Learn values, attitudes, knowledge, ways of being, thinking, speaking, and feeling.
- Training experiences.
- Vocational guidance process.
- Possibility of employment and self-employment.
- Transition between university and the world of work.

On the other hand, it is extremely important to supervise these preprofessional practices, since according to Puig (2010) three basic functions can be identified in supervision: administrative (service management), educational (training, psychotherapeutic paradigms), and support (professional role). However, the development of the student's professional skills stands out as its primary function, highlighting an adequate use of communication, knowledge, technical skills, clinical reasoning, emotions, values, and a reflection on daily practice with an ethical responsibility for all those involved.

The not only educational value of supervision, training and support in the development of competencies specific to the profession is undoubted; especially when providing a mental health service, learning has an extraordinarily significant value.

The Practice of Clinical Supervision in Psychotherapy

Practice Models

In Mexico, generally the supervision models that are used in practice, considering the taxonomy proposed by Consoli et al. (2017), would correspond to the first and second generation.

According to these authors, "the supervision models conceptualized as first generation bring together those that are based on psychotherapy approaches that incorporate theoretical principles, technical practices and the relational roles of client and therapist; In such a way that, psychotherapeutic theory and supervisory learning are aligned" (p. 8). In this way, in Mexico it is common for clinical supervision to depend on the psychotherapeutic approach on which both training and professional practice are based.

On the other hand, Consoli et al. (2017) state that second-generation models "are based on the combination of factors, processes and perspectives of common practices including the application of the contextual psychotherapy model" (p. 9). Within these second-generation models, one of the lines of work includes "models that emphasize competencies, which focus on the knowledge, skills, attitudes, and values required to develop specific clinical skills within which they emphasize evidence, examine, develop, and evaluate measurable results in supervisory practices" (p. 9).

Another classification that could help us conceptualize supervision models in Mexico is the one proposed by Daskal (2008), who proposes three types of models: evolutionary, problem-solving, and analysis of inconsistencies.

1) Evolutionary models are based on the idea that psychotherapists go through different stages in their professional development; steps that must be taken into account to adapt the methodologies to the process of the supervised. These described stages are divided into three main ones: beginner, middle stage of development, and advanced therapists; supervisors must possess certain specific skills and competencies during each of these stages.

With beginning students, the supervisor should focus on the strengths and weaknesses of the supervisees, as well as provide a role model, structure, clarity of techniques, and validation of their own perceptions or delivery of alternative concepts through positive feedback.

Supervisees in a medium stage need supervisors to maintain a flexible position, attentive and at the same time respectful of the knowledge they have acquired, encouraging their autonomy and creativity. At this point, supervisors' criticisms can be more direct in terms of suggestions for types and ways of intervening.

Finally, the supervision of advanced stages focuses on the ways to evaluate technical instruments and also the development of the patient. Requiring attitudes of humility from supervisors, respect for experience and diverse perspectives, ability to establish a dialogue with their supervisees; focusing on the strengths and weaknesses of the supervisee, thus somewhat reducing the direct participation of supervisors.

2) Problem-solving model starts from the premise that the supervisee is facing a problem before the user, which prevents him from advancing towards the goal. Following this logic, the supervisor contributes to detecting the variables that make up the supervisor's problem and helps him reach his potential, develop hypotheses, use instruments, relate facts and fill information gaps.

   The problem according to the model arises when the desired state cannot be reached immediately. The characteristics that may be present in a problem are (Funke, 2003 as cited in Daskal, 2008):

   - Complexity: The problem is multifactorial and multifaceted, causing the person to perceive himself as excessive, making it necessary to synthesize or reduce the available information.
   - Network operation: Each part of the problem is interrelated and it is important to recognize the functioning of the network system.
   - Own dynamics: The problem has a changing condition, so the time factor must be considered as variable.
   - Transparency: To understand the problem it is necessary to actively seek out the information that you do not have about the problem.
   - Multi-targeting: The problems often contain incompatible or contradictory factors, therefore, the goal has to be very well defined.

3) Inconsistencies analysis model is based on the principles of Integrative Psychotherapy of Klaus Grawe (2002 as cited in Daskal, 2008), who, part of the definition of four basic needs of the human being, as a cause of psychic disorders that cannot be satisfied. These needs are divided into: need for guidance and control, attachment and belonging, increased and protection of self-esteem and need for pleasure and avoidance of displeasure.

   Applying these principles in supervision, it is intended to detect difficulties or inconsistencies regarding: therapeutic work, the therapeutic relationship, their personal capacities to treat the case and the joy and pleasure in the work of the supervised (Grawe, 2006 as cited in Daskal, 2008). This allows the model to be applied regardless of the orientation of the supervised, it also offers a structure that allows the definition of goals and resources to achieve them.
4) On the other hand, based on the experiences of graduate programs in universities, specific models have been proposed, such as the Supervision Model for Professional Practice in Clinical and Health Psychology, proposed by Carbajal et al. (2019), academics of the Faculty of Psychology of the UNAM. This model aims to link vocational training and the provision of psychological services to different populations to the current Curriculum Plan. This is a competency-based model, whose main theoretical paradigms are socioconstructionism, gradual transfer of responsibility, learning-by-doing, situated cognition, and accompaniment.

   This model is composed of the following stages:

   1. Planning: The objectives, scope, activities, scenarios, and supervision modality are identified. Likewise, the competences that the student will acquire and

under.what modality and requirements the supervision will be carried out are described, the sessions are also assigned a date and the supervised ones are communicated.
2. Frame: Communication with the student to make their knowledge of what was planned, as well as the role of the supervisor and the consent of the student.
3. Development: It encompasses the following monitoring modalities: exposure, modeling, testing, and feedback.
4. Evaluation: It promotes the identification and measurement of the scope and achievements of supervision; it must be done based on what is established in the planning, return to the definition of competent performance of the student and identify the level of demand of the moment of formation. It applies to both student performance and student perception of supervisory performance.

From this model, supervision favors the development of professional competencies because supervised practices aim to highlight the commitment to train critical, responsible, reflective, ethical psychologists capable of applying and generating knowledge in psychology through self- awareness, autonomy, and self-care.

As can be seen, the line of work in the supervision models for the training of psychologists and psychotherapists is one of the main ones in many of the university programs, both undergraduate and graduate, so it is one of the greatest strengths in our country. However, it is important to mention that few certified educational institutions have systematized and published such supervision models for professional training and psychotherapists, among those published are the Universidad Iberoamericana (Montes de Oca, 2017); UNAM both in the Faculty of Psychology (Urbina, 1989, Ayala & Vázquez, 2001; UNAM, 2009; Diaz, 2010; Valenzuela, 2011; Carbajal et al., 2019; Jiménez y Rivera, 2019), the Faculty of Higher Studies of Zaragoza (FES Zaragoza, 2010) and the Faculty of Higher Studies of Iztacala (López & Porras, 2019); the National Polytechnic Institute (Guerrero, 2019); the Autonomous University of Baja California (UABC/UNAM, 2013–2015); Universidad Panamericana (UPN, 2012); and Universidad de Colima (CENEDIC, 2012).

Conducting Supervision Sessions

So far we have talked about the contexts in which supervision occurs, the social needs it seeks to cover and how educational institutions have sought to structure models that put all this into practice. Now we will take a look at how supervisors direct their work to meet the training and accompaniment needs in the supervision they provide, always taking into account that these may differ to a wide degree.

As mentioned above, the most common supervision in our country occurs in the training of psychotherapists in graduate programs, so the most common format of supervision is group supervision and most of the time it is linked to some subject or model of psychotherapy; therefore, the way in which this supervision is carried out still depends very much on the model of psychotherapy on which the training is based, the most common being narrated supervision (self-report) followed by live supervision in Gesell chambers. For this, different mechanisms of analysis of the sessions are used, which can range from real-time communication with the therapist to written reports or transcripts sometimes accompanied by recordings of the session to be supervised. This is often complemented with scales of satisfaction and/or feedback of the users attended in these sessions as well as the clinical record that should reflect the professional management of said case.

The following are some elements that are common in supervisory practices and that give structure to the practice of this profession.

First Stage of the Supervision

At the beginning of supervision, the framing, which is often taken as equivalent to the supervision contract, is usually done verbally and may include some academic program and/or written institutional regulations of the professional practice to be carried out. This framework ideally includes the way in which the supervision will be carried out, the professional profile of the supervisor, the work format, the periodicity (which is usually weekly), the objectives set, the way to evaluate them, and the formats to be used. It is worth mentioning that the confusion between what should include the therapeutic framework (between the therapist and the user), the practical training program (the way the academic program to which the supervised practice belongs is to be staged) and the supervision contract is still very common. That is why, elements such as: the objectives of supervision, the supervisory relationship that is sought to be created, what can be expected from the supervisor and what is to be expected of the supervisee depending on his/her degree of training and the program in which she/he will be supervised and the ethical or institutional regulations that must be observed, may go unnoticed or ignored in a large proportion of supervised practices.

During the Supervision

In the case of live supervision, there is usually a Gesell chamber or two rooms communicated through camera and microphone so that the supervisor and the rest of the therapeutic group or team can observe the session, often an intersession is made before finishing the session with the client so that the therapeutic team can give feedback to the therapists (one or two in the case of cotherapy) before closing the session. Once this is over, there is a supervision session directed by the supervisor in which sometimes the whole in training group participates to propose the conceptualization of the case, the search for clinical strategies and the professional management of the therapists in charge of the case. It is at this stage of supervision that ideally we work both with the management of the clinical case, and with the scaffolding of the clinical competences of the therapists. In Mexico, the interrelationship between both tasks is increasingly understood, although since, as mentioned above, the models we follow of supervision often follow the first-generation models, it may happen that the main focus is on the management of the clinical case and not necessarily on the clinical competencies of the therapist.

In cases where there is a focus on enhancing the clinical competencies of the supervised therapist; this is given session by session and we can observe their professional evolution in real time, in addition to encouraging the professional growth of the therapeutic team in a vicarious manner. At this point there may be exercises or educational strategies aimed at developing clinical competencies demanded by the case being addressed.

Example

Supervised: I have been preparing the next couple session with Alan and Nancy, I reviewed the recording and the article of the cycle of vulnerability that we were talking about the last supervision and I would like to talk about it with you to clarify what I understood.

Supervisor: Sure, tell me what you've been thinking about and we can figure it out together.

Supervised: I want to talk to them about when they are angry and how that does not allow for dialogue and reflection. I prepared some questions to differentiate what surges when there is understanding, empathy and negotiation and what is obstructed when they react to the vulnerabilities that are touched in their discussions and they react defensively.

Supervisor: I think it could be very useful to them, I remember that after the last session with them you talked about how sometimes it is difficult to talk about these things in therapy because they get upset and argue; Have you thought about how you could approach it this time?

Supervised: In the article you sent me it talked about what to do in impasses and I was thinking of addressing it with a specific example to be able to talk about how they could decide that this conflict should be handled differently, maybe put it in slow motion and review it in parts to see how each of them reacts and that they can take responsibility for what they are doing and be able to review at the same time how that makes the other person feel. Then maybe begin to clarify with them some differences; This is violence, this is power, this is control, but also point out the moments in which they understand and connect and look for other ways they can connect and negotiate their desires and needs. Can I show you the questions I prepared?

Supervisor: I think the first part is a very good idea Sara, I imagine that the part of pointing out what violence, control or power is has to do with what we talked about last time about limiting the intimidating behaviors that Alan sometimes has. Is that so?

Supervised: Yes, because I kept thinking that it hasn't been easy for me to point it out so clearly for fear of him getting angry, but after the session in which we were able to talk about it, I think he is more receptive and we need to ground it in examples when he resorts to these power tactics.

Supervisor: I also agree with you and I think it is very important that it be exemplified; However, it seems to me that you raise two very important issues that can be complex; How would you feel if we could think about making a two-session plan that addresses these topics one by one so that it doesn't become too complex to be responsible for taking everything into account in one session?

Supervised: In fact it sounds better to me because I do worry about getting lost in the session because I want to cover a lot.

Supervisor: Of course, the priority would be that both topics serve as a guide for you to understand what is happening in the relationship that does not allow for a better dynamic, and that while you understand it, they can also have more clarity about what is happening and how to change it, don't worry, you don't have to feel like you have to have everything clear from the beginning.

Supervised: I do feel sometimes I have to be clear about everything from the beginning and sometimes that can paralyze me a little.

Supervisor: It is normal to feel a lot of responsibility in the session, but we have seen that when you take a more horizontal position you feel more comfortable and flow more with them, so we can think that it is a good resource to go to.

Supervised: Okay, it does make me feel more comfortable, and so I would like to focus a little more on the cycle in this session and maybe that will open the way more easily to talk about violence.

Supervisor: Perfect, now, do you want us to look at some of the questions you prepared so that they can be a kind of guide for you in the session?

The previous example shows a conversation between one of the authors of the chapter in a supervision scenario for psychotherapists in Family Therapy training at the master's level. Of course, it proposes a path of many possible ones in supervision, but it helps us make visible that in clinical supervision different levels of competencies are addressed at the same time, ranging from the use of specific techniques or theories, the management of information in the sessions, the use of hypotheses to guide the therapeutic work, the analysis of the case session by session combined with the evolutionary analysis of the therapy and the management of the professional level of the supervised person and the respective insecurities that may arise among many other possibilities.

After Supervision

Usually between supervision sessions, therapists and the team are in charge of updating the clinical record and completing the forms in which supervision is supported. These may include, session reports, institutional formats, logs, case analysis, analysis exercises, transcripts of the session and/or search for information or creation of materials to use in future sessions.

Finally, at the end of the period of supervision (usually one or two semesters), supervisees must usually deliver the evaluation resources that the program requires such as theoretical work, case analysis reports, logs and the complete clinical record, among others. This is complemented by summative feedback (face to face in the best cases), which allows the supervisee to gradually integrate the supervisor's feedback, and that creates evidence of the supervision received by the therapist and his professional development.

In the case of narrated supervision, the dynamics can be very similar, with the difference that the supervisees have specific dates scheduled every 1 or 2 weeks, generally, to review the cases they are carrying out in their clinical practices; in this modality, video or audio recordings of the sessions may be required.

Supervisory Relationship

Watkins (2013) reports that the supervisory working alliance is composed of three core elements: the supervisor-supervisee link, the objectives established in collaboration that guide the supervision process, and the tasks agreed in collaboration that facilitate the pursuit of the achievement of supervisory objectives.

Regarding the supervisor-supervisee relationship, clinical supervision in Mexico is generally based on an academic relationship, hence, it is common for the supervisory alliance to be subordinated to the teaching relationship and the therapeutic alliance. This situation may involve risks in the supervisory relationship, as very few supervisors establish a clear framing of the supervisory relationship specifically. Thus, we have, in broad terms, a group of clinical supervisors who, depending on the therapeutic model they practice and supervise, derive the type of relationship that they must have with their supervisees and even the objectives they seek to meet in supervision. On the other hand we have those supervisors who, focused on the competencies they want to develop in their supervisees, seek to create a relationship that allows this development. This last group would include not only those who are seeking to generate or strengthen clinical competencies, but those who, due to the supervision program they direct, are seeking to scaffold specific theoretical or professional competencies of psychotherapy training.

Regarding the objectives and tasks agreed in collaboration that facilitate the achievement of supervisory objectives, Watkins states that these involve: mastery of specific skills; broaden the understanding of consultants; increase awareness of the problems of the process; increase self- awareness and impact on the process; overcoming personal and intellectual obstacles to learning and mastery; deepen understanding of concepts and theory; provide a stimulus for research; and maintain service standards. In this regard, we can observe that, in the models that have been published in Mexico so far, many of these elements are covered in different ways and to different degrees in the most common supervisions in our country. It is worth clarifying at this point, that an important area of improvement is that these objectives are established in collaboration with the supervisee, since it is generally the supervisors who decide what is going to be sought to achieve; still focusing many times on the management of the case or on the objectives of the subject to which supervision is anchored as a practice and not directly on the construction of therapist competencies.

Training Clinical Supervisors in Psychotherapy

Finally, we must emphasize that exercising clinical supervision in a context in which there is no specific legal framework or academic structure for the training of supervisors presents many challenges in the day to day of our professional practice and therefore there are efforts that are being carried out continuously so that the regulation of clinical supervision is increasingly clearer both in academic institutions and in the legal and regulatory context of the country.

Until now, in Mexico, clinical supervisors are primarily experienced professionals with expertise in the specific field of clinical psychology, but not necessarily with formal training in clinical supervision. This, on the one hand, arises from the still scarce culture of training supervisors for the development of supervisory competences based on clear theoretical-methodological models; thus, confusing clinical and teaching expertise with competencies and supervisory performance.

On the other hand, the above generates that the training alternatives for supervisors are quite scarce, coupled with the fact that there is little differentiation between the functions, activities, responsibilities and scope of the academic staff of practice scenarios, psychotherapists, tutors, and supervisors. Generally, psychotherapists with competent and outstanding performance may be hired as part of the teaching staff to supervise on-site clinical practices in psychotherapy. However, both clinical supervision in psychotherapy and academia in supervision are subject to university training processes and usually have some seminars, courses and workshops that are eventually organized as part of their updating and teacher training. Some of the offers that have been launched so far in our country come from specific educational institutions, which offer training in the supervision models they use and that provide the opportunity for clinical supervisors with most experience to share their knowledge and expertise with those who are beginning to exercise clinical supervision or want to do so. Although this is very valuable, we still need to systematize and formalize alternatives for training supervisors, considering specialized programs, focused on the training and development of supervisory skills. As well as continuing to promote the training of highly qualified personnel in mental health services, so issues such as certification and membership are priorities in the mental health services that need to be provided to our communities.

Due to gaps in formal training, certification, and mandatory membership requirements for clinical supervisors professionals bear the responsibility of constantly seeking, in Mexico or other countries, opportunities to enhance their competencies in their areas of expertisse, and in recent years, in specific supervisory competencies. As much of the supervision they offer is in academic contexts; many of them have credentials in educational training and have become clinical supervisors after having certain years of experience as psychotherapists and very commonly as undergraduate and/or postgraduate professors in clinical psychology. Likewise, they must have the same degree or an academic degree higher than that in which they supervise and present proof of their credentials to the institutions in which they practice. Most of the time the supervisor exercises as a psychotherapist the same clinical model in which he/she supervises clinical practice, although there are exceptions in which his professional profile allows him to supervise in interdisciplinary contexts.

On the other hand, in daily practice, it is very common that through the same institution in which supervision takes place or through the continuous training courses that supervisors take, collaboration and professional support groups are created through which options for co- supervision, supervision of supervision, continuous training, review of problems in professional competence, search for educational strategies, creation of instruments, and even emotional containment are provided when required.

Ethical Issues and Challenges

As Villafuerte (2021) mentions, Mexico does not have certifying bodies at the national level or legislation regarding clinical supervision in psychotherapy. However, as mentioned above, the AMOPP since 2009 has made efforts to promote the certification of psychotherapists with international standards through a partnership with the NBCC. In these efforts, it has also sought to certify clinical supervisors, although this is still an incipient work. However, as it is not an obligation to practice within clinical psychology, few health professionals obtain this certification. This suggests the need to create laws that promote continuous professional updating and evaluation with the aim of improving clinical practice (Villafuerte, 2021).

On the other hand, Carbajal et al. (2019) include a section on "Ethical and legal aspects" in the publication of the Supervision Model for Professional Training in Psychology, where it is described that in Mexico both training and practice in clinical psychology and psychotherapy is governed by both the General Health Law and the Code of Ethics of the Psychologist and make some recommendations for protective actions for supervisors, supervised, and persons served:

1. Do not supervise beyond one's own competences as a supervisor.
2. Choose carefully the supervision model(s).
3. Avoid dual relationships.
4. Evaluate the competence of the supervisee.
5. Be available for monitoring.
6. Formulate a robust monitoring program.

7. Be aware of professional considerations of supervision.
8. Monitor honestly and with integrity.

An In-House Supervisory Approach

Throughout this text, many of the particular conditions of clinical supervision in psychotherapy in Mexico have already been mentioned. We believe this is important because much of the research and models proposed about clinical supervision, as well as suggestions for best practices, have come from countries that have contexts different from our own. This.

creates the illusion that other countries practices become a kind of parameter with which we must contrast what we do, as if the contextualization of professional practices were annulled. However, the present book arises from the need to change this illusion of emptiness in which our profession is exercised, to rescue both those contextual and structural factors that exist in the Latin-American context around supervisory practices, as well as the best practices that occur thanks to these specific cultural and social contexts. We believe that Mexico and Latin-American countries have much to contribute in the dialogue of clinical supervision because of those characteristics that unite us as Latinos and that make us unique as countries.

Significant challenges remain, particularly in establishing standardized regulations and structured training for clinical supervision in psychotherapy, but our strengths lie precisely in the fact that despite the lack of these conditions, we have managed to take care of the standards of our profession and we continue to feedback what we have learned to continuously improve.

The collaborations that are being achieved between professionals and national institutions, as well as the international alliances that are increasingly stronger, generate a very prosperous panorama for clinical supervision and the use of shared knowledge. Mexico and Latin America have always been characterized by their gregarious cultures and brotherhood which come from a rich and very challenging history and we are sure that this will be a pillar for the future growth of our profession.

References

Amarís, M., Acuña Reyes, E., & Quintero González, S. (2019). *Intervening to repair: Recovery of dignity and mental health in contexts of violence*. Universidad del Norte.

Autonomous University of Baja California / National Autonomous University of Mexico. (2013–2015). "#Collaborative networks in teacher training and evaluation". Financing of the Teacher Improvement Program (PROMEP).

Ayala, H., & Vázquez, F. (Eds.). (2001). *The professional training of the psychologist in the field of health, education, social processes and organizations: The internship in general psychology of the Faculty of Psychology of the UNAM*. UNAM.

Belle, D., & Doucet, J. (2003). Poverty, inequality, and discrimination as sources of depression among U.S. women. *Psychology of Women Quarterly, 27*(2), 101–113.

Benjet, C., Medina-Mora, M., Borges, G., Zambrano-Ruiz, J., & Aguilar-Gaxiola, S. (2009). Youth mental health in a Popolous City of the developing world: Results from the Mexican adolescent mental health survey. *The Journal of Child Psychology and Psychiatry, 50*, 386–395.

Carbajal, M. T., Diaz, N., Felix, V., Gutierrez, M., Hagg, C., Hernandez, L., Jimenez, V., Morales, S., Paredes, H., Rodriguez, T., Ruiz, V., Torres, K., & Valenzuela, A. (2019). *Supervision model for training in professional practice in psychology*. UNAM: Faculty of Psychology.

Chamber of Deputies LXV Legislature. (2023). Bulletin No. 3680. Mental disorders increase in Mexico; population between 15 and 20 years old, the most vulnerable. Retrieved April 17, 2023, from http://www5.diputados.gob.mx/index.php/camara/Comunicacion/Boletines/2017/Mayo/26/3680-Incrementan-trastornos-mentales-en-Mexico-poblacion-entre-15-y-20-anos-la-mas-vulnerable

Consoli, T., Grazioso, M., Fenández, M., & Cobar, A. (2017). Monitoring today: What we know and need to know. *Psychologists Magazine, VII*. 20th Special Edition, 6–19.

Coordination of Educational Psychology, UNAM. (2009, August). *Academic programs of the integral practices modality. Practical training system. Booklet*. National Autonomous University of Mexico: Faculty of Psychology. Survey for students on the curriculum. Synthesis of results. UNAM.

Daskal, A. (2008). Putting the magnifying glass on clinical supervision. *Revista Argentina de Clínica Psicológica, XVII*(3), 215–224. ISSN: 0327-6716.

De Lebl, B. (2000). Clinical supervision. *Revista Ciencia y Cultura, 8*, 87–95. http://www.scielo.org.bo/scielo.php?script=sci_arttext&pid=S2077-33232000000200009&lng=es&tlng=es of Mexico, Mexico

Diaz, N. (2010). *Model for the training of psychology professionals in the care of gender violence against women in the couple. (Unpublished PhD thesis)*. Faculty of Psychology, UNAM, Mexico.

Domínguez, J., Merino, F., Moreno, R., González, J., Sánchez, J., & Vera, J. (2007). The practicum of psychology in the european higher education area. Retrieved February 3, 2017, from http://www.uab.cat/document/PracticumEEES_2007,0.pdf/

Encyclopedia humanities. (2023). Mexico. Retrieved April 17, 2023, from https://humanidades.com/mexico/#ixzz7xriwS1bV

Faculty of Higher Studies Zaragoza. (2010). *Proposal for modification to the plan and study programs of the degree in psychology (face-to-face system)*. National Autonomous University of Mexico.

Falender, C., & Shafranske, E. (2014). Clinical supervision: The state of the art. *Journal of Clinical Psychology: In Session, 70*(11), 1030–1041. https://doi.org/10.1002/jclp.22124

Foss-Kelly, L., Generali, M., & Kress, V. (2017). Counseling strategies for empowering people living in poverty: The I-CARE model. *Journal of Multicultural Counseling and Development, 45*, 201–213.

Guerrero, D. (2019, October). Supervised internship at the Polytechnic Institute.

Jiménez, M. E., & Rivera, O. R. (2019). *Proposal of guidelines for training in professional practice in psychology that considers the observations received from professors of both divisions*. Faculty of Psychology: UNAM.

Kneppe, W. J. (2018). Early childhood education students! Perceptions of community college online practicum experiences from a competency-based education Perspective. ProQuest.

https://search.proquest.com/openview/8607bc488d91076e7b76ce48ba5f4622/1?pq-origsite=gscholar&cbl=18750&diss=y

López, G., & Porras, K. (2019, October). Project to promote personal development.

Medina Mora, M., Real, T., & Sarti, J. E. (2015). *Depression and other psychiatric disorders*. Academia Mexicana de la Ciencia.

Mexican Association of Psychological Orientation and Psychotherapy, A.C. (2011). *Code of ethics 2011* (1st ed.). AMOPP, A.C.

Mexican Society of Psychology. (2015). *Code of ethics of the psychologist* (5th ed.). Trails.

Ministry of Foreign Affairs. (2023). Basic data of Mexico. Retrieved April 17, 2023, from https://embamex.sre.gob.mx/nigeria/index.php/es/mexico-informacion/datos-basicos

Montes de Oca, S. (2017). *Manual of pre-professional practices*. Department of psychology. Universidad Iberoamericana. CDMX.

National Association of Universities and Institutions of Higher Education. (2023). Part One. Higher Education in Mexico. Retrieved April 17, 2023, from http://publicaciones.anuies.mx/acervo/revsup/res029/txt1c.htm

National Center for Digital Publishing and Development of Education Technologies (CENEDIC). (2012). University of Colima. Retrieved from http://cenedic.ucol.mx/paginacenedic/index.php?option=com_content&view=article&id=18&Itemid=24

National Council for the Evaluation of Social Development Policy. (2020). Multidimensional Measurement of Poverty in Mexico 2018–2020. https://www.coneval.org.mx/Medicion/MP/Documents/MMP_2018_2020/Pobreza_multidimensional_2018_2020_CONEVAL.pdf

National Institute of Statistics, Geography and Informatics [INEGI]. (2010). Retrieved May 19, 2019, from https://www.inegi.org.mx/temas/discapacidad/

National Institute of Statistics, Geography and Informatics [INEGI]. (2020). Mexico in figures. https://www.inegi.org.mx/app/areasgeograficas/

National Pedagogical University (UPN). (2012). Professional practices. Retrieved from: http://www.upnmochis.com/practicas.html

Orrego, S., Hincapié, G. M., & Restrepo, D. (2019). Mental disorders from the perspective of trauma and violence in a population-based study. *Colombian Journal of Psychiatry*.

Puig, C. (2010). On supervising and supervision in social intervention. *RTS Revista de Treball Social, 189*, 49–64.

Ramirez, L., & Ramos, C. (2016). Learning to be a psychologist: Identity transitions in the university classroom. *Revista de la Educación Superior, 45*(179), 41–53.

Saiz, L. Á., & Susinos, R. T. (2017). "#You Gave Us the Confidence to Speak." The University supervisor in a reflective practicum. *REICE. Revista Iberoamericana sobre Calidad, Eficacia y Cambio en Educación, 15*(1), 55–69. https://www.redalyc.org/articulo.oa?id=551/55149730004

Urbina, J. (Ed.). (1989). *The psychologist: Training, professional practice and prospective*. UNAM.

Valenzuela, C. (2011). *Importance of psychotherapeutic supervision in the training of the clinical psychologist. Master's Thesis*. Faculty of Psychology, UNAM.

Villafuerte, A. (2021). Profile and competencies of the clinical supervisor: Who supervises and how?. Chapter 2. Clinical supervision in psychotherapy: A guide to best practices. Compiler Tena, A. (2021). Vesalius.

Watkins, E. (2013). The supervisory alliance as quintessential integrative variable. *Journal Contemporany Psichotherapy, 44*, 151–161. https://doi.org/10.1007/s10879-013-9252-x

World Bank. (2023). Mexico: overview. Retrieved April 17, 2023, from https://www.bancomundial.org/es/country/mexico/overview

Zabalza, M. A. (2013). The practicum in university education. *Giornale Italiano della Ricerca Educativa., VI*(10), 127–141. ISSN 2038-9744.

Zalaquett, C. P., & Ivey, A. E. (2018). The role of neuroscience in advancing social justice counseling. In *Counseling for social justice* (pp. 191–203). American Counseling Association Foundation.

María Antonia Carbajal Godínez is a Systemic Therapist and Clinical Supervisor with a gender perspective. She has a degree in psychology and a master's degree in Family Therapy from the National Autonomous University of Mexico (UNAM), with diplomas in Family Violence and Human Rights and training in Systemic-Dialectic Psychotherapy aimed at the development of clinical skills. She has taught courses at the bachelor's level since 2014 and master's level since 2019. She has served as an academic-administrative technical secretary in the Coordination of the Dr. Guillermo Dávila Psychological Services Center of the Faculty of Psychology. She has participated in multiple conferences and media on issues of systemic therapy, clinical supervision in psychotherapy, and gender-based violence. In recent years, she has accumulated over two hundred hours of training in clinical supervision and is co-author of publications in this field. Today she is Professor and Systemic Clinical Supervisor in the Master's Residency in Family Therapy at UNAM and in the private sector with more than four hundred hours of experience in individual and group supervision.

Verónica Ruiz González is a child and adolescent psychologist and psychotherapist with more than 17 years of clinical experience. She completed her bachelor's and master's studies in psychology with a residency in Child Psychotherapy from UNAM. She is currently pursuing her PhD studies at the University of the Americas in Mexico City. She is an academic, tutor, supervisor in the Child Psychotherapy Residency at the Faculty of Psychology, UNAM from 2005 to date. From 2013 to 2021, she was head of the "Dr. Julián Mac Gregor y Sánchez Navarro" Community Center. From August 2022 to date, she is the head of the "Dr. Guillermo Dávila" Psychological Services Center linked to the Faculty of Psychology, UNAM. She has 17 years of experience as an on-site supervisor at the "Dr. Guillermo Dávila" Psychological Services Center of the UNAM and in private groups. She has participated in several research projects about delinquency, anger control in children, child abuse, child psychotherapy, violence, positive parenting, and training in supervised professional practice, as well as participated as speaker in various national and international conferences. She is the compiler and author of the book "Supervision Model for Training in Professional Practice in Psychology," Editorial UNAM (2019); co-author of the books: "Clinical supervision in psychotherapy. A Guide to Best Practices" (2021); "Narrative Therapy Practices for Children and Their Families" (2018); and "Child Psychotherapy with Play. Clinical Cases of Modern Manual" (2010). President and co-founder of the International College of Child Psychology, CDMX, and Specialties Yolopath.

Antonio Tena-Suck since 1983 Edgar Antonio Tena Suck holds a doctoral degree and has been a professor in the Department of Psychology at the Universidad Iberoamericana. He was also Director of the Department of Psychology at the Universidad Iberoamericana, Mexico City from 2008 to 2015. He has also led many programs such as Coordinator of the bachelor's degree in psychology at the UIA and Coordinator of the Postgraduate Program in Psychology at the UIA, as well as was Visiting Professor at the Department of Counseling & Human Services of the J.A. Panuska College of Professional Studies at the University of Scranton, PA. He co-directed the TIES/ENLACES program, National Researcher SNI level 1 (National System of Researchers). He was also Director of the Department of Psychology at the Universidad Iberoamericana, Mexico City 2008–2015. He has held leadership roles such as president of the CNEIP (National Council for Teaching and Research in Psychology) in the period 2015–2019 and president of FIAP (2018–2021). He is currently the coordinator of the University Wellness Clinic at IBERO CDMX.

Supervision of Mental Health Service Providers Working with Latine Populations in the U.S.A.

Andrés J. Consoli, Maira Anaya-López, Iliana Flores, Himadhari Sharma, Isabel López, Evelyn A. Melendez, and Yvette Ramírez-Gutiérrez

Vignette

Therapist: I am working with a 55-year-old Latino patient who is experiencing stress because his youngest daughter has legal problems with her boyfriend. Everything was going well, but something that caught my attention was that the patient started crying during the session and I realized that I had never seen a Latino man cry in my presence.

Supervisor: And how did you feel at that moment?

Therapist: Well, the truth is, I felt a little uncomfortable. In that moment, I realized that I hadn't really experienced someone who looks like my dad or my uncles crying in front of me. The truth is that I didn't expect to feel this way.

Supervisor: It is good to be attentive to our reactions and what comes up for us with our clients. You recognized the influence that some of your experiences and relationships may have on your clinical work, allowing you to keep in mind the cultural dimension. By reflecting on this, you can be more mindful of how to present yourself in future sessions.

The order in which the first four co-authors are listed reflects their level of contributions; the rest of the co-authors are arranged alphabetically.

A. J. Consoli (✉) · M. Anaya-López · I. Flores · H. Sharma · I. López
E. A. Melendez · Y. Ramírez-Gutiérrez
The Building Bridges Collective, University of California, Santa Barbara, CA, USA
e-mail: aconsoli@ucsb.edu; manayalopez@ucsb.edu; ilianaflores@ucsb.edu; Himadri@UCSB.edu; isabellopez@ucsb.edu; eamelendez@ucsb.edu; yramirez00@ucsb.edu

M. P. Grazioso et al. (eds.), *Clinical Supervision in Latin America*,
https://doi.org/10.1007/978-3-031-82373-2_4

Contextual Considerations

We summarize mental health professional practice and supervision in the U.S.A. with the hope that the information will benefit colleagues both within and outside of the U.S.A., particularly with regard to work with *minoritized* and, therefore, *vulnerized* populations. We focus on cultural aspects in the service with Latines, underscoring bilingual (English/Spanish) challenges bound to come up when delivering psychotherapy and supervising its practice.

Language is addressed as an eminently cultural element. Readers are encouraged to intentionally and systematically consider cultural values and norms throughout psychotherapy and supervision. The chapter advocates for and articulates ways to formalize bilingual supervision, by providing specific guidelines for its provision and institutionalization as part of the professional development process. We detail not only the strengths but also the shortcomings of supervision as practiced in the U.S.A., as it relates to its bicultural and bilingual delivery.

Institutional Matters in the U.S.A.

License to Practice

Licenses and requirements vary across the various professional backgrounds of psychotherapists. Psychologists in the U.S.A. are required to complete a doctoral-level degree through either a Ph.D. or a Psy.D. program, focused in clinical, counseling, and/or school psychology. Therapists can also complete master-level training through one of multiple degree pathways, such as clinical social work, marriage and family therapy, and professional clinical counseling. Providers of mental health treatment done primarily through biomedical methods, must complete a medical doctorate (M.D.) and a specialization in psychiatry or become a registered nurse practitioner who specializes in psychiatry.

In order to provide psychotherapy in the U.S.A. professionals must complete the appropriate educational requirements and be properly accredited through a license for independent practice. Currently, there are no licenses at the national level, only at the state level, which means that requirements for licensure can and do vary from state to state. While some states grant reciprocity based on an individual license in another state, the provider is required to complete all necessary steps to be licensed in the state where their clients reside. Nonetheless, a relatively new interstate agreement, known as PsyPact (Psychology Interjurisdictional Compact; https://psypact.org), facilitates the practice of telepsychology and the temporary in-person, face-to-face practice of psychology across state boundaries, albeit not all the States in the Union are signatories to it. But, to practice psychotherapy independently, all these professionals must have earned the required education, received supervised training, engaged in supervised professional experiences, and passed the requisite exams for professional license.

Licenses for the independent practice of professional psychology are regulated by the Board of Psychology of each state (in California, www.psychology.ca.gov). It is worth noting that the Board is part of the State Office of Consumer Affairs (www.dca.ca.gov). This Board is markedly different from what is typically considered a *Colegio de Profesionales* in Latin America. The Board, being part of the consumer affairs office, has, as its main mission, to look after psychotherapy consumers by ensuring that the laws that govern the profession and its practice are complied with by all professionals, including supervisors, supervisees, and practitioners alike. These laws are created by the State government and contained largely, but not exclusively, in the Business and Professions Code (https://leginfo.legislature.ca.gov).

Certification to Supervise

Supervision is a professional service that takes place within a contract, one that must be signed in advance and rigorously observed (https://tinyurl.com/y47ufu9n). The contract must make explicit a planned and structured development program, with an increasing level of complexity. It should include the expectation of socialization of supervisors into the profession (e.g., through mentoring, didactic exposure, role modeling, vicarious learning). The contract emphasizes the paramount responsibility of the supervisors, that is, ensuring the well-being of the clients who receive the services of their supervisees. Supervisors must have a current license, have received supervision training (six initial hours, followed by 6 hours of professional development in supervision every 2 years), and provide no less than 1 hour of weekly supervision to each supervisee for every 10 hours of service. Meanwhile, supervisors must work in the same place where their supervisees do, and not receive monetary compensation from the supervisees for supervision services, although it may be part of the professional role in the organization at which they work. Supervisors should not agree to supervise a relative or people who were their patients.

In California, psychologists who want to provide supervision must have an active license for no less than 2 years and have completed a course on supervision whose content is regulated by the state of California and provided by duly accredited instructors. Every 2 years, supervisors must complete no less than 6 hours of professional development in supervision (typically in the form of additional coursework) as part of the 36 biannual hours of continuing professional development (CPD; formerly known as continuing education, or CE) required to renew the license. The Board maintains a list of what are considered best practices in the context of supervision, which serve to guide both supervisors and supervisees (https://tinyurl.com/cz772jmx).

Latine Populations in the U.S.A.

According to the U.S. Census Bureau, Latine populations are considered an ethnicity, based on geographic origin, and include a broad group of people who can be of any race, such as Afro-Latines (https://tinyurl.com/44zr92tx; Adames et al., 2021). The Bureau specifies that "origin may be viewed as the heritage, nationality group, ancestry, or country of birth of the person or the person's parents or ancestors prior to his or her arrival in the United States" (https://tinyurl.com/2s4zsun4). Although the Bureau indicates that the terms "Hispanic, Latino, and Spanish" could be applied interchangeably to these populations, there are historical, sociodemographic, and political arguments that distinguish them. Added to this are arguments related to gender inclusion that, over time, has been reflected in the use of Latino/a, Latin@, Latin*, Latinx and, more recently, Latine (Campos et al., in press).

Demographically, Latine populations in the U.S.A. have shown considerable expansion: 2000—12.5% of the total U.S. population, 2010—16%, 2020—18.7%. It is projected that by 2060, 28% of the U.S. population will be Latine (https://tinyurl.com/3t9deadz). Latine populations constitute the largest minority; 60% of them are of Mexican origin and almost 10% are Puerto Rican. People of Salvadoran, Cuban, and Dominican origin make up the next 12%, with each group representing 4%. The largest number of Latines are in California (15,750,000) and Texas (11,400,000), and in the cities of New York, Los Angeles, Houston, San Antonio, and Chicago.

Considering the very important place that language occupies in psychotherapy ("the talking cure"), it is worth emphasizing that Spanish is the second most spoken language in the U.S.A., after English, and that, approximately 42 million people speak it. Therefore, to appreciate the needs of Latine populations related to psychotherapy and supervision, as well as access and utilization of mental health services, issues related to bilingual professional training and service delivery in Spanish are fundamental. Still, it is important to remember the colonial roots and the colonizing nature of Spanish.

With respect to mental health needs in the U.S.A., it is estimated that one in five people has a mental illness, while one in twenty people has a severe mental illness (www.nami.org/mhstats). The incidence of mental disorders among the Latine population in the U.S.A. is comparable to national averages. However, significant differences are observed in the percentage of access to, and use of, mental health services among needy populations according to race and ethnicity: 52% of non-Latine White people have done so, compared and contrasted with 35% of Latine populations with the same needs. The reasons that have been considered are several, but they are centered on inequalities, inequities, and social injustices, including the notable lack of proportional representation of Latine populations among mental health professionals, the shortage of trained personnel to provide mental health services in languages other than English, and the inadequate number of facilities that offer treatment in Spanish in the U.S.A. Specifically, with regards to the proportional representation of Latines among mental health professionals in the U.S.A., it is estimated that only

7% of licensed professional psychologists identify as Latine, while only 5.5% of psychologists speak Spanish (American Psychological Association, 2022). Meanwhile, between 2014 and 2019, the percentage of establishments with professionals who speak Spanish decreased by 17.8% (Pro et al., 2022).

Multiple political and social movements have contributed negatively to the current situation. In particular, the "English Only" movement dismantled bilingual education programs in schools, while anti-immigration laws and policies did their part to limit the diversity of qualified personnel. These laws and policies find their origin in xenophobic attitudes. Such attitudes are important to keep in mind in psychotherapy and supervision, since they can help appreciate and understand the reluctance to seek services, the reasons for consultation, and some of the issues to be discussed with clients and supervisees.

Codes of Ethics Relevant to Professional Practice and Supervision

The American Psychological Association (APA) developed the first version of its code of ethics in 1953 and has published nine versions to date. The current version, known as the Ethics Code and titled *Ethical Principles of Psychologists and Code of Conduct* (www.apa.org/ethics/code), was developed in 2002, with amendments in 2010 and 2016. The Ethics Code is undergoing substantial revisions at the moment (see www.apa.org/ethics/task-force) to include a clear social justice and human rights emphasis, among other features. It is worth contrasting the APA code with others, such as that of the American Counseling Association (ACA, www.counseling.org). The latter offers greater details and is ordered according to what are the most important aspects of professional work, starting with the therapeutic relationship (https://tinyurl.com/46vfak3p). We would like to emphasize that an important function of all ethics codes is to inform and educate consumers of professional services, as well as the general public, considering that the latter are potential consumers. This function is based on the motto "an informed consumer is a better consumer." Unfortunately, it is difficult to access Spanish versions of the codes in the U.S.A., or one must pay for them. For example, although the National Association of Social Workers (www.socialworkers.org) has an official version of the code in Spanish, it requires payment to access it.

Supervision in the APA Ethics Code

While the APA Ethics Code does refer to supervision, it does so only as one among many other roles that psychologists can play, both as providers of supervision (supervisors) and as consumers (supervisees). The overall document is divided into two parts, one addressing the ethical principles psychologists are expected to uphold (e.g., nonmaleficence, beneficence), and another specifying the code of conduct expected of professionals. The latter includes, for example, the prohibition of sexual conduct by supervisors with their supervisees. In another example, supervisors are required to establish a supervisory evaluation process and make this process explicit at the beginning of the supervisory relationship. However, the APA Ethics Code lacks a section dedicated entirely to supervision, which stands in contrast to the ACA Ethics Code. The latter includes a lengthy and detailed section on supervision; it underscores the priority that supervisors must give to the well-being of the clients being treated by their supervisees, the role of multicultural competencies, and the importance of respect for diversity. Moreover, the ACA Ethics Code discusses the crucial role of informed consent in supervision; this is in line with the previously mentioned motto, in this case "an informed supervisee makes for a better supervisee" and for a better supervisory experience.

The National Latinx Psychological Association Ethical Guidelines

The National Latinx Psychological Association (NLPA; www.nlpa.ws) developed the Association's own Ethical Guidelines (National Latinx Psychological Association, 2020). They are based on an eminently relational and collective perspective on people. To do this, the NLPA resorted to several foundations, including the Mayan expression In Lak'ech Ala K'in (approx. "I am you and you are my other me"), the African principle of consubstantiation (approx. "I am because we are, and therefore I am"), and collective consciousness (i.e., connections across generations). The Ethical Guidelines articulate nine principles including justice, understood as equity in distribution, and advocacy for it, as well as social conscience. Among the various examples offered in the document, supervision in the same language in which mental health services are provided figures prominently. In other words, supervision in English when services are rendered in Spanish is considered unethical.

Culture and Diversity Issues

In addition to the NLPA Ethical Guidelines, the APA Office of Ethnic Minority Affairs has published the Guidelines for providers of psychological services to ethnic, linguistic, and culturally diverse populations (American Psychological Association, 1993). This document emphasizes the need for psychologists to recognize the limits of their own cultural competencies and the importance of sharing information written in the patient's language. These guidelines emphasize the need for continued education and training on how to increase and improve services for communities that receive the fewest benefits and where the quality of those benefits is particularly low. These responsibilities extend to the supervisors and instructors who train their supervisees and graduate students. The APA has also published an updated version of its Multicultural Guidelines; these Guidelines are characterized by an ecological approach, emphasizing context and identity (American Psychological Association, 2017). The previous version (American Psychological Association, 2003) emphasized the importance of diversity and multiculturalism, both in individuals and groups; it underscored the role of culture in the way that individuals and groups identify themselves and how they relate to others, whether in the U.S.A. or at a global level. The 2017 version highlights intersectionality, that is, the presence and interaction between two or more social factors in the same person.

APA has published guidelines focused on issues related to race and ethnicity (American Psychological Association, 2019). These guidelines arose from the documentation of health disparities among ethnic minorities when compared to the Anglo-Saxon population in the U.S.A. (U.S. Department of Health & Human Services, 2011). The guidelines establish that psychologists must have knowledge, awareness, and skills to work with ethnic minority populations. Furthermore, psychologists must pay attention to the diversity within each community, considering multiracial identities, gender, sexuality, social class, religious beliefs, and (dis)abilities. One of the guidelines regarding education and training highlights the experiences of supervisees of color and how race, racism, or racial identity has impacted the relationship with their supervisors and the effectiveness of that relationship (American Psychological Association, 2019). Specifically, with respect to clinical and supervisory work, psychologists are expected to avoid all types of racial or ethnocultural biases, and to engage in as well as model self-reflection on their own racial identities. Another guideline indicates that psychologists should strive to recognize the influence of race and ethnicity in all aspects of their professional activities. This includes a developmental process in which therapists appreciate racial and ethnocultural influences on their own identities and professional activities, beginning with training and continuing with their professional practices, whether as educators, supervisors, and/or researchers. In this chapter's opening vignette, you can recognize the personal experiences that the therapist mentioned to her supervisor—the fact that her client cried in front of her, something she was not used to seeing in a Latino man. The supervisor demonstrated the ability to normalize the therapist's reaction despite the fact that the therapist was surprised by her own reaction. The supervisor transformed the experience into a learning moment, honoring issues of ethnicity and gender.

Implicit in all of these guidelines is the importance of cultural humility (Tervalon & Murray-García, 1998). The idea of cultural humility is to make cultural competence a more attainable goal through multicultural education and training. Even when a therapist or supervisor share identities (e.g., cultural, religious, linguistic) with a patient or supervisee, the provider likely will not completely know the personal cultural experiences of the patient or supervisee. Thus, remaining humble, self-reflective, and curious with all patients and supervisees is essential. It is about committing to practicing self-reflection and self-assessment, as well as caring about the structural power differences that exist in the therapeutic and supervisory relationships. Supervisors should model cultural humility with their supervisees, while encouraging and inviting them to incorporate it into their clinical work.

Modes of Supervision

In the U.S.A., the primary mode of supervision is through one-on-one interactions between a supervisor and supervisee. To become license eligible, most states require that a training psychotherapist provide 3000 hours of Supervised Professional Experience (SPE) that include at least 1 hour per week of individual supervision with the primary supervisor who, in turn, must be a licensed practitioner and qualified supervisor. This hour is typically face-to-face with the primary supervisor. Within the SPE framework, up to 10 hours of service provision per week can be supervised in this way. The regulations permit up to 44 hours of SPE per week, but these must include 4 hours of supervision. Essentially, for every 10 hours of service provision, 1 hour of individual supervision is required. While the initial hour must be individual and with the primary supervisor, subsequent hours may be conducted individually or in groups, either by the "primary supervisor" or by properly trained "delegated supervisors" (who are mental health professionals but not necessarily licensed psychologists). The rationale for a primary supervisor who shares the same professional identity (i.e., psychologist) is one of pertinent socialization into the profession. Group supervision is also another mode of supervision that is acknowledged by SPE regulations. Group supervision is limited to eight participants and can be conducted via teleconference if the primary supervisor deems it appropriate for the supervisees' needs.

Outside the SPE regulations, peer supervision can occur in either dyads or groups, functioning more like a consultation and support network among colleagues with shared interests and needs. NLPA runs a peer support group, specifically for professionals providing services in Spanish. This group is recognized as one of NLPA's Special Interest Groups (SIGs), and focuses on the challenges faced by bilingual clinicians and aspiring psychologists, as well as issues related to bilingualism within Latine populations in the U.S.A. The Bilingual Issues in Latinx Mental Health SIG meets regularly as a consultation group, conducting discussions in Spanish while fostering a sense of community and support for bilingual clinicians and aspiring psychologists.

Strategies for Ensuring Client Well-Being

Supervisors must strike a delicate balance between their primary responsibility of protecting client well-being and their secondary responsibility of fostering supervisees' competence and professional growth (APA, 2015). Several strategies have been identified as crucial for achieving these goals through supervision. In particular, supervisors need to develop their own competencies by obtaining formal education and training, understanding the ethical and legal aspects of supervision, receiving supervision on their supervisory practices, engaging in self-evaluation and reflection, recognizing their limitations, seeking consultation when needed, and affirming best practices (Association for Counselor Education and Supervision, 2011).

Supervisors must establish and maintain effective working relationships with their supervisees (Barnett et al., 2007; Goodyear et al., 2014; Lawson, 2017). A written contract must be used to lay the foundation for this relationship, clearly outlining the roles, tasks, and responsibilities of both parties, as well as the performance expectations for supervisees. Supervisors should directly observe supervisees' performance and provide constructive feedback to foster supervisees' efficacy in enhancing client well-being. Additionally, it is essential for supervisors to develop and maintain their multicultural competencies and support their supervisees in doing the same, particularly when working with clients from ethnic minorities, such as Latines in the U.S.A. Supervisors must also be adept at managing power dynamics in their relationships with supervisees, and in the supervisees' relationships with their clients (Hernández & McDowell, 2010; Reynaga-Abiko, 2010). Nurturing these relationships is essential for creating a safe environment where supervisees feel comfortable engaging in open communication with their supervisors. For example, in the case of a White supervisor and a non-White Latino supervisee, the latter might tolerate racist comments from the supervisor as the supervisee may feel that they cannot question their White supervisor's behavior due to multiple power differences, and the fear of being reprimanded or receiving a negative evaluation. In other words, a supportive atmosphere encourages supervisees to communicate honestly. For instance, in situations where there is a racial power dynamic at play, such as between a White supervisor and an Afro-Latine supervisee, the quality of the relationship becomes even more significant. If the supervisor makes inappropriate comments, a strong, respectful relationship might make the supervisee feel more comfortable addressing these issues. Conversely, a strained relationship could lead to the supervisee tolerating such behavior out of fear of retaliation if they were to voice their concerns.

An essential competency skill when working with diverse communities, especially in multicultural contexts, is the use of languages beyond English. This is particularly relevant in relationships such as those between supervisors and supervisees or therapists and clients, where the use of Spanish, for example, can significantly impact communication. Addressing cultural nuances, such as understanding metaphors, using pertinent *dichos* (sayings), and determining the right level of formality, can affect the effectiveness of these interactions (Consoli & Flores, 2020; Lugo, 2021). In fact, Pérez-Rojas et al. (2019) highlight that bilingual clients who can converse with their therapists in both English and Spanish experience enhanced expression and understanding, leading to more positive therapeutic outcomes, and a stronger therapeutic alliance.

Culturally competent supervisors must recognize the impact of cultural values on their Latine supervisees and clients, actively seeking opportunities to address potential issues (Field et al., 2010). To drive meaningful change in services with diverse populations, supervisors must rigorously develop their own reflective skills to identify and manage personal biases, preventing these biases from affecting their work. Furthermore, they should mentor their supervisees in building these crucial self-awareness skills. Supervisors are tasked with monitoring and evaluating competence, guiding supervisees through remediation when necessary, and, in extreme cases, facilitating a dignified exit for those unable to acquire the essential skills for practice. This role as gatekeepers is crucial for protecting clients, the public, and the profession as a whole (APA, 2015; Barnett et al., 2007).

Opportunities for Supervisors to Obtain Training

Professional development opportunities in supervision are both extensive and diverse. Doctoral programs typically include at least one course on supervision, and advanced doctoral students may have the opportunity to gain experience by supervising their junior peers. During the predoctoral internship year, students frequently supervise master's students or those at earlier stages of their doctoral journey. Post-graduation, newly minted psychologists continue to refine their supervisory skills while accumulating the required SPE hours in roles as postdoctoral fellows. Additionally, they often participate in supervision groups, where they collaborate with instructors or primary supervisors to discuss and assess their supervisory practices.

After psychologists secure their independent practice license and maintain it for 2 years, they can become primary supervisors, as long as they meet the requirements for supervision. For example, as mentioned in California this includes an initial training of at least 6 hours and update courses every 2 years. This mandate has led to a sizable industry of supervision courses and training across various levels—introductory, intermediate, and advanced. However, there is a notable shortage of supervision training focused on Latine populations. This issue is compounded by the limited number of bilingual, specifically Spanish- speaking, mental health professionals in the U.S.A. The most typical situation is that supervisors who do not speak supervisees' other languages, such as Spanish, supervise aspiring psychologists who are providing bilingual services. This creates the difficulty of having to rely on the therapists themselves to translate what their clients say. In cases where supervisors speak Spanish, the vast majority have not received professional training in Spanish - let alone in supervision- , making it difficult for them to express themselves professionally in Spanish.

The State of Supervision Research in the U.S.A.

Research on supervision has evolved for the past several decades, primarily focusing on several key areas: the impact of supervision on the supervisor-supervisee relationship, supervisee competence, client outcomes, and the factors that influence and moderate these effects, as well as the characteristics of both supervisors and supervisees (Lawson, 2017; Watkins et al., 2021).

Several of these studies have highlighted both productive and unproductive characteristics of supervision. Productive characteristics include: (1) supervisors addressing the immediate concerns of supervisees, (2) providing specific feedback, (3) offering specific guidance regarding more severe clinical dilemmas, and (4) honoring supervisees' concerns about the impact their personal life experiences may have on the clinical encounter (Lawson, 2017; Millán, 2010). In general, unproductive characteristics of supervision include: (1) supervisors' lack of availability to meet the basic needs of supervisees (e.g., not having an hour of supervision available per week), (2) the absence of a supervision contract, (3) not directly supervising the sessions provided by supervisees, and (4) engaging in a power struggle in the supervisor-supervisee relationship (Hernández & McDowell, 2010; Lawson, 2017; Reynaga-Abiko, 2010).

Research has shown that supervision significantly enhances supervisee competence when certain strategies are employed. Specifically, the benefits increase when supervisors use role- playing and collaborative feedback tailored to working with Latine clients, assess supervisees' comfort with Spanish-language proficiency, help develop Spanish vocabulary for mental health terminology, and resort to alternate cultural paradigms and/or translate and adapt established interventions (Consoli et al., 2022; Lawson, 2017; Lugo, 2021; Pérez-Rojas et al., 2019).

Although there is evidence that supervision positively impacts clients (Lawson, 2017), researchers face challenges in measuring its effect on specific treatment outcomes. Effective supervision often involves culturally relevant modifications, accommodations, and a demonstration of cultural humility (Lugo, 2021). Additionally, the identities and intersectionality of these identities among supervisors, supervisees, and clients play a crucial role in shaping supervision and treatment outcomes. Reynaga-Abiko (2010) identified factors such as norms, trust, communication, time, socioeconomic status, spirituality, and ethical issues (e.g., boundaries, gift-giving) as significant influences on the effectiveness of supervision.

Practice Concerns in the U.S.A.

Effective Training Models for Latine Mental Health

One key issue in supervising mental health services with Latine communities in the U.S.A. is the need for specialized training opportunities that address the diverse and urgent needs of these communities. Crucial skills include multilingual capabilities among researchers, clinicians, supervisors, educators, and mentors working with Latine and Spanish-speaking individuals. This section highlights exemplary programs that provide students the opportunity to receive education, clinical training, and supervision designed to effectively serve these communities, as illustrated in the initial vignette. Despite the existence of such programs, the demand far outstrips the available resources and opportunities (Consoli et al., in press).

One of the longest-running programs in the U.S.A. is offered by Our Lady of the Lake University (OLLU) in San Antonio, Texas. OLLU developed a Certificate in Psychological Services for Spanish-Speaking Populations, which includes bilingual courses, supervision, and other experiences and opportunities for cultural immersion abroad. The courses in this program cover Latine psychology and other relevant content areas, including cultural, social, political, historical, economic, linguistic, and institutional analysis. It is important to highlight these aspects of the program because they present an integrative approach where language is understood as a cultural element and tool embedded in a sociocultural context that gives it meaning. This sharply contrasts with programs that only focus on the use of Spanish without paying attention to the rest of the training, as if it were merely a matter of translation.

Another program that trains students in culturally relevant research and service is the Specialization in Research and Psychological Services in Spanish (SLPSR) at the University of Oregon (UO) in Eugene, Oregon. This specialization focuses on developing students' linguistic and multicultural competencies, as well as their general understanding of Spanish-speaking populations in the U.S.A. The SLPSR includes four general objectives and ten competencies (see https://tinyurl.com/56239as7). Aliento, the Center for Latinx Communities at Pepperdine University's Graduate School of Education and Psychology, offers a master's in clinical psychology with a program focused on Latine communities. Aliento prepares students to meet the educational requirements for family and couples' therapists and professional clinical counselors in California (www.gsep.pepperdine.edu/Aliento). It is important to note that Aliento provides training in clinical, cultural, and linguistic aspects involved in serving the U.S. Latine population. Another noteworthy program is the Master of Science in the Department of Counseling at California State University, Fullerton (CSUF). The emphasis on Latinecommunities within the CSUF master's program is known as Ánimo (https://tinyurl.com/yc7nb4e9), and it includes supervision in Spanish.

Relationships

APA outlines specific guidelines for the supervisory relationship that focus on: (1) create a cooperative relationship that fosters the competence of supervisees; (2) specify the responsibilities of supervisors and supervisees, including expected competencies and individual goals of the supervisees; and (3) regularly monitor supervisees' progress and the effectiveness of the supervisory relationship, addressing proactively any issues that arise (APA, 2015). Supervisors are expected to take the initiative in discussing cultural differences that may be affecting the supervisory relationship and strive to build a trusting relationship that can support the intrinsic challenges of supervision. Supervisors are to be explicit about the goals they have for their supervisees and pay close attention to the goals that the supervisees have for themselves.

Given the increase in supervisees representing greater racial and ethnic diversity, several articles have focused on the supervisory relationship between individuals who identify as ethnic minorities (e.g., Jernigan et al., 2010; Millán, 2010; Reynaga-Abiko, 2010). The study by Jernigan et al. (2010) demonstrated the importance of discussing racial identities with supervisees to strengthen professional supervisory relationships. Simply talking about race is not enough to understand the experiences individuals have with their racial identity. Since there may be differences within the groups with which one identifies, it is important to recognize how this appears between clients and therapists, and between supervisees and supervisors. It is necessary to discuss these experiences to genuinely consider how to integrate cultural aspects into the supervisory relationship.

Millán (2010) and Reynaga-Abiko (2010) shared personal stories about their perspectives on the supervisory relationship, as well as ways to advance professional practices attentive to multicultural issues. Both Millán (2010) and Reynaga-Abiko (2010) emphasize the importance of creating a trusting relationship that allows for enough closeness to share more personal aspects with their supervisees. Although there may be some initial uncertainty on the part of the supervisees, they eventually appreciate the importance of discussing cultural identities. This contributes to a deeper supervisory relationship and has implications for the therapeutic relationship between supervisees and their clients.

Ethical Issues and Challenges

One of the main objectives of clinical supervision in the U.S.A. is to assess and monitor the well-being of clients. However, ethical issues and challenges often arise that can jeopardize clients' well-being. One common challenge is bilingual supervision, specifically supervision in Spanish. Receiving supervision in Spanish is an essential part of training supervisees to maintain and ensure the well-being of monolingual, Spanish-speaking clients (Field et al., 2010; Fuertes, 2004). The shortage of supervisors trained to provide bilingual supervision creates an additional burden for bilingual supervisees. Specifically, bilingual supervisees end up doing extra work to prepare for a session in Spanish and then translating the session into English during supervision, as well as writing their notes and translating treatment plans into Spanish (Biever et al., 2004; Gonzalez et al., 2015). Meanwhile, the risk of using incorrect clinical terminology increases when competent bilingual supervision is not provided. Similarly, multicultural competencies developed in psychology's education and training programs ought to reflect the communities in which professionals-in-training work (https://tinyurl.com/46vfak3p); sadly, this is often not the case. Regarding the needs of Latine communities in the U.S.A., education and training should include not only an increase in the development of clinical skills in both English and Spanish but also a curriculum that is inclusive of bilingual pedagogy (Mezquita, 2020). Peters et al. (2014) highlight that many Latines prefer mental health services in Spanish but struggle to find qualified professionals. This underscores the urgent need for bilingual training and culturally competent education for mental health professionals dedicated to serving these communities. However, this presents an ethical challenge as very few programs provide the bilingual training necessary to meet the needs of Spanish-speaking communities in the U.S.A.

Information Gathering in Supervision

There is a wide range of existing practices in how supervisors gather information about what is happening in the treatment of clients receiving services by their supervisees. This spectrum ranges from retrospection to live supervision. Supervision through retrospective content provided by supervisees is the most common form of access to material related to clients being treated by supervisees. This content may come in the form of case notes or descriptions offered by supervisees during supervision. However, Ladany and collaborators have documented the limitations of this modality (e.g., Ladany et al., 2016). More useful and effective forms of supervision begin with adding voice recordings, progressing to video recordings, live recordings via an electronic platform (e.g., Zoom, Google meet), and even one-way (also known as two- way) mirror live supervision. Previously known as the "bug-in-the-ear," wireless earpieces have also allowed supervisors to communicate privately with their supervisees while the latter provide psychotherapy. The use of an electronic platform and wireless earpieces has made it feasible and relatively accessible for supervisors to provide specific suggestions to supervisees during a session (e.g., using the chat function in an electronic platform to send a timely message to the supervisee). Nonetheless, the realities of supervision offered in training centers, typically housed within universities, compared and contrasted with supervision in community care centers are notably distinct, largely due to costs, especially equipment and personnel expenses.

Regarding information gathering by supervisors when supervisees provide services to Latine populations, the modalities remain the same. However, if supervisees provide services in Spanish and supervisors do not speak it, the more advanced and effective supervision options are practically eliminated, even when using subtitling and automatic translation functions in an electronic platform. This significantly hinders the professional development of supervisees, places an unnecessary burden on them, and raises numerous professional, ethical, and legal concerns (Fuertes, 2004; Mezquita, 2020; Peters et al., 2014; Trepal et al., 2019). Specifically, it limits the ability of supervisors to carry out their duties, reducing the overall effectiveness of their work, shortchanging the supervisees' development, and ultimately the quality of the services rendered to the client. For example, monolingual, English-speaking supervisors supervising services rendered in Spanish cannot take advantage of the pluses involved in observing sessions through a one-way mirror as they are unable to understand the content of the exchanges. Moreover, supervisors who do not speak the language in which services are being rendered miss the opportunity to use a wireless earpiece to provide specific suggestions to supervisees, including the use of certain professional terms in Spanish that supervisees may need during the session. From a risk management perspective, monolingual supervisors who do not speak Spanish in a context where services are being rendered in Spanish, or even Spanglish, create a high-risk and clearly inappropriate situation, perpetuating discrimination in access to services of equal quality to those available to English-monolingual populations.

Checklist of Best Supervision Practices

The APA (2015) published a set of guidelines aimed at guiding the provision of clinical supervision in the U.S.A. According to this publication, supervisors must have adequate education, training, and experience to assume their responsibilities. At the outset of supervision, supervisors should outline the roles and expected behaviors, both of themselves and their supervisees. They should communicate and articulate the responsibilities, goals, and competencies expected of supervisees, typically through a written contract.

According to these guidelines, supervisors should aim to create, maintain, and value a collaborative relationship with supervisees, especially in promoting their competencies. Supervisors are expected to meet with their supervisees for at least 1 hour weekly to provide individual supervision. They should also monitor the professional performance and development of their supervisees, providing clear evaluative feedback, both affirmative and growth- promoting, on their performance. When conflicts arise between supervisors and supervisees, supervisors should take the initiative and dedicate the necessary time to discuss the conflict, thus assuming responsibility for their roles. If necessary, supervisors should consult with other colleagues. Supervisors must respect diversity dimensions as considered in professional ethics codes, as well as individual differences that may exist between supervisors and supervisees, ensuring supervisees feel encouraged and safe to discuss these differences with their supervisors. Meanwhile, supervisors must ensure the welfare of clients assigned to their supervisees.

Appropriate Supervision Approach for Your Country

The practice of supervision in the U.S.A. has specific characteristics when it comes to providing services to Latine communities. To appreciate these characteristics, we offer a typical example of supervision: Vanessa is a bilingual Mexican therapist living in the U.S.A. She participates in a supervision group led by a Mexican American psychologist who is monolingual in English, Dr. Garcia. Vanessa works with Carlos, an immigrant client from Costa Rica who is monolingual in Spanish. This situation poses a linguistic challenge as Vanessa uses Spanish with Carlos and most of her clients, who prefer to speak in Spanish or are monolingual in Spanish. Dr. Garcia cannot advise Vanessa on linguistic nuances when conveying information or making interventions with her clients. Therefore, Vanessa must do extra work outside supervision meetings to determine the best course of action with her Spanish-speaking clients. This is a common experience, albeit an unethical one, among therapists in the U.S.A. who provide services to Spanish-speaking communities.

In addition to linguistic concerns, there are cultural and countertransference issues. The APA Guidelines (American Psychological Association, 1993) mentioned previously emphasize that psychologists should recognize ethnicity and culture as significant parameters for understanding psychological processes. Challenges may emerge from not recognizing cultural values when a therapist from an individualistic background works with a client from an allocentric or collectivist one. For instance, a Latino father from a collectivist background may want to focus on problems related to his family as a group compared to individual issues. In therapy, he may want to explore how a potential divorce could affect his family members and show little interest in prioritizing the exploration of his individual goals or areas of self- improvement. An understanding of these cultural value differences in the therapeutic setting between providers and clients would be important to avoid erroneously misdiagnosing or misinterpreting certain client's behaviors as resistant to treatment in order to provide culturally responsive care. Moreover, psychologists are expected to interact in the language requested by clients. In cases where psychologists do not speak the language of clients and there is no realistic option to refer them, clients should, at the very minimum, be offered the services of interpreters with cultural knowledge and appropriate professional training.

A Relevant Supervision Model

The Multicultural Developmental Supervisory Model (MDSM; Field et al., 2010) emphasizes the importance of providing culturally sensitive supervision within ethnic group dyads (e.g., Latine-Latine dyads). The MDSM is based on developmental theories such as the Supervision Complexity Model, the Comprehensive Development Model, the Multicultural Competence Model, and the conceptualization of Latine identity development in the U.S.A. Each of the theories and frameworks incorporated into the MDSM makes this supervision model unique. For example, the Latine identity model is essential in the MDSM as it helps understand from which state a particular supervisor operates and how it can influence the dyad and affect how the supervisee interacts with their client. The MDSM emphasizes the importance of language and diverse cultural values and practices characterizing Latine communities in the U.S.A. (Barnett et al., 2007; Lugo, 2021).

Analysis

For the purpose of this analysis, we will examine the example of Vanessa and Dr. Garcia using the MDSM model. Dr. Garcia will have to identify cultural differences between Mexican and Costa Rican cultures so that Vanessa can be properly supervised. Furthermore, both Vanessa and Dr. Garcia must consider and reflect on the wide variety of cultural aspects within Mexican and Costa Rican cultures (intracultural variations reflected in our choice to write these terms in the plural form), and the debates on national identities. It is crucial to remember the importance of personal and idiographic reflections, where Carlos, Vanessa, and Dr. Garcia are appreciated as cultural beings. Meanwhile, Dr. Garcia must consider the significant difficulties that exist when therapy is provided in a language she does not speak, as well as the risk management, legal, and ethical issues involved in Dr. Garcia's choice to supervise services in a language Dr. Garcia does not speak let alone has not received discipline-specific professional training on.

Next Steps in Clinical Supervision in the U.S.A.

While the practice of clinical supervision in the U.S.A. has evolved considerably since its inception, that is not so much the case when it comes to its pertinent application with racial and/or ethnic minorities in this country. The current status of supervision differs significantly from what one might and should expect. This is the case not only in supervising the provision of services to such minorities but also in supervising professionals who identify as minorities, among supervisors who also identify as such, between supervisor-supervisee dyads belonging to those minorities, and in supervision groups where racial, ethnic, and cultural identities are diverse. The limited development of supervision in these areas accentuates what is called the *minorization* of racial and ethnic minorities. This underscores the need to consider the issue as a social injustice in the professional context.

As with the development of multicultural competencies in clinical practice, it has been primarily professionals identifying as racial and/or ethnic minorities the ones who have advanced knowledge in multicultural supervision. Historically, supervision research did not take into account the racial, ethnic, and cultural dimensions of supervisees or supervisors, nor of the supervisory encounter itself, partly because the dominant discourse in the profession was a hegemonic one from professional bodies considered majorities in the U.S.A., reflected in the expression "*white heterosexual male power and privilege*" (WHMP and pronounced wimp, according to the articulation of this construct by Dr. Janet Helms; it is worth noting that wimp is an informal derogatory term referring to weakness, cowardice, insecurity, and/or passivity of a person or group).

In general terms, the social concerns that characterized the 1960s and 1970s in the U.S.A., particularly regarding civil rights, led to contextualization and critique of racism, exposing the notable absence of minority professionals (people of African, Asian, Latine, and Indigenous descent). In the 1980s and 1990s, criticisms focused on sexism, while multicultural appreciation was emphasized, leading to questioning of knowledge sources in the profession, but only marginally with respect to supervision. In the twenty-first century, pluralism (the coexistence of diversity) and intersectionality (the existence of multiple identities in one person) have been accentuated. Although these developments are notable in professional practice, they are beginning to be addressed in supervision.

While it has been individuals identified as racial and/or ethnic minorities who have advanced the study of racial, ethnic, and cultural differences in supervision, being a minority does not exempt people from prejudice or racism. Specifically, this matter has only recently begun to be explored among Latine populations in the U.S.A. and among Latine professionals. It concerns exposing the colonizing roots in dominant psychological discourse, the need to decolonize professional psychology education and clinical supervision, and the urgency to recognize and dismantle the racism and colorism prevailing in Latine populations in the U.S.A., expressed in the marginalization of Indigenous peoples and Afro-Latine individuals (Adames et al., 2021).

References

Adames, H. Y., Chavez-Dueñas, N. Y., & Jernigan, M. M. (2021). The fallacy of a raceless Latinidad: Action guidelines for centering blackness in Latinx psychology. *Journal of Latinx Psychology, 9*(1), 26–44. https://doi.org/10.1037/lat0000179

American Psychological Association. (1993). Guidelines for providers of psychological services to ethnic, linguistic, and culturally diverse populations. *American Psychologist, 48*(1), 45–48. https://doi.org/10.1037/0003-066X.48.1.45

American Psychological Association. (2003). Guidelines on multicultural education, training, research, practice, and organizational change for psychologists. *American Psychologist, 58*(5), 377–402. https://doi.org/10.1037/0003-066X.58.5.377

American Psychological Association. (2015). Guidelines for clinical supervision in health service psychology. *American Psychologist, 70*(1), 33–46. https://doi.org/10.1037/a0038112

American Psychological Association. (2017). Multicultural guidelines: An ecological approach to context, identity, and intersectionality. http://www.apa.org/about/policy/multicultural-guidelines.pdf

American Psychological Association. (2019). APA guidelines on race and ethnicity in psychology: Promoting responsiveness and equity. https://www.apa.org/about/policy/guidelines-race-ethnicity.pdf

American Psychological Association. (2022). Demographics of U.S. Psychology Workforce [Interactive database]. https://www.apa.org/workforce/data-tools/demographics

Association for Counselor Education and Supervision. (2011, April 22). Best practices in clinical supervision. https://tinyurl.com/6j4hr3h2

Barnett, J. E., Erickson Cornish, J. A., Goodyear, R. K., & Lichtenberg, J. W. (2007). Commentaries on the ethical and effective practice of clinical supervision. *Professional Psychology: Research and Practice, 38*(3), 268–275. https://doi.org/10.1037/0735-7028.38.3.268

Biever, J. L., Castaño, M. T., González, C., Navarro, R.-E. L., Sprowls, C., & Verdinelli, S. (2004). Spanish-language psychotherapy: Therapists' experiences and needs. In S. P. Shohov (Ed.), *Advances in psychology research* (Vol. 29, pp. 157–185).

Consoli, A. J., & Flores, I. (2020). The teaching and training of bilingual (English/Spanish) mental health professionals in the US. In G. Rich, A. P. López, L. Ebersöhn, J. Taylor, & S. Morrissey (Eds.), *Teaching psychology around the world* (Vol. 5, Chap. 35, pp. 441–454). Cambridge Scholars.

Consoli, A. J., López, I., & Whaling, K. M. (2022). Alternate cultural paradigms in Latinx psychology: An empirical, collaborative exploration. *Journal of Humanistic Psychology, 62*(4), 516–539. https://doi.org/10.1177/00221678211051797

Consoli, A. J., Ramírez-Gutiérrez, Y. , Anaya-López, M., López, I., & Meléndez, E. A. (in press). El entrenamiento: Training necessities and opportunities to advance bilingual mental health competencies. In M. Campos, Y. Mejia, & A. J. Consoli, *Forging caminos: Pathways to becoming a bilingual (English/Spanish) mental health professional*. American Psychological Association.

Field, L., Chavez-Korell, S., & Rodríguez, M. M. D. (2010). No hay Rosas sin espinas: Conceptualizing Latina-Latina supervision from a multicultural developmental supervisory model. *Training and Education in Professional Psychology, 4*(1), 47–54. https://doi.org/10.1037/a0018521

Fuertes, J. N. (2004). Supervision in bilingual counseling: Service delivery, training, and research considerations. *Journal of Multicultural Counseling and Development, 32*, 84–94. https://doi.org/10.1002/j.2161-1912.2004.tb00363.x

Gonzalez, L. M., Ivers, N. N., Noyola, M. C., Murillo-Herrera, A., & Davis, K. M. (2015). Supervision in Spanish: Reflections from supervisor-trainee dyads. *The Clinical Supervisor, 34*(2), 184–203. https://doi.org/10.1080/07325223.2015.1058208

Goodyear, R., Lichtenberg, J. W., Bang, K., & Gragg, J. B. (2014). Ten changes psychotherapists typically make as they mature into the role of supervisor. *Journal of Clinical Psychology, 70*(11), 1042–1050. https://doi.org/10.1002/jclp.22125

Hernández, P., & McDowell, T. (2010). Intersectionality, power, and relational safety in context: Key concepts in clinical supervision. *Training and Education in Professional Psychology, 4*(1), 29–35. https://doi.org/10.1037/a0017064

Jernigan, M. M., Green, C. E., Helms, J. E., Perez-Gualdron, L., & Henze, K. (2010). An examination of people of color supervision dyads: Racial identity matters as much as race. *Training and Education in Professional Psychology, 4*(1), 62–73. https://doi.org/10.1037/a0018110

Ladany, N., Friedlander, M. L., & Nelson, M. L. (2016). Addressing skill difficulties, deficits, and competency concerns. In N. Ladany, M. L. Friedlander, & M. L. Nelson (Eds.), *Supervision essentials for the critical events in psychotherapy supervision model* (pp. 57–84). American Psychological Association. https://doi.org/10.1037/14916-004

Lawson, C. (2017). What makes supervision helpful? A review of research. In D. Pickvance (Ed.), *Cognitive analytic supervision: A relational approach* (pp. 53–68). Routledge.

Lugo, B. L. (2021). Spanish-English bilingual supervision. In M. Polanco, N. Zamani, & C. D. H. Kim (Eds.), *Bilingualism, culture, and social justice in family therapy* (pp. 61–68). Springer Nature. https://doi.org/10.1007/978-3-030-66036-9_9

Mezquita, S. V. (2020). *Evaluating the effectiveness of the training and supervision provided to Spanish/English bilingual graduate students* (Order No. 28087051). https://www.proquest.com/dissertations-theses/evaluating-effectiveness-training-supervision/docview/2437760701/se-2

Millán, F. (2010). On supervision: Reflections of a Latino psychologist. *Training and Education in Professional Psychology, 4*(1), 7–10. https://doi.org/10.1037/a0016977

National Latinx Psychological Association. (2020). Ethical guidelines of the National Latinx Psychological Association. *Journal of Latinx Psychology, 8*(2), 101–111. https://doi.org/10.1037/lat0000151

Pérez-Rojas, A. E., Brown, R., Cervantes, A., Valente, T., & Pereira, S. R. (2019). "Alguien abrió la puerta:" The phenomenology of bilingual Latinx clients' use of Spanish and English in psychotherapy. *Psychotherapy, 56*(2), 241–253. https://doi.org/10.1037/pst0000224

Peters, M. L., Sawyer, C. B., & Guzman, M. (2014). Supporting the development of Latino bilingual mental health professionals. *Journal of Hispanic Higher Education, 13*(1), 15–31. https://doi.org/10.1177/1538192713514611

Pro, G., Brown, C., Rojo, M., Patel, J., Flax, C., & Haynes, J. (2022). Downward national trends in mental health treatment offered in Spanish: State differences by proportion of Hispanic residents. *Psychiatric Services, 73*(11), 1232–1238. https://doi.org/10.1176/appi.ps.202100614

Reynaga-Abiko, G. (2010). Opportunity amidst challenge: Reflections of a Latina supervisor. *Training and Education in Professional Psychology, 4*(1), 19–25. https://doi.org/10.1037/a0017052

Tervalon, M., & Murray-García, J. (1998). Cultural humility versus cultural competence: A critical distinction in defining physician training outcomes in multicultural education. *Journal of Health Care for the Poor and Underserved, 9*(2), 117–125. https://doi.org/10.1353/hpu.2010.0233

Trepal, H., Tello, A., Haiyasoso, M., Castellon, N., Garcia, J., & Martinez-Smith, C. (2019). Supervision strategies used to support Spanish-speaking bilingual counselors. *Teaching and Supervision in Counseling, 1*(1), 3. https://doi.org/10.7290/tsc010103

U.S. Department of Health & Human Services. (2011, March 23). Report on minority health activities. https://minorityhealth.hhs.gov

Watkins, C. E., Jr., Vîşcu, L. I., & Cadariu, I. E. (2021). Psychotherapy supervision research: On roadblocks, remedies, and recommendations. *European Journal of Psychotherapy and Counselling, 23*(1), 8–25. https://doi.org/10.1080/13642537.2021.1881139

Andrés J. Consoli (he, him, él) is a bilingual (English/Spanish) faculty member in the Department of Counseling, Clinical and School Psychology at the University of California, Santa Barbara. He is a fellow of the American Psychological Association (APA) and past president of the National Latinx Psychological Association, the Inter-American Society of Psychology, and the Western Association for Counselor Education and Supervision. Dr. Consoli received the Inter-American Psychologist Award for distinguished contributions to the advancement of psychology in the Americas and the Excellent Contribution Award for outstanding contributions to international research, program development, and teaching/mentoring by the International Counseling Psychology Section of APA's Division 17. With over 100 publications on bilingual professional development, access to and utilization of mental health services, and more, Dr. Consoli is the lead editor of the Comprehensive Textbook of Psychotherapy: Theory and Practice (Oxford University Press), co-author of CBT Strategies for Anxious and Depressed Children and Adolescents: A Clinician's Toolkit (Guilford Press), and coeditor of Forging *Caminos*: Pathways to Becoming a Bilingual (English/Spanish) Mental Health Professional (American Psychological Association).

Maira Anaya-Lopez is a bilingual (Spanish/English) doctoral student in counseling psychology in the Clinical, School, Counseling Psychology program at the University of California, Santa Barbara (UCSB). Maira earned a master's degree in psychology from California State University, Los Angeles and a second master's degree in Counseling Psychology from UCSB. Broadly speaking, Maira's interests include examining access to and utilization of culturally congruent mental health services and resources for underserved communities. In addition, she is interested in exploring disparities in mental health and health care services for Spanish-speaking Latino communities with a specific interest in families of children with autism. She is also interested in bilingual and professional training for students seeking to provide bilingual and culturally congruent mental health services.

Iliana Flores is a bicultural (Mexican-American) and bilingual (English/Spanish) psychologist working in the California Department of Corrections and Rehabilitation. Dr. Flores completed her doctorate in Counseling Psychology from the Counseling, Clinical, and School Psychology program at the University of California, Santa Barbara. She completed her predoctoral internship in the Cognitive-Behavioral Therapy and Dialectical Behavior Therapy (CBT/DBT) track in the Department of Psychiatry and Behavioral Sciences at the University of Texas Health Science Center, San Antonio. Dr. Flores' clinical and research interests broadly include Latine mental health, the training and development of bilingual (English/Spanish) mental health professionals, access to and utilization of mental health services among racial and ethnic minority populations, and the adaptation of evidence-based treatments to meet the needs of culturally diverse populations.

Himadhari Sharma (she/they) identifies as a bilingual (Hindi/Urdu/English), bicultural cisgender (Asian Indian/American) second-generation immigrant. Dr. Sharma is currently a postdoctoral fellow at the University of California, Berkeley Counseling and Psychological Services. She earned a doctoral degree in counseling, clinical, and school Psychology with an emphasis in counseling psychology at the University of California, Santa Barbara in 2024. Dr. Sharma's work, both clinical and research, focuses on serving minoritized groups, with an emphasis on South Asian and South Asian American communities. Dr. Sharma's current interests include increasing access to, utilization of, and development of culturally humble and social justice-oriented mental health services to support minoritized communities, bilingual and social-justice rooted mental health support, training, and supervision, adaptation and development of culturally rooted evidence-based treatments as well as intercultural/international psychology.

Isabel López is a bilingual (English/Spanish) Ph.D. candidate in counseling psychology at the Department of Counseling, Clinical and School Psychology at the University of California, Santa Barbara. She is completing her predoctoral internship at Arizona State University Counseling Services, and will graduate with her PhD in 2025. Her clinical and research interests focus on access to, and utilization of, mental health services among underserved communities - particularly Latine populations. She is interested in exploring facilitators for accessing care, and barriers to care, to improve outreach and engagement with mental health services for diverse communities. As the proud daughter of immigrants, of both Bolivian and Mexican descent, Isabel is passionate about increasing culturally diverse representation and cultural responsiveness in her research and clinical work. She is dedicated to improving language accessibility in both areas by conducting research in Spanish and providing therapy in Spanish.

Evelyn A. Melendez is a bilingual (Spanish/English) doctoral student in the Department of Counseling, Clinical and School Psychology at the University of California, Santa Barbara. With a master's degree in psychology from California State University, Los Angeles, Evelyn's academic trajectory reflects her commitment to addressing mental health disparities within underserved communities, with a particular focus on the Latine population. Passionately dedicated, Evelyn is committed to conducting research and providing therapy in both English and Spanish, with the goal of improving accessibility and inclusion in mental health services. Her research interests revolve around examining attitudes and utilization of mental health services, with the goal of identifying bridges and overcoming barriers that prevent effective use of these services. Through her unique perspective as a proud first-generation college student and daughter of Mexican immigrants, Evelyn aims to contribute meaningfully to the ongoing conversation about mental health disparities and accessibility within underserved communities.

Yvette Ramírez-Gutiérrez is a bicultural (Mexican-American/Chicana) and bilingual (English/Spanish) cisgender pansexual woman from Sacramento, California, and daughter of immigrants from Mexico. She is also a first-generation doctoral student in the Department of Counseling, Clinical and School Psychology with an emphasis in Counseling Psychology at the University of California, Santa Barbara. Her clinical and research interests aim to focus on cultural humility and social justice while exploring Latino mental health, interpersonal violence, domestic violence, policy advocacy, comprehensive health care, as well as access to and utilization of mental health services, especially for underserved communities (e.g., low-income communities, Spanish-speaking communities).

Part III
Clinical Supervision in Central America and the Caribbean

The Cultural, Professional, and Regulatory Context of Supervision in Cuba

Bárbara Zas Ros

There is no professional recognition of the exercise of psychological supervision, in the context of the professional practices of professional relations of psychological help in Cuba.
The professional practice of supervision is very isolated, infrequent, and always associated with the psychological service that is provided institutionally and free of charge.
Psychological supervision in Cuba is not characterized by having certification processes that guarantee its exercise.

Psychological supervision in Cuba at the undergraduate level is only taught in the context of the subject of Psychological Orientation, for students trained at the Faculty of Psychology of the University of Havana. An optional subject is offered in the same faculty. In the postgraduate program there is a proposal for a training course for supervisors, with very low demand for students.
As the practice is not systematized, the frequency that monitoring occurs is difficult to specify. In the undergraduate training space described above, previously contracted supervision sessions (four) are offered in the context of the subject. For the optional subject there are ten sessions of work in supervision. Supervision practices, when they occur, are usually done in groups.

The development of research in the field of Clinical Supervision in Cuba is highly deficient.
The Operational Model of Psychological Supervision, a second-generation model, is the first proposal developed, which has been developed in Cuba, from an investigative process deployed for more than ten years, with the use of grounded theory as a research method

Characterizing the context of the practices of professional psychological help relationships[1] in Cuba requires an understanding that aligns with the sociohistorical fabric in which they develop in the diverse landscapes of the "many Cuba's of

[1] Professional psychological help relationships: It is a direct interaction between two or more people, which is established as a relationship between them, through a professional practice, in order to help in the resolution of a problem of the order of the psychological, promoting changes in said order (Calviño, 2000).

B. Zas Ros (✉)
Center for Psychological and Sociological Research and University of Havana, Havana, Cuba

M. P. Grazioso et al. (eds.), *Clinical Supervision in Latin America*,
https://doi.org/10.1007/978-3-031-82373-2_5

today".[2] This influences the ongoing processes of subjective changes that occur in the population. The increase in economic and social heterogeneity has led to increased subjective diversity, marked by symbolic expressions and the emergence of new social actors along with highly complex processes of social reintegration.

This premise imposes, that we think of an exercise of psychotherapy and psychological guidance in our country, as "professional scientific performance", dominantly social and vindicating constructive social practices, which has been [...] "the very condition of its origin, its performance and the very meaning of its exercise as a discipline committed to a project that transcends it" (Calviño, 2016, p. 11).

In the research carried out by Henríquez and Corral (2014), it is concluded that [...] "the economic, political and social context, the therapeutic currents, the institutional demands, the characteristics of the community of professional practice, the spaces of interrelation with other professionals, the personal experience and motivation of the therapists [...]" (p. 29), are factors that have a high influence on the daily work of therapists.

Psychotherapy and psychological counseling are the primary forms of professional psychological help practiced in our country. These services are not offered privately. Professionals who have completed their Bachelor of Psychology (psychology graduates) and specialists in Psychiatry (coming from a medical background) are the recognized personnel for providing services in public institutions (healthcare, education, community), with open access to the population. This condition has influenced the approach, humanistic and ethical principles, and accessibility to these services, setting them apart from other countries where public and private practices coexist. For Zaldívar et al. (2004), practicing psychotherapy in the public sector [...] "It involves the harmonious integration of various therapeutic resources [...] as well as the participation of a care team where psychotherapy is one more service that is provided to the population and covers the demands [...]" (p. 297).

Rodríguez (2008) recognizes that the Cuban school of psychotherapy is constituted by a diverse set of therapies from different models, which harmonize the professionals who engage in a social practice centered around the human being. According to this author, all therapies have meeting points, and what justifies the diversity in approaches to patients is the uniqueness in the expression of human suffering, and based on this, the possibility of finding resources and relief from emotional discomfort in specific forms of therapy.

García (2013) also confirms the idea that they try to apply different psychotherapeutic methods and that professionals [...] "participate in the attempt to achieve a professional practice oriented to integration and convergence (in the configuration of models that assimilate the experience of other paradigms) and not to uncritical eclecticism [...]" (p. 207).

[2]"One Cuba, many Cubas", was the name of the National Symposium of the Center for Psychological and Sociological Research held in Havana in 2015.

It would be extensive to refer to all the variety of trends and models of professional relations of psychological help currently applied in Cuba. Just to cite some examples of more recent published works that range from the application of Lacanian psychoanalysis (Laje & Bedevia, 2017), systemic reflective family psychotherapy (Fraga & Araujo, 2015), large group psychotherapy (Rodríguez, 2016), combined and interactive care systems (Argudín, 2015), and group psychotherapeutic programs for minors (Castellanos, 2016), one has an idea of the wide and varied spectrum of ways of doing.

However, García (2013) summarizes that, in the work of psychotherapy in Cuba, there are a series of common elements that are taken into account in the approach to the different modalities of work, such as the active character of the individual [...] "and its cultural involvement in the process of psychological integration and disintegration" [...] "the significance of education in the subjective expression of the person" [...] and [...] "the role and place of the subject's personality in the psychotherapeutic process [...]" (p. 207).

On the other hand, García (2013) points out, that work is also being done on the foundation of psychotherapy from a historical and cultural perspective, which conceives psychological development as a complex process, which originates in the subject's social and cultural context throughout their history, mediated by experience (Roche, 2012; Echemendia, 2014; Cueli, 2018).

Another characteristic of professional relationships in Cuba is the variable duration of establishment (Calviño, 1998, 2000; Henríquez & Corral, 2014).

In this regard, Calviño (1998) identifies some conditions that influence the marked tendency to establish processes of Orientation and Psychotherapy in Cuba, with a shorter duration. These could be: national cultural and psychological peculiarities; living conditions that make it difficult to maintain prolonged treatments, frequent and time-consuming transfers; the institutional organization of the psychologist's work with a multiplicity of tasks and functions associated with the characteristics of the organizations where they work.

The Referential Scheme of Multiple Alternative (ERAM), emerges as a model of psychological orientation, with a work scheme that contains as a methodological principle the temporal delimitation, as well as the action on the probable (the problem), the emphasis on the relationship and interpersonal communication between the counselor, and the orientee and the search for changes to productive relationships (Calviño, 2000).

It is important to note that the Referential Scheme of Multiple Alternative is taught as a fundamental model in the training of Cuban psychology professionals, which guarantees at least basic training in a particular way of doing psychological guidance and working preventively (Molina, 2013).

The issue of training in professional relations of psychological help is another problem existing in the Cuban context. In the training of the psychology professional, basic subjects of General Psychotherapy and Child and Adolescent Psychotherapy are taught in the undergraduate (level), as well as in the Master's Degree in Clinical Psychology. Specialists in psychiatry also have this type of content in their teaching programs. However, this basic training is not enough.

Roche (2012) recognizes that many professionals express dissatisfaction with the existing training in the country, related to psychotherapy, and describes it as self-taught. Rodríguez (2016) states that [...] "there is no certification that accredits such condition, nor exclusive work as a psychotherapist [...]" (p. 185).

The absence of an updated code of professional ethics, its existence only as a project that has not been completed and that does not have institutionally established legal support (Calviño, 2000; Roca, 2013), is another example of the great problems that are confronted. The process of creating a code of professional ethics for Cuban psychologists began in 1986. This process has gone through several stages, until the final project proposal that was approved in the National Assembly of affiliates of the Cuban Society of Psychology, on December 11, 2012, which is the one that is counted as a reference at present.[3]

In this draft code of professional ethics, it is recognized within the fields of action of the practice of psychologists, psychological guidance, and psychotherapy, however, supervisory practices have no recognition. They are absent, they are not named, they do not constitute a requirement for the exercise of professional relationships of psychological help.[4]

Thus, when characterizing the current state of psychological supervision practices in Cuba, this is an essential element that reflects their conceptual, instrumental, methodological, formative, and investigative "nonrecognition", and the consequent absence of accreditation or certification processes of the same. This is a great weakness and limitation.

Why has supervision not found a space of recognition in the reality of the professional practice of the psychologist in our country? What have been the main obstacles to the implementation of this practice?

Zas (2004) states that, among some of the causes and obstacles of the insufficient recognition of the exercise of supervision in Cuba, could be: the lack of tradition in this type of practice; the guild imaginary of "not being necessary", since patients have been worked and cared for without having supervised, as a habit and systematic work style; the non-creation and existence of daily institutional spaces and working time dedicated to this work, as it is not required as a requirement of quality or improvement of psychological services; the scarce existence of training spaces in indigenous methodologies or work models; the association of supervision as a practice awarded especially to psychoanalysis and the absence of participation in constructive supervision, experienced positively, that start from psychotherapeutic work frameworks or Psychological Orientation similar to those that predominate in Cuban professional practice.

This scenario has resulted in limited development in training processes for professional psychological help that utilize supervision. There is also a lack of

[3] Agreement No. 4 of the National Assembly of Affiliates of the Cuban Society of Psychology, held December 11, 2012, at the Central University of Las Villas Marta Abreu, Santa Clara.

[4] The current directive of the Cuban Society of Psychology, is currently reviewing the document presented in 2012, with the aim of updating it, to proceed to its discussion in the guild, and subsequent legal settlement.

specialized training in supervision-related topics and in preparing individuals to take on the role of supervisors (Zas, 2018b).

The review of testimonies of recognized experts in the field of professional relations of psychological help in Cuba, provides information on some specific experiences of supervision associated especially with the training in some models of psychotherapy and the training of the psychology student in the clinical area. These experiences are mainly situated between the 1960s and the earlier years of the present century (Pérez, 2007). Dr. Isidoro Baly noted: "[...] the therapists who have worked most in psychotherapy under supervision are Acosta Nodal in orthodox psychotherapy of psychoanalysis, Bustamante in the cultural psychotherapy, Hiram Castro in modification of predispositions, Cristina Cunill in psychoanalysis [...] Oscar Ares. They were all supervising in psychotherapy" (Pérez, 2007, p. 32).

Dr. Aurora García said: "[...] Those of us who have somehow dedicated ourselves to the clinic here at the Faculty of Psychology of the University of Havana, have done supervision in some way [...] only that this supervision of which I speak, has been done from empirics and necessity [...]" (Pérez, 2007, p. 33).

The non-systematicity in the professional practice of supervision and in specialized training on this subject, has resulted in scarce theoretical production and scientific research on it in the context of Cuban psychology (Zas, 2018a). However, in the last 20 years there have been some moderate advances, which have been made explicit in a set of publications, as well as in presentations at Psychology congresses held in our country.

Organizing training processes in supervision is a strategy that has been applied in an incipient way. In 2011, the insertion of supervision as didactic training began, in the subject of Psychological Orientation, in the Faculty of Psychology of the University of Havana, and in September 2013, supervision began in the Faculty of Psychology of the University of Havana, with the teaching of the optional subject of Psychological Supervision in the fifth year of the career (Zas, 2015, 2018b).

Another experience of applying supervision as a training strategy is the one carried out at the University of Oriente to contribute to the development of professional skills for psychological care in clinical and health practice, specifically in the subject of Family Counseling. In this context, a group supervision is carried out, promoting reflection in action, and reflection on the reflective action of clinical practice (Mercerón, 2018). This space promotes a process of personal and professional growth favoring the role-person unity.

The projections regarding the training of psychological supervisors who attend to the professional development of psychologists in the exercise of their practices, has been an intention that has had its most recent materialization in the organization of a postgraduate course (Zas, 2018b).

The Supervisor Training Program attached to the Faculty of Psychology of the University of Havana, has been developed in its first version, within the framework of a project of the Provincial Psychology Group of Pinar del Río (Gutiérrez et al., 2018), which aims to systematically offer supervision spaces to psychology professionals in that province (Zas, 2018b).

Soteras (2017) refers to the training of supervisors in the psychotherapeutic technique of Eye Movement Desensitization and Reprocessing (EMDR), certified in Cuba by EMDR Europe. This certified group has monitored the training process of this particular technique in different provinces of the country.

In summary, we can affirm that the supervision modeling that occurs in the training practices of Psychology in Cuba, contains two aspects: supervision as an instrument to facilitate the processes of training in Psychology, and the training of psychological supervisors who attend the professional development of psychologists in the exercise of their practices.

It cannot be affirmed the existence of a prevalence of one model or another of supervision in the practices of psychotherapy and psychological guidance in Cuba. The experiences reported are isolated and punctual, with an emphasis on group supervision. During the COVID-19 period, remote supervision was reported for the first time in a group format (Zas & Molina, 2021).

As a report of psychotherapeutic practice, Ortiz (2018) conducted an investigation where he used psychodrama methodology as a resource for supervision in psychotherapy. It states that this application allows to incorporate fundamental aspects of supervision, coming from different psychotherapeutic approaches, and the contributions of the Cultural Historical Approach, to understand the process of subjective change of the supervised.

Fraga and Araujo (2015) refer to the systematic use of supervision in the practices of the systemic reflective family therapy model that they apply in the hospital environment.

There has been a slight trend since 2005 in some groups of professionals and psychology students towards progressive demands aimed at promoting training spaces and supervision spaces associated with professional practice. This has led to systematizing the theoretical-methodological and practical references according to the level of progress that has the theme of psychological supervision in the rest of the world, and in accordance with the original ways of understanding and organizing professional aid relationships in Cuba.

For these reasons, the result of the first and only existing research in the country is registered in 2021, where a theoretical model of supervision of indigenous production is proposed, which guides or explains ways of doing supervision in the context of professional relationships of psychological help: the Operational Model of[5] Psychological Supervision (Zas, 2021). The research process deployed for more than 10 years with the use of grounded theory as a research method, managed to identify and substantiate all the contents and theoretical links chosen for the construction and proposal of the model, from the study of several sample groups linked to the practice of supervision.

---

[5]Operational: It is the pertinent, the productive. The elaboration of an operative hermeneutic implies the analysis and inductive construction from reality, from everyday practices, in the "pragmatic space" (Calviño, 1998, p. 12). It would be to think about the effectiveness of the operations, their procedures, the skills and technical resources used and the "set of theoretical - conceptual representations that articulate in situ the operations that are carried out" (Calviño, 1998, p. 12).

Psychological Supervision Operating Model

The Operating Model of Psychological Supervision is a second-generation model because it is built from an operational pragmatics that essentially integrates the contributions that come from a set of models generated from a specific psychotherapeutic orientation, as well as from models focused on a developer and/or processual perspective (Zas, 2021, 2024).

It is proposed as a work model that promotes reflections to promote processes of improvement in the various supervisory actions that are undertaken, that can be implemented in the current context of psychological practices in Cuba, with methodological indications that facilitate its implementation. Let it serve to act.

We will stop at his presentation, because it contains the answers to a series of essential aspects related to the present and future of the development of psychological supervision in Cuba.

The structuring components of the Operating Model of Psychological Supervision are: the essential dimensions that determine the founding principles on which the model is based; the basic core composed of the roles of the supervisor and the *supervisor*, the professional relationship they establish, as well as the organizational component of the supervision process; and the formative proposal that could favor the teaching of supervision as a resource to promote the professional development of psychologists who are dedicated to the practice of professional relations of psychological help in Cuba (Diagram 1).

The existence of multiple dynamic interrelationships between each of the structural elements indicated determines the specificities at the two levels of operation of the model: an operational explanatory level of the way in which the realization of a supervision process should be conducted and a substantive explanatory level of the essential elements to be considered in the supervisory training process.

The three foundational dimensions of the operating model are: the epistemological dimension; the ethical dimension; and the processual dimension. They interact

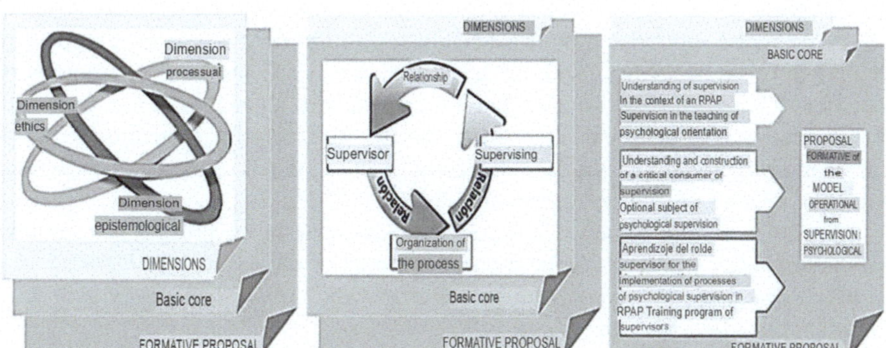

Diagram 1 General structure of the Operating Model of Psychological Supervision. Own elaboration

in a dynamic of permanent coexistence, and their principles complement each other to define the way of functioning of the professional relationship of supervision in the exercise of the general training, evaluative, collaborative, and preventive functions, which are intended with this resource (Zas, 2021, 2024).

In the *epistemological dimension*, the foundations on which the process of knowledge construction that occurs in the relationship between supervisor and *supervising is erected*. The proposed model is based on a pragmatic-operational construction, with an operative and convergent epistemology (Calviño, 1997, 1998, 2000). This involves considering a set of premises in the establishment of the monitoring process.

The first is the analysis of the convergence of the models of professional relationships and psychological help that the participants carry in a supervisory relationship. It is important to identify them as underlying the application of strategies and resources to promote changes and transformations in the subjects and groups receiving psychological care (Zas, 2021, 2024).

The second is the reflections of the participants in the relationship on the criteria to implement supervision practices in a work model, which implies: review the entire theoretical-methodological arsenal existing in the participants of the supervision process and locate it in relation to professional identity, type of practice, type of professional experience, the need to design or choose a specific mode of training, and the social context where all these experiences are occurring (Zas, 2021, 2024).

The third is the active participation of those involved in a monitoring process, in agreement, assuming and sharing a relevant, useful supervision model, consistent with the social essence and with the type of practices that are established.

A fourth premise would be the essential reflection by the participants in the processes of supervision and training in supervision, of an approach to the knowledge of the diversity of supervision models, a reevaluation of the integrations that the operating model proposes, and a critical reformulation.

The reflective-critical and constructive-integrative component that makes up the epistemics of the operating model, starts from the premises enunciated, thus favoring in the participants an assumed understanding of the usefulness of the supervision process.

The assumed supervision model declares a position on the type of relationship that is professed between supervisor and *supervising*. A dialogical epistemology is assumed to be a favoring resource that prevents the establishment of non-balanced power relations between the *supervising* and the supervisor. An intention to carry out monitoring processes aimed at achieving well-being (of supervisors, *supervisees, beneficiaries of support relationships) (Zas,* 2021, 2024*)*.

The complementarity between those who participate in the process has a nominal intentionality that leads to the use in the model of supervising, *to highlight the active character of the same in the process of knowledge, favoring their professional and personal growth.*

The developing perspective of the model promotes experiential learning from a common task as an operational structuring of the supervision process, where the action of intermediate supervision as an instrument carried out from the functions of the supervisor, generating nearby areas of development[6] necessary to be able to execute actively and independently the tasks linked to the provision of professional psychological help services (Zas, 2021, 2024).

In summary, the monitoring process would be based on a constructive-participatory-dialogic- operational character in its knowledge production practice.

The elaboration of the Operational Referential Conceptual Scheme (ECRO)[7] of the model is an essential part of it. The essential conceptual challenge is the definition of psychological supervision.[8]

In *the ethical dimension* of the model, the premise of the need to consider, given the little mastery and technical training in the role of supervisors and the lack of experience in supervision that prevails in professionals, the preparation and training of supervisors to identify the main problems and ethical dilemmas that appear in the relationship, stands out as a premise from the ethical principles that the model embraces and from the prior evaluation of the context in which the professional relationships of psychological help are occurring.

The inclusion of the ethical dimension in the Operating Model of Psychological Supervision then contains normative ethical principles that must be considered during the establishment of a relationship of psychological supervision[9] and principles related to the identification and management of ethical problems and dilemmas in supervision. Both edges are interconnected.

In each supervisory relationship that is established, ethical standards must be made known and must be erected between *supervisor* and supervisor (supervisee)

---

[6] Proximal zone of development, defined as "*the distance between the actual developmental level determined by independent problem-solving and the potential developmental level determined by problem-solving under adult guidance, or in collaboration with more capable peers*" (Vygotsky, 1978, p. 86).

[7] ECRO (operational referential conceptual scheme) is understood as the organized set of universal concepts that allow an adequate approach to the particular object, serving as a frame of reference for the application and promotion of a creative or adaptive modification to the reality with which it is interacting (Pichon-Riviere, 1985).

[8] In this sense, supervision in Psychology is visualized as a work instrument of those professionals who carry out actions of professional psychological help in different modalities and areas (psychotherapy, psychological guidance, community, organizational, educational orientation), being a resource aimed at improving professional work, and a collective action in order to achieve better performance.

Psychological supervision is a collaborative, formative, evaluative, and preventive professional relationship. It is established individually (between two psychology professionals, or between a professional and a student) or in a group. Whoever assumes the role of supervisor, must be able to perform it responsibly, and favor a relationship that leads to an overlapping of views, with the active participation of the *supervisor*, in the learning process that occurs. This process includes aspects related to the use of the technical resources of psychology, as well as the work of containment and elaboration of personal experiences that may hinder the professional relationships of psychological help provided (Zas, 2021).

[9] The normative ethical principles of professional relations of psychological help are referred to in the draft code of ethics that is in the process of being reviewed by the Cuban Society of Psychology. These principles serve as a basis for determining the normative ethical principles existing in the relationships that are established in the processes of psychological supervision.

(between *supervisees* if it were a group work modality and between supervisors who share workspaces or training). As part of the employment contract, they must manifest themselves in forms of agreement as a permanent topic to be addressed throughout the process. In supervisory training processes, this principle is equally valid.

Ethical standards in supervision are also expressed in the duties and rights of *supervisors and supervisors*, which must be exercised and assumed in the supervisory relationship, must be made explicit in the contractual elements, must be observed, and must demand compliance, thereby inviting dialogue about authentic practice.

The social responsibility assumed by those who carry out professional relationships of psychological help, and those who assume the supervision of this practice becomes even more complex, to the extent that the psychosocial problems that court the reasons for requesting help become more conflictive. There is no doubt that these contradictions are reflected in the reasons for consultation and in the emotional experiences that people bring to their encounters with psychology specialists.

At the same time, the impact of scientific and technological development linked to human health problems has favored the emergence of dilemmatic situations that imply decision-making conflicts for the applicants for help and for the psychologist himself, who is summoned to accompany this type of process, issues that have been addressed from the perspective of Bioethics (Delgado, 2011).

The technical resources of psychology, which at other times in the development of this science were effective in providing possibilities and alternatives to aid seekers, may today be insufficient for these purposes. This situation calls for questioning, revision, renewal, adaptation, and, in some cases, an integration of them with resources from other disciplines.

On the complex scenario that has been presented, is that the analysis of problems and ethical dilemmas is based on the model of psychological supervision.

The ethical problems that may arise in the exercise of psychological supervision in Cuba may have their origin both from the exercise of the role of the supervisor and the supervisor. Both deposit their values and moral development in a relational encounter. In the same way, ethical responsibility in the results of the process must be built and assumed from the aforementioned roles.

From another point of view, the student or professional who comes to ask for supervision also has no experience in this type of relationship, so the impact of the word "supervision" can leave him trapped in a power relationship, which will not bring him the necessary benefits for his professional development (in this aspect, the interrelation with the principles assumed in the epistemological dimension is essential to work on this problem).

Initially, an ethical problem may arise from the transgression of any of the ethical values that determine the relational norms in the supervisory process.

An analysis of the ethical problems linked to the responsibility of the participants in the supervisory relationship from the differentiation of their roles could begin by focusing on the figure of the supervisor. The specialist in psychology, whose purpose is to assume the role of supervisor of professional relations in psychological help, taking into account the current state of the practices that we have described, must carry out a reflective process that allows him to self-evaluate and respond to a set of concerns that can serve as a guide to channel this work of personal analysis: Am I qualified to call myself a supervisor and exercise that role? What kind of supervisor am I?

Assuming the role of supervisor without training for it, is an act of professional irresponsibility, a source of serious ethical problems, which harm the participants and break the development of the profession. Trained supervisors must also self-assess the limits of the fields of action they are *supervising*, learn to recognize the absence or deficiency of experience on a topic being worked on and seek the help of other colleagues when required.

They should question the personal tendencies of the *supervisees*, the fascination that they, as supervisors, provoke due to their expertise, the overall evaluation of external factors, the undervaluation of the personal, the autochthonous, the infatuation with novelty, and the fascination with the cloying discourse of seductive words. They must cultivate humility.

Supervision is conducted by recognizing the discrepancies and the points of convergence between the supervisor and *the supervisor* regarding cultural, racial, social class, sexual orientation, gender, and differentiated power differences in the supervisory relationship, as sources generating possible ethical issues in the relationship. It becomes an ethical problem to select a model that reproduces power dynamics harmful to the integrity of the *supervisees*.

The role of supervisor is to be the bearer and depository of a power, or aid to the determined situation that is supervised. This is not the ethical problem. The problem is when that power is used as an authority to override *the supervisor, when it is used to "convince" that* the supervisor's method, "his their model", "his their way of seeing", "is the form to be assumed".

The relationship of supervision as a space preceded by a work ethic and an ethic of the human and of human relationships, becomes an instrument for the training and facilitation of the development within the type of student and professional described. This function should be intentionally utilized as a resource, and it is the responsibility and duty of the supervisor to exercise it.

In this fusion integration with everyday practices, intentional training during the supervision processes will necessarily have to address the presence of ethical dilemmas of which the *supervisor* may carry.

Ethical dilemmas in supervision can occur between supervisor and supervisee, often related to what is called multiple relationships. These dilemmas can arise from conflicts that occur when intimate or sexual relationships develop between *the supervisor* (*supervisee*) and the supervisor, or when therapeutic relationships are established within supervision spaces, to cite some examples (Neufeldt, 1999; Bernard & Goodyear, 2009; Montalvo & Espinosa, 2011).

They are also presented on the part of supervisees as a consequence of their involvement with psychosocial issues and technological developments in contemporary Cuban society.

There is an ethical expectation in the behavior of specialists in psychology, regarding their role in the psychosocial transformation processes occurring in today's Cuba. This expectation is giving a rise to the dilemmas in the participatory encounter that is aspired to which.

The ethical dilemma is healthy, since it denotes an adequate humanistic formation, an indicator of professional growth, a recognition of social problems and the influence of technology in practice, and a development of self-evaluation as an indispensable moment to undertake supervision processes; a processed decision-making.

The recognition of problems and ethical dilemmas in supervision processes allows us to be in contact with a real psychology professional, in situation, and willing to do everything possible to engage in dialogue in the pursuit for higher-quality professional helping relationships.

The contents of the epistemological and ethical dimensions, the processual dimension of the supervision model *is based and interrelated.* The inclusion of this dimension in the model, aims to emphasize the recognition of supervision as a process in itself, distinct from other professional processes in Psychology. This contains the production of a relationship and interaction of specific roles, as well as the performance of tasks within a continuous flow of successive actions and peculiar moments that, correlatedly, they lead to the production of a set of effects (Holloway, 1995; Bernard & Goodyear, 2019).

Three processes to be considered in supervision contained in the model are distinguished: the process that occurs within the establishment of a professional relationship in supervision, the formative processes in supervision, and the development process that could be promoted to extend the application of psychological supervision in the context of professional relations of help in our country. The supervision process must be in accordance, in all cases, with the actual capabilities of the participants and the existing conditions in the various specific and general contexts that they occur in.

Once the foundational dimensions of the model have been presented, it is necessary to highlight the understanding of each of the elements (in the core structural framework) of the Psychological Supervision Operating Model. This will be crucial for the functionality of the supervision processes (Zas 2021, 2024).

In this sense, the first element to be presented is the supervisory relationship, which takes place according to the moments of the general process and contains phases that must be recognized and facilitated: an initial phase for framing the working alliance, a phase for developing the relationship, and a phase for closing the established relationship.

The transition from one phase to another of the relationship occurs through a dynamic process where a set of complex interactions occur. These interactions triggered in one way or another, depending on the peculiarities existing in those exercising corresponding roles of supervisor and *supervisee*. These existing peculiarities are determined by the confluence of a set of factors contained in each of these roles. Understanding and identifying these factors are essential for assessing their impact on the quality of the supervisory relationships that are fostered.

Regarding the role of the supervisor, an important element to consider in the model is that the factors that will be pointed out constitute essential axes to be included in the training intention that is assumed. Training in the role is an essential premise for it to be executed. The factors to be considered in the supervisor's role would be linked to technical conditions necessary to perform the role and linked to personal and identity-related conditions and characteristics.

Among the technical conditions that are required to fulfill the role of a supervisor is to possess a mastery in the exercise of professional relationships of psychological help. This condition is essential, as well as the level of experience in this type of practice, knowledge of the diversity of models and theories of RPAP, prior experience in individual and/or group psychotherapy, and the types of areas where they have practiced. An initial assessment on these determinants is important to ensure the effectiveness of the supervisory relationship.

However, the aforementioned element is insufficient, because it is necessary for a supervisor to master a supervision model acquired through a formal training process. An in-depth study of supervision models, as well as reflection on the proposed integration into the operating model, are essential for this purpose (Zas, 2021, 2024).

The experience in the exercise of the role of supervisor is crossed by a level of development reached in the realization of self-evaluation and self-correction processes related to the supervisory actions carried out by the supervisors.

Proficiency in the executing supervisory functions[10] and designing and implementing supervisory strategies and tasks is an essential element that determines what happens in the supervisory relationship. The functional dynamics of the supervisor involve acting with both flexibility and precision in choosing which role to assume in response to emerging supervisory demands, add period. The supervisor's confidence in selecting the relevance of each function at any moment relies on their precision in defining the focus or area of supervision that is most essential to address (Bernard & Goodyear, 2019) considering the supervisee's professional level (Zas, 2021, 2024).

The supervisor must maintain the technical intent of the supervisory relationship, in order to make it effective.

The factors linked to the conditions and personal and identity characteristics are referred to the personological particularities and the diverse identity that the supervisor carries. The operating model considers that a better relational attitude of the supervisor occurs when they are flexible, dynamic, assertive, patient, humble, committed, respectful, ethical, responsible, motivating, and a listening person.

The supervisor must then have a clear representation of their role, be someone to engage with and respect the position of a supervisee enriched by a different perspective. They should be a person with professional experience that sets them apart not

[10] The model recognizes three functions of the supervisor that are integrated into a functional dynamic during the supervision process, and that adjust to the characteristics of the type of supervision process that is developed. These functions are: educators, advisors or consultants and those of exploration, containment and emotional support. This proposal integrates and contextualizes with the data, the contributions basically of Holloway (1995) and Neufeldt (1999).

hierarchically, but in terms of a different interpretation. A professional with the ability to establish effective communication and empathy, without ambiguities, that fosters expression, recognizes individual differences, and respects supervisee's pace.

A supervisor who, according to Watkins (2020), has a "transformational mindset". These descriptions are embedded in the aspirations expressed by the participants, in the monitoring processes studied.

The self-knowledge and self-awareness on the part of the supervisor regarding their identities: social, cultural, professional, gender, religious, as well as their sexual orientation, age, socioeconomic status and political beliefs, affect the relationship with their *supervisees*, and are fundamental aspects to be considered in the analyses of the relational dynamics within the supervision process (Bernard & Goodyear, 2019; Falender & Shafranske, 2017; Goodyear & Falender, 2017).

It is also important to consider how these factors affect the emergence of countertransference processes in the supervisor. If they occur, they will require attention due to their impact on the course of the professional relationship.

The factors to be considered in the role of *the supervisor* influence the supervisory relationship are: the motivation and commitment to participate in the supervision process, the Referential and Operational Conceptual Scheme (ECRO) that carries with respect to the professional relationships of in Psychological Help, the level of experience and professional development achieved, the type of participation they assume as consumers of supervision, their personal conditions to perform in the execution of self-evaluation and self-disclosure, and the personal and identity conditions and characteristics.

In the supervisory relationship, the teaching of how the supervisor *can play a more active and participatory role in the supervision process is encouraged, how* they can contribute from the fulfillment of their functions, with the achievement of a useful, functional, healthy, and satisfactory learning experience.

The emphasis of the operating model is that the relationship between supervisor and *supervisee* constitutes a working alliance. This alliance demands a distribution of functions among the participating roles, which must be configured and organized, and where the ethical determinants described in the dimensions of the model will be considered permanently. Two technical conditions that determine the course of this work alliance, in addition to the factors indicated by the supervisor and the *supervisee*, are functional asymmetry[11] and optimal distance[12] (Calviño, 2018).

The supervisory relationship transcends its properly technical aspect, which is essential, establishing itself as a complex process of elaboration of each of the

[11] The functional asymmetry corresponds to the process of specifying the functions of the subjects involved in the supervisory situation. There is a common task and two roles that are different. The notion of functional asymmetry marks the difference of roles, not from the notion of power, but from functional difference (Zas, 2021).

[12] Optimal distance as subjective distance is nothing more than "the limit of empathic proximity that determines in each case, situation, and relationship, that the professional exercise of supervision is possible, acceptable, and effective" (Calviño, 2018, p. 81).

participants based on their own roles in it, becoming an "always innovative and creative act, which seems to be born in each new exercise" (Calviño, 2018, p. 84).

The organization of the supervisory process, within the context of the operating model refers to the way in which all the conditions must be prepared to initiate and maintain the process that occurs within the establishment of a supervisory professional relationship, as well as the proposed supervisory training processes (Zas, 2021, 2024).

The professionalism of the supervision processes requires that participants have knowledge on the conditions necessary to ensure their effectiveness. This process is not improvised. Supervisors who foster psychological supervision relationships, as well as institutions involved in this type of practice, should consider the following essential aspects to begin and sustain the experience: particularities of the context and scope where the proposed supervision process takes place, the goals pursued, selected supervision modality, establishment of a contract between the parties involved in the process, implementation of the supervision process according to the contract, evaluation of the process carried out, and preparation of the closure (Zas, 2021, 2024).

The establishment of a contract between the parties involved in the process is the essential organizational and normative resource of the supervisory relationship (Bernard & Goodyear, 2019). In the case of the operating model, this contract can be made verbally or in writing between the parties, depending on what may be most pertinent. The essential thing is that it becomes a resource of framing, agreements and ways of proceeding, to ensure the effectiveness of the entire process undertaken.

The supervision contract is essential in all forms of supervision and is applicable to all contexts and areas where it is decided to engage in this type of professional relationship. It is established during the initial phase of the relationship. The first working session in any supervisory relationship contains the joint development of the relational contract between the parties as a means of formalization and commitment to it.

The contract includes: the framework of the participants' ECRO, the agreements on the overall objectives of the monitoring process to be conducted, the goals to be achieved, the selection of the working modality and its distinctive features, and the determination of the general monitoring procedure for attaining these objectives. According to the modality of the work selected: the time, frequency and structure of the sessions, the modes of presentation of the situations to be monitored, the conformity with the procedures, the methods of evaluation, and the ethical standards of the relationship.

The monitoring process begins, once all the aspects indicated have been agreed, and there is a consent with the proposal by the parties involved. During the course of the relationship, if it is necessary to rework any aspect, an analysis of the situation is carried out and that particular aspect is reevaluated.

Consequently, with the dimensions and structure of the Operating Model of Psychological Supervision, the operational procedures of this model are established.

The forms of operation of the operating model refer to how all the necessary actions take place within the supervision process. They serve as the operational guidelines to consider based on the working principles of the model, outlining the dimensions and considerations within the Operating Model of Psychological Supervision.

The model considers the forms of operation to provide supervision to conduct processes that occur within the establishment of a professional supervisory relationship and the operational procedures to enhance supervision training.

In the forms of operation to provide supervision, a primary aspect to[13] consider in the operating model to facilitate the understanding of its operation is that, in order to actualize a professional psychological supervisory relationship, it is necessary to follow a sequence that allows for the maintenance of the internal logic of the process. This involves paying attention to the moments within the supervision process that are relevant to each moment, as well as articulating the internal sequence in the sessions, the inter-session links, and the production of the expected effects.

It is important to emphasize that if the mode of work is group-based (face-to-face or distance), it is necessary to consider variables related to the group process and the characteristics that arise from group dynamics and collective learning within the overall supervision process.

If the mode of work is remote (individual or group), challenges related to technological difficulties are considered as threats to the fulfillment of the agreed times, affecting the dynamics within the sessions. When these difficulties arise, it is important to manage the presence of discomfort in the participants. The work must be resumed where it was interrupted, reworking together until the meeting point is found to give continuity to the process of the session, or to the process in general.

If working in asynchronous remote modalities, the times agreed in the contract for the determination of the general durability of the process and the particularities of the structure of the sessions will be considered.

A second aspect how the supervisor simultaneously applies the contents of the dimensions of the mode and ensures all the conditions and the performance of their functions during the session, so that the supervisory relationship produces the expected effects. As this happens, *the* active and critical supervisor of the process learns to execute its functions.

In the group work modality (face-to-face or remote), from the group's emergent dynamics, the focus shifts to what is agreed upon and the group objective to address. The conscious verbal contributions of the participants, the emotional states experienced by them, the patterns of their behaviors witnessed, are the group patterns to be observed and serve as a guidance to the supervisor on the functions to be fulfilled.

If the group work modality is remote individual or group, adjustments are made to the instrumental resources applied, considering the specific technological medium that is being used. This includes taking advantage of the possibilities of the medium to enrich the resource being utilized.

[13] Only the general characteristics described in each of the computers referred to will be mentioned. The Psychological Supervision Operating Model more accurately describes each of the corresponding contents.

The third aspect aimed at facilitating the understanding of the model's functioning focuses on the importance of verifying the performance in the supervisory relationship, role functions, and how they are learned and executed. This assessment should consider a set of indicators observed from both roles.

These indicators are useful for the supervisee's self-assessment *processes* and for the systematic and closing evaluation processes that occur during the supervisory relationship.

In the group work modality (face-to-face or remote) the indicated indicators are maintained, which must be analyzed according to the contribution of the participants to the group processes and to the group task facilitated by the coordination of the supervisor or the supervision team.

In the remote work modality (individual or group) one of the challenges lies in the difficulty to read nonverbal signals that could express important elements to consider about the supervisory alliance, which are not always perceivable. This should be considered in the evaluations of each session and in the evaluations of the closing phase of the process. Building a relationship of trust can have an impact on a more accurate assessment of the necessary indicators.

The fourth essential aspect to manage to handle the functioning of the supervisory relationship is the supervisor's knowledge and mastery, linked to the articulated use of each of the strategies, tasks, and instrumental resources. Having about the actions taken and what is expected to be achieved with each procedure, as well as having expertise in that essential operation, allows the model to be put into action.

In the group work modality face-to-face or remote the facilitation also involves the creation of options that emerge from group processes. The purpose of the intervention is oriented to elaborating productive ways of perceiving, analyzing, and constructing options by the members of the group. This involves active and respectful listening, energizing work from the group, as well as the application of joint elaboration resources.

In the remote work modality (individual or group) the systematic use of instrumental support resources such as messages, images, links, videos enrich the work and expands the possibilities to illustrate the modeling of intervention techniques. It is important to take advantage of the possibility of written records of all work sessions, in order to encourage their rereading by all participants and thereby facilitate new reflective processes that may occur from this action.

Paying attention to the interrelation of the four aspects indicated, serves as a reference to promote the functioning of a supervisory relationship within the operating model.

Regarding its role in promoting training in supervision, the Operating Model of Psychological Supervision acknowledges the importance of contributing to the preparation of these groups of students and professionals in Cuban psychology through training programs focusing on the theoretical knowledge and practical aspects (Zas, 2021, 2024).

Diagram 2 illustrates how this operation considers the existence of different levels of supervisory training, which can be achieved within the model. Each level of training corresponds to objectives that encompasses various levels of complexity

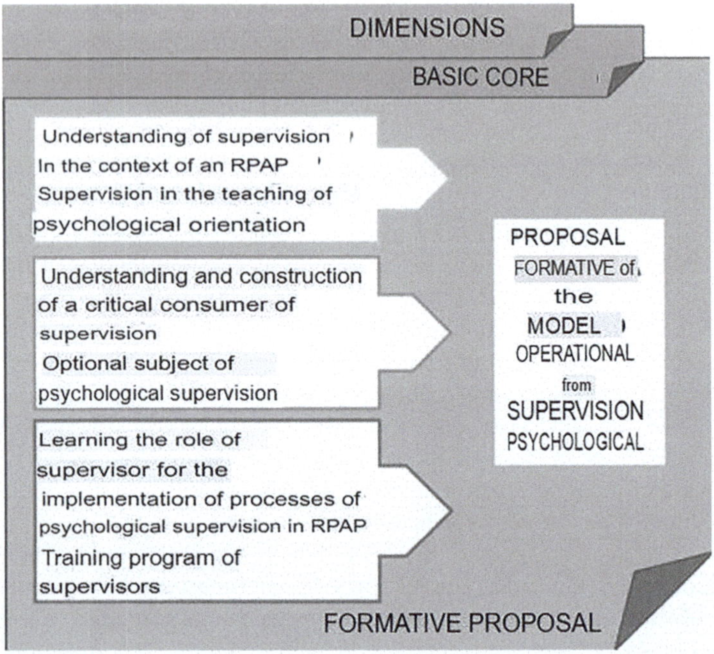

Diagram 2 Training proposal of the Operating Model of Psychological Supervision. Own elaboration

relating to the knowledge and application of supervision as a professional relationship.

The training proposal intends to initially include existing spaces within the training programs for psychology professionals and introduce additional ones; both as part of the regular curriculum and in postgraduate studies.

The goal intention of incorporating the model's concepts into undergraduate psychology training programs is to ensure that students, from the beginning of their learning process in providing professional psychological assistance, understand the importance of complementing this professional work with a supervisory relationship. This supervisory relationship serves as a facilitator for executive learning processes aimed at improving the quality of psychological help provided.

The level of basic training in supervision has been incorporated into the curriculum of the "Psychological Orientation" course within the Psychology program at the University of Havana, as previously mentioned. The supervisory training process encompasses the assimilation of the fundamental conceptualizations and the existing essential models, accompanied by the experiential learning of participation in a supervisory experience focused on the design of psychological counseling interventions. Instructions for the entire procedure of integrating supervision into the course, for both professors and students, are included as part of one of the Practicum's contents.

The level of specialization in psychological supervision has been integrated into the curriculum of the elective course "Psychological Supervision", offered in the Psychology program at the University of Havana. It is intended with this specialization, that students become aware and committed to the importance of receiving supervised assistance in their various professional activities and enhance the quality of their future practice professionally. This involves understanding their active role as supervisees and recognizing their elective choices regarding the supervision model to be employed.

The development of participants' professional identity is encouraged, emphasizing the importance of care and responsibility for their future performance based on ethical principles and respect for other professionals in the field. This includes reflecting on the recognition of their true abilities, knowledge, attitudes, as well as their limitations and emotional implications, and how these factors influence the course of their professional actions when establishing RPAP in different work settings.

The third level of professional training (for the supervisor role) is a proposal that carries significant professional responsibility. Providing the possibility to applicants for supervision, to choose the supervisor, necessarily implies and consequently with the fundamentals of the operating model, offer the possibility of professionally training psychologists to assume the role of supervisors.

The Supervisor Training Program consists of two stages or phases in its implementation. The general objectives of the training are aimed at: promoting the learning in the students regarding theoretical frameworks, fundamental concepts, and foundational knowledge related to the supervisory role in professional relationships, identifying the technical and personal conditions necessary to develop for the professional role of supervisors, integrate theory and professional development zones to the work style as a supervisor, and strengthen the professional identity of the supervisor role.

The training program is the result of a theoretical and methodological integration of various references derived essentially from the Supervisory Training Model of Bradley and Whiting (Bradley, 1989), together with the Neufeldt model of supervision strategies (1999), and some elements of the methodology of the Training Program that supported the experience of the MADIBA Learning Community (Rodríguez-Mena et al., 2015), based on the exposed contents of the operating model.

The program integrates intentional practice, group reflective processes, self-reflection, and ongoing corrective feedback to enhance functions as a supervisor in Professional Relations of Psychological Help.

It is essential to consider two initial conditions, which must be previously agreed upon the participants in the program: in the first phase of the course, assume a proactive role, multiplying what has been learned and with availability to participate in shaping, structuring, and contextualizing their learning experiences. This phase involves constructing the group ECRO on the structuring and assimilation of the supervision model to be used. In the second phase, assume the commitment to contribute to the group work process, performance experiences in the role of supervisors, which will be evaluated according to the model's references.

Another important element to clarify is that the course's design does not aim for an automatic replication of the operating model, but rather seeks to integrate the adoption of a specific supervisory approach based on the fundamentals within the model.

The training program involves a process of knowledge building and group learning among the participants, serving as a model for the kind of relationship that should be fostered from the role of supervisor in the practice of psychological supervision. Cooperation, collaboration for the co- construction of meanings and the emergence of spaces that enhance development, as well as the quality of group interaction, will determine how effectively the potentialities are taken advantage of according to the formation of this role.

Learning situations are designed to operationalize the training approach, focusing on developing the technical and personal skills necessary for proficiency in the role of a supervisor and for designing and implementing supervision strategies and tasks.

The structure of the program is based on three components for training in the role of supervisor: conceptual-reflective (concepts, models, and technical resources), experiential (role training), and integrative (integrating theory to experience in the exercise of the role and areas of professional development).

The Process of Developing Psychological Supervision in Cuba

Trying to visualize the future of psychological supervision in Cuba, the representation of a process that has already begun indisputably, would allow to delimit several stages to happen.

Stage 1: Awareness and Screening

The current stage in which we find ourselves in at the moment, can be described as a screening phase. This phase is aimed at providing information and persuading groups of students and professionals about the importance of supervision in the field of Psychology. It also helps convince institutions that trains psychologist about the necessity of incorporating supervision training practices.

Professionals and students should be encouraged to present content and develop experiences that promotes an understanding of supervision processes rather than viewing it as an obligation. It is recommended to prioritize experiences involving group supervision, because they are more collective and collaborative, yielding positive results. Within this stage, it is also essential to develop and disseminate the resources available to facilitate the necessary learning and training processes, and providing access to information about supervision models to aid in relevant concepts. It is very convenient to form study and discussion groups that propose a conceptual elaboration of the subject. The implementation of the thematic contents in the undergraduate and postgraduate curricula of psychology training is essential.

Promoting training will lead to the development of an advanced group of individuals who can serve to be valuable and systematize knowledge in the field of psychology.

It is essential to raise awareness regarding the inclusion and recognition of professional supervision practices, as well as their corresponding training processes, in the next revisions and updates of the code of ethics of psychology professionals in Cuba.

Stage 2: Assembly and Systematization

In the second stage of assembly and systematization, supervision mechanisms should be set up within the "institutional routines". This process requires the involvement of "supervisor trainers" who facilitate and demonstrate the performance of various tasks. Specialized training in the role of supervisors is essential for this exercise, so at the same time specialized training in this subject must be systematized, in order to achieve supervisors who respond to the idiosyncrasy and contextual peculiarities of the practices of professional relations of psychological help in our country. The assembly of this stage must be basically formative.

The training strategies in each institutional group will be tailored according to the specific characteristics of each one, and it will be established and agreed that it is not a process to evaluate professional work. Promoting lines of research on the subject of supervision would be necessary at the level of the training institutions, and at the level of the institutions that incorporate this type of professional relationship. Critical and thoughtful analysis of indigenous supervisory models that are designed and implemented is essential.

Stage 3: Recovery and Construction

The third stage of recovery and construction is based on the fact that every act of supervision should be revisited in the process vertically and longitudinally, individually and as a group. The supervision within a service, in an area, or with a work team, must assume as a task the continuous personal and group recovery. Here, too, lies its capacity for training and development. After a period of work, it is necessary to pause and observe what has transpired, where you are, and where you are now. A "supervision of supervision" is essential, which involves an exchange of experiences, of dialogue on the production of models, and the impact of supervision on the development of practices and formation of professional relationships of psychological help in our context.

This process needs to be projected and accompanied, it is part of the responsibility of the institutions that provide guidance on the formation and development of Cuban psychology.

References

Argudín, S. G. (2015). *Self-compassion. Psychotherapeutic approach*. Editorial Científico-Técnica.

Bernard, J., & Goodyear, R. (2009). *Fundamentals of clinical supervision* (4th ed.). Pearson Education, Inc.

Bernard, J., & Goodyear, R. (2019). *Fundamentals of clinical supervision* (6th ed.). Pearson.

Bradley, L. (1989). *Counselor supervisión. Principles, process, practice*. United States of America, Accelerated Development Inc.

Calviño, M. (1997). Fusions without confusion: From the tower of babel to practice. *Revista Cubana de Psicología, 14*(1), 11–15.

Calviño, M. (1998). Hurries and sanity in psychotherapy. *Cuban Journal of Psychology, 15*(1), 3–20.

Calviño, M. (2000). *Psychological counseling. Multiple alternative referential scheme*. Editorial Científico Técnica.

Calviño, M. (2016). Doing psychology with Cuba: A time of change in changing eras. *Puerto Rican Journal of Psychology., 27*(2), 10–30. http://www.ojs.repsasppr.net/index.php/reps/article/view/287

Calviño, M. (2018). Supervision. Functional asymmetry and optimal distance. In B. Zas (Ed.), *Supervisión y Psicología. Multiplying reflections and experiences* (pp. 71–87). ALFEPSI Editorial.

Castellanos, R. (2016). *Rationale of the group psychotherapeutic program for minor schoolchildren with emotional disorders: "Accompany you". (Thesis)*. Faculty of Psychology, University of Havana.

Cueli, M. (2018). *Contributions of the historical-cultural approach to the practice of the helping relationship: Case studies(Undergraduate thesis)*. Faculty of Psychology, University of Havana.

Delgado, C. (2011). *Towards a new knowledge. Bioethics in the contemporary revolution of knowledge*. Aquarius.

Echemendia, B. (2014). Psychotherapy and historical-cultural approach. Contributions and challenges. *James, 133*, 85–98.

Falender, C., & Shafranske, E. (2017). Competency-based clinical supervision: Status, opportunities, stresses and the future. *Australian Psychologist, 52*(2), 86–93. https://doi.org/10.1111/ap.12265

Fraga, R., & Araujo, E. (2015). Model of systemic reflective family therapy in a hospital setting in Cuba. In *Dialogues for transformation: Experiences in therapy and other psychosocial interventions in Ibero-America* (Vol. 1, pp. 143–161). Taos Institute Publication.

Garcia, R. (2013). Psychology and psychotherapy in Cuba towards the present: Relevant theoretical figures and aspects. *Theory and Criticism of Psychology, 3*, 172–215.

Goodyear, R. K., & Falender, C. (2017). How can psychologists maximize their effectiveness as supervisors? Eight essential conditions. *Journal of Psychologists Guatemala City, VII*(20), 83–96.

Gutiérrez, D., León, L., & Santos, N. (2018). Project of supervision of professional relations of psychological help. Memories VIII Intercontinental Convention of Psychology. Hóminis 2018. http://www.hominiscuba.com

Henríquez, P., & Corral, R. (2014). Approach to the characterization of psychotherapeutic practices with adults in a group of specialists in Havana. *Cuban Alternatives in Psychology, 2*(6), 22–29. http://www.alfepsi.org/wp-content/uploads/2014/09/alternativas-cubanas-en-psicologia-vol2-N%C2%B06.pdf

Holloway, E. (1995). *Clinical supervision: A systems approach to supervisions*. SAGE Publications, Inc.

Laje, C., & Bedevia, A. (2017). *Psychoanalysis in Cuba. Intervention before the real*. Scientific-Technical.

Mercerón, Y. (2018). Supervision as a formative strategy in the clinical and health practice of the student. Memories VIII Intercontinental Convention of Psychology. Hóminis 2018. http://www.hominiscuba.com

Molina, M. C. (2013). Psychological guidance as an intervention of choice in the face of the demands of the health system in primary health care. *Cuban Alternatives in Psychology, 1*(2), 79–84. https://www.acupsi.org/numero/12/vol-1-nm-2-2013.html

Montalvo, J., & Espinosa, M. (Eds.). (2011). *Supervision and systemic therapy: Proposed models and practical guidelines*. Ediciones Cree-Ser.

Neufeldt, S. A. (1999). *Supervision strategies for the first practicum*. American Counseling Association.

Ortiz, M. E. (2018). All roads lead to supervision. *Memories VIII Intercontinental Convention of Psychology*. Hóminis 2018. http://www.hominiscuba.com

Pérez, G. (2007). *Clinical supervision: An effective tool for the health psychologist in Cuba. (Undergraduate thesis)*. Faculty of Psychology, University of Havana.

Pichon-Riviere, E. (1985). *The group process: From psychoanalysis to social psychology*. Ediciones Nueva Visión.

Roca, M. (2013). *Clinical psychology. A view from human health*. Editorial Universitaria Félix Varela.

Roche, O. (2012). *Therapeutic practice from a historical-cultural perspective of psychological development. Thesis presented in option to the scientific degree Doctor in Psychological Sciences*. Faculty of Psychology. University of Havana.

Rodriguez, R. (2008). *Historical tour of the models in psychotherapy used in Cuba*. INTERPSYCHE. No. 1 February: http://www.psiquiatria.com.htm

Rodriguez, R. (2016). *Large group psychotherapy. Origin and development in Cuba*. Scientific-Technical.

Rodríguez-Mena, M., López, C., Corral, R., Lorenzo, K., Pomares, W., Lago, C., et al. (2015). *The learning community "MADIBA". Memoirs of a Journey*. Aquarius Publications.

Soteras, M. P. (2017). History of EMDR-Cuba. http://www.emdr-es.org

Vygotsky, L. S. (1978). *Mind in society: The development of higher psychological processes*. Harvard University Press.

Watkins, C. E. (2020). The psychotherapy supervisor as an agent of transformation: To anchor and educate, facilitate and emancipate. *American Journal of Psychotherapy, 73*(2), 1–6. https://psychotherapy.psychiatryonline.org/

Zaldívar, D., Vega, R., & Roca, M. (2004). *General psychotherapy*. Félix Varela.

Zas, B. (2004). Clinical supervision: A developmental need for health psychologists in Cuba. *Journal Alternatives in Psychology, IX*(10), 30–39.

Zas, B. (2015). Training in psychological supervision: peculiarities of its development in the preparation of the professional of Psychology in Cuba. *Revista Integración Académica en Psicología, 3*(7), 39–47. Retrieved from http://integracion-academica.org/antriores/16-volumen-3-numero-72015/84

Zas, B. (2018a). Psychological supervision in Cuba: Current state of its development. *Obtained from Academic Integration in Psychology, 6*(18), 48–58. http://www.integracion-academica.org/28-volumen-6-numero-18-2018

Zas, B. (2018b). Supervision in psychology: Challenges in its employment as a resource for training and professional performance. In B. Zas (Ed.), *Supervisión y Psicología. Multiplying reflections and experiences* (pp. 8–28). ALFEPSI Editorial. http://www.alfepsi.org/libro-supervision-y-psicologia-multiplicando-reflexiones-y-experiencias/

Zas, B. (2021). *Construction of an operating model of psychological supervision. Dissertation*. Faculty of Psychology of the University of Havana.

Zas, B. (2024). La supervisión psicológica: Propuesta de un modelo de actuación. *Revista Cubana de Psicología, 6*(9), 62–82. http://www.psicocuba.uh.cu

Zas, B., & Molina, C. M. (2021). Psychology professionals: Immune to Covid-19? Updating the need for psychological supervision. *Magazine News in population, 17*(33) January-June ISSN (on-line) 1817-4078 RNPS: 2106 ISSN (print) 2308-2984 RNPS: 0638.

Bárbara Zas Ros holds a Psychology License obtained in 1985 and has specialized in Health Psychology since 1997. She earned a master's degree in clinical psychology in 2000 and a PhD in Psychological Sciences in 2021. She is an Assistant Researcher and Assistant Professor at the Faculty of Psychology of the University of Havana. She served as the Director of Psychology Services at the "Hermanos Ameijeiras" Clinical Surgical Hospital from 1993 to 2001. Currently, Dr. Zas Ros is an Assistant Researcher at the Center for Psychological and Sociological Research, where she heads the Psychosocial Health Studies Group. She has held several leadership roles, including President of the Havana Provincial Group of the Cuban Society of Psychology (2013–2019) and President of the Orientation Section of the Cuban Society of Psychology (2015-Present). She is also the Executive Secretary of ULAPSI (2021-Present) and the Regional Leader of the Caribbean Area for the International Society for Policy Research and Evaluation in School-Based Counseling. Dr. Zas Ros is the author of several books, including "Manual of Group Sports Practices" and "Multipliers Manual of the Psychosocial Transformation Program Centered on Psychology: Multiplying Reflections and Experiences."

Approaching Clinical Supervision in Guatemala

Meri Lubina, María Alejandra Auyón, Ana Alicia Cobar, and Maria del Pilar Grazioso

Dedication *Our gratitude to the community that continues to enrich the field of clinical supervision in Guatemala.*

Approaching Clinical Supervision in Guatemala

The Cultural, Professional, and Regulatory Context of Clinical Supervision in Guatemala

Despite advancements in supervision practice, the chapter points out the need to improve regulatory mechanisms, such as the qualificaitons and certifciaiton of supervisors, which have not progressed at the same pace. This highlights a significant gap that could limit the quality and consistency in the training of mental health professionals. The social constructivist approach proposed in the analysis emphasized that, to address current challenges, it is essential to consider the political, economic, and social dimensions influencing supervision. This approach could facilitate a more comprehensive understanding of how supervision training and practice should be strcutured in the Guatemalan context. Finally, the chapter highlights the tension between the growing demand for mental health care and the limited training opportunites and resources available. This challenge underscores the urgency of developing strategies to expand training and supervision capacity in the country, ensuring an effective response to the population needs. Currently, clinical

We have no conflicts of interest.

M. Lubina (✉) · M. A. Auyón · A. A. Cobar · M. P. Grazioso
Asociación Proyecto Aigle Guatemala, Universidad del Valle de Guatemala, Guatemala City, Guatemala
e-mail: mlubina@proyectoaigle.org.gt; melubina@uvg.edu.gt; aauyon@proyectoaigle.org.gt; maauyon@uvg.edu.gt; aacoma@proyectoaigle.org.gt; aacobar@uvg.edu.gt; mpgrazioso@proyectoaigle.org.gt; mpgderod@uvg.edu.gt

M. P. Grazioso et al. (eds.), *Clinical Supervision in Latin America*,
https://doi.org/10.1007/978-3-031-82373-2_6

supervision is practiced across clinical, academic, and research fields in Guatemala. Much of this work is conducted through our affiliations with Asociación Proyecto Aiglé Guatemala, a nonprofit organization based in the city, Universidad del Valle de Guatemala, a private higher education institution; and various international universities where we offer training and continuing education courses. Our journey has evolved over several years of training and professional development, during which we have assumed diverse leadership roles in training and the internationalization of supervision (Grazioso et al., 2021).

In addressing supervision as a field of action within the country, we recognize the necessity of considering its development, which has emerged from a complex interplay of existing realities in its co-construction, application, and transformation. For instance, an integrative approach that emphasizes "the role of context on human behavior," "social justice," "liberating practices," "self-determination," "universal design," and a "respectful relationship with the environment" (Fernández-Álvarez et al., 2016) highlights the challenges and opportunities that are shaping the field of supervision in Guatemala.

The ongoing interactions between supervision and the sociocultural context foster social exchanges that are continually advancing mental health supervision through counseling, psychology, psychiatry, and psychotherapy. This development acknowledges the existing multicultural complexity in supervision and the intersection of professional identities evident in both practice and research (Peters, 2017). Given these diverse realities and their formal and informal operationalization, the contributions of supervision in Guatemala are often advancing at a pace that exceeds that of regulatory practices.

In the following section, we present two vignettes, one in a dialogue format, illustrating various contextual factors that can influence supervision processes in Guatemala. These factors relate to institutional, cultural, and regulatory frameworks, connecting supervision in Guatemala with international contexts and highlighting the interconnections that arise from broader settings.

Vignette 1

Emilia García (fictitious name), graduated with a *licenciatura* degree in clinical psychology from a private university and has been an active member of the Colegio de Psicólogos de Guatemala for the past 8 years. She is currently studying a master's level degree in family and couples' psychotherapy, endorsed by a foreign university. She describes the psychotherapy model that guides her work as integrative . She works at her private practice, located in Guatemala City, offering group supervision to four professionals, charging fees for these services of around 100 quetzales (the country's currency) per participant. The supervision sessions offered are online, in group format, and the group meets once every 15 days.

The supervisee group is composed of three psychologists who work in different settings: educational, clinical, and hospital contexts. They requested supervision services out of personal motivation with the goal of becoming more competent, resolving ethical dilemmas, receiving feedback, feeling more confident and to learn from other cases and colleagues. The request of this group is increasingly reflected in other groups seeking supervision, however, there are no guidelines that regulate supervision in the practice of psychotherapy and the supervisor relies on available training, previous supervision experiences and on accessible, national and international literature to guide supervision. Emilia's relationship with past supervisors was not entirely satisfactory and she has remained a bit distant from them after graduation. This has contributed to Emilia, eagerly awaiting the supervision offered by the master's program she is currently enrolled in, to continue strengthening her skills as a supervisor.

Reflecting on this vignette, if Emilia came to consult you, what feedback would you give her to improve her supervisory practice while carrying out her role as a supervisor? And as a supervisee? What would you recommend to her considering the context described? What questions would you ask to guide your recommendations? Would you rely on Emilia's sociocultural context or your own context when transferring these recommendations? Finally, what literature would you recommend aiding her in this process, if you consider it relevant?

Vignette 2

The following vignette in a dialogue form, which may be experienced in any psychotherapeutic supervisory setting, helps us illustrate an excerpt from an interaction between supervisor and supervisor related to multiculturalism, diversity in the development of supervisory competencies and in analyzing the multiple identities that are related to the context in which it is implemented. Furthermore, it may function very differently in its application, in other countries in the Latin American region and across various groups and communities in the country.

Supervised therapist: I am thinking about the possibility of making a case transfer…, because I see that the case is not moving forward and…, I feel frustrated.

Supervisor: How do you feel thinking about that possibility?

Supervised therapist: Of transferring the case? I feel that I do not have the necessary skills to work with this case… Maybe I would need to study a master's degree, I don't know if in Guatemala or, perhaps abroad. Something more specific. I've already reached my limits, and I really feel like I've put in all my effort and am unable to move forward.

Supervisor: Is that the reason why you want to transfer the case?

Supervised therapist: I think so. He would benefit from another therapist with postgraduate training and perhaps more years of experience. You know, being young, all the stereotypes that are present. Maybe, I also need to advance further in my professional career, now that I am young and in another country with more opportunities. Don't you think?

Supervisor: I understand. Do you think the patient is benefiting from your care, in some way?

Supervised therapist: Well yes… we have built an alliance, he manages to regulate himself more, but we always return to his same complaint, "Women *in this country don't understand that as a man, you are not used to talking about difficult issues in order to resolve them.*" I feel like he is not seeing me as a professional because of my age and obviously because I am a woman.

Supervisor: What you are noticing, is it yours or does it come from the patient?

Supervised therapist: What do I feel? That's mine. He hasn't told me anything specific about it or of me, as a person or as a therapist. However, I am a woman and if I try to get us to talk about difficult topics, such as his alcohol dependency and the rejection he has felt at work because of the way he speaks and behaves with others, he shuts down. He is becoming more and more isolated.

Supervisor: What emotions are there in you? How are you connecting with your patient in this sense?

Supervised therapist: I feel angry, but I didn't tell him that. I didn't know how to handle it. Also, I'm worried. I mentioned that saying "I don't know" doesn't help.

Supervisor: It may be that you feel that he is not moving, and it makes you angry to see that he does not react. Perhaps, you're worried that this could strain the alliance.

Supervised therapist: The alliance? How can I see that? What does it have to do with him not wanting to talk about what is happening to him?

Supervisor: Possibly it has to do with the way you have worked on collaborative agreements with your patient. Perhaps working towards objectives, on tasks to be performed or through the emotional bond between you.

Various actions, contextualized within cultural, professional, and regulatory frameworks, influence supervisory functions and inform this dialogue. A universal perspective might consider the effectiveness of transferring a case to another therapist, emphasizing the necessary competencies and meta-competencies involved. Conversely, a more localized perspective would prompt us to examine the roles of the therapist, supervisee, and supervisor within the specific social, institutional, and organizational systems that underpin mental health care services in the country, particularly in response to community needs. This approach would also encourage us to appreciate the interconnectedness of gender, ethnicity, and training in Guatemala, exploring for example, sociocultural dimensions that shape therapeutic (Vides Porras, 2008) and supervisory alliances (Lubina, 2016).

For instance, should we openly discuss anger in supervision and therapy, or could this be perceived as disrespectful given the therapist's personal style and the asymmetrical nature of the therapeutic and supervisory relationships? Is it appropriate to address anger freely, particularly when considering the dynamics of a male patient and a female therapist, and the implications of gender and sexuality (Toro-Alfonso, 2009) within Guatemala's diverse context? How might the therapist, residing in the country's city, interpret the experiences of a patient from a rural southwestern region? Furthermore, how can supervisors enhance their effectiveness (Goodyear & Falender, 2017a, 2017b) and create conducive conditions for supervision? What are the potential consequences for the patient's well-being if no alternative therapist are available for case transfer? In other words, how do we navigate the various elements that arise in the supervisory relationship within this contextual framework?

We emphasize the importance of approaching this chapter from a social constructivist perspective, critically assessing the current context of clinical supervision in Guatemala. A multitude of social interpretations of professionalism shape this process, considering political, economic, and social dimensions at both the individual level and in relation to the values and cultures (Martimianakis et al., 2009) embedded in training programs, institutions, and professional organizations. As a collective of professionals trained both locally and internationally, we acknowledge that these experiences inform our supervisory practices from diverse lenses that may not be universally applicable or unique to the country.

The environments in which supervision and psychotherapeutic practices occur are deeply intertwined with the realities of mental health, characterized by its pluricultural and multilingual nature. Supervision operates within varied conditions, shaped by historical contexts and lived experiences that reflect both the professionalization of mental health and its potential for healing or oppression. As supervision evolves into a distinct field, supervisors are increasingly trained in specific competencies relevant to the Guatemalan sociocultural, ecological, and regulatory landscape.

At first glance, our efforts to expand professional access may appear limited due to the scarcity of resources, accessibility of mental health services, and socioeconomic barriers to professional training and development. These challenges often contrast sharply with the growing demand for mental health care and well-being in the population. The evident growth and expansion of supervision may seem paradoxical; however, this reflects the developmental trajectory of supervision across various contexts, including global trends. Supervision practices continue to transform Guatemala's mental health landscape in compelling ways.

Institutional Issues

License or Certification

Psychology is governed by the Compulsory Membership Law, which stipulates that obtaining a university degree enables professional practice. Legal authorization must be secured from the relevant professional association, which entails compliance with membership obligations. As such, the practice of psychology is regulated by the Colegio de Psicólogos de Guatemala a nonprofit labor association that mandates membership for university-trained professionals, as required by the Political Constitution of the Republic of Guatemala. Obtaining a licenciatura degree from accredited universities, followed by recognition from the Colegio de Psicólogos de

Guatemala Association, is a step forward toward promoting practices aligned with institutional norms regarding supervision.

Despite this framework, recent international publications indicate that programs specifically designed to provide supervision, along with their requisite hours and qualification standards, are still being developed (Falender et al., 2021). The number of professionals qualified to assume supervisory roles is notably limited, and there is considerable diversity in their training backgrounds. For instance, some supervisors have received training through theoretical-practical courses included in their master's and doctoral programs, while others may have pursued informal self-training in response to contextual demands or to support students and colleagues.

Consequently, the regulation of supervision primarily originates from the organizations and institutions in which it is practiced. While there has been a shift toward improved qualifications and certifications for supervisors in recent years, comprehensive research on the topic remains scarce. However, certain initiatives are emerging from university institutions and associated groups. It is anticipated that formal and diverse proposals regarding qualifications and accreditation in supervision will continue to develop in the coming years.

Within institutional frameworks and professional associations, many psychologists supervise their peers. Often, supervisors rely on their years of experience, highlighting the current deficiencies in formal qualifications and accreditation for supervision. In other contexts, formal training in supervised practice is mandatory, with varying requirements regarding the number of hours of practice or formal training in supervision. Although some institutions and organizations offer supervisory training, the criteria and expectations for the roles of supervisor and supervisee can vary significantly. This disparity indicates that the regulatory framework for qualification and certification has not kept pace with the growing practice of supervision. Currently, several professional groups and associations are striving to address this need at both undergraduate and postgraduate levels, as well as in ongoing professional training.

Ethical Codes

The practice of psychology is guided by the Ethical Code of the Colegio de Psicólogos de Guatemala, which is based on the Declaración Universal de Principios Éticos para Psicólogos (the Universal Declaration of Ethical Principles for Psychologists) (Jurado & Grazioso, 2022). This code emphasizes values that aim to provide optimal care, grounded in respect for the dignity of individuals and communities (Colegio de Psicólogos de Guatemala, 2010).

Within the "Scope and Limits" section of this code, supervision is specifically mentioned as part of the training activities in which psychologists engage, framed within defined professional, academic, and scientific relationships (Colegio de Psicólogos de Guatemala, 2010). The ethical framework emphasizes the principle of competent care, focusing on the well-being of clients through the promotion of competence, self-awareness, and the delivery of quality services. The code also addresses the management of conflicts of interest in supervisory relationships, emphasizing the need to avoid exploitation for personal or business gain (Colegio de Psicólogos de Guatemala, 2010). This underscores the ethical considerations inherent in the supervision process.

University Training for Psychologists Who Wish to Provide Psychotherapy

According to Law 30 of 1992, el Consejo Superior Universitario (the Superior University Council) serves as the highest governing body for higher education. Its responsibilities include: (a) defining academic and administrative policies and institutional planning, (b) overseeing the academic, administrative, and financial organization of educational institutions, (c) ensuring compliance with legal provisions and institutional policies, (d) modifying institutional statutes and regulations, and (e) appointing and removing the rector as per the institution's statutes and budget approvals.

Currently, the Universidad de San Carlos de Guatemala is the only state university, responsible for: (a) directing, organizing, and developing higher education and state university professional education, (b) promoting cultural dissemination, (c) fostering research, and (d) participating in the resolution of national issues. Established over 200 years ago, private universities have emerged as independent institutions with legal status, allowing them the freedom to create faculties and institutes, develop academic programs, and carry out educational activities. Consejo Superior Universitario (Superior University Council) is the entity that authorizes the establishment of new universities and ensures the maintenance of academic standards in private institutions.

As of 2019, el Instituto Nacional de Estadísticas (the National Institute of Statistics) reported 38,950 university graduates, with 44% earning technical degrees, 48% at the licenciatura level, 7% obtaining master's degrees, and less than 1% achieving doctoral degrees (Loarca, 2021). University education is generally limited in relation to the general population and scarce regarding participation in postgraduate programs. Despite being one of the largest economies in Central America, Guatemala's stability does not translate into significant reductions in inequality or poverty (Banco Mundial, 2023).

Eleven of the 15 existing universities offer training for psychologists in various fields of applied psychology and graduates practice across diverse academic and professional fields (Cárcamo & Escobar, 2015). These institutions employ various educational methodologies, including face-to-face, hybrid, and online formats (Klie & Grazioso, 2020).

Although all universities qualify new professionals, they do not grant the right to practice unless graduates obtain collegiate affiliation. Generally, these programs focus on scientific knowledge, promoting well-being, personal development, health, and quality of life. The interdisciplinary, multidisciplinary, and sometimes transdisciplinary nature of psychology characterizes the different branches and specializations offered.

As of April 12, 2023, el Colegio de Psicólogos de Guatemala reported 14,502 active members. Previous data indicated that the average age of professionals was 39, with approximately 7 years of service (González & Bolaños, 2015). This study noted that around 800 psychologists graduate annually, primarily from the country's capital (71%), with the remainder distributed across other departments. Most graduates specialize in General Psychology (65%), Clinical Psychology (26%), with smaller percentages in Organizational Psychology (4.5%), Educational Psychology (2.6%), and Social Psychology (1%), alongside even fewer in Sports and Forensic Psychology.

Most university training programs incorporate clinical practice centers that provide supervision. Ethical and critical perspectives are essential characteristics sought in the professional profiles of trainees, with a strong emphasis on developing competencies in prevention, treatment, evaluation, diagnosis, and research. Biopsychosocial approaches form the foundation of several programs and support the development of clinical competencies. In this training context, some programs include supervision, described as a supportive process for reflecting on doubts, challenges, strengths, and incorporating diverse perspectives from supervisors and peers (Cóbar, 2019). Other programs offer varied frameworks, conceptualizing supervision in multiple ways based on different approaches, explanatory models, and objectives, which are evident in supervision agreements, professional meetings, and interactions with clients, colleagues, and communities.

Culture and Diversity Issues Particularly Relevant in Guatemala

Guatemala is home to approximately 17.8 million people (Instituto Nacional de Estadística de Guatemala, 2024), with a population that is predominantly female, young, and characterized by significant socioeconomic diversity. This diversity is evident in urban and rural settings, reflecting disparities in living conditions, access to education, healthcare, and employment opportunities. Among the country's multicultural and diverse landscape, war, conflict, colonization, and struggles for independence have profoundly influenced mental health development and the evolution of psychology in the region (Klie & Grazioso, 2020).

Given this rich diversity, training and supervision present unique opportunities, including: (1) the use of multiple languages, (2) varying lifestyles and spiritual beliefs, and (3) differing interpretations of traditions related to mental health. These factors contribute to difficulties faced by therapists, including: (1) professional awareness of one's own values, biases, beliefs, attitudes, knowledge, and skills, (2) understanding the worldviews of clients and patient groups, and (3) developing culturally relevant interventions (Sue et al., 1992).

At the Latin American level, we encounter shared political barriers regarding service delivery, a limited number of mental health providers and services, widespread poverty, and restricted access to education (Fernández-Álvarez et al., 2020). These challenges underscore the urgent need to cultivate multicultural therapeutic competencies regarding supervisor training. The advancement of scientific knowledge, the regulation of practices, and the assessment of service quality and delivery are critical issues that impact psychotherapy and supervision, particularly in relation to culture and diversity. Addressing these conditions is essential, given their prevalence and professional relevance both locally and internationally.

Supervision Formats

Most training programs offer supervision primarily in group settings, with individual supervision available as needed, typically on a weekly to monthly basis (Cóbar, 2019). Currently, we provide hybrid supervision formats, online formats and face-to face supervision. Our collective experience evidenced that virtual supervision gained traction during the pandemic, transitioning from predominantly in-person sessions. At present, these formats present distinct strengths and challenges. Virtual supervision has enhanced accessibility, improved time efficiency, and facilitated ongoing education, leading to greater national, regional and international coverage and the integration of both practical and theoretical components. For instance, during the early stages of the COVID-19 pandemic, we collaborated with Colegio de Psicólogos de Guatemala enabling training courses on telepsychology.

Current initiatives include supervision in private clinics, available in both group and individual formats, as well as hybrid and face-to-face options. Supervision occurs in educational and hospital contexts, sometimes referred to by alternative names such as "team meetings" or "case monitoring." However, we face challenges consistent with those identified by the American Psychological Association (APA), including issues related to professional presentation, lack of formality, confidentiality risks, and insufficient proactive care (American Psychological Association, 2013).

Mechanisms to Guarantee Client Well-Being

In recent years, we have focused on shaping professional beliefs and values regarding client well-being. It is crucial to recognize that supervision relies on a shared comprehension of its definition, practice, models, and contexts (Consoli et al., 2017). We advocate for specific, gradual training in supervision. As Falender and Shafranske (2020) have indicated, professional development remains tied to client well-being and an informed understanding of clinical supervision, which in turn enhances practices, competencies, and effectiveness.

Within this framework, we prioritize the informed consent process between client and therapist, along with establishing supervision agreements or contracts with supervisees that clearly outline the professional services provided by the supervisor. Collaborating with experts, mentors, professors, and colleagues, we have translated and adapted various documents, presentations, and materials to facilitate this process. For example, we have contributed to the Spanish translation of *Fundamentals for the Clinical Practice of Competency-Based Supervision* (Falender & Shafranske, 2020) and the *Supervision Toolkit* (Bernard & Goodyear, 2014), which compiles questionnaires and scales to guide feedback and evaluation in supervision.

Supervisors bear the responsibility for ensuring both client well-being and the professional development of supervisees. This gatekeeping role enables supervisors to assess whether supervisees are prepared to advance in their academic programs in accordance with regulatory policies and institutional guidelines. Emphasizing self-care in supervision and among supervisors themselves is crucial for safeguarding client well-being. Gomar and Musso (2017) have emphasized the importance of addressing stress and its contributing factors, such as living conditions, vicarious trauma, and burnout in professional practice, while promoting self-care strategies.

The roles and responsibilities of supervisors can be complex and sometimes poorly defined in terms of regulation. Therefore, it is imperative to prioritize supervisors' self-care consistently. Each institution or organization that trains psychologists has established standards for credentialing, including the completion of a specified number of supervised hours, attainment of therapeutic competencies with practical evidence, and adherence to administrative requirements (e.g., managing files, databases, bibliographic resources). Compliance with the Ethical Code of the Colegio de Psicólogos de Guatemala is essential.

Methodologically, case discussions are integral to supervision, aimed at developing skills and informed practices across diverse approaches. These discussions help resolve ethical dilemmas, monitor cases, and strengthen the sense of security and support among supervisees and supervisors, allowing for mentoring relationships and expansive feedback from both peers and supervisors. This collaborative approach fosters professional growth, focusing on achievements and challenges, while also ensuring the ethical and clinical management of records and case files. Additionally, formative and summative evaluations are conducted to guarantee client well-being and to demonstrate the progress and development of supervisees.

Opportunities for Supervisors to Obtain Training

Our training experiences have provided valuable opportunities for self-development through various educational programs at multiple academic and community levels. We believe that fostering the supervisory relationship is crucial, as it promotes training opportunities for aspiring supervisors (Grazioso et al., 2021). Professionals seeking to enhance their skills often join our practice after participating in workshops, conferences, or supervision groups. Some trainees have also conducted graduation theses or dissertations specifically on supervision, contributing significantly to local research and professional practice in this area.

Training for supervisors is offered through university courses, nongovernmental organizations, and professional associations. One notable example is the training provided by Asociación Proyecto Aiglé Guatemala (Aiglé Association Project in Guatemala), affiliated to Fundación Aiglé (Aiglé Foundation), Argentina, which integrates supervision with teaching, research, and community practice in both urban and rural settings. These organizations collaborate with various entities to address mental health needs both locally and internationally, aiming to ensure effective services while supporting therapists (Fernández Álvarez et al., 2020). Additionally, supervision for supervisors is a recognized practice at both Asociación Proyecto Aiglé Guatemala (Aiglé Association Project Guatemala) and Universidad del Valle de Guatemala.

The State of Academia and Research in Supervision in Guatemala

The origins of supervision in Guatemala can be traced back to medical models, which have evolved into more comprehensive clinical models of psychology within a multicultural and interdisciplinary framework (Grazioso, 2015). At Universidad del Valle de Guatemala, supervision courses were integrated into the master's program curriculum in Counseling Psychology and Mental Health from 2000 to 2003, under the direction of Dr. María del Pilar Grazioso, who played a pivotal role as the first supervisor of the program. Gradually, some students began supervising their peers, and the focus on supervision became a fundamental aspect of postgraduate studies, establishing a foundation for future developments and fostering national and international collaborations in this field.

Table 1 Graduation work on supervision: Universidad del Valle de Guatemala

Author	Date	Thesis title (English translation)
Bran, M.	2006	Favorable and unfavorable factors in the supervision process of students of a Master program in Counseling and Mental Health (Bran, 2006).
Lemus, K. R.	2006	The use of multicultural skills by counselors in training within a supervisory session (Lemus, 2006).
Cazali, L.	2006	Experiences of group supervision: what are the needs that arise? (Lemus, 2006).
Cóbar, A.	2012	Exploring the experience of being supervised by graduates of the master's degree in Psychological Counseling and Mental Health at the Universidad del Valle de Guatemala (Cóbar, 2006).
Lubina, M.	2016	What did you like and what could you do differently? A contextualized study of the supervisory alliance (Lubina, 2016).

As supervision has expanded, contextualized research has emerged, driven by the interests of graduated professionals seeking to deepen their understanding of supervision. To date, seven studies have been reported on clinical supervision, alongside others focusing on educational supervision at both the master's and doctoral levels. Universidad del Valle de Guatemala has produced five qualitative studies at the master's level and two doctoral dissertations on supervision (Table 1).

At the doctoral level, two dissertations have specifically focused on supervision. The first dissertation, conducted by Cóbar (2019), explored supervision in psychotherapy, presenting a professional consensus among expert supervisors in Guatemala City. The author offers a definition of supervision that enhances understanding and contextual interpretation:

> Supervision is a human encounter between an expert and a less experienced individual, wherein support, training, and evaluation processes occur. The objective is to meet the training and informational needs of supervisees, ensure the quality of services provided, and foster a sense of community. It is acknowledged that building a connection with the supervisee facilitates successful supervision, while a lack of engagement may lead to ineffective outcomes. Furthermore, it is crucial to incorporate the necessity for self- training among supervisors and to address the potential risks of social insecurity in this context.

This definition provided a valuable, contextual framework drawn from the country's academic landscape and the perspectives of experienced supervisors, contributing to a more nuanced understanding of the topic.

The second dissertation, conducted by Lubina (2021), examines the strengthening of supervision in Guatemala from the perspective of a group of supervisees. This study aimed to understand how supervision is practiced among psychologists in Guatemala and the implications of these practices, utilizing a constructivist grounded theory approach. A significant finding revealed that at least 22.5% of participants, who had received supervision or were currently undergoing it, reported not having clinical supervisors. The analysis identified key themes regarding negative critical incidents associated with supervisor behavior, including: (1) transgression of boundaries, (2) ineffective feedback, and (3) poor evaluations concerning both the supervisee and the patient. Conversely, critical events perceived as highly beneficial to supervisees included: (1) the supervisor's role, (2) effective feedback, and (3) constructive evaluations of both supervisees and patients.

In 2019, Cóbar et al. published a qualitative study in the *Brazilian Journal of Psychotherapy*, assessing the supervision model used in the Programa de Maestría en Consejería Psicológica y Salud Mental de la Universidad del Valle de Guatemala (Master's Program in Psychological Counseling and Mental Health at Universidad del Valle de Guatemala). Analysis provided, stemmed from 14 interviews with program graduates and resulted in a definition of supervision as a learning and evaluation process facilitated through "acompañamiento" (accompaniment) and feedback. The study highlighted the impact of supervision on client outcomes and underscored the necessity for defining, guiding, and standardizing supervision practices. Key characteristics identified as essential to effective supervision included respect, support, guidance, listening skills, trust, communication skills, responsibility, empathy, openness, respect for diversity, feedback, learning, and structure. The authors indicated that this research had opened avenues for further studies in academic, community, professional, and training contexts beyond the confines of this program, with potential applicability in other Latin American settings.

Another article by Fernández-Álvarez et al. (2019) addressed the literature gap concerning remote supervision within the Latin American, psychotherapeutic, training program of Fundación Aiglé Argentina (Aiglé Foundation Argentina). This study presented perspectives from both Argentina and Guatemala, illustrating training experiences that shed light on the strengths and weaknesses of technology-assisted supervision. In 2017, the journal *Psychologists*, published by the Colegio de Psicólogos de Guatemala, featured a special edition dedicated to supervision (Consoli et al., 2017). This issue included contributions from several national and international professionals discussing essential contextual components in supervision practices. This journal expanded the understanding of supervision as a multicultural and diverse field, emphasizing the alignment of key constructs such as the supervisory relationship, working alliance, effective practices, and personal factors that shape supervision.

Additionally, in 2013, Lemus García published an article in this same journal, emphasizing the necessity of supervision for clinical psychologists in Guatemala. The author outlined the various actions involved in supervision and the ethical considerations associated with it, highlighting the benefits of supervision as a space for sharing experiences and challenges, as well as fostering professional development for supervisees, supervisors, patients, and communities. Since 2016, Universidad del Valle de Guatemala has co-coordinated interuniversity meetings, fostering an investigative and practical spirit in case formulation presentations and supervision. These gatherings and related discussions allow students and supervisors to present case conceptualizations, generating reflections on the learning experiences and challenges that enhance mental health care and the supervision process.

Supervision has also been approached from an educational standpoint, viewed as a supervised professional practice that, while not always directly related to clinical supervision, enriches the field through the exchange of information and evidence generated. Table 2 illustrates some of the topics addressed.

Practice Issues

Practice Models

Currently, there are no systematic studies at the country level that investigate the dominant models of supervision practice in Guatemala. However, Fernández-Álvarez (2017) provided a valuable regional perspective, highlighting influential theoretical models across Latin America. He noted the "dominant but not exclusive" influence of European and North American models, particularly those rooted

Table 2 Educational field research and supervised practice

Author	Date	Topic (English translation)
Sandoval	2015	Group supervision, theoretical and historical background, forms of application and interviews with experts
Girón Cifuentes	2012	Pedagogical support of the educational supervisor in teaching performance
De la Roca	2012	Efficacy of final year clinical psychology students in relation to supervised professional practice
Portillo	2012	The importance of school supervision in strengthening educational quality in the municipality of Jalapa, department of Jalapa
Campos	2008	Perception of practitioners in clinical psychology from Universidad Rafael Landívar who do their internships at the Landivarian Center for Psychological Practice and Services on the patient-therapist relationship during their supervised practice experience
Castellanos Álvarez	2008	Personal style of the therapist in clinical psychology Students who carry out supervised practice
Sotomayor	2004	School supervision as an administrative attribution of the director to strengthen educational quality
Chacón	2001	Evaluation of the educational supervision process, in the department of Santa Rosa
Esquivel Rivera	1995	Supervision within an active education process: The new unitary school
Rubio	1992	Proposal to convert school supervision into technical-pedagogical advice
Aldana	1991	School supervision of pedagogical counselors in the process of curricular adaptation in the department of Jutiapa
Enríquez	1987	Deconcentration and administrative decentralization of educational supervision in the south-eastern region of Guatemala
López	1981	Educational supervision in Guatemala. Current state of school supervision in Guatemala

in psychoanalysis, humanistic-existential approaches, cognitive- behavioral methods, and systemic frameworks. Simultaneously, he discussed how these models, including psychodynamic, cognitive-behavioral, humanistic-existential, systemic, and integrative approaches, had been disseminated across the continent through expert consensus. This work clarified other relevant approaches and interventions in the region, such as therapeutic groups, psychodrama, and community-based applications, which are particularly vital within the supervision context in Guatemala.

Supervisory Relationships

In supervisory relationships, key issues often arise around interactional components, collaborative development, and the influence of sociocultural contexts, ethics, competence, and meta-competence. Based on our experience, a productive starting point for these relationships has been to open discussions regarding supervisory dynamics, their relationship to supervision itself, and the interactions among all parties involved. Grazioso et al. (2021) emphasized the need to explore both the implicit and explicit hierarchies present in the relationships between supervisors and supervisees, as well as to focus on how these hierarchies can transform through professional development cycles. These authors also highlighted the importance of addressing the multiplicity of roles that emerge in these relationships.

Identifying specific, nationwide situations that characterize the development of supervisory alliances remains challenging. In the special edition of the Psychologists journal (Consoli et al., 2017), Lubina et al. (2017) discussed various contextual challenges and aspects affecting supervisory alliances. They stressed the importance of reflective practice aimed at enhancing the quality of supervision training, ensuring deep connections to the country's context. Castañeda and Cóbar (2017) further addressed issues related to repair and rupture within supervisory relationships, examining their ties to power dynamics and authority from cultural perspectives relevant to Guatemala. They advocated for a nuanced analysis of power in supervision, considering sociocultural factors such as privilege, identity, and worldviews that can significantly influence the supervisory relationship.

Multicultural competencies and diversity present additional opportunities in establishing respectful supervisory relationships and understanding the impact of biases, prejudices, and stereotypes in practice. Defining what it means to be a supervisor and to supervise others can be complex (Falender & Shafranske, 2020). Contributions from cultural humility in psychotherapy supervision (Zhang et al., 2022), the relevance of multiculturalism and diversity in supervision (Falender et al., 2014), and the dimensions of supervisory relationships (Bernard & Goodyear, 2014) enhance our understanding of supervision as a practice that assumes a social justice role in a multicultural county level context like that in Guatemala. Consequently, the implicit power dynamics, cultural differences, and varied objectives within supervision (Falender & Shafranske, 2020) are particularly relevant when addressing supervisory alliances, tensions, and ruptures.

Based on our experience, the evaluative component of supervision, along with the frequency and quality of participation, requires careful consideration regarding supervisory relationships. This includes addressing subjectivity and objectivity in feedback processes, where the levels and contexts of training are crucial. The dynamics of the supervisory relationship encompass various factors, including the frequency of sessions, consistency, and systematic participation by supervisees. Some professionals engage actively in supervision throughout different phases of their academic training but may choose to discontinue during their professional development after graduation or early professional development. Conversely, some supervisory relationships persist over time, maintaining a focus on managing alliance tensions and ruptures. However, it remains challenging to specify the benefits gained regarding supervisee professional development or the quality and effectiveness of the therapeutic alliance with clients.

Verification Resources from Best Practices of Supervision

From an international perspective, several instruments (Bernard & Goodyear, 2014) are available for application in supervision, which can be particularly useful in specific contexts within Guatemala. However, the credentials of supervisors in the country still requires clearer identification, monitorization and regulation as resources to enhance implementation and effectiveness become available. Clarity will largely depend on regulatory frameworks and future research aimed at establishing supervision as a distinct field that aligns with local practices.

We acknowledge that the practice of supervision under informed consent requires greater support and training in context. This encompasses the identification of best practices, the development of competencies (including the competence to supervise), management of rights, and the well-being of clients, as well as the professional responsibilities and institutional obligations of those providing supervision.

Key aspects to consider when regulating supervision include the frequency of supervision sessions, the number of participants involved, the methods employed for supervision, and the feedback processes utilized. The sociocultural context is also critical, as it interacts with the legal, economic, and professional frameworks of the country. Addressing these factors can enhance the effectiveness, fairness, and respectfulness of supervision, ensuring its integrity, especially in relation to content, information processing, and the effective evaluation of supervision training programs. Typically, materials that guide feedback processes include informal questionnaires, practice records, adaptations of existing instruments, observations of recorded sessions, on-site supervision, client satisfaction surveys, and supervision toolboxes (Bernard & Goodyear, 2014). These resources deserve increased attention from supervisors, as they contribute to the well-being of society at large, clients, and to the effective professional growth of supervisees and supervisors. Consideration of diverse needs, unique situations, and varying levels of competence remains essential.

We are committed to strengthening supervisory alliances, key in supervisory relationships. Ethically, it is imperative to promote training in multicultural competencies that address diversity effectively. This challenge involves being mindful of different worldviews related to health, well-being, and quality of life, particularly as they pertain to confidentiality practices. This includes informed consent processes, safeguarding records, and discussing cases within protected supervisory contexts. Several dilemmas we have encountered compel us to thoughtfully consider the power dynamics between supervisees and supervisors and their impact on the supervisory relationship. It is essential to engage in discussions about how power is granted, earned, and shared, fostering a greater awareness of boundaries between supervisors and supervisees. This approach encourages us to avoid collusion and clarify expectations, thereby enhancing the training and professional development.

A Country-Appropriate Supervisory Approach

Based on our experiences and comprehension of supervision practices in our country and other countries, we find that the practice of supervision in Guatemala can be particularly unique in its organization and structure, reflecting the specific context in which it operates. Integrative community approaches to supervision appear to be well-suited for Guatemala. The connection between culture and practice enhances the supervisory relationship and aligns with the common dimensions of supervisory alliances, particularly from a group perspective. However, achieving established objectives can be complex, influenced by various contextual factors that may differ significantly from those in other regions.

In conclusion, we recognize that we are navigating a relatively new field of action-research. Our journey—spanning over two decades as supervisees, supervisors, and supervisors of supervisors— has provided valuable insights into the multidisciplinary nature of supervision and its evolving emphasis within the country.

Next Steps in the Progression of Clinical Supervision in Guatemala

The current supervision landscape encourages us to consider future steps and stages. Despite years of progress, we are at times, only beginning to understand the foundations of supervision in the country. A new generation of plans and approaches for supervision training is emerging, often discussed in national and international publications and conferences. These proposals aim to integrate clinical supervision practices while expanding on specific research topics relevant to our context.

Significant developments are evident, including increased opportunities for the supervision of supervisors, interconsultation in clinical supervision, and the effective use of telesupervision. These prospects motivate us to engage further actions in training and supervision programs. The emphasis on clinical supervision is growing nationwide, although perhaps not at the pace we desire. It is evolving in response to the challenges and advancements we face. For example, the lack of regulatory frameworks around supervision remains a critical area for improvement, directly impacting the quality of services provided.

Historically, the practice of psychotherapy in Latin America and its theoretical models have been shaped by diverse professional approaches (Fernández-Álvarez, 2017), often viewed through Western lenses (Falender et al., 2021). The supervision models typically employed in Guatemala reflect the region's sociocultural complexities. However, adhering to specific supervision models has not been a normative expectation for many Guatemalan professionals. Numerous practitioners have yet to engage in clinical supervision due to limitations in trained supervisors, available supervision spaces, collaborative content, evaluation processes, and research opportunities. From a multicultural and diversity perspective, the relationship between supervision and Guatemalan cultures remains insufficiently explored regarding its contextual relevance and effectiveness.

Defining supervision—clinical supervision and supervision in psychotherapy—has historically posed significant complexities, influenced by international practices (Milne & Watkins, 2014). It is challenging to rigorously trace how supervision models have been applied and developed in clinical practice. As a group of Guatemalan professionals dedicated to supervision, we have embraced an integrative model in our applied practice, recognizing that a one-size-fits-all approach is inadequate. We continue to deepen our understanding of supervision and cultural interactions in Guatemala. As we do so, we value Falicov's (2014) perspective, which positions the client as an expert who informs the therapist, with the supervisor facilitating the supervisee's exploration of the client's needs and contexts.

Advancing supervision as a valid and reliable approach in Guatemala faces important challenges rooted in its formation and its becoming. We see the necessity of developing, implementing, and evaluating consistent supervision models tailored for our context. We have been prompted to consider whether psychotherapy supervision is perceived as a foreign practice. This question and its accompanying discussion remain significant. In response, we are committed to moving forward with practices informed by local research and training. We recognize the pressing need for effective supervision, especially considering the cultural, educational and professional barriers that limit access for many Guatemalans. Supervision has profoundly impacted our practices, offering insights into progress while also highlighting persistent challenges, humbling us. Learning more fuels our hope for the development of consistent and relevant supervisory approaches in Guatemala. Our journey in seeking supervision has led us to valuable discoveries. It has become clear that pursuing effective supervision in Guatemala involves navigating various risks at multiple levels, as we engage in processes of interaction and collaboration across different contexts.

Acknowledgments We want to acknowledge all mentoring relationships in supervision encouraging collaborative, supervisee stances and challenging supervisor roles and identities across Latin America. Our heartfelt gratitude to Dr. Hector Fernandez-Alvarez and the legacy he has left behind for many others. He continues transforming our learning from each other, invigorating our professional stances. His immense strength, capacity and keen interest in opening our collective spirit grows, reminding us of what is truly valuable and hopeful in doing supervision.

References

American Psychological Association. (2013). Guidelines for the practice of Telepsychology. *American Psychologist, 69*(9), 791–800.

Banco Mundial. (2023, abril). Guatemala Panorama General. [Guatemala Overview]. https://www.bancomundial.org/es/country/guatemala/overview#:~:text=Luego%20de%20un%20fuerte%20repunte,2%20por%20ciento%20en%202023

Bernard, J. M., & Goodyear, R. K. (2014). *Fundamentals of clinical supervision* (5th ed.). Pearson Education.

Bran, M. (2006). *Factores favorables y desfavorables en el proceso de supervisión de estudiantes de un programa de Maestría en Consejería y Salud Mental: un estudio fenomenológico* [Favorable and unfavorable factors in the supervision process students in a master's program in counseling and mental health: A study phenomenological]. Trabajo de graduación, Universidad del Valle de Guatemala.

Cárcamo Duarte, A. G., & Escobar Martínez, A. C. (2015). La psicología en Guatemala, un poco de historia y actualidad [Psychology in Guatemala, a little history and current events]. *Psychological Information, 109*, 72–85. https://doi.org/10.14635/IPSIC.2015.109.9

Castañeda, T., & Cóbar, A. (2017). Matices de poder y autoridad en la supervisión clínica en Guatemala [Power and authority nuances in clinical supervision in Guatemala]. *Revista Psicólogos, 7*(20ª), 20–28.

Cazali, L. (2006). *Experiencias de una supervisión de grupo: ¿cuáles son las necesidades que se presentan? [Experiences of group supervision: what are the present needs]*. Trabajo de graduación, Universidad del Valle de Guatemala.

Cóbar, A. (2012). *Explorando la experiencia de ser supervisado en egresados de la maestría en Consejería Psicológica y Salud Mental de la Universidad del Valle de Guatemala* [Exploring the experience of being supervised in graduates of the master's degree in psychological counseling and mental health from the Universidad del Valle de Guatemala]. Trabajo de graduación, Universidad del Valle de Guatemala.

Cóbar, A. (2019). *La supervisión en psicoterapia: Consenso profesional de supervisores expertos de la ciudad de Guatemala [Supervisión in psychotherapy: Professional consensus of expert supervisors of Guatemala City]*. Doctoral dissertation, Universidad del Valle de Guatemala.

Cóbar, A., Cazali, L., de Staebler, I. E., Grazioso, M. P., & Gallardo-Cooper, M. (2019). Modelo Integrativo de Supervisión: Construyendo la identidad profesional en el campo de la Consejería Psicológica en Guatemala. [Integrative supervision model: Building a professional identity in the field of counseling psychology in Guatemala]. *Brazilian Journal of Psychotherapy, 21*(2), 1–20. https://doi.org/10.5935/2318-0404.20190018

Colegio de Psicólogos de Guatemala. (2010). Código de ética [code of ethics].

Consoli, A. J., Grazioso, M. P., & Musso, A. (2017). Colegio de Psicólogos Guatemala. *Revista Psicólogos, 7(20ª)*, 3–108.

Falender, C., Goodyear, R., Duan, C., Al-Darmaki, F., Keeyeon, B., Ciftci, A., Ruiz Gónzalez, V., Grazioso, M. P., Humeidan, M., Xiaoming, C., Kagnici, D. Y., & Partridge, S. (2021). Lens on International Clinical Supervision: Lessons Learned from a Cross-National Comparison of Supervision. *Journal of Contemporary Psychotherapy, 51*, 181–189. https://doi.org/10.1007/s10879-021-09497-5

Falender, C., & Shafranske, E. (2020). *Práctica Clínica de la Supervisión, basada en competencias. [Supervision clinical practice, based on competencies]*. GiuntiEOS Psychometrics, S.L.

Falender, C. A., Shafranske, E. P., & Falicov, C. J. (2014). *Multiculturalism and diversity in clinical supervision: A competency-based approach* (pp. xv–296). American Psychological Association.

Falicov, C. J. (2014). Psychotherapy and supervision as cultural encounters: The multidimensional ecological comparative approach framework. In C. A. Falender, E. P. Shafranske, & C. J. Falicov (Eds.), *Multiculturalism and diversity in clinical supervision: A competence-based approach* (pp. 29–58). American Psychological Association. https://psycnet.apa.org/doi/10.1037/14370-002

Fernández Álvarez, H., del Pilar Grazioso, M., & Kirszman, D. (2019). Distance supervision in the Aiglé Foundation's Latin American psychotherapy training program. *Journal of Clinical Psychology, 75*(2), 282–291.

Fernández-Álvarez, H. (2017). Psicoterapia en un mundo emergente. El paisaje de América Latina [Psychotherapy in an emerging world. The Latin American landscape]. *Revista Argentina de Clínica Psicológica, XXVI*(3), 255–260.

Fernández-Álvarez, H., Consoli, A. J., & Gómez, B. (2016). Integration in psychotherapy: Reasons and challenges. *American Psychologist, 71*(8), 820–830. https://doi.org/10.1037/amp0000100

Fernández-Álvarez, H., Grazioso, M. D. P., Kirszman, D., Lubina, M., & Goodyear, R. (2020). Responding to the mental health needs of underserved Latin Americans. In J. Zimmerman, J. E. Barnett, & L. F. Campbell (Eds.), *Bringing psychotherapy to the underserved: Challenges and strategies*. Oxford University Press.

Gomar, K., & Musso, A. (2017). Propuesta de intervención de autocuidado para supervisoras utilizando técnicas experienciales [Self-care intervention proposal for supervisors using experiential techniques]. *Revista Psicólogos, VII*(20a), 49–58.

González, G., & Bolaños, V. (2015). Perfil del psicólogo/a de Guatemala: Hallazgos del Colegio de Psicólogos de Guatemala [Profile of the psychologist from Guatemala: Findings from the College of Psychologists of Guatemala]. *Revista Psicólogos, IV*(16), 51–65.

Goodyear, R. And Falender, C. (2017a). How can psychologists maximize their effectiveness as supervisors? *Revista Psicologos VII* (20), 83–96.

Goodyear, R., & Falender, C. (2017b). ¿Cómo pueden los psicólogos/as maximizar su efectividad Como supervisoras/as? Ocho condiciones esenciales [how can psychologists maximize their effectiveness as supervisors? Eight essential conditions]. *Revista Psicólogos, VII*(20a), 83–97.

Grazioso, M. P. (2015, August 4–10). *Contemporary trends in the supervision process in Guatemala* [Presentación powerpoint]. Conferencia Anual de la Asociación Americana de Psicología, Toronto, Canadá.

Grazioso, M. P., Lubina, M., & Cóbar, A. A. (2021). Perspectivas sobre el desarrollo de la supervisión clínica en Guatemala [Perspectives on the development of clinical supervision in Guatemala]. In A. Tena Suck (Ed.), *Clinical supervision in psychotherapy: A guide to best practices*. Vesalius.

Instituo Nacional de Estadística de Guatemala (2024, March, 25). *Daily Archives: 25 de marzo*. https://www.ine.gob.gt/2024/03/

Jurado, A. M., & Grazioso, M. P. (2022). Code of ethics of Guatemala based on the universal declaration of ethical principles for psychologists. *APAW, 4*(3), 35–45.

Klie, M., & Grazioso, M. P. (2020). Current context of the teaching of psychology in Guatemala. In G. J. Rich, L. A. Padilla Lopez, L. Ebersohn, J. Taylor, & S. M. (Eds.), *Teaching psychology around the world* (Vol. 5, pp. 70–88). Cambridge Scholars Publishing.

Lemus, K. R. (2006). *El uso de destrezas multiculturales por consejeras en entrenamiento dentro de una sesión de supervisión. [The use of multicultural skills by counselors in training within a supervision session]*. Trabajo de graduación, Universidad del Valle de Guatemala.

Lemus, G. M. (2013). Supervisión. Una herramienta necesaria Para el psicólogo clínico en Guatemala [Supervision. A necessary tool for the clinical psychologist in Guatemala]. *Revista Psicólogos, II*(8), 24–27.

Loarca, H. (2021, May). ¿Cuántas personas logran graduarse de la universidad en Guatemala? [How many people manage to graduate from university in Guatemala?] I am 502. https://www.soy502.com/articulo/casi-39-mil-personas-obtuvieron-titulo-universitario-101476#:~:text=Fueron%20contabilizadas%20212%2C150%20mujeres%2C%20lo,es%20decir%20unas%2021%2C812%20personas

Lubina, M. (2016). *¿Qué te gustó y qué harías diferente? Un estudio contextualizado de la alianza en supervisión [What did you like and what could you do differently? A contextualized study of the supervisory alliance]*. Trabajo de graduación, Universidad del Valle de Guatemala.

Lubina, M. (2021). *Fortaleciendo la supervisión clínica a través de la perspectiva del supervisado en Guatemala [Strengthening clinical supervision through supervisee perspectives in Guatemala]*. Disertación doctoral, Universidad del Valle de Guatemala.

Lubina, M., Cardona, S., & Rodas, P. (2017). Enfoque sobre las alianzas de supervisión. [Focus on working alliances in supervision]. *Revista Psicologos, 7*(20th), 29–38.

Martimianakis, M. A., Maniate, J. M., & Hodges, B. D. (2009). Sociological interpretations of professionalism. *Medical Education, 43*(9), 829–837.

Milne, D. L., & Watkins, C. E. (2014). Defining and understanding clinical supervision: A functional approach. In C. E. Watkins & y Milne, D.L. (Eds.), *The Wiley International handbook of clinical supervision* (pp. 3–19). Wiley Blackwell.

Peters, H. C. (2017). Multicultural complexity: An intersectional lens for clinical supervision. *International Journal for the Advancement of Counselling, 39*, 176–187.
Sue, D. W., Arredondo, P., & McDavis, R. J. (1992). Multicultural counseling competencies and standards: A call to the profession. *Journal of Counseling & Development, 70*(4), 477–486.
Toro-Alfonso, J. (2009). *Perspectivas sobre Género y Sexualidad en Guatemala: Hacia una sociedad respetuosa de la diversidad [Perspectives on gender and sexuality in Guatemala: Towards a society respectful of diversity].* UVG, GTZ.
Vides Porras, A. (2008). El estilo personal del terapeuta guatemalteco en el interior del país. [The personal style of the Guatemalan therapist in the interior of the country]. (Trabajo de graduación, Universidad del Valle de Guatemala). http://repositorio.uvg.edu.gt/xmlui/123456789/2618
Zhang, H., Watkins, C. E., Jr., Hook, J. N., Hodge, A. S., Davis, C. W., Norton, J., Wilcox, M. M., Davis, D., & DeBlaere & Owen, J. (2022). Cultural humility in psychotherapy and clinical supervision: A research review. *Counseling and Psychotherapy Research, 22*(3), 548–557.

Meri E. Lubina has earned a licenciatura degree in general psychology, a master's degree in counseling psychology and mental health and a PhD in Applied Psychology, awarded by Universidad del Valle de Guatemala. She holds a specialization in family and couple psychotherapy with a cognitive behavioral orientation and a certification in clinical supervision, awarded by Fundación Aiglé, Argentina. She works as a psychotherapist, psychologist, counselor, clinical supervisor, and teacher at the Asociación Proyecto Aiglé Guatemala and Universidad del Valle of Guatemala. Her research and publishing interests are in clinical supervision and applied psychology. She is a member of

Alejandra Auyón is a specialist in family and couple psychotherapy with cognitive behavioral orientation from the Aiglé Argentina Foundation/Maimonides University, Argentina (2015). In addition, she holds a master's degree in counseling psychology and mental health (2011) and a licenciatura degree in psychology from Universidad del Valle de Guatemala (UVG) (2007). She holds certification in clinical supervision from Fundación Aiglé. She has training in the integrative cognitive model, which has allowed her to understand people from their beliefs, thoughts, values, culture and how they connect with their emotions and attitudes. She has worked individually and in groups, responding to demands related to grief, trauma, emotional disorders, violence, chronic diseases, difficulties in the life cycle, eating disorders, among others. She has been a college teacher (since 2011) in the undergraduate degree in psychology at the UVG and the postgraduate degree in psychological counseling and mental health. In addition, she has been a supervisor in the practice of clinical health and clinical cases both at the undergraduate and graduate levels. She worked for 11 years (2004 to 2015) in a clinic of the San Juan de Dios General Hospital that cares for pediatric patients living with HIV.

Ana Alicia Cobar holds a PhD in applied psychology, a master's degree in psychological counseling and mental health, and a licenciatura degree in psychology from Universidad del Valle de Guatemala. She holds asSpecialization in Family and Couple Psychotherapy with Cognitive Behavioral Orientation from Fundación Aiglé, Argentina and Universidad de Maimonides, Argentina. Internships at the Ackerman Family Institute in New York. Director, teacher, and supervisor in the Department of Psychological Counseling and Mental Health. Professor in the Department of Applied Neuropsychology and in the master's degree in Community Counseling at the Universidad del Valle de Guatemala. She is a member of the Aiglé Guatemala Project Association where she conducts her private practice as a psychotherapist and counselor for adults, couples, families, as well as providing clinical supervision. Areas of interest in research and publication are counseling, well-being and quality of life, self-management competencies, clinical supervision, crisis care, and expressive arts interventions. Member of the College of Psychologists of Guatemala, Inter-American Society of Psychology, Guatemala Chapter and American Psychological Association.

Maria del Pilar Grazioso has expertise in pediatric development and learning, community mental health, prevention, gender, multiculturalism, higher education, psychotherapy, counseling, and supervision. She has held administrative, research, teaching, and clinical positions, as well as professional duties in higher education and private practice. She developed graduate programs and began formal training in supervision at the university level in Guatemala. She has publications and recognition for her leadership and contributions to the development of Psychology having leadership positions at the international level. She is currently co-coordinator of the Aiglé Guatemala Project Association and is a researcher affiliated with the Universidad del Valle de Guatemala and Maya Health Alliance/ Wuqukawoc.

The Cultural, Professional, and Regulatory Context of Clinical Supervision in Puerto Rico

Norka Polanco Frontera, Marielly González Chardón, Keishalee Gómez Arroyo, Hiradith Menéndez, Marcos Reyes Estrada, and Yaritza López Robledo

Vignette

A clinical psychology doctoral intern is preparing for supervision. Ten minutes prior, she reviews the notes from last week's sessions, going over the caseload to identify which ones will be discussed and outlining a list of questions. Her supervision occurs every Tuesday, although sometimes the supervisor changes the day. Her supervisor is a doctor in clinical psychology who graduated 5 years ago.

In addition to her role as a supervisor, she works part-time at the same facility she supervises. Therefore, she knows the population her intern attends. On some occasions, she supports the clinic with administrative tasks and teaches in a graduate clinical psychology program. During some supervisions, she looks tired; however, she is always prepared. Her intern admires and respects her and sometimes discusses her with other people in the clinic. The intern usually remarks: "I do not know how she does it, but she supervises me."

The supervision lasts for 1 h. The practice center is an interdisciplinary clinic where all types of cases arrive, though most of the services offered by the clinic are

N. Polanco Frontera (✉) · M. González Chardón · H. Menéndez · Y. López Robledo
Ponce Health Sciences University, Ponce, Puerto Rico
e-mail: npolanco@psm.edu; mariellygonzalez@psm.edu; hmenendez@psm.edu; ylopez@psm.edu

K. Gómez Arroyo
Institute of Psychological Research, University of Puerto Rico, Río Piedras Campus, San Juan, Puerto Rico
e-mail: keishalee.gomezarroyo@upr.edu

M. Reyes Estrada
Albizu University, San Juan, Puerto Rico
e-mail: mareyes@albizu.edu

M. P. Grazioso et al. (eds.), *Clinical Supervision in Latin America*,
https://doi.org/10.1007/978-3-031-82373-2_7

medical. The office space for the supervision is small, but it is enough for them to talk comfortably and privately.

The intern decided that she would start by consulting a new patient's case; she had only conducted the initial interview. When the supervision begins, she immediately greets her supervisor. The intern tells her supervisor how nervous she is because she is unsure if she did the interview well and does not know if she followed all the recommendations she received in their previous session. She also told her supervisor that the clinic's power had gone out that day because it was raining, so she had not been able to complete the progress notes: "I am aware that I am behind; I promise you that I am doing everything I can to move forward."

She was going to continue, but before she could, the supervisor interrupted her and said: "I am aware that you have a lot of administrative work, that you are only in your second year, and that you are still learning to integrate all the recommendations. I imagine you must be tired and worried about your execution. I also noticed that you started talking and are hardly breathing. What do you think about taking a few seconds to breathe before continuing?

Remember, in order to focus and be organized during supervision, it is essential that you are present and clear about what you need. Let us make a schedule to organize our time. I want us to talk about how you feel and the barriers you have encountered this week. You can present the case to me using the guide we discussed last week, and we can evaluate the information you have to identify the following steps to take, including the choice of the intervention model and the external barriers you had last week, such as difficulties in electricity services. In addition, we can add any pending issue to the agenda."

Context of the Vignettes

This vignette represents the clinical supervision processes in Puerto Rico from the point of view of the supervisor. It reflects the context and circumstances of supervision, and describes the setting and the supervisor's experience. In Puerto Rico, one of the everyday contexts of supervision is that those who supervise are the same psychologists of the centers where they work. In terms of format, the most common practice is for supervision to be carried out weekly and in one-hour meetings. However, there are other ways to supervise. It depends on the supervisor's training level and their employer's Graduate Program. The vignette also shows how most people who exercise the supervisory role do not do so exclusively; they play multiple roles, which can be successful yet tiresome.

The vignette also reflects the value given to interpersonal relationships in Puerto Rico. In purely content-focused supervision, there is not necessarily room for supervisory agendas to explore how the person being supervised is doing and what other aspects of that person's life may be impacting their performance. In the vignette, the supervisor uses the beginning of the session to listen without interrupting, prioritizing the human aspect and creating the space to develop their relationship. With its reference to power outages due to rain, the vignette also shows the social circumstances of people living in Puerto Rico. After Hurricane Maria made landfall on the island in 2017, electricity problems have been frequent and have impacted all aspects of people's daily lives, including how we teach psychology and supervision processes.

Sociopolitical and Cultural Context

The context in which academic work is performed is not exempt from political and social processes. In the case of Puerto Rico, the development of research, training, and practice responds to historical, social, economic, and political forces (Bernal, 2013). It is important to highlight that Puerto Rico occupies a position of political, social, and economic subordination to the United States. With the end of the Spanish-American War in 1898, the American colonial period began, and with it, multiple political and social changes occurred on the island. Therefore, Puerto Rico went from being a colony of Spain to being a colony of the United States. This historical aspect distinguishes the development of psychology education and practice in Puerto Rico, and consequently, supervision.

According to Bernal (2006), the United States' administration initiated a wave of programs that impacted the economic, educational, and social aspects of Puerto Rico's inhabitants. A public education system was established, and in 1900, the Normal School was founded, and eventually, the University of Puerto Rico in Río Piedras (UPR-RP) (Bernal, 2006). Professional training in psychology was carried out abroad, particularly in the United States (Bernal, 2006; Jacó-Vilela et al. 2022), leading to the influence of imported models and practices. This historical fact is relevant to understanding the context in which the practice of psychology began, since the first people who practiced the profession in Puerto Rico were mostly trained in the United States and began to apply their training here. No documentation was found describing the aspects of supervision at that time. However, it is understood that they also learned the supervisory aspects they received and later practiced. These historical data suggest that the development of the practice of psychology and clinical supervision in Puerto Rico is related, from its inception, to the influences received from the models used and developed in the United States. The first influence in Puerto Rico of the first psychologists who were trained in the United States is their use and application of the models, the structure of teaching, and the structure of training learned abroad. In addition, the legal and ethical-legal structure is based on North American training, such as the importance of having malpractice insurance. Furthermore, the influence of the APA (American Psychological Association) model has persisted. Although not all graduate programs in clinical psychology are accredited by APA, its influence is still present, including aspects related to supervision. While there is a local code of ethics in Puerto Rico, most schools also teach and use the APA Code of Ethics. That direct influence impacts our vision of psychology, science, and training. It also influences the models of therapy that are taught.

The first psychology courses on the island emerged at the end of the nineteenth century (Manual Junta Examinadora de Psicología, 2018). For example, the Center for Higher Education of the Ateneo Puertorriqueño was founded for the study of psychology, among other disciplines. Between 1966 and 1967, the first graduate programs at the master's level emerged at the UPR-RP and the Psychological Institute of Puerto Rico (now Albizu University). Nevertheless, other psychology programs on the island were developed, such as the Inter American University of Puerto Rico (1937), the Pontifical Catholic University of Puerto Rico (1951), and the Carlos Albizu University (1967) (Boulon & Roca de Torres, 2016). Subsequently, between the 1970s and 1980s, doctoral programs began (Boulon & Roca de Torres, 2016). Over time, the programs and their academic offers have been increasing. Currently, there are six universities that have graduate programs in clinical psychology: (1) University of Puerto Rico, Río Piedras Campus (UPR-RP), (2) Albizu University (UA), (3) Pontifical Catholic University of Puerto Rico (PUCPR), (4) *Ponce Health Sciences University* (*PHSU*), (5) Inter American University of Puerto Rico (UIPR), and (6) Ana G. Méndez University (UAGM).

Table 1 illustrates milestones from the development of training programs on the island to what we know today.

In Puerto Rico, the practice and models of Clinical Supervision are closely linked to the development of graduate programs. The responsibility for ensuring the quality of professional psychological services is collectively held by training programs in higher education institutions, the Examination Board, and professional organizations. Below, we will review several regulatory aspects of the practice of supervision in our country.

Ethical Aspects of Clinical Supervision in Puerto Rico

In Puerto Rico, clinical supervision is anchored in ethical and legal principles as complex as the provision of direct services in clinical psychology. This ethical and legal basis for the practice of clinical supervision is critical given the crucial role that supervision plays in shaping the professional conduct expected in clinical training in Puerto Rico. Two codes of ethics primarily govern the practice of clinical supervision: the Code of Ethics and Professional Conduct, which includes Standards for Services Through Telepsychology and Procedural Rules for Disciplinary Matters in the Practice of the Profession, established by the Puerto Rico Board of Psychologists Examiner (2022), and the Code of Ethics of the Puerto Rico Psychological Association (2021) (see Table 2). In addition, most clinical psychology training programs, especially those accredited by the APA, integrate the "APA Ethical Principles of Psychologists and Code of Conduct" (American Psychological Association, 2017) as part of the practice of clinical supervision. Although the three

Table 1 Moments in the history of the development of psychology programs

• 1934–1965: Beginning of clinical psychology in Puerto Rico.
• 1948–1951: Founding of the (PUCPR) and its first psychology courses. In 1949, a concentration in psychology was offered at UPR-RP. In addition, Carlos Albizu Miranda and Norman Matlin founded the Psychological Institute of Puerto Rico, located in Santurce, and the first clinic of services and training in the clinical area (also known as the Caribbean Center for Postgraduate Studies).
• 1953, Jorge Dieppa and Carlos Albizu Miranda were the first Puerto Rican clinical psychologists. Both earned their doctorates in philosophy with a concentration in clinical psychology from Purdue University.
• 1958–1962: Dr. Juan Nicolás Martínez directs the psychology program of the Faculty of Social Sciences of the UPR-RP. The university offers a program of 30 graduate credits that does not lead to a degree, and in 1963, the Department of Psychology was established, promoting the offer of additional courses.
• 1960–1970: Development of government programs aimed at the prevention of drug addiction and alcoholism, among others.
• 1963: The federal law for the establishment of community mental health centers in Puerto Rico is approved. The legislation was intended to promote access to mental health services.
Given the great demand and the limitation of professionals offering psychological services, the applied psychology training center opened. This is probably what promoted the development of graduate programs.
• 1963: The psychology program was added to the Faculty of Social Sciences at UPR-RP.
• 1966: Fifteen students began in the general psychology program with an emphasis on clinical services at UPR-RP under the direction of Abigaíl Díaz de Concepción.
• 1966–1967: The first graduate program in psychology with an emphasis on clinical services began. The offer was at the master's level at the UPR-RP and the psychological Institute of Puerto Rico (now Albizu university). Later, between the 1970s and 1980s, doctoral programs began.
• 1967: Founding of Albizu university as a private institution (UA). This program offered a master of science degree in clinical psychology.
• 1972–1974: Albizu university became a pioneer and offered a doctor of philosophy (PhD) degree in clinical psychology, industrial/organizational psychology, and general psychology. Five years later, they added a doctor of psychology (PsyD) degree in clinical psychology.
• 1986: Under the interim direction of Dr. Edwin Fernández Bauzó, a PhD in general psychology that includes four specializations was introduced in the UPR-RP. In that same year, the University Center for Psychological Services and Studies (CUSEP) of the Department of Psychology was founded, under the direction of Dr. Guillermo Bernal.
• 1994: Accreditation of the clinical Psychology programs (PhD and PsyD) of UA by the APA.
• 1998–1999: The *Ponce School of Medicine* (now, *Ponce health sciences university, PHSU*) develops the graduate program in psychology under the direction of Dr. José pons Madera. Currently, this private institution offers a PsyD and a PhD in psychology with foundations in neuroscience and clinical Health Psychology. In addition, the PUCPR introduces a PhD in clinical Psychology and a PsyD in clinical psychology.

(continued)

Table 1 (continued)

• 2000–present: The University of Turabo (now Ana G. Méndez university, UAGM) opened a Master's program in psychological counseling, directed by Dr. María López Pagán in 2000. A year later, the doctoral program in psychological counseling was created at both the metro
Campus and the San Germán Campus of the Interamerican University of Puerto Rico (UIPR). In 2004, PHSU's PsyD program received APA accreditation, becoming the second institution in the country to receive this recognition. The PHSU PhD program received the APA accreditation in 2014. Between 2019 and 2020, the graduate program in psychology at UPR-RP received accreditation from APA.

(Junta Examinadora de Psicólogos de Puerto Rico, 2018, Boulon-Díaz & Roca de Torres, 2016)

Table 2 Description of the codes of ethics and laws that regulate the practice of clinical supervision in Puerto Rico

Code of Ethics and Law in Puerto Rico	Description of the Code of Ethics and Law	Aspects related to the practice of clinical supervision
Code of Ethics of the Psychological Association of Puerto Rico	The Puerto Rico Psychological Association (APPR) is the leading organization that brings together psychology professionals in Puerto Rico. The code of ethics presented by this professional body promotes the highest standards of the practice of psychology in Puerto Rico through a comprehensive and rigorous document on all aspects of the practice of psychology in Puerto Rico.	In "Guide 6," under "teaching and supervision," the APPR code of ethics describes the duties and conduct expected of professionals in the exercise of clinical supervision.
Code of Ethics and Conduct Standards for services through telepsychology and rules of procedure for disciplinary matters in the practice of the profession of psychology in Puerto Rico	The Board of Examiners of Psychologists in Puerto Rico is the body that ensures compliance with the laws, rules, and regulations of the practice of psychology. The Code of Ethics of the Examining Board provides the basis for the professional conduct expected under Act No. 96.	Chapter III, principle X, details the duties and responsibilities of professionals in clinical supervision. The requirements for this practice in Puerto Rico are specified, including remote supervision. Article 21 details the exercise of telesupervision.
Act No. 96 of June 4, 1983	Act No. 96 establishes the Board of Examiners of the Profession of Psychology to regulate the profession's practice in Puerto Rico. In light of this law, the Examining Board establishes the rules and procedures for psychology practice.	Act No. 96 specifies in its articles the processes for licensing professionals to practice psychology, which is required to exercise clinical supervision.

codes present overlapping information, they allow for a broad and deep understanding of the ethical practice of clinical supervision in Puerto Rico.

In their role as clinical supervisor, each professional recognizes responsibilities to educate and supervise the development of competencies and conduct of future professionals in Puerto Rico. To achieve this, codes of ethics specify the role of each clinical supervisor to stay up to date in their areas of expertise and comply with the documentation pertinent to the supervision process so that it accurately reflects the current and science-based material on the practice of clinical psychology. This allows students to promote the importance of scientific knowledge and respect for the profession. In addition, a clinical supervisor who urges their students to stay up to date with scientific evidence promotes an evolution of the practice of clinical psychology tempered by emerging challenges (Beck et al., 2014).

In their role as clinical supervisor, each professional must ensure that clear and precise ethical and professional boundaries are maintained with each student. The relationship between supervisor and student is one of power and influence that impacts the practice of the profession. Considering the diverse context of Puerto Rico, where there are high levels of poverty and inequity, it is of greater importance to recognize the impact of these inequities on the process of clinical supervision with students. In view of this, it is of crucial importance that each clinical supervisor be thoughtful and careful in their actions, distancing themselves from any intimate, sexual, or direct authority relationship, even with the student's consent. This type of behavior profoundly lacerates the triad relationship between supervisor, student, and patient, significantly impacting the parties and the expected modeling of each clinical psychology professional (Previdi & Vega, 2020).

Recognizing the diversity and multiculturalism among the students in training in Puerto Rico, it is essential to respect the dignity and recognize the values of all people in clinical supervision. In view of this, a space for equitable training and inclusion in matters of race, ethnicity, sexuality, and gender diversity, among others, must be promoted. In addition, students in Puerto Rico may be fluent in Spanish or English. Sometimes there is proficiency in both languages and/or a preference for one language over the other. This situation represents an example where the clinical supervisor must carefully employ affirmative strategies to recognize these diversities and intersectionalities in the supervision process. On the other hand, the clinical supervisor is sensitive to social and contextual movements to advance the rights of vulnerable populations in Puerto Rico, understanding their relationship with psychology training on the island. By recognizing and addressing diversity and multiculturalism in clinical supervision, we demonstrate an ethical and effective practice among students in training.

The Examining Board of Psychologists, in its most recent review of the code of ethics, details the rules on the practice of telepsychology in Puerto Rico. Article 21 specifies the expected practices of supervision through telepsychology. It details that telesupervision should not be the only means of communication between supervisor and student. In addition, telesupervision should be used to supervise skills and competencies that have been previously supervised in person. Although the potential of remote supervision in Puerto Rico has been documented, the exclusive use of this modality should not be relied upon. Thus, the code of ethics specifies that the use of remote supervision is limited to 50% of the total hours required for clinical supervision in a practice setting. Also, all clinical supervisors who use telesupervision must comply with the minimum standards of this practice, which include determining the convenience of this modality, being attentive to the inherent risks in the use of this technology, ensuring the well-being of the supervisee and patient, establishing alternative means of communication, and establishing written agreements on the use of telemonitoring (Rodríguez-Díaz et al., 2020).

Legal Aspects of Clinical Supervision in Puerto Rico

When referring to the legal aspects that regulate the practice of clinical supervision in Puerto Rico, they are governed by the "Law that regulates the exercise of the profession of psychology in Puerto Rico"; Act No. 96 of June 4, 1983, as amended. Similarly, the General Regulation of the Board of Examiners of Psychologists number 9314 regulates the practice of the profession in Puerto Rico in its various roles, including that of clinical supervisor. It should be noted that these documented regulations are aligned with the Board's revisions and amendments to the law, so psychologists are encouraged to maintain a continuous update of the law and its regulatory stipulations. Among the most relevant aspects to consider for the practice of clinical supervision in Puerto Rico are the following: (1) to be a licensed psychologist, (2) to be competent regarding the area in which supervision is offered, (3) to follow the stipulations that regulate the number of hours, (4) to keep records and documentation of the supervision process, and (5) to complete an informed consent and protect the confidentiality of what is discussed.

A review of the manuals suggests that, in practice, all programs have a practice and supervision contract. However, only UA's Program was identified as having informed consent for supervision (Clínica de la Albizu, 2015). The objective of internship contracts or informed consent is to establish the objectives of supervision from the beginning of the process and provide formality and structure. On the other hand, although it is not explicitly required as part of what is regulated by the Examining Board, it is highly recommended to have professional malpractice insurance when exercising the role of clinical supervisor. Not all universities have a requirement that the people they supervise have malpractice insurance, however, all universities have insurance, and most programs have insurance for their students. Therefore, supervisors are covered by these insurances.

In Puerto Rico, clinical supervision within the practice of psychology is regulated by laws and government entities, as previously mentioned. Act No. 96 of June 4, 1983, as amended, establishes the guidelines for exercising the functions of clinical supervision. The license to practice as a clinical supervisor is a mechanism that allows the competent authorities to validate the competence, training, and experience of psychologists who wish to assume this critical role in the training of future colleagues. Clinical supervisors have considerable responsibility, as they guide and evaluate the performance of doctoral students in their clinical practice, which directly impacts the quality of psychological service provided to individuals and communities.

Regarding competence and its link with legal aspects, it should be noted that the quality of supervision is highly mediated by the supervisor's competence in their area of specialization. The supervisor has an ethical and legal responsibility to ensure that the services provided under his or her supervision meet professional and ethical standards. Lack of competence in the supervised area can result in inadequate supervision, which can lead to unethical practices or clinical negligence, exposing supervisors to legal liabilities. This competence in the field allows the practitioner to comply with the laws and regulations that govern the practice, ensuring that the clinical supervision meets professional and legal expectations.

It is crucial to ensure that the stipulated number of supervision hours is met according to the academic program where the supervision process is being offered. Although the number of required hours of clinical supervision for doctoral students in clinical psychology in Puerto Rico is not generally specified, each institution establishes its requirements and agreements. For this reason, to know the detailed requirements of the hours dedicated to supervision and the corresponding formats (individual, group, etc.), it is suggested that you refer to the specific manuals of each program. Similarly, in the case of required documentation, it is suggested that the requirements established by each university for the training process, as well as the clinical practice manuals of each program, be reviewed.

Informed consent is a crucial aspect in the process of clinical practice in psychology and, therefore, in the supervision of this role. It ensures that people are fully informed and voluntarily agree to participate in specific processes or receive certain services, as well as their circumstances. In the context of clinical supervision, informed consent can ensure that students and supervisors fully understand their roles, responsibilities, and the boundaries of the relationship. In addition, it helps protect the confidentiality and rights of the clients with whom students interact.

As previously mentioned, though it is not an explicit requirement of clinical supervisors, it is highly recommended that they have professional malpractice insurance. Fulfilling this responsibility is tied to legal and ethical risks that should not be underestimated when exercising this role. Reasons to consider having malpractice insurance include: protecting against claims that may arise from a patient or supervised student and maintaining professional integrity, as the insurance reflects the supervisor's commitment to professionalism and demonstrates that he or she is prepared to respond appropriately to an incident, and protecting finances from the potential of being involved in legal litigation.

Evaluation of the Current State of Supervision in Puerto Rico

To achieve the objectives, the catalogs and online information about clinical psychology graduate programs in Puerto Rico were reviewed and key personnel from one of the universities was interviewed.

Format, Structure, and Best Practices *of Supervision Sessions*

Supervision models are categorized into four main groups: Models Based on Psychotherapeutic Currents, Developmental-Based Models, Process Models, and Second-Generation Models which incorporate the Evidence-Based Competency-Based Model (Villafuerte-Montiel, 2020). In Puerto Rico, graduate programs in Clinical Psychology predominantly favor the Competency-Based Model (Pontifical Catholic University of Puerto Rico, n.d.; Mambrú-Tavarez, 2022; Department of Psychology: Faculty of Education and Behavioral Professions Inter Metro, n.d.-a; Albizu University, n.d.-a, n.d.-b; School of Behavioral and Brain Sciences, 2022a, 2022b, 2022c; Graduate Program in Psychology—Department of Psychology, Faculty of Social Sciences, n.d.; A. Plaza, personal communication, October 15, 2023). This trans- theoretical approach offers a systematic, integrative, and meta-theoretical framework, providing guidelines applicable to various clinical training formats and psychotherapeutic approaches, favoring the adaptation and integration of different educational currents (Bernard & Goodyear, 2019).

Graduate programs also emphasize a balance between theory and practice, highlighting ethics, cultural sensitivity, and the use of evidence-based interventions (Pontifical Catholic University of Puerto Rico, n.d.; Department of Psychology: Faculty of Education and Behavioral Professions Inter Metro, n.d.-b; Albizu University, n.d.-a, n.d.-b; Mambrú-Tavarez, 2022; School of Behavioral and Brain Sciences, 2022c; Graduate Program in Psychology—Department of Psychology, Faculty of Social Sciences, 2022; A. Plaza, personal communication, October 15, 2023). These principles are aligned with the Competency-Based Model, which prioritizes the professional's ability to apply theory in practice, under ethical standards and solid scientific principles (Bernard & Goodyear, 2019). Although this alignment prevails in the revised manuals, some universities have distinctive characteristics, such as a religious or ecumenical orientation, which gives them a particular focus (Pontifical Catholic University of Puerto Rico, n.d.; Inter-American University of Puerto Rico, n.d.).

Supervision models in Puerto Rico are complemented by various intervention models including cognitive, behavioral, contextual, humanistic, and psychodynamic therapies. APA- accredited programs in the region promote evidence-based therapies and aligned intervention model supervision practices (Falender & Shafranske, 2017).

Supervision Format and Frequency

The Competency-Based Model mainly uses three formats of supervision: individual, group, and distance (Campbell, 2006). According to Campbell (2006), the individual supervision format is more prevalent. In addition, these sessions are usually weekly, and last a minimum of 1 h, focused on various aspects related to clinical practice. The group supervision format involves weekly meetings of a group of supervisees directed by one or more supervisors for a two-hour minimum (Bernard & Goodyear, 2019).

The Competency-Based Model utilizes individual, group, and distance supervision formats, mainly with weekly sessions of at least 1 h for individuals and 2 h for groups (Campbell, 2006; Bernard & Goodyear, 2019). According to Campbell (2006) and Bernard and Goodyear (2019), group supervision advantages as saving time and costs, vicarious learning, exposure to a variety of clinical cases, and sharing and normalizing experiences. Still, it has limitations, such as the lack of individualized attention that they sometimes require, the aspects of confidentiality of information, and the possibility of attending to group dynamics that could interrupt the learning process (Bernard & Goodyear, 2019).

The adoption of remote supervision has increased, particularly during the Covid-19 pandemic. Utilizing electronic media like telephones and computers establish this method as one of the most commonly used and of greater expansion (Phillips et al., 2021). This format allows for greater flexibility and access to resources, transcending geographical barriers. Despite its advantages, remote supervision poses challenges regarding quality of communication, technical problems, and data security (Rousmaniere et al., 2014).

In Puerto Rico, the three supervision formats are utilized (Department of Psychology: College of Education and Behavioral Professions Inter Metro, n.d.-b; Psychology Internship Program, n.d.; Clínica de la Albizu, n.d.; School of Behavioral and Brain Sciences, 2022a, 2022b; Graduate Program in Psychology—Department of Psychology, Faculty of Social Sciences, 2022; A. Plaza, personal communication, October 15, 2023). Each supervision format is conditioned by the context of where the supervision takes place, access to resources, and program specifications. For example, the format can vary depending on the student's training year and their competency development needs.

The graduate programs' manuals reveal that the frequency of supervision sessions typically fluctuates between 1 and 3 h per week (Department of Psychology: Faculty of Education and Behavioral Professions Inter Metro, n.d.-a, n.d.-b; Psychology Internship Program, n.d.; Clínica de la Albizu, n.d.; School of Behavioral and Brain Sciences, 2022a, 2022b; Graduate Program in Psychology—Department of Psychology, Faculty of Social Sciences, n.d.; A. Plaza, personal communication, October 15, 2023). It was also noted that the duration and frequency of supervision may vary based on the level of clinical training. Duration and frequency of supervision adhere to APA guidelines, which abide by the competency-based model. Following the Covid-19 pandemic, remote supervision sessions have become more frequent (Phillips et al., 2021). The APA's Commission on Accreditation (CoA) has provided increased flexibility for remote supervision, resulting in a significant impact on accredited programs and adjusting to maintain training quality in light of pandemic-related challenges (American Psychological Association Commission on Accreditation, 2023).

Supervision Techniques and Methods

Various supervision techniques are utilized in Puerto Rico, with their use and frequency varying across programs and their access to resources (Department of Psychology: Faculty of Education and Behavioral Professions Inter Metro, n.d.-b; Psychology Internship Program, n.d.; Clínica de la Albizu, n.d.; School of Behavioral and Brain Sciences, 2022a, 2022b; Graduate Program in Psychology—Department of Psychology, Faculty of Social Sciences, 2022; A. Plaza, personal communication, October 15, 2023). These techniques align with APA recommendations (APA, 2014). The supervision techniques identified in Puerto Rico are: (1) Recordings (audio/video), using standardized and/or simulated patients; (2) Live supervision (co-therapy); (3) Direct observations of the interventions; and (4) Modeling. Notably, PHSU was a pioneer in the use of using standardized and/or simulated patients in Puerto Rico, led by Dr. José Pons, which distinguished the program. Currently, the UA also uses this strategy.

Additionally, several monitoring methods, such as case consultations, review of progress notes, and direct observations of interventions, are implemented following APA recommendations, and the implementation depends on program-specific resources and requirements. The programs' manual information obtained for this project reveals that all supervision methods are recommended by APA (Department of Psychology: Faculty of Education and Behavioral Professions Inter Metro, n.d.-b; Psychology Internship Program, n.d.; Clínica de la Albizu, n.d.; School of Behavioral and Brain Sciences, 2022a, 2022b; Graduate Program in Psychology—Department of Psychology, Faculty of Social Sciences, 2022; A. Plaza, personal communication, October 15, 2023). The supervision methods employed are (1) Case Consultation (UPRRP, UA, PUCPR, PHSU); (2) Review of progress notes and transcripts (UPRRP, UA, PUCPR, PHSU); (3) Review of psychological reports (UA, PUCPR, PHSU); (4) Supervision of data (test scores) (UPRRP); (5) Recordings (audio/video) (UPRRP, UA, PUCPR, PHSU, UIPR); (6) Live Supervision (co-therapy) (UA, PUCPR, PHSU); (7) Direct observations of interventions (UPRRP, UA, PUCPR, PHSU, UIPR); (8) Observations through a one-way mirror (UA, PHSU, UIPR); (9) Observation during team meetings (UPRRP, UIPR); (10) Consultation with other supervisors (PUCPR, UPRPR, UIPR); (11) Consultation with team members and other staff (UPRRP, UA, PUCPR, UIPR); (12) Standardized/Sham Patients (PHSU, UA, UAGM); (13) Clinical Interaction Discussion (UA, UPRRP); (14) Self-report (UPRRP, UA, PUCPR, UIPR); and (15) Electronic (zoom, chat, text) (UA, PUCPR, PHSU).

Supervisory Training

Supervisor training in Puerto Rico accentuates a strong commitment to APA's supervisory guidelines, promoting a comprehensive, culturally competent, and ethical practice (APA, 2014). It was found that all graduate programs in clinical psychology in the region include a supervision course as a standard requirement to ensure that supervisors have a theoretically based preparation (Department of Psychology: College of Education and Behavioral Professions Inter Metro, n.d.-a, n.d.-b; Psychology Internship Program, n.d.; Clínica de la Albizu, n.d.; School of Behavioral and Brain Sciences, 2022a; Graduate Program in Psychology—Department of Psychology, Faculty of Social Sciences, 2022). Furthermore, the renewal requirements for the license to practice psychology mandate specific training hours dedicated to ethical considerations and promoting equity, respect, and non-discrimination, as well as specialized training in clinical areas (Departamento de Salud de Puerto Rico, 2024).

At the moment, the resources available to enhance supervisory skills are limited to a series of online courses offered by APA and a recently introduced supervisory certification by UA, providing 24 h of direct training and continuing education (Albizu University, n.d.-a, n.d.-b). Some programs lead training initiatives for individuals who supervise their students. For instance, PHSU conducted an eight-hour contact training session last year, which was approved for continuing education and is anticipated to be repeated annually (Ponce Health Sciences University, 2023). Also, PUCPR has a structured training plan for their supervisors in their programs. Additionally, they have academic and clinical supervisors (A. Plaza, personal communication, October 15, 2023).

This situation reflects the efforts being made to uphold and enhance the competencies of psychologists, which in turn benefits students in training by complying with the recommended standards. However, the lack of additional resources highlights a significant opportunity to expand supervisor training, consequently elevating the quality and efficacy of clinical and supervisory services in Puerto Rico, in line with the competency-based supervision practice endorsed by educational institutions on the island.

Evaluation Process

According to the manuals and gathered information about the programs, it is evident that all training programs in Puerto Rico use formal documentation to assess their trainees' progress (Department of Psychology: College of Education and Behavioral Professions Inter Metro, n.d.-b; Psychology Internship Program, n.d.; Clínica de la Albizu, n.d.; School of Behavioral and Brain Sciences, 2022a, 2022b; Graduate Program in Psychology—Department of Psychology, Faculty of Social Sciences, 2022; A. Plaza, personal communication, October 15, 2023). All programs explicitly mention summative evaluations. Programs also describe additional assessments that seem to be formative, although it is not documented as such. The frequency of trainees' progress evaluations varies by academic program.

Recommendations for Practice in Puerto Rico

After analysis, it was concluded that the practice of clinical supervision in Puerto Rico differs positively from other countries because it is regulated. In Puerto Rico, the Office of Regulation and Certification of Health Professionals (ORCPS) and the Psychology Board ensure compliance with the expectations of people who practice psychology, including those who exercise clinical supervision. In addition, the law requires clinical psychologists to be licensed to practice the profession. Puerto Rico also has a code of ethics that outlines the duties and expected behaviors of those they supervise. In that sense, from an ethical and legal point of view, Puerto Rico has guides that both protect trainees and encourage the minimum of training for supervisors.

Regarding specialized training in supervision, although the courses offered by universities meet the teaching requirements to form the essential competencies, there is room for the development of greater and more continuous professional advancement programs that reinforce supervisory skills throughout time. As it is not mandatory to have continuing education credits in supervision, workspaces where clinical psychology students receive supervision can provide further specialized training for supervisors. Through this, they can frequently receive training that is aligned with the competency model, the specific populations they serve, or the models they use, allowing supervision training to be more adaptable and personalized. Training resources can benefit from greater customization to address the specific supervisory needs of different clinical and demographic contexts.

On the other hand, it is understood that although there is a strong foundation in theory and ethics, it may be necessary to incorporate more training in evidence-based supervision practices, ensuring that supervision strategies are up-to-date with the latest research in the field. In addition, as the team knows supervision should not only focus on meeting minimum standards but also on mentoring and long-term career development, it is an area that could be reinforced in the current curriculum. It is recommended that Clinical Psychology Programs review their curricula to ensure that mentoring is included in supervisory training. In summary, while Puerto Rico shows a commitment to supervision training aligned with APA standards, strengthening the depth and personalization of training and maintaining an ongoing focus on evidence-based practice are areas that could be further developed to improve the quality and effectiveness of supervision in clinical practice.

The regulations that guide the training of clinical psychologists in Puerto Rico are based on U.S. laws and regulations. Professionals must have doctoral postgraduate training to practice clinical psychology, and supervisors must be licensed to practice. While not all universities in Puerto Rico are accredited by APA, their influence is indisputable. In Latin American countries such as Chile, people practicing psychology do not require a doctoral degree and can obtain their license after finishing their bachelor's degree (Pesqueira et al., 2021). According to Pesqueira (2021), supervision has traditionally been exercised by professors and clinicians with extensive experience. Though, over the years, private local groups and associations have made efforts to regulate the practice of supervision.

This study was limited by the lack of published research documenting the practice of supervising clinical psychology trainees. Dissertations published in the academic programs were not reviewed. The information used was mainly obtained from university websites and one interview. The analysis of the material for this chapter suggests that more studies need to be developed that explore the supervisory experience and what needs to exist from the point of view of the supervisor, the supervised, and academia. The next step for this team will be to conduct further investigation using quantitative methods to document the experience, practices, needs, and training of clinical supervisors in Puerto Rico. Qualitative studies are also recommended for a deep exploration of their experiences. However, this project lays the groundwork for further efforts on documenting these processes in Puerto Rico. Sociocultural aspects, legal and ethical aspects, formats and structures of supervision, and education and training were documented. To the team's knowledge, this is the only book chapter that documents what has been published on Clinical Supervision in Puerto Rico.

References

Albizu University. (n.d.-a). Doctor of Psychology (Psy.D.) in Clinical Psychology. https://www.albizu.edu/san-juan/psyd/clinical-psychology/

Albizu University. (n.d.-b). Certification supervision in the professional practice of psychology- level 1. Professional studies and continuing education Program. https://www.eventbrite.com/e/cert-supervision-en-la-practica-profesional-de-la-, https://www.eventbrite.com/e/cert-supervision-en-la-practica-profesional-de-la-psychology-level-1%2D%2Dtickets-646033903797

American Psychological Association. (2014). Guidelines for clinical supervision in health service psychology. Retrieved from http://apa.org/about/policy/guidelines-supervision.pdf

American Psychological Association. (2017). Ethical principles of psychologists and code of conduct (2002, amended effective June 1, 2010, and January 1, 2017). https://www.apa.org/ethics/code/

American Psychological Association Commission on Accreditation. (2023). COVID-19: Updates and information. https://www.accreditation.apa.org/covid-19, https://www.asppr.net/_files/ugd/0522af_e47e99fb62544dab8af172690a46646c.pdf

Beck, J. G., Castonguay, L. G., Chronis-Tuscano, A., Klonsky, E. D., Mcginn, L. K., & Youngstrom, E. A. (2014). Principles for training in evidence-based psychology: Recommendations for the graduate curricula in clinical psychology. *Clinical Psychology: Science and Practice, 21*(4), 410–424. https://doi.org/10.1111/CPSP.12079

Bernard, J. M., & Goodyear, R. K. (2019). *Fundamentals of clinical supervision (6th ed)*. Pearson.

Bernal, G. (2013). 60 years of clinical psychology in Puerto Rico. *Interamerican Journal of Psychology, 47*(2), 213–228.

Bernal, G. (2006). La psicología clínica en Puerto Rico. *Revista Puertorriqueña de Psicología, 17*, 341–388.

Boulon Díaz, F., & Roca de Torres, I. (2016). Formación en psicología en Puerto Rico: Historia, logros y retos. *Revista Puertorriqueña de Psicología, 27*(2), 230–241.

Campbell, J. M. (2006). *Essentials of clinical supervision*. John Wiley & Sons, Inc. (Chapter 4).

Clínica de la Albizu. (n.d.). Internship program handbook 2022–2023. Albizu University, San Juan Campus. https://www.albizu.edu/wp-content/uploads/dlm_uploads/2023/09/CAIP-Handbook-2023-2024-1.pdf

Clínica de la Albizu. (2015). Manual de normas y procedimientos. Universidad Carlos Albizu.

Departamento de Salud de Puerto Rico (4 de enero de 2024). Orden Administrativa del Secretario de Salud para enmendar la Orden Administrativa Núm. 398–2018 que establece ciertos requisitos de educación continua requeridos para los profesionales de la salud. (OA Núm. 2024-583). https://www.salud.pr.gov/CMS/DOWNLOAD/8426

Department of Psychology: Faculty of Education and Behavioral Professions Inter Metro. (n.d.-a). Sequential Doctorate in Psychology (PSY.D.) Integrated combination. http://www.metro.inter.edu/secuencial/PSYD-Clinico-Consejeria-Psicologica.pdf

Department of Psychology: Faculty of Education and Behavioral Professions Inter Metro. (n.d.-b). [Unpublished information-Manual of the Combined-Integrated Internship Program in Clinical/Psychological Counseling and Clinical/School Psychology] Inter American University of Puerto Rico, Metropolitan Campus.

Falender, C. A., & Shafranske, E. P. (2017). Groundwork and rationale. In C. A. Falender & E. P. Shafranske (Eds.), *Shafranske, supervision essentials for the practice of competency-based supervision* (pp. 3–16). American Psychological Association. https://doi.org/10.1037/15962-001

Graduate Program in Psychology – Department of Psychology, Faculty of Social Sciences. (2022). [Unpublish- PhD in psychology in the area of emphasis in clinical psychology student handbook (2022–2023)]. Universidad de Puerto Rico, Recinto de Río Piedras.

Graduate Program in Psychology – Department of Psychology, Faculty of Social Sciences.(n.d.). Unpublished information- Manual of clinical training conditions]. University of Puerto Rico, Río Piedras Campus.

Inter-American University of Puerto Rico. (n.d.). Graduate Catalog 2023–2024: Religious Life Policy. https://inter.smartcatalogiq.com/en/2023-2024/graduate-catalog-2022-2023/general-information/religious-life-policy/

Jacó-Vilela, A. M., Vasconcellos, M. A. G. N. T., & Degani-Carneiro, F. (2022). La Revista Puertorriqueña de Psicología y la historia de la psicología en Puerto Rico. *Revista Puertorriqueña de Psicologia, 33*(1), 44–59. https://doi.org/10.55611/reps.3301.04

Junta Examinadora de Psicólogos de Puerto Rico. (2018). Manual de procedimientos de reválida y licenciamiento. Oficina de Reglamentación y Certificación de Profesionales de la Salud.

Law to Regulate the Practice of the Profession of Psychology in Puerto Rico, Law No. 96. (1983). https://bvirtualogp.pr.gov/ogp/Bvirtual/leyesreferencia/PDF/Salud/96-1983.pdf

Mambrú-Tavarez, V. (2022). [Unpublished information-manual of clinical practice and internship of the doctoral program in clinical psychology]. Ana G. Méndez University.

Pesqueira, M. I., Ramírez, I., Ceruti, P., et al. (2021). Practicing clinical supervision in Chile: Lessons from 28 years of training. *Journal of Contemporary Psychotherapy, 51*, 201–210. https://doi.org/10.1007/s10879-021-09494-8

Phillips, L. A., Logan, J. N., & Mather, D. B. (2021). COVID-19 and beyond: Telesupervision training within the supervision competency. *Training and Education in Professional Psychology, 15*(4), 284–289. https://doi.org/10.1037/tep0000362

Ponce Health Sciences University. (2023). Supervision processes: Models and Competencies. Continuing Medical Education Division [Unpublished information: PHSU Student Supervisor Training].

Pontifical Catholic University of Puerto Rico. (n.d.). Graduate catalog: Pontifical Catholic University *of Puerto Rico 2023–2026*. https://www.pucpr.edu/oficina-de-admisiones/formularios-de-admisiones/catalogos-academicos/

Previdi, I. L., & Vega, C. M. V. (2020). Health disparities research framework adaptation to reflect Puerto Rico's socio-cultural context. *International Journal of Environmental Research and Public Health, 17*(22), 1–11. https://doi.org/10.3390/IJERPH17228544

Psychology Internship Program. (n.d.). Psychology Internship Manual (2021–2022). Universidad Ana G. Mendez. https://documento.uagm.edu/programas/documentos/UAGM-G-PIP-Manual_2020-2021.pdf

Puerto Rico Board of Psychologists Examiner. (2022). Code of ethics and conduct standards for services through telepsychology and rules of procedure for disciplinary matters in the practice of the profession of psychology in Puerto Rico. https://www.salud.pr.gov/CMS/DOWNLOAD/7226

Puerto Rico Psychological Association. (2021). Code of ethics of the psychological association de Puerto Rico.

Rodríguez-Díaz, G., Reyes-Estrada, M., & Cepeda-Hernández, S. (2020). Experiences and considerations for clinical training in professional psychology programs in times of COVID-19. *Behavioral Sciences, 35*(1), 119–156. https://cienciasdelaconducta.org/index.php/cdc/article/view/35/35

Rousmaniere, T., Abbass, A., & Frederickson, J. (2014). New developments in technology-assisted supervision and training: A practical overview. *Journal of Clinical Psychology, 70*(11), 1082–1093. https://doi.org/10.1002/jclp.22129

School of Behavioral and Brain Sciences. (2022a). Psychology internship consortium. Information for Candidates. Ponce Health Science University. https://www.psm.edu/doc/sbbs/Consortium.pdf

School of Behavioral and Brain Sciences. (2022b). [Unpublished- doctoral program in clinical psychology (PsyD)- clinical training manual]. Ponce Health Science University.

School of Behavioral and Brain Sciences. (2022c). [Unpublished-*Student Handbook Psy.D. Clinical Psychology Program]*. Ponce Health Sciences University.

Villafuerte Montiel, A. L. (2020). Contemporary models of clinical supervision: New directions. *Multidisciplinary Health Research, 5*(1), 3. https://doi.org/10.19136/mhr.a5n1.4210

Norka Polanco Frontera is an associate professor in the Behavioral and Neural Sciences Program at Ponce Health Science University (PHSU). She is a clinical psychologist with expertise in suicidal behavior and non-suicidal self-harm, borderline personality disorder, disorders related to emotional dysregulation, and trauma. She is formally trained in Cognitive-Behavioral Therapy (CBT) and Trauma-Focused (TF-CBT) and Dialectical Behavior Therapy (DBT). She was the coordinator and supervisor of the PHSU DBT Training Program for 7 years. She is a supervisor of psychology doctoral students who train with the standardized patient technique. She is currently conducting research on experiences of stigma toward suicide in families with adolescents who have had suicidal behaviors. In addition, she has had research experiences related to DBT and people with borderline personalities. She is a research member of the APTECO Working Group (affiliated with the Latin American Association of Cognitive and Behavioral Therapies).

Marielly González Chardón is a clinical psychologist and faculty member of the Clinical Psychology Doctoral Program at Ponce Health Sciences University, Puerto Rico. She is pleased to contribute to this important work. Her experience in clinical psychology has been forged over the years since she completed her PsyD in 2008 and obtained her professional license in 2009. In her professional practice, she has offered services to a broad population, including preschool programs and programs focused on health psychology. For the past 9 years, she has supervised students at the doctoral level, a facet of her career that she has enjoyed. Clinical supervision is enriched through a Certification in Supervision in the Professional Practice of Psychology and her role as part of a training team for supervisors of clinical psychology students at Ponce Health Sciences University.

Keishalee Gómez Arroyo is a Clinical Psychologist and Assistant Researcher at the Institute for Psychological Research (IPsi) at the University of Puerto Rico, Río Piedras Campus (UPR-RP). She coordinates the Child and Adolescent Support Project, supported by a SAMHSA grant, and is part of the National Child Traumatic Stress Network of the United States. Her role includes supervising psychology graduates students and co-supervises clinical psychologists. Dr. Gómez is a National Certified Provider and Supervisor in Trauma-Focused Cognitive-Behavioral Therapy, she is also certified in Health Psychology, Mindfulness. Also, she has training in Systemic Family Therapy, EMDR, ACT, CBT, TCTSY, and other therapeutic modalities. Currently, she is pursuing a Higher University Diploma in Clinical Supervision at El Salvador University and Aiglé Foundation in Argentina.

Hiradith Menéndez holds a doctorate in clinical psychology from the Ponce School of Medicine. She is also certified in "Primary Care Behavioral Health" from the University of Massachusetts Medical School. Currently, she is an Associate Professor at Ponce Health Sciences University, where she has been offering courses and supervising and collaborating on doctoral student research for 13 years. For the past 8 years, Dr. Menéndez has participated as a supervisor of the Dialectical Behavior Therapy (DBT) Program at the Center for Psychological Services, and for the past 2 years, she has served as the Program Coordinator. She has formal training in various treatment models, including DBT, DBT-Adolescents, DBT-Prolonged Exposure, ACT, Emotion Efficacy Therapy (EET), TF-CBT, and CBT, among others. Dr. Menéndez is an official trainer of the General Psychiatric Management (GPM) model of the Gunderson Personality Disorders Institute at McLean Hospital. Additionally, she is a psychologist at CPTET-Ponce under the PCPP Program.

Marcos Reyes-Estrada is currently director of the Doctoral Program in Clinical Psychology at Albizu University. Dr. Reyes-Estrada received his PhD from the Ponce Health Sciences University and completed his postdoc in Primary Care Mental Health Integration at VA Caribbean Healthcare System. His current research focuses on integrated primary care, health care provider training, health disparities, and SUD/OUD. Dr. Reyes-Estrada is interested in using innovative training strategies to improve the practice of healthcare providers. He has expertise in qualitative, quantitative, and mixed methods. He has received funding to study HIV/AIDS stigma among Puerto Rican nurses and to develop specialized training in integrated care and SUD/OUD.

Yaritza M. López-Robledo earned a PhD in Clinical Psychology from the University of Puerto Rico, Rio Piedras campus in 2009. She has received additional professional training in forensic practice in and outside Puerto Rico, which include topics such as custody, forensic interviewing of minors, expert testimony, and sexual abuse, among others. She is Dean of the School of Behavioral and Brain Sciences at Ponce Health Sciences University (PHSU). She maintains a private practice in clinical psychology with a forensic focus and offers specialized courses and training in the field, both in and outside the PHSU program. She has presented at scientific forums inside and outside Puerto Rico, on topics of sexual abuse and mistreatment of minors, simulation, forensic interviews, and psychosis, among others. For the past years, her roles within PHSU include coordinating the Curriculum Committee for PHSU's graduate psychology programs.

Part IV
Clinical Supervision in South America

Clinical Supervision in Argentina

Mariana Maristany and Diana Kirszman

> *"...in my view, it is not advisable that therapists go about their work believing they have complete control of the situation, without room for questioning. It is not good for therapists or supervisors to adhere to an absolute truth, even at the highest levels of their development."*
> Héctor Fernández Álvarez, 2015 Reflections on supervision in psychotherapy
> *Psychotherapy Research*

Cultural and Professional Context in Argentina

Argentina is a country with a long tradition in the field of psychotherapy. Somewhere around the 1870s could be considered the beginning of our discipline in the country, with a marked proliferation of public and private psychiatric institutions. Initially, psychoanalysis served as the foundation for developments in clinical theory and practice, holding a significant place both nationally and internationally. Argentine psychoanalysts have been influential throughout Latin America and have played a key role in the leadership of the International Association of Psychoanalysis.

Over the past 160 years, the systemic, humanistic, and cognitive behavioral orientations have also developed, with publications, associations, training and education centered in each of these perspectives (Fierro et al., 2018). As other models emerged, the dominance of psychoanalysis in Argentina decreased without losing its significant prevalence (Korman et al., 2015).

M. Maristany (✉)
Fundación Aiglé, Buenos Aires, Argentina

Fundación Aiglé, CIUDAD DE BUENOS AIR, Argentina

D. Kirszman
Fundación Aiglé, Buenos Aires, Argentina
e-mail: fundacion@aigle.org.ar

M. P. Grazioso et al. (eds.), *Clinical Supervision in Latin America*,
https://doi.org/10.1007/978-3-031-82373-2_8

The latest published studies indicate that currently, psychotherapists are mainly grouped into two orientations: psychoanalytic (52.9%) and integrative (41.7%). A total of 94.6% of the psychotherapists surveyed in the capital city and the province of Buenos Aires, report working from these perspectives (Müller & Palavezzatti, 2015). The movement towards integration has taken on a very significant place represented by the integrative model in psychotherapy of Fernández Álvarez as one of the main developments (Fernández Álvarez, 1992).

Argentina is a country with a very broad and significant psychotherapeutic culture. It has the highest per capita proportion of psychologists in the world, with around 200 psychology professionals per 100,000 people and the vast majority specialize in clinical psychology in the private sector (Alonso & Klinar, 2016). We can also highlight that the vast majority of therapists undergo personal psychotherapy for more than 5 years in their lives, exceeding more than 10 years in a large proportion.

Receiving therapy in Argentina, particularly in urban centers, is very common. People seeking therapy often have multiple previous psychotherapeutic experiences. The high availability of psychotherapy generates high demand for it.

Given the above, the availability of clinical supervision has been, and continues to be, a very important part of the practice of psychotherapy. The supply and demand of supervision are very extensive in the field of education and training. As expressed by Fierro et al. (2018) "*supervision has come to be identified, in Argentina, as an instance that alone can replace both training and continuing education through specific postgraduate courses*" (pp. 18). The statement illustrates, that while supervision is widely recognized and utilized by therapists, it does not always occur within a formal educational or training framework.

Expert professionals who constitute themselves as supervisors, have developed competences as psychotherapists and/or teachers without having until now systematic training. Since 2023, we have in Argentina the development of a *Higher University Diploma in Clinical Supervision* that will involve the possibility of accessing systematic training.

We can now consider several examples that may be representative of the style of supervision developed in Argentina.

Vignette 1 Pablo is completing a residency in psychology at a public hospital, where he began seeing patients and has a group supervision space. The *residency* is a full-time postgraduate program. It is paid for by public entities and take place in mental health hospital settings. It lasts 4 years and includes clinical supervision spaces for residents in training.

The predominant orientation in public hospitals is Freudian or Lacanian psychoanalysis (Muller & Palavezzatti, 2015). Psychotherapists who are doing the residency and prefer to supervise from other orientations, can often seek alternative supervisions to integrate their hospital practice can be integrated with the perspective from which they wish to train.

The clinical situations they typically supervise involve moderate to severe severity cases. The people who seek consultation suffer traumatic situations involving violence and abuse with limited personal and contextual resources.

Vignette 2

Let's also consider Josefina, who graduated as a psychologist a few months ago and started a university specialization in psychotherapy and began seeing patients as part of the practice of such training. It has a weekly group supervision space.

In addition, she receives patient from various sources. One of them is through a network of therapists offering services on the web. Professionals are connected through this medium. Another source of referrals is health insurance systems (Social and Prepaid Works).

Currently, the level of demand, especially post-pandemic, has increased significantly for which Josefina and many other therapists receive a number (and variety) of patients who require supervision in the different areas of care.

This circumstance leads Josefina, like other therapists, to require more supervision time since regular weekly spaces are not sufficient given the number of patients in charge.

Situation 3

Yanina, graduated a few months ago with a degree in psychologist, and obtained her qualifying registration. She started seeing patients privately in her office. She feels insecure as she receives patients with very diverse problems and decides to call a teacher from her faculty to request a supervision space. She found her to be a very warm person and had a very good impression during the classes. Thus, she supervises individually and privately. It is interesting to observe the selection criteria that proves to be similar to when students seek personal therapy. Like the previous case, in addition to seeing patients privately, Yanina receives patients from the mentioned sources such as web networks or health insurance.

These examples are not isolated. These are situations that recur very frequently, and the solution approach depends on each professional.

Regulation and Training in Psychotherapy

Considering the previous examples, Pablo, Josefina and Yanina studied the degree in psychology, which is the enabling title to practice psychotherapy, supported by Law 23.277 of Professional Practice of Psychology. In addition, they must be registered with the Health of the Nation.

The exercise of psychotherapy has faced challenges in becoming an autonomous discipline (Falcone, 1997). Law 23.277 passed in 1985 regulates the conditions for the professional practice of psychology, enabling psychologists to conduct treatments independently. Before this law, psychotherapy was legally considered as a medical practice, and psychologists depended on psychiatrists to practice. Since the law's enactment, both psychologists and psychiatrists have been authorized to practice psychotherapy, though psychologists handle the majority of the practice.

Returning to Yanina's case, current regulations allow her to begin independent psychotherapy practice after earning her psychology degree and license. Until recently, there were no formal oversight bodies for psychotherapy practice or specific requirements regarding supervision hours to support professional practice.

In November 2022, normative 2282/2022 of the Ministry of Health (Boletín oficial de la Presidencia de la Nación, 2022) was passed to regulate the certification of the specialty in Clinical Psychology. Psychology professionals must now be accredited as specialists in Clinical Psychology through either the certification of special evaluation commissions, through a university specialist degree, through recognized scientific entities, or certification through professional residencies.

A mode of regulation of the practice of psychotherapy is established in which psychologists must accredit, at least, 5 years of graduation in a National or Private University recognized by the National State and 3 years of consecutive and immediate exercise prior to the date of application in the exercise of the Specialty in question. In all cases, the certification of seniority in the exercise of the specialty will require the fulfillment of minimum 20 h per week and 200 days per calendar year of certified activity.

In this sense, the framework of education and training in Clinical Psychology must be accredited through the certification of specialized evaluation commissions, or through a university specialist degree, through recognized scientific entities, or certification through professional residencies. It is a very important step in the regulation of the practice of psychotherapy that is likely to impact in the medium term, directly on the formal structuring of supervisory spaces.

Codes of Ethics

In Argentina, various codes of ethics guide professional psychology practice published by provincial collegiate and professional associations. The first ethics code was developed by the Federation of Psychologists of the Argentine Republic (FEPRA), approved by the Ordinary Assembly on April 10, 1999, and then modified in 2013. The so-called colleges of psychologists have as one of their main functions the establishment of a deontological code that regulates the professional activity of their members within ethical-moral margins. This code is developed or updated by the psychologists within the collegial association. In each Argentine province, psychologists are organized into "collegiate" groups, professionally united within that territory. These entities also regulate contracting terms, set minimum fees, and develop training and supervision spaces.

Each provincial collegiate association publishes its code of ethics, which can be consulted through their respective links:

https://colegiodepsicologos.org.ar/wp-content/uploads/2022/08/Codigo-de-Etica-de-la-FePRA.pdf

http://psicologos.org.ar/wp-content/uploads/2019/12/C%C3%B3digo-de-%C3%89tica-de-la-APBA.pdf

https://cppc.org.ar/wp-content/uploads/2022/05/CODIGO-DE-E%CC%81TICA-2016.pdf

These codes include sections related to the practice of psychotherapy particularly focusing on informed consent for treatment initiation, best practices for using evaluation methods and providing feedback to patients, documentation and storage of clinical material, the patient- therapist relationship, and all aspects of professional confidentiality.

The codes frame supervision practice within the functions of teaching and training of undergraduate and graduate psychology professional. Any training that is carried out on a regular or sporadic basis, in public or private institutions, or at private individual levels, must be guided by certain ethical rules that guarantee the training, and the academic level, of the teacher and supervisor. In the student-supervisee relationship, there should be careful attention to role asymmetry, adherence to professional ethics, and mutual respect. Psychologists will teach psychological techniques and procedures only to professionals with the appropriate credentials for their practice.

University Training for Psychotherapists

The education and training opportunities for psychotherapists are extensive and diverse. Undergraduate degrees are available nationwide, resulting in a high number of psychologists per capita. Clinical Psychology is the most popular specialization among psychologists.

The number of courses, diplomas, specialization careers, master's programs, and doctoral programs is substantial. Although advanced certifications can be endorsed by public or private universities, only specialization, master's, and doctoral programs are evaluated by a government agency known as CONEAU or National Commission for University Evaluation and Accreditation. Accreditation of these programs is mandatory and cyclical, requiring periodic renewal and improvements to maintain the validity of the degrees nationwide.

The accreditation standards can be found in the following link: https://www.coneau.gob.ar/archivos/publicaciones/CatalogoPosgradosAcreditados2022.pdf

Likewise, the degrees in psychology, accredited by the said organism, showing the category corresponding to each of them (A, B or C), can be accessed in the following link: http://www.coneau.gob.ar/buscadores/posgrado/buscar.php

There are 20 accredited Doctorates in psychology in national and private universities; approximately ten master's degrees mainly linked to psychoanalytic models and, to a lesser extent, cognitive and systemic models, and 19 specialization programs in psychoanalytic, cognitive, and integrative models, for children, adolescents, adults, and the elderly, and around topics such as family violence and gender.

Many of the public and private universities distributed in different parts of the country, including Buenos Aires Province, Autonomous City of Buenos Aires, Córdoba, Mendoza, San Juan, San Luis, Santa Fe, Tucumán.

Culture and Diversity

The majority of the Argentine population is of European descent, mainly Italian and Spanish, due to immigration in the early twentieth century. Unlike other Latin American countries, indigenous groups constitute only 3% of the population (National Institute of Statistics and Censuses [INDEC], 2010) (we do not have the updated data from the 2022 census). They consist of a diverse group of people who settle mainly in the border areas of the north and west of the country, with the Mapuche people being the largest group. It is important to highlight that a high percentage of the general population of the country lives below the poverty line (39.2%). Vulnerable populations receive less healthcare than necessary given the living conditions and context. In our country, they receive free care in public institutions, hospitals, or treatment programs offered by Non- Governmental Organizations (Fernández-Alvarez et al., 2021). Providing psychotherapy to low- income populations is challenging for both therapists and supervisors. The socioeconomic differences between therapist and patient are among the most complex issues to consider. Additionally, the resources available to therapists in urban centers contrast sharply with those in more remote areas, where certain recommended interventions may not be feasible due to a lack of professionals, such as psychiatrists for pharmacological treatments or intensive therapeutic programs and day hospitals. Supervision in these settings must consider the contextual resource limitations.

The code of ethics includes the need for nondiscrimination based on nationality, religion, race, ideology, or sexual preferences of its clients. Health professionals must be careful and prudent against notions that generate discrimination and stigmatizing labels, and be aware of their system of beliefs, values, needs and limitations, and the effect that these may have on their professional practice.

Training of Clinical Supervisors

Education and Training of Supervisors

Clinical supervision has been a concern of experts, for some time now, with publications on the subject dating back to the 1970s. Within the psychoanalytic tradition, supervision was an integral part of analytical training, framed within personal and didactic analysis. Served patients were supervised with analytic work done on the person of the therapist. Thus, personal analysis, didactic analysis, and supervision were articulated components of training in the psychoanalytic model. Supervisors were the expert psychoanalysts involved in didactic analysis, which implied, and still implies, a rigorous path ensuring their expertise within professional associations.

We find multiple publications that reflect from a clinical perspective, about the vicissitudes of supervision and *psychoanalytic education* (Grinberg, 1970, 1975; Casullo & Resnizky, 1993; Perrotta, 1978). The clinical and narrative approach predominate from this perspective.

In 2008, Héctor Fernández Álvarez published an influential article in the *Journal of the Association of Psychotherapy of the Argentine Republic* (APRA), which laid the groundwork for a shift towards evidence-based supervision. The article develops the state of the art in clinical supervision, and introduced, in our country, the need to consider supervision as a practice that requires both specific training by supervisors, as well as research. His publications have opened up knowledge regarding the different supervision models developed so far and have framed the supervision space as an evidence-based practice (Fernández-Álvarez, 2008, 2015, 2016; Fernández-Álvarez et al., 2018b, 2020; Kirszman & Fernández-Álvarez, 2021). Additionally, the Aiglé Foundation's training and education program launched a systematic program of supervised internships. Training workshops for supervisors were coordinated by Fernández Álvarez were developed from this perspective.

Although the objective of this chapter is not to detail what the training consists of, it is pertinent to mention the principles on which it is based. The four principles are:

1. The importance of providing information, help, guidance, as well as performing advisory work.
2. The importance of the alliance between the participants (supervisor and supervisee).
3. The value given not only to the generic principles of application but also to the personal and individual aspects of both the supervisor and the supervisee.
4. Consideration of sociocultural aspects regarding the systematic training of supervisors, in addition to the aforementioned workshops, the implementation by the Aiglé

Foundation of a university program in Clinical Supervision stands out. It is an initiative that will materialize during 2023, with the first university-level education in our country.

Research

Some research programs accompanied the development of evidence-based supervision programs. The adaptation of tests of supervisory alliance evaluations were developed (Santangelo & Conde, 2020; Fernandez-Alvarez et al., 2018a, 2018b). In psychoanalysis, there are developments that try to generate bridges between research and supervision through the analysis of patient content and therapist interventions (Luzzi et al., 2015).

Supervision Practice

Practice Models

Based on current developments, the predominant practice models today are psychoanalysis and integrative models (Müller & Palavezzatti, 2015). Likewise, both cognitive-behavioral, systemic, and humanistic orientations are prevalent models of practice. Supervision models are mostly set by the therapeutic model of the supervisor and/or the institution in where supervision takes place. Case formulation is organized according to the theory of mind, the psychopathological model, and the principles of change in each model. Supervisees usually choose supervisory spaces that align with their psychotherapy working model. Organizations and training programs, such as the Aiglé Foundation (Fernández-Álvarez & Garcia, 2019), that are based on a competency model (Falender & Shafranske, 2016).

In summary, it could be said that in our country there is not only one model of supervision and that they are mainly governed by models in psychotherapy rather than by models of supervision.

Monitoring Relationships

Similar to therapist/patient relationship, the Therapist/Supervisor Alliance is very important in order to achieve the expected results. The supervisor should be careful to distinguish an act/session of supervision from an act/session of personal psychotherapy. This distinction is subtle since it is appropriate to address issues in the supervisee's personal life which can easily influence the process. The supervisor's role is to delineate what can be addressed in supervision from what should be treated in a personal therapeutic setting (Kirszman & Fernández-Álvarez, 2021). In this sense, the supervisor's role is to promote the professional and personal growth of the supervisee by providing information, assistance, guidance, and advice. When it comes to potential ruptures in the alliance—similar to those in the patient-therapist relationship—the first step is to identify their causes. The supervisor's expertise will allow them to recognize tensions, impasses, and potential ruptures and help repair them (Watkins et al., 2019).

One way to reduce tensions is to highlight the values of the psychotherapist, helping them find their "best way to exercise the role of psychotherapist", while avoiding imposing the supervisor's own values, beliefs, and styles. This does not exclude pointing out weaknesses and locating aspects of greater insecurity, which will help the therapist improve and strengthen their performance.

Monitoring Format

There is a wide variety of supervision spaces available. Professional associations, such as the regional psychology associations, universities, and private institutions of different orientations offer supervision in different modalities (individual, group, face-to-face, and online). A survey of 200 therapists (not published) revealed that the vast majority participated in individual supervision and vertical supervision. A smaller percentage participated in group and horizontal supervision. Usually, individual supervisions last 1 h and group supervisions an hour and a half. The pandemic led to a significant expansion of online supervision. Fernández-Álvarez and Garcia (2019) examine the challenges, advantages, and disadvantages of remote supervision, especially regarding the use of technology and intercultural differences in the Aiglé Foundation's integrative psychotherapy training program, conducted throughout our country and Latin America.

Mechanisms to Ensure the Well-Being of Clients

Supervision takes place in different types of institutional frameworks (hospitals, professional associations, collegial associations, private institutions) and also as "independent" supervision spaces outside institutional framework. These are therapists or teachers who offer supervision services and are chosen by therapists for their expertise and/or personal characteristics. Supervision included in training programs may have evaluation mechanisms depending on the program framework, especially in specialization careers with external evaluation by CONEAU, as supervised practice is part of obtaining a university degree. Clinical supervision, linked to professional associations or private institutions, can serve as "the guardian of the profession", by ensuring the correct application of specific techniques or therapeutic model. In contexts of "independent" clinical supervision, the evaluation of the supervisee depends exclusively on the supervisor's criteria. However, the regulation of supervisory activities is not systematized and requires improvement.

In extreme cases involving the assessment of iatrogenic practices by a therapist, ethical code can guide action, and the clinician may be reported to the relevant professional associations. Even though we have such protocol as a resource, there is no record of such procedure being utilized.

In extreme cases of evaluating the iatrogenic practice of a therapist, the criteria expressed in the code of ethics should be used to report the therapist to the corresponding professional associations. Although we have this resource, there are no known cases where this procedure has been utilized. As long as we do not have a regulatory body of supervisors and general evaluation criteria, the level of development and adequate evolution in the training of therapists will continue to depend on different institutional frameworks or individual criteria.

How Do Supervisors Obtain Information to Provide Feedback to Supervisees?

The way the supervision material is defined will depend on each model of psychotherapy and the institutional setting in which it is conducted. The format for presenting material is determined by each supervisor or institution, structuring the case according to the variables that each psychotherapy model emphasizes as most important. For example: therapists in the Aiglé Foundation training program should note in their records: (a) session content; (b) therapeutic interventions; (c) development of the therapeutic alliance; (d) critical events; and (e) significant life events, which refer to life cycle-related events that are expected in development and are not necessarily pathological or dysfunctional (e.g., individual or group migrations, adoption processes, divorce sequelae, gender identity-related confusion, adolescence events, or older age-related events) (Kirszman & Fernández-Álvarez, 2021). However, supervisees often narrate without a specific structure.

In our country, live supervision through the Gesell Chamber was initially incorporated first by therapists with a systemic orientation, and later adopted by cognitive-behavioral and integrative orientations. Likewise, the use of recorded sessions and video recordings is also used and is another way to directly access session information without the mediation of the supervisee's construction. The use of systematic monitoring for evaluating the therapeutic process, using patient-centered feedback models, is unusual in our practice context. However, we have adapted instruments used in some clinical working groups. Héctor Fernández-Álvarez pioneered in introducing these methods for the process and outcome evaluation. The OQ-45 and OQ-30 are used as feedback tools to assess patient progress and supervisee development (Lambert, 2015; Maristany & Fernández Álvarez, 2010). Currently, CORE-10 and CORE-34 are being incorporated into patient monitoring at the Aiglé Foundation.

The personal style of the therapist (EPT-C) (Fernández-Álvarez, García, 2019) is also used for the initial evaluation of therapists who entering the Aiglé Foundation's training program and to assess the evolution of their style throughout the program. Another locally adapted test is the Working Alliance Inventory (WAI) (Gómez Penedo et al., 2015), a valuable tool for evaluating the therapeutic alliance and its use in supervision. Research on supervisory alliance instruments (Santangelo & Conde, 2020; Fernández-Álvarez et al., 2018a, 2018b) is underway. These instruments, although still under study, can be useful for assessing the supervision process and addressing difficulties, such as monitoring the supervisor.

Final Considerations: A Look to the Future

Our country has a long-standing tradition in the practice of psychotherapy and in upholding good practices. The expansion of psychotherapy research has underscored the need to develop evidence in our specific contexts. An integrative approach allows for greater flexibility in traditional “dogmas.” The legal and ethical frameworks serve as regulators and protectors for both patients and therapists. However, there is still significant room for improvement, particularly in the ongoing education and training of therapists.

Regarding clinical supervision, we can highlight some points to take into account for the improvement of the practice. One of the first issues to consider is the need to develop a code of ethics for clinical supervision. Just as there is a specific code of ethics for psychological evaluation [https://adeip.org.ar/codigo-de-etica], it would be helpful to have a specific code for the guidance of supervisees and supervisors.

Regarding ethical challenges in supervision, we can highlight some questions to reflect on. First, it is necessary to explain, through an informed consent, the scope of the supervision space such as the framework, the tasks to be developed, the mode of presentation of the materials, the fees, etc. Working with the human therapist implies, on many occasions, the inclusion of their emotional life in the work with patients. How necessary may it be to open up intimate aspects of the therapist? To what extent is it necessary to involve these intimate aspects in the supervisory space?

Confidentiality of patient material is a crucial consideration. Both supervisors and supervisees do not have agreed criteria regarding sensitive materials. The transmission of information through emails or WhatsApp can generate difficulties in professional confidentiality.

The asymmetric relationship between supervisor and supervisee is a concern for experts in this field. However, there are institutional contexts where situations of mistreatment or abuse of authority can arise, leaving supervisees without sufficient protection.

We are in a process where evidence-based supervision is gaining traction in the scientific community. There is a need for systematic training and the development of research programs to identify necessary changes for improving practice. The initiation of a university education program this year is promising.

There is still much work to be done, and we have outlined the directions guiding our efforts. Without a doubt, networking across the Americas unites us in a joint movement for this development.

The paths laid out for the future, and the content developed in this chapter, are the result of the reflections and shared teachings of our mentor, Héctor Fernández Álvarez (1944–2023). His legacy includes the importance of upholding scientific practices, building relationships, and embodying an attitude of humility and openness.

References

Alonso, M. M., & Klinar A. D. (2016, November). *Psychologists in Argentina. Quantitative survey* 2015. Presented at the VII International Congress of research and professional practice in Psychology, Buenos Aires, Argentina.

Casullo, A., & Resnizky, S. (1993). Psychoanalytic supervision: Shared clinical approach or reflections. *Journal of Psychoanalysis*, 1043–1052.

Falcone, R. (1997). History of a law the professional practice of psychology (Law 23.277) and its background. In L. A. Rossi et al. (Eds.), *Psychology before the profession. Yesterday's challenge: Instituting practices* (pp. 65–78). Eudeba.

Falender, C. A., & Shafranske, E. P. (2016). *Supervision essentials for the practice of competence-based supervision*. American Psychological Association.

Fernández-Álvarez, H. (1992). *Fundamentals of an integrative model in psychotherapy*. Paidós.

Fernández-Álvarez, H. (2008). Supervision in psychotherapy. *Journal of the Association of Psychotherapy of the Argentine Republic, 1*, 1–9.

Fernández-Álvarez, H. (2015). Supervision in psychotherapy. In H. Fernández-Álvarez (Ed.), *Integration and mental Health (3rd ed.)* (pp. 177–201). Desclee de Brower.

Fernández-Álvarez, H. (2016). Reflections on supervision in psychotherapy. *Psychotherapy Research, 26*(1), 1–10. https://doi.org/10.1080/10503307.2015.1014009

Fernández-Álvarez, H., & García, F. (2019). *The therapist's personal style*. Ed. Polémos.

Fernández-Álvarez, J., Molinari, G., Maristany, M., Fernández-Álvarez, H., & Rønnestad, M. H. (2018a). *Preliminary psychometric properties of the Spanish version of the brief supervisory alliance scale (Trainee Form)*. Poster presented at 49th Annual International Meeting of Society for Psychotherapy Research, 2018, Amsterdam, Netherlands.

Fernández-Álvarez, H., Grazioso, M. P., Kirszman, D. (2018b). Distance supervision in the Aiglé Foundation's Latin American Psychotherapy Training Program. *Journal of Clinical Psychology, 75*(2):282–291. https://doi.org/10.1002/jclp.22721

Fernández-Álvarez, H., Grazioso, M. P., Kirszman, D., Lubina, M., & Goodyear, R. (2020). Responding to the Mental Health Needs of Underserved Latin Americans. En J. Zimmerman, J. E. Barnett, y L. Campbell (Eds.). Bringing Psychotherapy to the Underserved. Challenges and Strategies. United States: Oxford University Press. Pp. 227–245.

Fernández-Álvarez, J., Molinari, G., Szewach, P., Bregman, C., Gómez, B., & Fernández-Álvarez, H. (2021). PATER: An integrative psychotherapy program for socio-economically deprived people in Argentina. *Journal of Psychotherapy Integration., 32*(1), 95–109. https://doi.org/10.1037/int0000258

Fierro, C., Fernández-Álvarez, J., & Manzo, G. A. A. (2018). Century of psychotherapy in Argentina*: Clinical psychology, psychoanalysis and recent developments. Journal of Psychology, 27*(2), *1–27*. https://doi.org/10.5354/0719-0581.2019.52310

Gómez Penedo, J. M., Waizmann, V., & Roussos, A. J. (2015). *Psychometric properties of the Argentine adaptation of the Brief Work Alliance Inventory – Patient version (WAI-SR-A): A confirmatory factor analysis* (Vol. 20, No. 1, pp. 49–62). *University of Buenos Aires. Faculty of Psychology. Research Institute; Research in Psychology*.

Grinberg, L. (1970). Problems of supervision in psychoanalytic education. *Journal of Psychoanalysis, 27*(3), 453–487.

Grinberg, L. (1975). *Psychoanalytic supervision*. Paidós.

Kirszman, D., & Fernández-Álvarez, H. (2021). Supervision as part of a training program for therapists. In A. Tena Suck (Ed.), *Clinical supervision in psychotherapy: A guide to best practices*. Editorial Versalius.

Korman, G. P., Viotti, N., & Garay, C. J. (2015). The origins and professionalization of cognitive psychotherapy in Argentina; American Psychological Association. *History of Psychology, 18*(5), 205–214.

Lambert, M. J. (2015). Progress feedback and the OQ-system: The past and the future. *Psychotherapy, 52*(4), 381–390. https://doi.org/10.1037/pst0000027

Ley 23277 para el ejercicio profesional de la psicología. Boletín oficial 25.806 – Buenos Aires, 15 de noviembre de 1985. Recuperado de https://www.argentina.gob.ar/normativa/nacional/ley-23277-1985-20059

Luzzi, A. M., Ramos, L., Bardi, D., & Slapak, S. (2015). Empirical research in psychotherapy and clinical supervision: Contributions to professional and academic training. In *Anuario de investigacións* (Vol. XXII, pp. 38–44). University of Buenos Aires, UBA, Secretaria de investigación.

Maristany, M., & Fernández-Álvarez, H. (2010). Evaluation of results in psychotherapy: Study of the psychometric properties of OQ-45.2, in Argentina (Unpublished article).

Muller, F., & Palavezzatti, M. C. (2015). Theoretical orientation and clinical practice: the psychotherapists of Buenos Aires. *Revista Argentina de Clínica Psicológica, 24*(1), 13–12.

National Institute of Statistics and Censuses [INDEC], (2010). Censo del Bicentenario Resultados definitivos, Instituto Nacional de Estadística y Censos (INDEC). Buenos Aires, Argentina. http://www.indec.gob.ar

Perrotta, A. (1978). Psychoanalysis and supervision: Attempt at theoretical unification. *Journal of Psychoanalysis, 35*(05), 973–1023.

Resolución 2282/2022. Boletín oficial de Presidencia de la Nación Argentina (noviembre 2022) Recuperado el 7-4-2023: https://www.boletinoficial.gob.ar/detalleAviso/primera/275049/20221104

Santangelo, P. R., & Conde, K. (2020). Supervisory relationship: Adaptation of the S-SRQ in Argentine psychotherapists. *CES Psico Magazine, 13*(3), 76–87. https://doi.org/10.21615/cesp.13.3.5. ISSN: 2011-3080.

Watkins, C. E., Hook, J. N., DeBlaere, C., Davis, D. E., Van Tongeren, D. R., Owen, J., & Callahan, J. L. (2019). Humility, ruptures, and rupture repair in clinical supervision: A simple conceptual clarification and ex tension. *The Clinical Supervisor, 38*(2), 281–300. https://doi.org/10.1080/07325223.2019.1624996. Advance online publication.

Mariana Maristany holds a PhD in Psychology and is a member of the Board of Directors of the Aiglé Foundation in Argentina. She is an Adolescent and Family Psychotherapist and Clinical Supervisor, as well as the coordinator of the area of adolescence and psychological evaluation at the Aiglé Foundation. Dr. Maristany also serves on the Board of Directors of the Argentine Association of Cognitive Therapy. She is an undergraduate and postgraduate professor at various universities, both in Argentina and abroad, including the National University of Mar del Plata-Aiglé Foundation, National University of San Juan, ADEIT-Valencia in Spain, University of Salvador, and Argentine Catholic University. Additionally, she is the Director of the Higher University Diploma in Clinical Supervision at the University of Salvador-Aiglé Foundation, a program created by Héctor Fernández-Álvarez. Dr. Maristany is the author of several scientific publications.

Diana Kirzman holds a PhD in Psychology and is a founding member and member of the Board of Directors of the Aiglé Foundation in Argentina. She is a Couple and Family Psychotherapist and serves as the Clinical Supervisor Coordinator of the Eating Disorders Program at the Aiglé Foundation. Dr. Kirzman is the Teaching Coordinator of the Specialization in Integrative Psychotherapy at the National University of Mar del Plata and the Aiglé Foundation in Buenos Aires, Argentina. She is also the Co-director and professor of the Multidisciplinary Master's Degree on Personality Disorders, Eating Disorders, and Emotional Disorders at the University of Valencia, Spain. Additionally, she is a guest lecturer at various national and international universities. Dr. Kirzman has authored several publications in her field.

Clinical Supervision in Brazil: Training and Challenges for Evidence-Based Practice

Carmem Beatriz Neufeld and Janaína Bianca Barletta

Among the primary training strategies for mental health professionals is clinical supervision, which is deeply ingrained in psychological training as a pedagogical practice. Due to its historical context (Milne & Reiser, 2018), the social representations and assumptions that have sustained this practice over the years (Falender, 2018), and the variety of theoretical approaches, clinical practice models, and didactics (Barletta & Neufeld, 2024), supervision does not have a single standard format and is carried out in various ways. Additionally, it is important to identify the context in which the supervised practice occurs, including the institution hosting the supervision and the ethical, regulatory, and political issues of a country or region, which influence how supervision is provided and who is eligible to conduct it (Bernard & Goodyear, 2014; Ferreira et al., 2021).

These factors shape the differences in the development of supervision as a specific professional activity and in the guidelines for the training of supervisors to become quite unique across different contexts and countries (Bernard & Goodyear, 2014; Ferreira et al., 2021). From this perspective, this chapter aims to describe how supervision in clinical psychology has developed in Brazil. To do this, a brief contextualization of psychotherapy in the country and its regulations will be provided, followed by examples of training and clinical supervision to then glimpse the training of supervisors, the proposals, and the current challenges.

C. B. Neufeld (✉) · J. B. Barletta
University of São Paulo, São Paulo, Brazil
e-mail: cbneufeld@usp.br

M. P. Grazioso et al. (eds.), *Clinical Supervision in Latin America*,
https://doi.org/10.1007/978-3-031-82373-2_9

Historical and Cultural Contextualization of Psychology and Psychotherapy in Brazil

A psychologist is a science professional dedicated to the study of human behavior and mental processes. In Brazil, the profession of psychologists has been regulated since 1962 (Brazil, 1962). To earn the title of Psychologist in Brazil, one must complete a five-year undergraduate degree in Psychology, which follows a generalist path, at a higher education institution recognized by the Brazilian Ministry of Education (MEC) (MEC Resolution No. 5, 2011). Furthermore, the psychologist must adhere to the code of ethics of the Federal Council of Psychology (CFP) [https://site.cfp.org.br/]), the supreme body of the Council System, which is also made up of the Regional Councils of Psychology (CRP). Together, the CFP and the CRP regulate and control the practice of the profession. Upon graduation, the psychologist receives a diploma, registers with the CRP, and can practice in any field of the profession.

Throughout history and up to this day, clinical activity continues to be the most sought-after and practiced by psychologists in Brazil (Barletta et al., in press). Therefore, psychotherapy is a widely practiced profession and follows the principles and duties regulating the practice carried out by psychologists, as described in CFP Resolution No. 13 (2022) and in accordance with the provisions of the Code of Professional Ethics for Psychologists (Federal Psychology Council, 2022). This resolution establishes criteria and parameters of psychotherapeutic practice, as well as highlights ethical dilemmas, which is excellent, because it outlines important aspects of this practice. On the other hand, in Brazil, while some activities are restricted to psychology—such as psychological evaluation and the use of psychological tests—others are not exclusive to this profession, such as psychotherapy itself. In this sense, Resolution No. 13 of the CFP (2022) only regulates the activity of psychotherapist psychologists. Moreover, although it is desirable for psychologists to specialize in their area of practice, it is not mandatory to practice the profession.

According to Neufeld and Carvalho (2017), psychoanalysis (which is not exclusively a psychologist's activity) established itself early as a strong pillar in clinical training in the country, influencing psychotherapeutic practice, professional training, and supervision. The authors also highlight that the profession's growth has occurred in a diversified manner in Brazil due to the geographical large size, which has consequently led to internal cultural, social, economic, development, and educational differences.

In this way, the following social representation of psychotherapy, how it works, and what its purpose is has spread in Brazilian culture: it's a conversational activity where the patient seeks a space to speak freely without direction, and the therapist maintains a contemplative stance. This representation reinforces therapists' inadvertent beliefs about possible rejection by people with characteristics of more structured therapies, including nonacceptance of the session agenda and action plans, which are typical aspects of cognitive-behavioral therapy (CBT) (Neufeld et al., 2021).

For example, Neufeld et al.'s (2021) research, which involved two focus groups—one with CBT professors/researchers and the other with therapists and graduate students—identified the perception that CBT may encounter some resistance in Brazil.

Respondents noted the closer therapeutic relationship, including personal contact, as characteristics associated with the Brazilian social structure that values kindness in interpersonal relationships, even in formal and work contexts. When observing role plays and videos demonstrating a clinical session in European or North American countries, where the therapeutic relationship is more assertive and less permeated by displays of affection, the perception is that the professional's stance should be more mechanical and rigid, which contrasts the Brazilian style.

Following the same line of reasoning, the interviewees indicated that the structure and systematization of the CBT therapeutic process do not fit the relationship model of Brazilian society either, which tends to be flexible regarding excessive formality and rules and does not adhere to rigid norms. Thus, it was noted that the therapist values a welcoming attitude (being quite empathetic) more than problem-solving (showing difficulty in assertiveness and directiveness), in addition to perceiving that structure, agenda, and action plans will not be well accepted by patients (Neufeld et al., 2021). Similarly, a survey conducted in 2011 with 245 Brazilian CBT therapists from different regions (Shinohara & Figueiredo, 2011) revealed some difficulties, such as shorter interventions, possibly due to the challenge of establishing specific therapeutic goals and more systematic therapeutic processes focused on problem-solving; consistent maintenance of session structure, which was occasionally set aside; utilizing resources such as action plans (homework) without incorporating them into the intervention process; and gaps in fostering patient participation in their own care, such as not encouraging them to take their own session notes. Additionally, Bakos and Kristensen (2013) highlighted that Brazilian culture tends to be less pragmatic.

Given that the construction of roles and functions' representations and understandings in a society, as well as one's own understanding of the *self*, are influenced by beliefs anchored in a specific sociocultural reality (Beck, 2004), it is necessary to review the values that support CBT to adapt them to different nationalities and their customs (Naeem, 2019). If this adaptation is not carried out, the intervention strays from local daily life and can sometimes be difficult to apply and accept in that context. Bakos and Kristensen (2013) reinforce this view by addressing the cultural context's influence on clinical supervision activities and proposals, their operationalization, and the significance of theoretical constructs.

The research conclusions previously cited (Neufeld et al., 2021; Shinohara & Figueiredo, 2011) indicated that there is a dichotomous, "all or nothing" understanding as if the structure and the programmed and organized activities would repel empathy, proximity, and flexibility. In this regard, it can be said that the beliefs spread among

Brazilian CBT therapists, professors, and supervisors are considered distorted, as culture and individual characteristics are essential elements to personalize care desirably and according to needs, making it flexible without losing the intervention's fidelity, that is, the theoretical axioms and the evidence base that supports the effectiveness of CBT (Barletta & Neufeld, 2024).

Given that respondents also indicated the importance of cultural adaptation but cited difficulty in carrying it out due to the lack of parameters and criteria, as well as the lack of national models and instruments (Neufeld et al., 2021), it is assumed that there is a certain gap in knowledge, skills, and attitudes for such adaptation among professionals. Continuous improvement fosters skill development based on evidence-based practice (EBP), strengthening therapist and supervisor training, increasing expertise, and culturally sensitive clinical activity guided by empirically supported treatments (Barletta & Neufeld, 2020).

Therefore, it is understood that a trained professional with this perspective has greater ease in considering social, cultural, and individual issues beyond the technical, scientific, conceptual, and philosophical aspects of CBT to adjust the therapeutic process more effectively and efficiently. However, it is still an incipient proposal in Brazil. It is highlighted that, due to the size of the country and its sociodemographic, epidemiological, economic, educational, and religious diversity, the literature (Bakos & Kristensen, 2013; Neufeld et al., 2021) emphasizes the variety of coexisting subcultures, including languages, interrelations, and habits, making impossible to establish a single standard or a generalization of actions.

Clinical Supervision in Brazil

We will present a vignette to illustrate a little what often happens in clinical supervision in Brazil.

Vignette:

Rubiana, a psychologist who graduated ten years ago, worked in Cognitive-Behavioral Therapy (CBT). In her desire to advance her knowledge, she started a clinical workshop in which the first activity was to write a retrospective of the supervisions she had received throughout her professional career. She described four different moments: (1) the clinical supervision she received during her undergraduate degree in psychology: over one academic year (four months in the first semester and four months in the second semester), there were 1 hour 40-minute meetings once a week with a group of 15 students. Each student dealt with four different clinical cases. Since there was no theoretical CBT course before the clinical practices, each supervised meeting proceeded as follows: the first 40 minutes were dedicated to discussing the text, and the remaining 60 minutes were assigned to three students who presented their cases and answered questions. Thus, after five supervised meetings, all the students had presented their work, and the round of presentations began again. Additionally, there were two theoretical exams and a report at the end of each semester. (2) Clinical supervision received during her specialization course: the (theoretical) course lasted over two years, with modular meetings, that is, there was class one weekend per month (Friday afternoon and all-day Saturday). Each module included supervision, so that during the last two hours of class on Saturday, a student would tell the class about their service, and the professor would provide guidance. The class was made up of 37 students, and the choice of who presented their case was voluntary, meaning a student might not present any case during the course. (3) Peer supervision: with some doubts about her practice over her career, Rubiana sought help from more experienced colleagues. Thus, she received occasional supervision to resolve doubts in the office of her supervisory colleague whenever needed. (4) Group supervision: she found a colleague through Instagram who offered online group supervision. In this supervision, there were ten slots for receiving direct supervision or 20 slots for participating as an observer (only listening to the cases presented by those being supervised, without contributing her own case). As an observer, she noticed that the supervisor had a specific agenda for each meeting, which was divided among the participants into the first five minutes, with 15 minutes for the case presentation and 30 for the discussion. Two people presented their cases at each meeting. Each supervised meeting lasted two hours. Then, in the remaining 20 minutes, a formative activity was conducted, leaving five minutes for summaries and feedback. In describing the supervisions she had received, Rubiana realized that there was no standard or format for clinical supervision in the country, that each supervisor relied on their personal experience, and that there had never been an evaluation of clinical skills and performance.

When discussing psychology in Brazil, the current criteria for providing clinical supervision in psychotherapy are also directly related to the undergraduate degree in psychology and registration with the CRP (CFP Resolution No. 3/2007). This resolution highlighted the importance of the code of ethics and class council's norms that must be followed during the supervision process. It was also deemed desirable for the supervisor to have more experience than the therapist, although it is not clear how much experience or if this criterion is even mandatory. Additionally, the supervisor is expected to be a trained professional, both theoretically and technically. For this, once again, experience as a psychotherapist is used to indicate their qualification for supervision (Barletta et al., 2021a), reinforcing the mistaken belief that a good therapist is automatically a good supervisor (Falender, 2018).

Given that psychodynamic and unstructured psychotherapies were primarily disseminated throughout the development of psychology in Brazil (Neufeld & Carvalho, 2017), the form of supervision compatible with the psychotherapeutic proposal also became the main model of this practice in the country. Consequently, clinical supervision in Brazil was based on a model that primarily uses the therapist's verbal report as a teaching strategy and the supervisor's background for guidance (Barletta et al., 2023), relying exclusively on personal experience in clinical practice and supervision (Bakos & Kristensen, 2013). This model does not develop the necessary skills for practicing CBT, as supervision in this format fails to address essential functions: formative, normative, and restorative (Barletta & Neufeld, 2020).

The formative function of supervision involves installing, developing, and refining the repertoire of clinical skills, including those described by Roth and Pilling

(2008): general, basic in CBT, technical, problem-specific, and meta-competence skills. The normative function, on the other hand, ensures quality control of the intervention, ethical and normative issues, and the management of clinical activity. Lastly, restorative function focuses on the well-being of the supervisee. It is important to highlight that if supervision does not fulfill these three functions, it can become inadequate or even detrimental to the therapist (Barletta & Neufeld, 2024).

In the undergraduate psychology program in Brazil, for students to become psychologists, they must complete a supervised professional practice internship, totaling at least 300 hours throughout the course, whether at a basic level or specific level (including the internship in psychotherapy). Given the wide range of theoretical orientations, practices, and work contexts, each program, though generalist, can place specific emphasis on various psychological practices (MEC Resolution No. 5, 2011). In article 20 of said resolution, it is defined that

> Supervised internships are sets of formative activities, programmed and directly supervised by faculty members of the training institution, aimed at ensuring the consolidation and articulation of established skills.

Therefore, formally, all undergraduate programs include supervision as a fundamental strategy for teaching professional skills. However, there are no specific criteria on how it is conducted, evaluated, or what didactic and pedagogical methodologies that can be used, as they vary according to the curriculum and are entirely based on the proposal of the supervisor who offers the internships and/or the educational institution. Velasquez et al. (2015) reinforced this understanding by stating that supervisions in clinical specialization courses in CBT, as a lato sensu postgraduate program, proved to be extremely varied when offered, without any standard, criteria, or similarity. According to the MEC, lato sensu postgraduate courses in Brazil aim to perfect the skills of professional practice required by the job market (MEC Resolution No. 1, 2007), but supervised internships are not mandatory.

It is highlighted that, as mentioned, due to the lack of more specific criteria for conducting clinical supervision and the low relevance and limited dissemination given to supervisor training (a topic that will be discussed later), and the inadequate beliefs about more structured therapies, such as CBT and EBP, supervision remains an activity focused on case consultation or, as indicated by Barletta et al. (2023), traditional supervision. These factors, in turn, perpetuate this culturally representative cycle of supervision as an activity that does not require more rigorous systematic training nor the concern (or knowledge) to ensure that supervision fulfills the formative, normative, and restorative functions.

The Training of Supervisors in CBT in Brazil

Historically, the development of clinical practice in Brazil maintained the idea that no specific training or education was necessary to practice as a supervisor. Campos (1998) carried out an analysis and identified a gap in the training of Brazilian supervisors, a situation that persisted for many years. Without formal training, supervisors continued to rely on their own supervision and clinical practice experiences (Bakos & Kristensen, 2013).

With little data on clinical supervisors in Brazil, two groups of researchers conducted an active search through online surveys to learn more about supervised practice in psychotherapy and the training of supervisors in the country. Based on a broader project, Gauy et al. (2015) profiled supervisors working in school clinics with different theoretical approaches. They identified that, of the 147 respondents, the majority were female (77.6%), had an average of ten years of experience in psychotherapy, mostly worked in private universities (56%), and resided in the South and Southeast regions of the country (78%). Barletta et al. (2023), aiming to understand the profile of Brazilian CBT supervisors, also found that, of the 180 respondents, the majority were female (77.8%), had an average 13.9 years of experience in psychotherapy and 7.4 years of experience in supervised practice, and were mainly based in the Southeast (32.9%), Northeast (28.9%), and South (22.2%) regions. Only 27.8% of the respondents reported having received any type of training as a supervisor, with 23.9% being specifically in supervision, while the rest were in clinical practice, research or other areas. Since there is still no certification of supervisors in Brazil and there are few guidelines on this practice, these two surveys provide an initial idea about the profile of those who practice supervision and reinforce the lack of formal training for this activity.

Currently, with the advancement of EBP and the pursuit for clinical excellence, the perspective of training and supervision offered to therapists, especially CBT, has been reviewed. For example, in 2014, the Brazilian Federation of Cognitive Therapies (in Portuguese, *Federação Brasileira de Terapias Cognitivas* [FBTC]) created the certification of cognitive therapists. In 2020, the Association for Evidence-Based Teaching and Supervision (in Portuguese, *Associação de Ensino e Supervisão Baseados em Evidências* [AESBE]) was founded to strengthen psychology training and promote the professionalization of supervised practice (Barletta et al., 2023).

AESBE aims to develop the first certification of clinical supervisors in CBT in Brazil in the medium term. These authors note, for example, that AESBE has already held two international symposia on teaching and supervision. Additionally, in recent years, there has been a modest increase in the offering of courses by private institutions for supervision training, as well as workshops on this topic, suggesting a growing interest and acceptance of psychology in supervision training. This understanding can have a medium- and long-term impact on the qualification of therapists and lead to greater expertise in offering adapted and contextualized CBT (Mendoza, 2017; Neufeld et al., 2021).

Examples of CBT Supervision Offered in Different Regions of Brazil

Although specific criteria for training and supervision in psychotherapy have not been formally and regularly described in the resolutions governing psychology in Brazil, there is a growing concern related to this issue within the professional community. In fact, despite slow progress, the national literature describes clinical CBT supervisions that highlight this importance. Generally, examples of clinical supervisions are associated with the context of formal and university teaching, whether at the undergraduate or postgraduate level, since, in Brazil, these are moments when there is an obligation (in the case of the undergraduate psychology program) or an expectation (in the case of postgraduate studies) that there will be supervised teaching and clinical practice (MEC Resolution No. 5, 2011).

As an example, in 2011, Barletta, Delabrida, and Fonseca described a clinical supervision offered at the undergraduate level of a private university in a northeastern state of Brazil. The 15 undergraduate students who participated were divided into two supervision groups, which lasted ten months. In total, 34 meetings were held, with an average duration of 3 hours and 40 minutes per supervised session. The supervision format followed a structure similar to that of the session, linking with the previous supervision, assessing the supervisee's mood, revisiting the action plan, and establishing an agenda that could include formative activities (experiential for self-practice and repertoire enhancement, observational model, evaluative to recognize strengths and identify weaknesses, or reflective), case discussions (based on cognitive conceptualization), review of theoretical concepts, and discussion of texts, among others. In the end, a new action plan for home practice was established, along with a summary and final feedback from the supervision. Additionally, the authors noted that the supervision process also had a structure like that of clinical intervention, with a shared contract drafted in the first meeting, establishing the educational goals to be achieved and the educational and evaluative activities to be used. Among the direct observation activities, two processes were identified: mirror room monitoring and session recording. In both cases, peer evaluation and self-evaluation were conducted using a list of knowledge, skills, and attitudes titled *AADPRT Cognitive Behavioral Therapy Competencies* (Wright et al., 2006).

Bakos and Kristensen (2013) also described CBT supervision offered in the undergraduate courses at two private universities in the south of Brazil. Similarly, and being widely used in university school clinics, the supervisions were conducted in groups, with weekly meetings lasting two to three hours. Supervisions began with a review of the key points from the previous session, although there was no set supervision agenda for each meeting. Clinical case presentations were based on forms filled out by students, including data collection: background, diagnostic hypothesis, and cognitive conceptualization. Therefore, each student had a specific time to present, debate, and clear up doubts about the progress of clinical care. Notable teaching strategies included: pre-reading and theoretical discussion, case formulations for the development of clinical reasoning and selecting appropriate intervention techniques for the presented demand, role-playing games, image exercises, demonstration videos, session recordings, and one-way mirror rooms. Additionally, the supervisors attended a session serving as a model for the students who observed in the mirror room. The authors noted that the supervised meetings did not include a final summary or feedback from the students, highlighting that this was an identified difference between the supervised practice offered and the literature in the area.

At the lato sensu postgraduate level in CBT, Gauy et al. (2023) described four different clinical supervision proposals offered in the central-west and southeast regions of Brazil, in the states of Goiás, Rio de Janeiro, Minas Gerais, and São Paulo. Of the proposals described, three followed a structure and tracked the therapist's development. Key features included:

1. In one course, there were four supervisors who formed the supervisory team and had received the same training. In this course, each therapist, in addition to their supervision, had to participate as an observer in another supervision offered by a different supervisor. The goal of this activity was to introduce the therapist to a different supervision style, minimize anxiety (since they would not have to participate or answer any questions), and focus on individual learning.
2. In two different courses, the therapist had to prepare for supervision by answering supervision questions in advance.
3. In three different courses, session recording was proposed as a teaching, evaluation, and feedback strategy, using the Cognitive Therapy Rating Scale (*CTRS*) (Young & Beck, 1980) or its revised version reviewed. In one of them, the literal transcription of the recorded session was also a complementary activity to direct observation, with written feedback and CTRS evaluation. In another, strategies such as group dynamics role-playing, and demonstration videos were used to train therapists in the use of the CTRS.
4. In two of the courses, the supervisor was also evaluated by the therapists using a Supervisor Competence Scale (*SCS*) (OCTC, 2009).

From the Training of Therapists to the Training of Supervisors: The Example of LaPICC-USP

Among the centers that offer training for CBT therapists and supervisors is the Cognitive-Behavioral Research and Intervention Laboratory (in Portuguese, *Laboratório de Pesquisa e Intervenção Cognitivo-Comportamental* [LaPICC-USP]), which holds significant importance and scope in the Brazilian landscape. As a laboratory that promotes training, intervention, and research, and being in a public university, it has a commitment to science, to the community, and to the dissemination of knowledge, as well as to access to and by various researchers and professionals. The LaPICC has offered training to CBT therapists since its creation in 2008. Initially, the primary supervisor was responsible for all undergraduate student

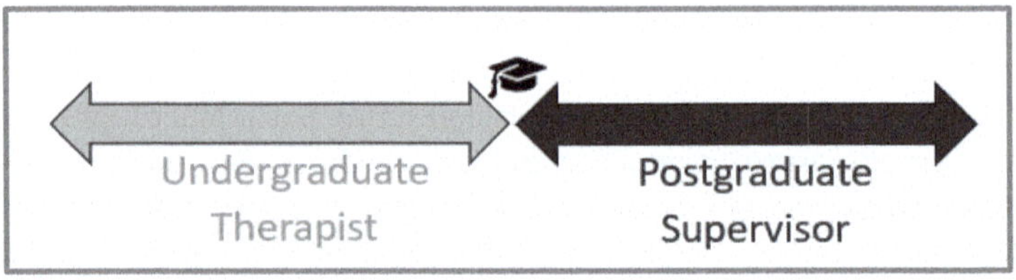

Fig. 1 Continuous training. Source: Chapter Authors

supervisions, while the first postgraduate students observed their supervision. As the team grew, the training gained structure and consistency, evolving into a continuous training proposal for therapists, from undergraduate students to supervisors, for students stricto sensu postgraduate— master's students and doctoral students (Fig. 1).

It should be noted that the training proposal, both for therapists and supervisors, was fundamentally based on Social Cognitive Theory, where younger students observed more advanced ones, both in intervention and supervision. Therefore, as the beginner student participates in the activity, they can see a model of how to perform the task, identify possibilities, and review difficulties. Throughout the observations, the student gradually acquires responsibility and autonomy (Barletta et al., 2021a, 2021b; Neufeld et al., 2022).

Model observation enhances the installation of behaviors and tasks as expected. Additionally, the sequential discussion of observations among peers and the primary supervisor can enrich the meanings, the sense of self-efficacy, and the understanding of the process. In the next step, when the student therapist or student supervisor begins the gradual execution of the activity, they are also accompanied by peers and receive feedback that helps refine their repertoire (Barletta et al., 2021a, 2021b; Neufeld et al., 2022, 2023).

Until 2020, before the Covid-19 pandemic, the LaPICC offered individual and group clinical internships for practice with children, adolescents, and adults. Third-year psychology undergraduate students could participate as observers, both in group interventions and in clinical supervisions. Fourth-year students have already carried out individual sessions or participated as co-therapists in group sessions and in clinical supervision. Fifth-year students conducted individual sessions or participated as therapists in group sessions (Neufeld et al., 2022, 2023).

Master's and doctoral students linked to the laboratory had generally already undergone supervised practice as therapists. In addition, postgraduate students are already trained professionals, so they can begin training as supervisors. One of the criteria for participating in this type of training is to be a licensed psychologist registered with a regional psychology council (CRP). Like therapist training, clinical supervisor training was also structured in developmental levels. Initially, the first hierarchical level was called "observing supervisor," and the apprentice's activity consisted of following the supervisions conducted by the so-called "assistant supervisors." Assistant supervisors were master's and doctoral students who had been in the learning process for longer and who were already in charge of conducting supervision. Sometimes they were also accompanied by so-called "monitoring supervisors," who had an intermediate level of development. This entire process was accompanied by the "primary supervisor," who supported and guided whenever necessary (Barletta et al., 2021a, 2021b; Neufeld et al., 2022, 2023).

With the measures required by the pandemic, supervision and clinical care were offered exclusively online, with some differences: intervention programs became lower and of medium intensity, shorter (six to eight sessions), and were available only to adults.

Innovatively, asynchronous clinical internships in CBT were also offered with a psychoeducational approach (Neufeld et al., 2022, 2023).

To strengthen the development of supervisors, since 2018, with the inclusion of a postdoctoral researcher at LaPICC, another activity was added: specific training for the role of supervisor. This means that, in addition to supervisory practices or their observations (depending on the supervisor's level of development) and the administrative, management, and consultation meetings with the primary supervisor, a formal supervisor training program was incorporated (Neufeld et al., 2022, 2023). This program—which is currently held once a year—includes:

- Discussion of evidence-based supervised practice theory and ethical and regulatory issues.
- Planning supervision according to the intervention program and the needs of undergraduate students.
- Debate and activities to manage relationship breakdowns in supervision.
- Practice in assessing and monitoring learning and skill development, including training on instruments such as the CTRS, the SCS (OCTC, 2009), and the Cognitive Behavioral Therapy Competency Scale-Group (ECTCCG) (Scotton & Neufeld, 2023).
- Practice in using various didactic-pedagogical strategies, such as session recordings, role-playing, psychoeducation, Socratic dialogue, etc.
- Practice in supervisory management, including structured supervision note-taking, document maintenance, directions, etc.
- Remote supervision practice, including applications, online resources, etc.

Current Challenges of Clinical Supervision in Brazil

The examples described are fundamentally important for developing the quality of both psychotherapists and clinical supervisors. However, it is understood that such initiatives are still limited in Brazil, accessible only to students and researchers linked to these institutions and to the faculty-supervisors who promote the training. Therefore, on the national level, it is perceived that the model where the supervised process focuses exclusively on the case, based on the therapist's verbal account and the supervisor's experience, continues to be repeated (Bakos & Kristensen, 2013; Barletta et al., 2023).

Therefore, we understand that one of the main challenges lies in changing the perspective on psychotherapy and clinical supervision at the national level. One of the necessary aspects of dissemination is understanding that evidence-based psychological practice is essential. In this sense, recognition must be spread that work activity based solely on the professional's experience (whether therapist or supervisor) is not only insufficient to ensure the expected results but can also cause harm and iatrogenic effects (Barletta & Neufeld, 2024).

One of the initial strategies has been the introduction of disciplines in master's and doctoral programs. As an example, in recent years, two pioneering disciplines have been offered in three stricto sensu graduate programs at the University of São Paulo, which, in turn, promote psychoeducation and the dissemination of good psychological practices: (a) the Practice of Evidence-Based Psychology (PPBE) discipline, which aims to strengthen concepts, research knowledge, and reflections on their impacts on

work activity, including clinical practice (Melnik et al., 2019) and (b) the discipline of Evidence-Based Supervision (SBE), offered in hybrid and online versions, which aimed to reflect on the knowledge, skills, and attitudes necessary for evidence-based supervised practice (Barletta et al., 2021b).

Additionally, there is a growing interest in supervisor training; however, the offering of specific courses is still incipient and sometimes reproduces nonevidence-based models. In this regard, increasing national production, encouraging interest groups on the topic, and strengthening the field seem to be paths that can help overcome the aforementioned challenges. Collective power can also be crucial for regulation or at least for obtaining consistent and generalized indicators of good practices in supervision and supervisor training. There is a long road ahead, but the way is open for collective efforts to build it.

References

Bakos, D. S., & Kristensen, C. H. (2013). Supervising cognitive behavioral therapy practitioners in urban Brazil. *Journal of Cognitive Psychotherapy: An International Quarterly, 27*(1), 42–50. https://doi.org/10.1891/0889-8391.27.1.42

Barletta, J. B., Araújo, R. M., & Neufeld, C. B. (2023). Survey of cognitive-behavioral therapy clinical supervisors' profile in Brazil. *Estudos de Psicologia (Campinas), 40*, e210072. https://doi.org/10.1590/1982-0275202340e210072en

Barletta, J. B., Delabrida, Z. N., & Fonsêca, A. L. B. (2011). Knowledge, skills and attitude in CBT: Perception of beginning therapists. *Brazilian Journal of Cognitive Therapies, 7*(1), 21–29.

Barletta, J. B., & Neufeld, C. B. (2020). New directions in clinical supervision in cognitive-behavioral therapy: Concepts, models and evidence-based strategies. In FBTC, C. B. Neufeld, E. Falcone, & B. Rangé (Eds.), *PROCOGNITIVE: TCC Update Program, cycle 7* (pp. 119–158). Artmed Panamericana.

Barletta, J. B., & Neufeld, C. B. (2024). Evidence-based clinical supervision. In J. L. Leonardi, R. Catelan, D. Josua, & E. Caetano (Eds.), *Evidence-based practice in clinical psychology: Theoretical foundations, methodological issues and guidelines for its implementation.* (pp. 342–367). Manole

Barletta, J. B., Rodrigues, C. M. L., & Neufeld, C. B. (2021a). Training supervisors in cognitive-behavioral therapy. *Brazilian Journal of Professional Guidance, 22*(1), 61–72. https://doi.org/10.26707/1984-7270/2021v22n106

Barletta, J. B., Versuti, F. M., & Neufeld, C. B. (2021b). From hybrid to virtual teaching: Report of teaching experience with the subject of Evidence-Based Supervision in the stricto sensu Brazilian postgraduate course. *Brazilian Journal of Cognitive Therapies, 17*(2), 79–86. https://doi.org/10.5935/1808-5687.20210020

Beck, A. T. (2004). Beyond belief: A theory of manners, personality, and psychopathology. In P. M. Salkovskis (Ed.), *Frontiers of cognitive therapy* (pp. 21–40). Psychologist's House.

Bernard, J. M., & Goodyear, R. K. (2014). *Fundamentals of clinical supervision* (5th ed.). Pearson Education.

Brazil. (1962). Lei n° 4119/62, of August 27, 1962. Available at http://site.cfp.org.br/wpcontent/uploads/2008/08/lei_1962_4119.pdf

Campos, L. F. L. (1998). *Education, supervision and training in clinical psychology*. EPU.

CFP Resolution n° 3/2007. (2007). Establishes the Consolidation of Resolutions of the Federal Psychology Council. http://site.cfp.org.br/wp-content/uploads/2007/02/resolucao2007_3.pdf

Falender, C. A. (2018). Clinical supervision - The missing ingredient. *American Psychologist, 73*(9), 1240–1250. https://doi.org/10.1037/amp0000385

Federal Psychology Council. (2022). Professional Code of Ethics for Psychologists. CFP Resolution No. 10/2005. https://site.cfp.org.br/wp-content/uploads/2022/06/WEB_29535_Codigo_de_etica_da_profissao_14.04-1.pdf

Ferreira, I. M. F., Almeida, N. O., Barletta, J. B., Versuti, F. M., & Neufeld, C. B. (2021). Criteria for accreditation/certification and training of Cognitive-Behavioral therapy supervisors around the world and the implications for the Brazilian context. *Brazilian Journal of Cognitive Therapies, 17*(1), 48–57. https://doi.org/10.5935/1808-5687.20210007

Gauy, F. V., Penido, M. A., Nicoletti, E., & Mendes, J. A. (2023). The training of cognitive-behavioral therapists at a lato sensu level. In C. B. Neufeld & J. B. Barletta (Eds.), *Teaching, training and supervision in psychology: An evidence-based perspective* (pp. 35–56). Artmed.

Gauy, F. V., Fernandes, L. F. B., Silvares, E. F. M., Marinho-Casanova, M. L., & Löhr, S. S. (2015). Profile of Psychology Supervisors in Brazilian School Services. *Psicologia Ciência e Profissão, 35*, 543–556

MEC Resolution No. 1/2007. (2007). Establishes standards for the operation of lato sensu postgraduate courses, at a specialization level. http://portal.mec.gov.br/cne/arquivos/pdf/rces001_07.pdf

MEC Resolution No. 5/2011. (2011). Establishes the National Curricular Guidelines for undergraduate courses in Psychology, establishing standards for the complementary pedagogical project for the Training of Psychology Teachers. https://normativaconselhos.mec.gov.br/normativa/pdf/CNE_RES_CNECESN52011.pdf

Melnik, T., Meyer, S. B., & Sampaio, M. I. C. (2019). Teaching experience report: The First Discipline in Brazil on the Practice of Evidence-Based Psychology Taught at the Psychology Institute of the University of São Paulo. *Psychology: Theory and Research, 35*, e35418. https://doi.org/10.1590/0102.3772e35418

Mendoza, W. R. C. (2017). Therapeutic skills and limitations in the application of third generation therapies in the Latin American context. *Brazilian Journal of Behavioral and Cognitive Therapy, XIX*(3), 260–273. https://doi.org/10.31505/rbtcc.v19i3.1067

Milne, D. L., & Reiser, R. P. (2018). *A manual for evidence-based CBT supervision*. John Wiley & Sons.

Naeem, F. (2019). Cultural adaptations of CBT: A summary and discussion of the special issue on cultural adaptations of CBT. *The Cognitive Behavior Therapist, 12*, e40. https://doi.org/10.1017/S1754470X19000278

Neufeld, C. B., Barletta, J. B., Lobo, B. O. M., & Mendes, A. I. (2023). Training as a teacher and supervisor in psychology: Challenges and possibilities. In C. B. Neufeld & J. B. Barletta (Eds.), *Teaching, training and supervision in psychology: An evidence-based perspective* (pp. 84–108). Artmed.

Neufeld, C. B., Barletta, J. B., Mendes, A. I. F., Amorim, C. A., Rios, B. F., Ferreira, I. M. F., & Szupszynski, K. R. (2022). Proposals for intervention and training of therapists and supervisors: Overview of the LAPICC USP online programs. *Brazilian Journal of Cognitive Therapies, 18*(1), 114–121. https://doi.org/10.5935/1808-5687.20220010

Neufeld, C. B., Barletta, J. B., Scotton, I. L., & Rebessi, I. P. (2021). Distinctive aspects of CBT in Brazil: How cultural aspects affect training and clinical practice. *International Journal of Cognitive Therapy, 14*, 247–261. https://doi.org/10.1007/s41811-020-00098-z

Neufeld, C. B., & Carvalho, A. V. (2017). Latin America. In S. G. Hofmann (Ed.), *International perspectives on psychotherapy* (pp. 121–137). Springer.

OCTC. (2009). Supervisor Competency Scale (SCS): A tool for promoting good practice in CBT supervision. https://www.octc.co.uk/wp-content/uploads/2017/11/SCS-July-2014.pdf

Roth, A. D., & Pilling, S. (2008). *A competence framework for the supervision of psychological therapies*. Retrieved October 10, 2010, from http://www.ucl.ac.uk/CORE/

Scotton, I. L., & Neufeld, C. B. (2023). Group psychotherapist skills: A narrative review. *Brazilian Journal of Psychotherapy, 25*(2), 103–119.

Shinohara, H., & Figueiredo, C. (2011). The practice of cognitive therapy in Brazil. In B. Rangé (Ed.), *Cognitive-behavioral psychotherapies: A dialogue with psychiatry* (pp. 33–39). Artmed.

Velasquez, M. L., Thomé, C. R., & Oliveira, I. R. (2015). Reflections on supervised clinical practice in specialization courses in cognitive-behavioral therapy in Brazil. *Journal of Medical and Biological Sciences, 14*(3), 331–337. https://doi.org/10.9771/cmbio.v14i3.14985

Wright, J. H., Basco, M. R., & Thase, M. E. (2006). *Learning cognitive behavioral therapy: An illustrated guide*. Artmed.

Young, J., & Beck, A. (1980). *Cognitive Therapy Scale: Rating Manual*. Unpublished manuscript. Center for Cognitive Therapy, Philadelphia, PA

Carmem Beatriz Neufeld is a psychologist with a master's and PhD in Psychology from the Pontifical Catholic University of Rio Grande do Sul, and a Post-Doctorate in Psychology from the Federal University of Rio de Janeiro. She is a Full Professor at USP (University of São Paulo) and a CBT psychotherapist certified by the Brazilian Federation of Cognitive Therapies (FBTC). Dr. Neufeld has also received training in Clinical Supervision from the Beck Institute. Currently, she is the Founder and Coordinator of the Cognitive-Behavioral Research and Intervention Laboratory (LaPICC-USP). She serves as the President of the Latin American Federation of Cognitive and Behavioral Psychotherapies (ALAPCCO) and is the founding past president of the Association for Evidence-Based Teaching and Supervision. Additionally, she is a former president of the Brazilian Federation of Cognitive Therapies (FBTC). Dr. Neufeld is the author of several books and articles on cognitive-behavioral therapy, clinical supervision, and group work. Email: cbneufeld@usp.br.

Janaína Bianca Barletta holds a master's degree in psychology from the University of Brasília (UnB/DF) and a PhD in Health Sciences from the Federal University of Sergipe (UFS/SE). She completed her postdoctoral fellowship in Psychology at the University of São Paulo (USP/RP). Dr. Barletta is a specialist in Clinical Health Psychology (UnB/DF), Cognitive-Behavioral Therapy (Silvio Romero Center for Higher Studies/Faculty of Medical Sciences of Minas Gerais - CESSR/FCMMG), and Clinical Psychology by the Federal Council of Psychology (CFP). She is a CBT psychotherapist certified by the Brazilian Federation of Cognitive Therapies (FBTC) and a Clinical and Health Supervisor with extensive training in the area. She is a collaborating researcher at the Cognitive-Behavioral Research and Intervention Laboratory (LaPICC-USP). She is also a founding member and President of the Association for Evidence-Based Teaching and Supervision (AESBE) for the term 2023–2026. Dr. Barletta has authored several book chapters and articles on cognitive-behavioral therapy, clinical supervision, and health psychology. Email: janabianca@gmail.com.

Cultural, Professional, and Regulatory Context of Supervision in Chile

Ivonne Ramírez Clavería, José Domingo Salvo Rivera, and María Inés Pesqueira Banderas

This chapter reviews and describes clinical supervision in Chile. To achieve this goal, supervisors working in different contexts and from different theoretical models in our country were interviewed to collect the broadest possible view. To begin with, it is necessary to say that in Chile supervision is a requirement in the training of therapists, either in undergraduate or clinical specialization; and is optional beyond training mandate. Nevertheless, its most vibrant expression occurs in informal or self-convened spaces, and although it is not a formal requirement, it is an instance required by therapists seeking greater learning and improvement. Being clinical supervision a very relevant practice in the evolution of psychotherapy in our country, a space highly valued and cared for by therapists, it has been minimally described and made visible in the formats and specificities in which it is practiced (Loubat, 2005).

This chapter is an effort, among others, to make its relevance more visible, show how it has been changing and propose guidelines for its evolution. We will begin by illustrating the extract of a supervision as often happens in our country, a clinician with a case in which he experiences difficulties consults with a professional with greater experience and a trajectory that it merits advising the difficulties in which the clinician finds himself, and a schedule is agreed between the parties, format and conditions in which the meeting will take place, without an economic cost but rather as a support between peers which accounts for the importance of these preexisting links between colleagues and the needs of belonging and self-care that these instances mean. In the same way, this implies that they are not instances of public knowledge and therefore requires greater care and rigor in the framing, roles of the participants and guarantee of the rights of the supervisee.

I. Ramírez Clavería (✉) · J. D. Salvo Rivera · M. I. Pesqueira Banderas
Centro MIP, Santiago, Chile
e-mail: mipesqueira@centromip.cl

M. P. Grazioso et al. (eds.), *Clinical Supervision in Latin America*,
https://doi.org/10.1007/978-3-031-82373-2_10

The following vignette corresponds to a supervision carried out in Santiago, by a supervisor of strategic systemic orientation who responds to the request for help of the supervisee with a case he attends to in a mental health center. The supervisor and the supervisee have known each other for years and have shared different academic instances, as well as previous supervision meetings. The case presented corresponds to a patient diagnosed with chronic depression with several hospitalizations and attended by a multidisciplinary team.

Therapist (T): Her theory of change is that she thinks she need something, but she says it doesn't exist.
Supervisor (S): That she needs something for her life...
T: But she thinks that doesn't exist, she says she's alive, but she feels materially dead, so it's like super shocking, she doesn't say it histrionically, she feels it, "I feel like I'm dead in life."
S: She is...
T: And she says, "I find this to be pure suffering, and if I died..."
S: It would be over... (Empathetic tone while both are nodding).
(At this time the supervisee expands on the interventions she has been performing in her treatment and the goals of the different professionals who oversee the case, also the difficulties of the patient who does not manage to persevere in any of the activities she tries to start).
(...) I think that at the level of your intervention with her you are doing very well, as you say, you have a good alliance, she feels that this is useful for her, and you are adapting your interventions to the stage of change in which she is, more so of reflection (...) She suffers from an illness, and a depression of this nature, is no small thing, and in that case she has to follow the instructions of the psychiatrist. But in other things, she is the protagonist of her life, and she can decide about her treatment, because deep down she does want to live, because she is the one who is already doing some things. On the other hand, I would like to prevent her from taking too many activities and leaving them all because she feels bad... I want to prevent her from falling again because the danger is that, at 25, she might lose hope of having a better life...
T: Or normal...
S: I wouldn't even say normal, because I think she's not a normal person, I would show her that she's very special, rather than seeing her as a depressive person, I would show her that she's a very special woman, because the things you tell me she's trying to do are very rare, very different. I mean, professional athlete?... That speaks to me about athletic skills, strength, and body... Also taking painting classes, which require a different set of skills... Studying for a degree...
She has a unique set of skills, so I wouldn't tell her you have to work with her on becoming 'normal'... How boring! Really dull!
T: Yes, but I haven't told her that... (they both laugh)
S: That is, if you are going to tell me "You are going to become a very special person, and maybe, you will be able to be a tremendous contribution to life, to others... Well! Maybe I'll buy it. Maybe I will get the will to have that sense of life... So, I think you have to co-construct with her a sense of future, where she can become a very special, rare and different person.

Institutional Issues

License or Certification

To practice psychotherapy in Chile it is required to have an undergraduate degree in psychology awarded by a university recognized by the State (Biblioteca del Congreso Nacional de Chile, 2009a). It should be borne in mind that the field of Psychology is recognized in a generalist way. That is, regardless of the specialties that universities offer in their undergraduate programs (clinical, labor, educational, community psychology, etc.), having the title of psychologist is a sufficient legal requirement to practice psychotherapy (Library of the National Congress of Chile, 2009b). On the other hand, regarding clinical supervision, there is currently no legal regulation governing specialization or its practice.

It is important to note that, between 1994 and 2017, there was a period of greater regulation while the National Commission for the Accreditation of Clinical Psychologists Specialists in Psychotherapy (CONAPC) was in operation. This guideline required specific training requirements, having received psychotherapy and membership in trade unions. Failure to comply with this certification did not prevent the practice of psychotherapy, but it was required by the public health system insurance (FONASA) for the coverage of benefits and, in many cases, to work as a psychotherapist in a public institution. Similarly, many universities established as desirable, and sometimes exclusive, attribute the accreditation of CONAPC for the hiring of supervising professors of undergraduate clinical practices.

Codes of Ethics

The College of Psychologists of Chile has a Code of Professional Ethics, drawn up in 1996 and its latest version published in 1999. Its objective is to regulate the professional work with emphasis on the proposal of action criteria that places ethics as a central issue in the performance of the professional role. However, it should be noted that it does not have specific indications for the practice of psychotherapy or clinical supervision (College of Psychologists of Chile, 1999).

On the other hand, it should be noted that Decree Law No. 3,621, issued in 1981, which eliminates the ethical tuition of the Professional Associations and repeals the obligatory nature of this tuition by professionals, leaving this tuition in charge of the Ordinary Courts of Justice. In August 2005, constitutional reforms were approved that revalidated the ethical tuition of Professional Associations over their associates, however, nonassociated professionals remain outside their jurisdiction (Winkler et al., 2007).

In the absence of control, universities and training centers have a crucial role in the ethical training of professionals. It should be noted in this regard that the Code of Professional Ethics is usually included in the undergraduate curriculum of the Psychology career and is also considered to regulate research designs.

University Training for Psychotherapists

Chile was the first country in Latin America to open the field of psychology, in 1946, by founding the school of psychology of the University of Chile, belonging to the State of Chile (Urzúa et al., 2015). Later, in 1954, the second school of psychology was founded by the Pontificia Universidad Católica de Chile, under the Archbishopric of Chile. Both institutions were the only ones to offer the career of Psychology until, in 1981, the General Law of Universities was issued, favoring from that moment a proliferation of schools and programs of psychology (Urzúa et al., 2015).

Currently, for a population of almost 20 million people, there are 48 universities that teach the undergraduate career of psychology, 15 of them state-based and 33 private (MINEDUC, 2023). These universities teach the degree in 83 campuses distributed throughout the country, 24 of them in the capital and 59 in the different regions. In total, 11,568 new students were enrolled in the first year of studies at different universities (MINEDUC, 2024).

The National Council of Education, under the Ministry of Education, is the body responsible for establishing the quality standards of curricula and certifying which universities can offer the degree (Biblioteca del Congreso Nacional de Chile, 2009a). Undergraduate programs comprise a total duration of ten semesters, which are divided into six semesters of general psychology, two semesters of specialization in a specific field (Clinical, Educational, Organizational Psychology, etc.) and one or two semesters of professional practice. To be accredited in the field of psychology by the Ministry of Education, it is indicated that professional practices are supervised, without specifying the format, in such a way that this depends on the resources and decisions of each university. Thus, it is possible to find formats of individual supervision, of one supervisor per student, in meetings of one hour per week and, in other cases, groups of up to eight students per supervisor, in meetings with a duration of two hours (M. Aravena, personal communication, March 2023).

Culture and Diversity Issues Particularly Highlighted in Chile

Chile is the longest and narrowest country in the world, with 4270 kilometers in length and an average width of 180 kilometers (Gob.cl, n.d.). To the north it has the driest desert in the world, and to the extreme south a rainy climate and rugged geography, with areas that have little or no connectivity by land. This geographical condition influences, on the one hand, that there is a great diversity in terms of lifestyles and subcultures throughout the country. And, on the other hand, added to various historical, political, and social variables, have led to the densest urban centers, as well as political, economic, and academic activity, to organize from and around the capital, located in the central area of the territory (Montecinos, 2005). Likewise, towards the extremes of the country there are populations with scarce access to services, and training programs, including this condition also to psychotherapy and clinical supervision.

One way to address the lack of specialists and training opportunities in isolated areas has been to attract professionals to reside or provide services from other parts of the country, through State economic programs and incentives and private foundations. However, this means that therapists or supervisors providing services in such contexts are not necessarily familiar with the specific living conditions of the consultants.

On the other hand, Chile has a high social inequality, ranking 24th out of 159 countries with available data, with greater inequality (Lambeth et al., 2019). At the same time, places of residence, studies, leisure, etc. tend to be organized in such a way that there is little integration between people of different socioeconomic and cultural levels (Criteria, Metlife and Pride Connection, 2022). In this way, it is common for therapists and supervisors to know little about the living conditions of people of low socioeconomic status, and the type of benefits they receive through state institutions or private nonprofit foundations.

In another order of things, awareness of diversity is an issue that has been acquiring relevance from 2017 to date, given different government initiatives that have favored inclusion, such as the guarantee of rights for people with disabilities or the equal marriage law, among others. According to the Criteria survey (Criteria, Metlife and Pride Connection, 2022), 70% of Chileans consider that the visibility of diversity is a contribution to the public debate. Various initiatives have been incorporating the concept such as inclusion of women in management positions, parity in government bodies, mandatory inclusion of workers with disabilities in companies and inclusion of sexual minorities or indigenous populations However, this greater expression of diversity does not always translate into acceptance, let alone inclusion, of such groups. Even so, according to the same study, 76% of respondents think that discrimination is done in Chile and 72% think they prefer to surround themselves with people with similar characteristics (Criteria, Metlife and Pride Connection, 2022).

As for disability in our country, there is still a long way to go on inclusion. It is estimated that in Chile, 13% of the national population are people with disabilities (SENADIS, 2015). Now there are public policies willing to promote inclusion and have proliferated the approval of laws that guarantee the rights of people with disabilities and others that favor inclusion, for example, Law 21.015 (Biblioteca del Congreso Nacional de Chile, 2017) establishes a legal reserve of jobs for people with disabilities and establishes financial sanctions for companies that do not comply with this requirement. From this, some universities have developed special units to facilitate inclusion in students and work staff and have included elective branches on the subject.

On the other hand, with respect to sexual diversity, private organizations promoting the inclusion and promotion of mental health in the LGBTIQ+ population have developed technical guides to support psychotherapy and the development of culturally competent therapy that are available to the public through their websites (Andiloro et al., 2013; Martínez et al., 2018). Similarly, some researchers have developed recent research on the barriers to the practice of quality psychotherapy with LGBTIQ+ population (Tomicic et al., 2021), or the relationship between internalized stigma and mental health in this population (Martínez et al., 2022). Both studies agree that there is a growing concern about this issue and that, at the same time, there is still much to be developed so that mental health and the rights of all people are properly protected.

In the field of clinical supervision, diversity is a topic that has progressively gained interest even when it lacks sufficient technical guidance or research. However, there are supervision initiatives and specific study groups on cultural diversity and sexual diversity. Different practical guides and techniques developed by private organizations promoting inclusion are also available to therapists and we have been able to verify that these are part of the contents of the programs in different supervisor training centers.

Supervision Format

In Chile, different supervision formats are used, namely: group, individual, face-to-face or online. Supervision in these formats can also be carried out directly and indirectly. With direct supervision we refer to the format in which supervisors can observe and intervene live in the development of psychotherapy sessions, as is the case of client care in a unidirectional vision mirror, or by participating in the same video call in cases of online attention and supervision. This format implies that the supervisor can participate by intervening in the process, also acting as a model for the therapist when intervening, and finally, delivering feedback contingent to the therapist's practice. On the other hand, with indirect supervision we refer to any format where supervision occurs at a time other than the development of the sessions, through different methods of reporting the therapeutic processes. This format has a lower cost in time and economic resources, is based on the therapist's report of the case and sometimes includes recorded or transcribed record of what happens in session and works on the construction that the therapist is having on the case and his experience as a therapist facing the situation he is posing. This distinction in supervisory modalities allows for different competency development objectives and demands different resources for the supervisor or the organizations that provide it.

In most cases, in the case of therapist training as well as in institutions dedicated to the provision of psychotherapy services, an indirect and group supervision format is usually used. In the case of postgraduate training programs, it is possible to observe direct supervision more frequently, but the group format is usually maintained, given that most theoretical approaches privilege the incorporation of different perspectives, over other advantages that individual supervision could offer. And, finally, the supervision of advice or supervision between professionals, where a therapist asks for a second opinion regarding a case to another professional, voluntarily, to seek professional excellence and avoid stagnation, is given as a rule in an indirect format, either individual or group.

On the other hand, each of these examples of supervision can be given in both, a face- to-face and an online format. Although in recent years, in the context of the COVID-19 pandemic, the online care and supervision format has become considerably widespread, the face-to-face modality continues to be the most common format.

Mechanisms to Ensure the Well-Being of Clients

In Chile, supervisors of therapists in undergraduate practice are legally liable for any damage caused by these to their clients. In the case of qualified therapists, who are undergoing postgraduate training, they are legally responsible for their own clients, however, their supervisors could also be subject to legal claims for professional malpractice (Pesqueira et al., 2021). On the other hand, the role of supervisors to decide if someone can advance in their training as a therapist is comparatively reduced in respect to Western countries of the northern hemisphere (Falender et al., 2021). As we noted above, the field of psychology is recognized by the state in a generalist sense. That is, although a supervisor could fail the clinical practice of an undergraduate student, hindering graduation in his degree, a student could also choose to complete his last years of the career in courses of a specialty other than clinical (e.g., labor, educational, etc.) and, even so, be legally authorized to practice psychotherapy without having previous clinical experience or having received supervision. In this sense, the function of *gatekeeping* for the practice of psychotherapy is given, mainly, by the fulfillment of the general academic requirements of the undergraduate programs of the Psychology career. On the other hand, for postgraduate clinical training programs, there are currently no national evaluation standards, leaving it to the discretion of each program to resolve the approval or failure of students according to their own criteria.

Additionally, in institutional contexts for the provision of psychotherapy services, both public and private, it is common for there to be formal instances of case supervision within the teams. However, there are no regulations to ensure that this happens, nor the frequency, format, methodology, or who should conduct them. In such situations, the role of supervisor is usually exercised by a member of the team that holds the position of manager, another member of the team endowed with recognition for seniority, training, leadership, etc. Or, an external professional, hired for such purposes. In all these cases, the supervisor may or may not have formal supervisory training.

Opportunities for Supervisors to Obtain Training

There are currently several clinical supervision training opportunities in place. However, access to them is no different from the concentration of population that characterizes our country. In Chile, most training opportunities are in the capital. By 2017, the accreditation commission had 839 accredited supervisors in Santiago and 118 in the rest of the country (Pesqueira & Esquivel, 2018). Therefore, as can be expected, there is a significant training deficit that has recently been addressed by the increase in online training and supervision spaces. As for financing, this is paid for by the training supervisors themselves and the financial support efforts delivered by each training center.

The training of supervisors has at least three sources that have been formalized over time. The first will be called self-taught training, this coincides with the first supervisors in Chile, who adhered to a model of psychotherapy, strengthened their clinical skills in practice and have transmitted them to other colleagues in training, either in academic instances or work teams. Self-taught supervisors have a demonstrable clinical and academic background, as well as peer validation that supports them. (M. Aravena, personal communication, March 2023; Daskal, 2017; Loubat, 2005). This type of training is still current to this day; these supervisors transmit their knowledge in therapist training centers, universities or clinical centers.

The second opportunity for supervisor training will be called tutorial training. In this training you learn the trade of supervision under the guidance of one or more supervisors. A progressive approach to the execution of supervision is generated through participant observation, modeling, and bibliographic recommendations. They are trainings chosen by trust and are not always remunerated economically, the training is agreed based on the mutual benefit of learning and support in the growth of the organization. Many times, they are a consequence of the strengthening of the institutions in which clinical practice and supervision are developed that identify the need to generate new leadership roles or heads that assume the role of supervisor (L. Gutiérrez, personal communication, April 11, 2023; S. Campos and S. Bernales, personal communication, March 10, 2023). They are supervisors who have broad institutional support and have contributed to developing supervision in our country, facilitating the proliferation of supervisors who have also been participating in the growing need for supervision and training of therapists, either in undergraduate or postgraduate training.

Finally, there are formal supervisory training programs. They are programs with a defined structure that articulate a learning process that includes theoretical and practical contents of supervision, meta-supervision, and ethical aspects related to this activity. The emergence of these programs has to do with the regulatory requirements that once existed, and, although there is no longer such regulation, some of these programs continue to operate today. These programs have been developing a third generation of supervisors more up to date in the contents of supervision and are differentiating clinical supervision from teaching roles or therapeutic interventions.

The State of Academia in Supervision in Chile

Academic research on clinical supervision is still limited and has generally been developed from specific initiatives of authors or work teams that report their work system or a particular supervision experience, without constituting a sustained research development over time. It is possible to group most of the articles published in indexed journals into two categories, namely: (1) Description and discussion of general aspects of supervision in Chile (Araya et al., 2017; Daskal, 2008) and (2) Description of experiences and practices of specific teams (Bernales, 2010; Boetsch & Grez, 2019; Carrasco & Díaz, 2011; Ceruti & Ibaceta, 2014; Céspedes & Puentes, 2014; Ibaceta & Santana, 2014; Jara & Vidal, 2004; Leon, 2022; Pesqueira & Esquivel, 2018; Pesqueira et al., 2019, 2021; Ramirez et al., 2020; Taboada & Rivas, 2021).

Recently there has been an emergence of more stable research groups concerning clinical supervision. For example, in the context of the Integral Service of Psychology, corresponding to the clinical-teaching field of the Universidad del Desarrollo, Ximena Pereira oversees conducting research related to supervision. Carola Perez and Daniela Saralegui are some of the academics who have developed research in this service, which is in the process of being reviewed for publication (C. Perez, May 31, 2023; D. Saralegui, personal communication, June 2, 2023). Currently, ongoing research focuses on describing therapists' experience of attending and being supervised in the use of a specific model of psychotherapy that they have called the Multilevel Model (X. Pereira, personal communication, May 8, 2023). Another example is the case of the Training Center in Psychotherapy and Coaching, Centro MIP, which has published three articles that describe and discuss theoretically different aspects of its supervisory style (Ceruti & Ibaceta, 2014; Pesqueira et al., 2019, 2021). Additionally, in this center there is a team dedicated to research on feedback in psychotherapy and clinical supervision, which has published about the implementation and use of the PCOMS system in psychotherapy and supervision, in the context of the postgraduate program of Training in Brief Psychotherapy of said center (Ramirez et al., 2020). And, additionally, it has developed a specific instrument for supervisory feedback regarding the quality of each meeting (Ramirez et al., 2018). On the other hand, the Chilean Institute of Family Therapy possesses the magazine, De Familias y Terapias, where it is possible to find articles developed by faculty and students of its supervisor training program on different experiences in supervision (Boetsch & Grez, 2019; Ceruti & Ibaceta, 2014; Céspedes & Puentes, 2014; Ibaceta & Santana, 2014; Jara & Vidal, 2004; Leon, 2022).

Practice Issues

Practice Models

Using the classification developed by Bernard and Goodyear (2018) we could say that, predominantly, in Chile supervision is based on theoretical models of psychotherapy, considering as the most predominant the psychodynamic, systemic and cognitive behavioral models. Although there are no studies that reflect figures and based on the largest number of therapist training centers and universities, it could be said that psychodynamic and systemic models are the ones with highest activity in terms of clinical supervision, especially in undergraduate.

However, from a historical perspective, we observe that over the years there has been a growing tendency to incorporate contributions from different models of psychotherapy into supervision. Around the 1970s and 1980s of the last century, there was a tendency for each school of psychotherapy to function as a fiefdom isolated from others. In this way, within the same clinical field, it was common for therapists to be supervised separately, according to their theoretical model of psychotherapy, there being even different agreements regarding care, consistent with each model and each supervision. Later, between the 1980s and 1990s, from a greater influence of the constructivist paradigm and the consensus from empirical research that all psychotherapy approaches have similar results, an integrative trend began to take place. Currently, although clinical supervision still operates predominantly from theoretical models of psychotherapy, there is more openness to the different models being integrated into the field of care, emphasizing on the other hand, the importance of other aspects such as understanding the cultural, sociopolitical and relational context in which it is nested, both supervision and psychotherapy. Therefore, there are currently joint clinical supervision between therapists who have different working methods according to the needs of care and conversations are opened about what type of therapist or model could help in each case, in the same way more transversal agreements of operation have been created and a growing validation of empirical evidence in supervision and psychotherapy.

On the other hand, this predominant form of supervision, based on the different theoretical models of psychotherapy, in practice adapts, to a greater or lesser extent, to the different contexts and objectives of supervision. As Fernández Álvarez (2008) points out, these objectives can be classified into: (a) Education and training, (b) Orientation or therapeutic help, and (c) Institutional advice. As an example, a systemic supervisor who is in a training context, is likely to help the therapist think about expanding the consulting system by asking questions, helping him exercise his contextual analysis skills. On the other hand, if the supervision is given in the context of orientation, the questions will probably inquire how the therapist decides the consulting system and what is the emotional resonance when realizing that the father has not been included in the consultation. Or, if supervision is in the area of institutional counseling, which is geared towards achieving certain outcomes, the supervisor is likely to simply give a directive to include the excluded family member in the consulting system.

In this regard, we have the impression that there is considerable variability in how much supervisors adapt the development of supervision to different possible situations and objectives. A prerequisite for this to happen to a greater extent is for supervisors to be sensitive and have sufficient distinctions in this regard. This tends to occur more frequently in training programs for qualified therapists, where the training objective is more explicit, or when supervisors have specific training in supervisory models, beyond their expertise in a certain theoretical model of psychotherapy. When this is not the case, it tends to adopt, often by *default*, a format and objectives of an orientation or therapeutic help. Another scenario where it is common to observe a format and objectives other than orientation is in institutional contexts, especially on occasions in which the role of supervisor overlaps with that of head of a clinical team, often performed by professionals from areas other than psychotherapy. In these cases, supervision has an emphasis on administrative matters (number of sessions, waiting lists, etc.).

However, it is worth noting some efforts to systematize the practice of supervision that integrate theoretical principles of psychotherapy models, with supervision models based on the development of therapists and their competencies. An example of this is the Center for Training in Psychotherapy and Coaching, MIP. This work is characterized by a strategic systemic view focused on resources, which has been described in different articles (Ceruti & Ibaceta, 2014; Pesqueira et al., 2019, 2021; Pesqueira & Esquivel, 2018), and which describe the practice of supervision identifying three purposes (ensuring the well-being of therapists and consultants, ensuring the quality of psychotherapy and supervision services and strengthening the professional development of the supervisee), three principles (excellence, inalienable leadership and intervention) and three central procedures of reciprocal influence in the supervision process (supervisor adjustment, co-construction of meanings and active feedback). Another example is the Chilean Institute of Family Therapy, which has developed a form of supervision characterized by a contextual, relational, and resource-focused view (Boetsch & Grez, 2019). Based on these characteristics, for example, they have established some procedures, such as promoting the inclusion in the supervisory instance of all the people who work directly with the cases, a system for monitoring supervised cases, consideration of the subjectivity of the supervised in the co-construction of the relational space with their consultants, and special care to legitimize the perspectives and realities of the consultants, etc. (S. Campos & S. Bernales, personal communication, March 10, 2023). Finally, we find the conceptual proposal of theoretical trans integration made by Araya et al. (2017). In this article, the authors collect and integrate criteria that guide the development of supervision, according to supervisors, recognized as experts in Chile, of different theoretical orientations.

Monitoring Relationships

In Chile, great importance is attached to the link between supervisor and supervisee. Supervisees need to feel supported, contained, and guided, to feel that supervision is contributing to them. In addition, it is valued when the supervisor offers from the beginning a clear structure regarding their way of working and what is wanted to be achieved in supervision, for example, the role of each of the participants, use of certain patient records, etc. (Zamorano, 2012).

In general, it can be said that the supervisory relationship is hierarchical because there is someone who needs help and who expects to be helped, attributing that power and expectation to the supervisor. Naturally this becomes more complex depending on the supervision format and there are individual styles within each relationship (Araya et al., 2017). In the development of therapists, a very significant role is given to the supervisor (Zamorano, 2012) of whom anecdotes are remembered, leaving an inspiring mark on the path of the therapist, where bad experiences also leave a mark on the supervisee.

As is well known, interventions in supervision influence the development of the partnership. Many times, these are organized and oriented according to models, needs of the case and styles, both supervisor and the supervisee. In this sense, it is predictable that there are "miscalculations" in the design of supervisory interventions that trigger breaks in the alliance. Therefore, it is very important that even when there is a hierarchy in the role of the supervisor, he is aware of adapting to the context and needs of the supervisee (S. Campos & S. Bernales, personal communication, March 10, 2023); in this sense, it should be noted that "the capacity for influence is not attached to the role of supervisor but must be earned each time or at least not lost" (Pesqueira et al., 2019, p. 33).

In terms of alliance development, a differentiating aspect is whether the supervisor is elected or assigned. When the supervisee chooses the supervisor, he has reasons to grant confidence that account for his aspirations, motivations, and awareness of his own needs that, if detected by the supervisor and legitimized, is more likely to give a respectful and synergistic flow of this alliance. In assigned supervisors, these aspects must be built to establish the necessary power of influence, which implies striving to jointly build the motivation and needs of the supervisee, clarify expectations and put together a co-constructed framework.

Another source of tension in the Alliance in formative supervision is when the role of supervisor is combined with requirements for summative evaluation (qualification) or decision-making typical of the leadership role. This overlapping of roles raises the power differences already existing in the hierarchical nature of the helping relationship (Pesqueira & Esquivel, 2018). It has been discussed how the convergence of these roles could interfere with the openness with which supervisees could reveal errors or doubts regarding their cases, unprotecting their clients and closing learning opportunities as therapists (Pesqueira & Esquivel, 2018; Pesqueira et al., 2019). To address this potential conflict of roles, some institutions have taken steps to separate them, so that supervision is not a formal evaluation instance. However, today, each institution is free to resolve this issue in its own way.

Regarding alliance ruptures and its repairing, it is necessary to point out that in our country there is a tendency to avoid conflicts, "turn the page quickly" in order not to jeopardize authority figures and the sense of security that emanates from them (Moulian, 1997). In this sense, in supervision many times for fear of losing the bond, validation or the encounter, the tension of the alliance accumulates, and the ruptures are set, which eventually leaves the supervisor with the responsibility of opening it or not, sometimes remaining, on the part of the supervisee, unresolved conflicts and the possibility of withdrawal in the relationship. Finally, either the relationship ends, or it is sustained by finding an individual adaptation that prioritizes the maintenance of the *status quo*, sustaining the tension that the relationship implies.

Based on our experience, when supervisory conflicts are resolved so that both parties understand what is happening, feel legitimized and are active in agreeing on a new version of the alliance, it is not only repaired, but strengthened. Then trust improves, the relationship is horizontalized and it is possible to renew the choice of that professional bond. Thus, the ability of the supervisor and the supervisee to face and manage a conflict allows the development of good supervision practices.

Ethical Issues and Challenges

From what we have described so far, one of the ethical challenges that we can identify, for example, occurs in working with people of low socioeconomic status, or who live in geographically isolated areas where it is common for both therapists and supervisors to be more like each other than to their consultants. In this way, not only is the possibility of biases that lead to define as deficient or pathological what is different, but it is also difficult to identify when this is happening. In the same way, many themes that make sense from the academy may not be relevant or applicable to the characteristics of a given population, for example the view of attachment on motherhood, is often based on assumptions of context of social support or customs widely validated in the field of international psychology but that are not necessarily present in a given reality and may be visions that do not fit to the reality of a population or group (S. Campos & S. Bernales, personal communication, March 10, 2023).

Another issue of ethical tension is guaranteeing patients that their therapists and supervisors have sufficient specialization to address their difficulties, considering that currently it is just enough to graduate from the psychology career to practice psychotherapy and supervision (H. Esquivel, personal communication, March 10, 2023). However, this tension is broader than the specific situation in Chile, as different international research has offered evidence that certification, by itself, does not ensure that the necessary skills are available and/or that these are applied in practice (Walkman & Williston, 2015). This is a tension that we believe is complex to resolve where, both the absence of regulation and its excess seem problematic, and we do not know reliable criteria that allow us to establish at what point between both extremes it would be convenient to place ourselves (H. Hirsch, personal communication, March 24, 2023).

How Supervisors Get Information to Provide Feedback to Supervisees

In most contexts, supervision is developed indirectly, and the most common means used by supervisors to offer their comments is the supervisee report. For this, it is possible to observe a wide variety of methods and styles (Araya et al., 2017); some of them more structured, such as the use of clinical records, ad hoc guidelines for the presentation of cases, partial or total transcripts of a session, etc. And others less structured, such as free reporting by the supervisee regarding therapy. On the other hand, the observation of sessions, either live or through audio or video recordings, is usually used mostly in contexts of postgraduate training or specialization in specific models of therapy, with a special emphasis on the instructional objective of providing feedback for the development of skills or learning of the model by the therapist.

As far as we have come to know, methods of self-reporting by consultants are rarely included in supervision. In contexts where these are applied, most of the time they are used for research purposes, or to evaluate the general functioning of a certain program or clinical team. In very few places they are used by supervisors or therapists in the service of reviewing therapy processes while they are still in development. One of the few exceptions we know of is the case of the Psychotherapy and Coaching Training Center, MIP, which trains its supervisors and graduate students in the use of the PCOMS system and uses its reports routinely in the direct and indirect supervision of cases (Ramirez et al., 2020).

Supervisory Best Practices Checklist

Given the wide diversity of formats and types of supervision, the following list applies specifically to the training supervision of therapists in an undergraduate context. The following list is based on the recommendations developed by Ellis et al. (2014):

- *Has the appropriate credentials as defined by the supervisor's discipline or profession:* Credentials exist, even though there is no regulation, as long as supervisors adhere to the training criteria agreed upon by CONAPC and to the tradition of vast clinical experience and sufficient academic training.
- *Has the appropriate knowledge and skills for clinical supervision and awareness of its limitations:* Frequently.

- *Obtains informed consent for supervision or uses a supervision contract:* Frequently.
- *Provides a minimum of one hour of individual face-to-face supervision per week*: Supervision is usually given one hour per week for each student. However, some universities are flexible about whether this happens in an individual format or in groups of up to eight students.
- *Observes, reviews or monitors the supervisee's therapy/counseling sessions (or parts thereof):* Moderately. It is common to use transcripts of recordings and in some occasions live observation. However, including these methodologies depends on the supervisor's preferences and the resources of each institution.
- *Provides fair, respectful, honest, ongoing, and formal evaluative feedback to the supervisee*: Frequently.
- *Promotes and invests in supervisee well-being, professional growth, and development:* Frequently.

A Supervisory Approach Appropriate for Your Country

As we mentioned earlier, the geographical characteristics of our territory, long and narrow, surrounded by sea and mountains, always presents a connectivity challenge between the ends of the country and a tendency to concentrate resources and training opportunities in the capital or in urban centers. Given this concentration we could say that in most of the universities where the field of psychology is taught there are experiences of clinical supervision with adequate and homogeneous standards that are replicated throughout the country. Supervision is then perceived as a useful, supportive of clinical practice and it could be said that it is sought by therapists at the end of their career as a space for development, exchange, support and belonging. In more informal supervisory spaces, it is common for the practice of supervision to have a quality of enjoyment, of bonds that are strengthened both from the practice itself, and from having a space and characteristics that make it welcoming; it is common, for example, to eat together or share a coffee.

In our country there is respect for authority and order at the level of social representation (Riffo-Pavón et al., 2021). As an example, Chile has a tradition of hyper-presidential political organization in which trust is placed in authority as the central power and order and organization are expected of it. This social representation could accentuate the natural asymmetry of the supervisor's role. Therefore, in clinical supervision it is especially relevant that the supervisor develops broad communication skills and acquires an active role in learning about the experience of the supervisees to allow the expression of conflicts and tensions in the alliance early; and thus facilitate the resolution of possible ruptures.

Another issue to consider, that is a consequence of our geography, has to do with the appearance of natural disasters, namely: floods, earthquakes, tsunamis, and mega forest fires. These disasters influence the need to join efforts of individuals to be able to respond to crisis, which favors a solidary character and a normalization of clinical practice and *ad honorem* supervision. Additionally, therapists and supervisors who are helping in crisis are often part of the phenomenon; something similar to what was experienced in most of the world during the periods of confinement due to COVID-19. In this sense, it is especially important that clinical supervisors promote self-awareness and self-care of therapists, as well as the activation of networks and work teams.

On the other hand, as mentioned above, there are different ways to become a clinical supervisor in Chile. However, there is no regulation or consensus currently in force to certify that a supervisor has sufficient competences. Although in our country there were attempts at regulation, and there is nothing to prevent this from happening again, currently, there does not seem to be sufficient institutional legitimacy or legislative support to sustain this type of regulation. In addition, as the strategic model points out, it is important "not to repeat the ineffective solution attempted" (Watzlawick et al., 1992) because a general measure is not easy to sustain in such a diverse country with inequality of opportunities. On the other hand, it is highly necessary that the discipline continues to be perfected to guarantee the appropriate practice of psychotherapy and supervision. A way out of this is the legitimization and validation of peer work, to the extent that supervisors share our supervisory practices, expose successes and failures, triangulate different ways of intervening in a case, make our trajectory transparent, and put as a central objective the care for the role of the supervisor, rigor and excellence in the performance of supervision.

Another standard of adequate supervision that is recommended in the checklist of Ellis et al. (2014) is that of one hour per week per supervised, this criterion, although it is adequate for the training of therapists in undergraduate, is not necessarily sustainable in the different realities of the country. On the other hand, in our experience, the group format also has an enhancing effect on learning among therapists, allows to more extensively supply the shortage of supervisors supply and is compatible with the different supervision formats. However, it requires an adequate management of group dynamics, climate and framing of confidentiality among the participants.

In another area, in prevailing Western models of clinical supervision, evaluation is mentioned as an important aspect of the supervisor's role. Agreeing that evaluation is a relevant aspect, it is necessary to add feedback from the supervisee to the supervisor as a source of potential improvement in supervision. This allows the supervisor to refine the knowledge about how their interventions are perceived and increase awareness about their performance compared to the supervised (Pesqueira et al., 2019). Although the supervisor has sufficient expertise, we can say that the supervisee is an expert in their needs and context. Thus, it is possible to think of supervision as a service "tailored" to the supervisee (Pesqueira et al., 2021). For this, questions can be asked that facilitate feedback or more formal methodologies for evaluating the quality of the supervisee's quality of experience.

Next Steps in the Evolution of Clinical Supervision in Chile

As noted above, the regulation of psychotherapy and clinical supervision in Chile has seen a rise, a decline, and incipient search for new agreements. In this regard, the current situation offers advantages, disadvantages, and opportunities. On the one hand, the entity that oversaw the guidlines of training and practice was dissolved, however, the agreements reached regarding minimum standards of professional competence continue to be applied largely by training centers. Additionally, the process of reaching a higher level of associativity and agreements is a path already traveled, which could be traveled again.

On the other hand, it could be argued that less rigid regulations could also contribute to adapting training opportunities and supervisory practice to the different local realities throughout the country, where some standards, although widely shared, could be thought of more as a desirable horizon than as a necessary condition. In a country like ours, it is a challenge to maintain formal requirements associated with quality standards and, at the same time, not to generate barriers in terms of training opportunities for people living in geographically distant or isolated areas of the capital.

Additionally, we consider as a strength that in our country there is a culture of valuing supervision as a fundamental instance, both development and self-care of therapists. And, on the other hand, getting to occupy the role of supervisor, usually occurs as a result of having the recognition of peers, either by professional career, leadership skills, level of training, etc. In a context of less regulation, it is important to consider that relationship and service contracts tend to be more implicit than in a formal space. However, it is not because it is self- convened that it is devoid of rigor.

When thinking about the future for supervision in Chile, one not too far from now, we would like to see supervisors united in the mission of sharing experiences on the different ways of doing supervision. In this sense, it is worth recognizing one of the great achievements of CONAPC: bringing together supervisors and faculty thinking about the improvement of our discipline, seeking the development of consensus and reviewing local and international experiences. Thus, it seems relevant for us to build a future rescuing the achievements of previous efforts and today more than ever we need the human and professional exchange of supervisors who, thinking together, can undoubtedly improve the supervision of our country and enhance the efforts that each one makes in isolation. The actions that could be undertaken to this end are:

- Development of local research that contemplates the characteristics of clinical supervision in different contexts of care. And, at the same time, enhance the dialogue of local research with the current limitations and questions of international research. Given the current state and characteristics of supervision in our country that we have described in this chapter, we believe that research in Chile has the potential to be a contribution, among other topics, regarding cultural influences in the practice of supervision, development of supervisory skills, use of self-report and feedback, development of psychometric instruments and effectiveness in group supervision.

- Strengthen the collaboration between those who practice clinical supervision in Chile through exposure in national and international congresses so that this task allows to generate networks and a work agenda that evolves consensus and new developments.
- Practice and disseminate clinical supervision so that we deepen the knowledge of this trade and stimulate the development of therapists during the development of professional life. Examples of this could be the development of discussions on clinical supervision, relieving clinical supervision as a topic of seminars or congresses or meta-supervising their work among supervisors, etc.
- More supervisor training programs and funding support for this purpose. Programs that deepen the formation of relevant competences for supervision considering, for example, general guidelines (APA, 2015), as well as the emphasis on relevant aspects given the local culture. These competencies could include training in giving and receiving formative feedback, skills to raise difficult conversations, open and repair tensions in the alliance, evaluate and train in therapeutic competencies, etc. On the other hand, develop competency training and feedback systems within the organizations in which it supervises clinical practice.

Finally, in the preparation of this chapter we have been able to collect a list of good practices for the different formats that are currently in place. Some of these are:

- Direct patient information: Use of files with textual information of the case, use of scales of self-report of patients on well-being, therapeutic alliance, etc.; include other case reporters, direct supervision, or recording of sessions. Different possible forms according to the supervision formats.
- Identification of the supervisee's own resources, context of care or work team in which it is attended to strengthen and empower the supervised (S. Campos and S. Bernales, personal communication, March 10, 2023; Pesqueira et al., 2019).
- For supervision within institutional care settings, identifying the institution's goals as part of the supervisory process. For example, actions aimed at reducing waiting lists, number of sessions and referral times, all in alignment with a supervisor who can help to achieve these goals (Hirsch, H., personal communication, March 24, 2023).
- Leveraging new online meeting technologies, record supervision sessions, and increase opportunities for peer supervision or sessions with more experienced supervisors who can observe and review the recorded supervision interventions (Pesqueira et al., 2019).

- Throughout the realization of this article we have been able to observe that supervision in Chile has had an evolution in the professionalization of this discipline, it has been an important training strategy in clinical practice, of specific knowledge of interventions, greater understanding and collaboration between different theoretical approaches and ways of doing therapy; greater openness to integrating evidence into clinical work and recently the existence of supervisory training programs. This book is a contribution in this direction as it tries to visualize the supervision in Latin America and a greater knowledge of the phenomenon in dialogue and contrast with the state of the art of research at the international level which can undoubtedly contribute to the development of supervision in our country.

- At the end of this chapter, we would like to thank the contributions received by each of the supervisors interviewed for the preparation of this work and the generosity of their willingness to articulate ideas for the future of supervision in Chile. These conversations were a pleasant experience, which renewed in our minds the conviction that these efforts of dialogue, review, and reflection are also sources of inspiration and challenge to new developments for clinical supervision.
- We thank the supervisors and researchers in supervision who contributed to the realization of this chapter, sharing their experiences and knowledge through different interviews:
- *Marcela Aravena, Sergio Bernales, Cecilia Brahm, Sylvia Campos, Héctor Esquivel, Lucio Gutiérrez, Hugo Hirsch, Cristina Moya, Ximena Pereira, Carola Perez, Daniela Saralegui, María Inés Winkler.*

References

American Psychological Association APA. (2015). Guidelines for clinical supervision in health service psychology. *American Psychologist, 70*(1), 33–46. https://doi.org/10.1037/a0038112

Andiloro, L., Peralta, P., & Salgado, M. (2013). *General Guidelines for the Care of Lesbian, Gay, Bisexual and Trans Children and Adolescents for Mental Health Professionals. Gender Studies Unit.* Center for Studies and Attention to People CEAP, School of Psychology, Adolfo Ibáñez University. https://todomejora.org/bibliodiversa?categoria=todos

Araya, C., Casassus, S., War, C., Except, D., Zapata, J., & Krause, M. (2017). Criteria that Chilean clinical supervisors consider relevant when supervising: A qualitative study. *Revista Argentina de Clínica Psicológica, 26*(1), 47–58.

Bernales, S. (2010). Notes on couples therapy and video supervision. *Revista Argentina de Clínica Psicológica, 19*, 45–56.

Bernard, J., & Goodyear, R. (2018). *Fundamentals of clinical supervision* (5th ed.). Pearson ed.

Boetsch, T., & Grez, C. (2019). Chilean Institute of Family Therapy: 35 years in the training of therapists. *Of Families and Therapies, 46*, 21–28. https://doi.org/10.29260/DFYT.2019.46A

Carrasco, B., & Díaz, C. (2011). Therapist person workshop: ICHTF group supervision. *Of Families and Therapies, 31*, 27–34.

Ceruti, P. E., & Ibaceta, F. (2014). Supervisory practices in the center of specialists in strategic intervention. *Of Families and Therapies, 37*, 69–87.

Céspedes, L., & Puentes, C. P. (2014). Supervision in a group context: Reflections from the intersubjective perspective. *Of Families and Therapies, 36*, 109–126.

College of Psychologists of Chile. (1999). *Code of Professional Ethics.* http://colegiopsicologos.cl/wp-content/uploads/2021/06/1999-Codigo-de-Etica-2nd-Edition.pdf

Criteria, Metlife and Pride Connection. (2022). *What are we talking about when we talk about diversity?* https://www.prideconnection.cl/Presentacion-estudio-Metlife-Pride-Connection.pdf

Daskal, A. (2008). Putting the magnifying glass on clinical supervision. *Revista Argentina de Clínica Psicológica, 17*(3), 215–224.

Daskal, A. (2017). Supervisions. In A. M. Daskal (Ed.), *The person of the therapist* (pp. 105–117). Ediciones UC Santiago de Chile.

Ellis, M., Berger, L., Hanus, A., Ayala, E., & Swords, E. (2014). Inadequate and harmful clinical supervision: Testing a revised framework and assessing occurrence. *The Counseling Psychologist, 42*(4), 434–472.

Falender, C., Goodyear, R., Duan, C., et al. (2021). Lens on international clinical supervision: Lessons learned from a cross-national comparison of supervision. *J Contemp Psychother, 51*, 181–189. https://doi.org/10.1007/s10879-021-09497-5

Fernández Álvarez, H. (2008). Supervision in psychotherapy. Buenos Aires: *Revista de APRA,* 1. Retrieved June 02, 2023, from https://apra.org.ar/wp-content/uploads/2020/10/Supervision-in-Psychotherapy-Fernandez_Alvarez_1.pdf

Gob.cl. (n.d.). *Our country*. Government of Chile. https://www.gob.cl/nuestro-pais/

Ibaceta, F. J., & Santana, A. I. (2014). Supervision as promotion of the care of teams that work in reparation of sexual assaults: Delimitation of a proposal. *Of Families and Therapies, 37*, 23–39.

Jara, M. C., & Vidal, C. (2004). The training of family therapists and the therapist's family of origin: The work in the workshop of the therapist's person in the IChTF. *Of Families and Therapies, 18*, 85–93.

Lambeth, G., Otero, C., & Vergara, D. (2019). *Inequality is a political decision*. CIPER. https://www.ciperchile.cl/2019/12/10/parte-ii-la-desigualdad-es-una-decision-politica/#:~:text=El índice de Gini para,desigualdad de ingresos en Chile.

Leon, L. (2022). Supervision processes in serious abuse reparation programs. *Families and Therapies, 52*, 17–34.

Library of the National Congress of Chile. (2009a). Law 20.370 of 2009. Establishes the General Law of Education. https://www.bcn.cl/leychile/navegar?idNorma=1006043

Library of the National Congress of Chile. (2009b). Decree 16 regulation on records relating to individual health providers Ministry of Health; Undersecretariat of Assistance Networks. https://bcn.cl/3dest

Library of the National Congress of Chile. (2017). Law 21.015 of 2017. Encourages the Inclusion of People with Disabilities in the World of Work. http://bcn.cl/20zja

Loubat, M. (2005). Supervision in psychotherapy: A position based on clinical experience. *Journal of Psychological Therapy, 23*, 75–84.

Martínez, C., Tomicic, A., Dominguez, M., & Spuler, C. (2022). Internalization of stigma in LGB people: Analysis of its impact on mental health and the search for psychotherapeutic help in Chile. *Psychological Therapy, 40*(1), 49–69. https://doi.org/10.4067/s0718-48082022000100049

Martínez, C., Tomicic, A., Gálvez, C., Rodríguez, J., Rosenbaum, C., & Aguayo, F. (2018). *Culturally competent psychotherapy for work with LGBT+ patients. A guide for psychotherapists and mental health professionals*. Center for Studies in Clinical Psychology & Psychotherapy, Diego Portales University (CEPPS-UDP).

MINEDUC. (2023). Career Finder. My futuro.cl. Retrieved June 02, 2023, from https://www.mifuturo.cl/buscador-de-carreras/?tipo=carrera

MINEDUC. (2024). *Informe de Matrícula en Educación Superior en Chile 2024*. Retrieved August 15, 2024, from https://educacionsuperior.mineduc.cl/wp-content/uploads/sites/49/2024/07/2024- MATRICULA-VF-1.pdf

Montecinos, E. (2005). Background on the historical relationship centralism and decentralization in Chile. *Revista Venezolana de Gerencia, 10*(31), 443–462. https://doi.org/10.37960/revista.v10i31.10398

Moulian, T. (1997). *Chile actual: Anatomía de un mito*. Lom- Arcis, Eds.

Pesqueira, M. I., & Esquivel, H. (2018). The supervision of psychotherapists, from a systemic approach. Experiences in the Chilean clinical environment. *Electronic Journal of Psychology of the FES Zaragoza-UNAM, 8*(15), 35–40.

Pesqueira, M. I., Ramírez, I., Ceruti, P., & Carter, J. (2021). Practicing clinical supervision in Chile: Lessons from 28 years of training. *Journal of Contemporary Psychotherapy, 51*, 201–210. https://doi.org/10.1007/10879-021-09494-8

Pesqueira, M. I., Ramírez, I., Ceruti, P., & Salvo, D. (2019). What and how of the inalienable leadership of the clinical supervisor. *Of Families and Therapies, 46*, 29–45. https://doi.org/10.29260/DFYT.2019.46B

Ramirez, I., Except, D., Uribe, L., & Uribe, P. (2018). *Feedback and quality assessment in clinical supervision*. Paper presented at the 15th Chilean Congress of Psychotherapy, Reñaca, Chile.

Ramirez, I., Except, D., Uribe, L., & Uribe, P. (2020). Implementation of systematic alliance feedback and therapeutic outcomes in a training center: Opportunities and challenges. *Of Families and Therapies, 49*, 91–108. https://doi.org/10.29260/DFYT.2020.49F

Riffo-Pavón, I., Basulto, Ó., & Segovia, P. (2021). The Chilean Social Outbreak of 2019: A study from social representations and imaginaries in the press. *Revista mexicana de ciencias políticas y sociales, 66*(243), 345–368. https://doi.org/10.22201/fcpys.2448492xe.2021.243.78095

SENADIS. (2015). In M. A. Figueroa & H. Inostroza (Eds.), *Disability and mental health: A vision from SENADIS*. ISBN: 978-956-8441-05-0. https://www.senadis.gob.cl/descarga/i/3179/documento

Taboada, M., & Rivas, M. (2021). A supervisory experience based on the therapist's internal dialogue, according to Peter Rober's model. *Of Families and Therapies, 50*, 67–88.

Tomicic, A., Immel, N., & Martinez, C. (2021). Experiences of psychological and psychotherapeutic help of young LGBT survivors of suicide processes. *Inter-American Journal of Psychology, 55*(1), 1–24. https://doi.org/10.30849/ripijp.v55i1.1453

Urzúa, A., Vera-Villarroel, P., Zúñiga, C., & Salas, G. (2015). Psychology in Chile: Analysis of its history, present and future. *Universitas Psychologica, 14*(3), 1141–1158. https://doi.org/10.11144/Javeriana.upsy14-3.pcah

Walkman, S. H., & Williston, M. A. (2015). The role of vulnerability and peer-supervision in establishing clinical competency. *Psychotherapy Bulletin, 50*(1), 14–17.

Watzlawick, P., Weakland, J., & Fisch, R. (1992). *CHANGE training and solution of human problems*. Editorial Herder.

Winkler, M. I., Pasmanik, D., Alvear, K., & Reyes, M. I. (2007). When psychological well-being is at stake: The ethical dimension in the professional training of psychologists in Chile. *Psychological Therapy, 25*(1), 5–24.

Zamorano, M. (2012). *Descriptive analysis of the perception of the group supervision space of a center of specialists in strategic intervention* [Master's thesis not published]. Gabriela Mistral University.

Ivonne Ramírez Clavería is a psychologist from the Pontificia Universidad Católica de Chile and holds a master's degree in clinical psychology from the same university. She is a clinical supervisor dedicated to the training of supervisors. Ivonne teaches undergraduate and graduate courses and has published on topics such as clinical supervision, feedback, and indicators of change in psychotherapy. She is a specialist in Brief Psychotherapy, trained in Strategic Coaching, and has trained at the ICCE International Center of Clinical Excellence as a therapist and FIT supervisor. Currently, Ivonne is a clinical supervisor at Universidad del Desarrollo and is dedicated to private psychotherapy practice. Email: ivonnerc@gmail.com.

José Domingo Salvo Rivera is a psychologist from the Pontificia Universidad Católica de Chile and holds a PhD in Psychotherapy from the same university. He is a clinical supervisor and an undergraduate and graduate professor, specializing in Strategic Systemic Therapy. Dr. Salvo has published works on clinical supervision, routine outcome monitoring and working with client's resources in psychotherapy. He is a professor and clinical supervisor of the Brief Psychotherapy Training program and serves as the Research Coordinator at the Psychotherapy and Coaching Training Center, MIP. Also, he is currently a professor, clinical supervisor, and researcher on therapist training at the San Sebastián University. Email: jdsalvo@gmail.com.

María Inés Pesqueira Banderas is a psychologist from the University of Chile. She has been engaged for over 30 years in supervisors' training and supervision. She is the founder and director of the Center for Training in Psychotherapy and Coaching, MIP, and the EAS Chile clinic. She is a specialist in Strategic Cognitive Behavioral and Systemic Psychotherapy and has trained at the ICCE International Center of Clinical Excellence as a therapist and FIT supervisor. María Inés has published on clinical supervision in Chile and on the principles and style of supervision developed at Centro MIP. Email: mipesqueira@centromip.cl.

Clinical Supervision in Colombian Psychology: Current Status

Mónica Novoa Gómez

Introduction

Clinical supervision is an essential moment for the development of the necessary skills for clinical psychology and psychotherapy. It allows the consolidation of academic learning, attitudes, knowledge, and skills needed for the profession (Novoa-Gómez et al. 2019a; Falender, 2014a; Martino et al., 2016), improves the quality of clinical care (Reiser & Milne, 2014); and, due to its pedagogical modality, the student articulates theory and intervention to strengthen both therapeutic and research competencies (Ballesteros de Valderrama et al., 2019).

While teaching clinical skills, the supervisor explores and evaluates the supervisees' observations, feelings, and thoughts (Tomlin et al., 2014; Watkins & Scaturo, 2013) to make sense of them in the framework of the clinical care process.

Supervision models establish a series of objectives concerning the relationship between supervisor and supervisee that are based on education and training, management, development, and evaluation of the latter's work (Milne, 2009b; Rodolfa et al., 2013) so that the supervisee can receive support if needed (Callaghan, 2006a; Milne, 2009b), receive in-training and be evaluated on the development of specific competencies (APA, 2015; Callahan et al., 2017; Falender, 2014b; Rodolfa et al., 2013, Rosenbluth et al., 2016) while seeking the well-being and protection of the consultant (APA, 2015; Bastidas-Bilbao & Velásquez, 2016; Bernard & Goodyear, 2014; Callaghan, 2006a; Falender, 2014b; Milne, 2009b; Newman, 2010; Reiser & Milne, 2014).

Falender et al. (2004) posit competencies as a habitual and judicious use of communication, knowledge, technical skills, clinical reasoning, emotions, values, and reflections that are used in practice and further summarized as knowledge, skills,

M. Novoa Gómez (✉)
Fundación Universitaria Konrad Lorenz, Bogotá, Colombia

M. P. Grazioso et al. (eds.), *Clinical Supervision in Latin America*,
https://doi.org/10.1007/978-3-031-82373-2_11

and attitudes (Falender, 2014b) that require systematic feedback for their development (APA, 2015; Carmel et al., 2016; Newman, 2010).

The training of professionals in psychology requires not only the theoretical and conceptual skills imparted in the educational training process but also implies that these become evident in practice. In congruence, researchers such as González et al. (2021) indicate that the experience of the clinical professional is not so relevant, since if he/she has not had an effective supervision and previous training that allows him/her to transmit this knowledge to the student, the professional could present difficulties when interacting with his/her supervisees since he/she will present deficiencies in developing, modeling, and molding certain skills that guarantee competence to practice in the clinical context.

Professional and Regulatory Context of Supervision in Colombia

In contrast to the prolific regulatory development of supervision in other parts of the world, especially in Europe and Australia, in Latin America developments are incipient and mainly of a theoretical or documentary type (Novoa-Gómez & Córdoba, 2019; Castañeda-Quirama & Velásquez-Castrillón, 2021; Bastidas-Bilbao & Velásquez, 2016; Bautista, 2014; Hernández, 2008; Rodriguez & Niño, 2006 in Colombia; Loubat, 2005 in Chile; Wielenska & Oshiro, 2012 in Brazil). This level of production may be related to a low level of regional attention to supervision.

In Colombia, of the regulations governing training programs, Decree 1527 (Presidency of Colombia, 2002) defines the standards in the professional training of psychologists; and Resolution 3461 (Ministry of Education, 2013) establishes the specific guidelines for assessing the quality of programs. The normative guidelines derived from them determinate that the semesters of professional practice are an enforceable requirement to guarantee quality training and that these must be supervised by psychologists specialized in each of the scenarios, cores, and professional domains (Echeverry Gallo, 2018).

The internship is a pedagogical strategy structured by higher education institutions, which aims at academic training in the provision of health services (Decree 2376 of 2010). In addition, Decree 1075 of 2015 determines an obligation of university institutions to ensure that the professional has the competencies established by Law 1090 of 2006 to perform in the workplace, which is justified in the evaluation of curricular content by the chambers of the National Commission for Quality Assurance of the Ministry of National Education—CONACES. Consistently, psychology academic programs include semesters of professional practice integrated into their curricula and are usually carried out in the last semesters of the course.

Despite the breadth of the concept of health in psychology and the epistemological and theoretical inconsistencies expressed by the discipline itself regarding equivalence with the medical model, CONACES values clinical psychology and psychotherapy, health psychology and neuropsychology as exclusive to the health sector, and requires universities to ensure that students' academic practices conform to the teaching-service model, typical of medicine and related disciplines, to integrate university training with the provision of health services in hospitals, medical centers, clinics, and institutions providing health services. In summary, psychology programs have a curriculum that promotes the development of competencies that are fundamental in the processes of assessment, diagnosis, and intervention; responding to the requirements made by the Ministry of Education, Health and Social Protection regarding the training that a student must have to carry out his or her practice process in the clinical and health field (Norcross, 2004; Narváez, 2016). The requirement of the National Ministry of Education to psychology undergraduate programs to implement the supervision of clinical practices in order to obtain operating permits is based on the idea that psychology is a mental health profession, referring to its dimension of problems and disorders, as was relevant in the messages and studies derived from the health and social emergency by COVID-19. This normative proposal is aligned with international initiatives that highlight the complexity of the functions performed by the psychologist, it also points out the need for the student to have a continuous accompaniment by a professional-supervisor who guides the execution of clinical processes, thus ensuring a collaborative learning that promotes a praxis with a higher level of competence (Benatuil & Laurito, 2015; Corlett, 2015; Jalil & Gómez, 2016; Rodríguez & Fernández, 2014).

According to data from the observatory of the Colombian Association of Faculties of Psychology (ASCOFAPSI) and the National Higher Education Information System (SNIES), 136 undergraduate and 108 graduate programs in psychology are registered in the country. Very few of these postgraduate programs are offered in the distance or virtual modality. To practice the profession of psychology, which includes psychotherapy and clinical practice, in Colombia it is necessary to have an undergraduate university degree in psychology issued by a university duly recognized by the Ministry of National Education, which is regulated by Law 1164 of 2007, which also establishes the requirements for hiring and removal of health professionals, including psychologists. The practice of psychology is regulated by Law 1090 of 2006, which establishes the requirements for obtaining a license to practice psychology, one of which is participation in continuing education and clinical supervision programs. In addition, psychologists must be included in the National Registry of Health Professionals (RETHUS), which is a public database in which all psychology professionals who meet the legal and ethical requirements to practice the profession are registered. To be included in this registry, one must have a degree in psychology from a university and work in the clinical area.

In Colombia, several associations and organizations promote training, dialogue and learning on topics such as clinical supervision, competencies in the training of psychologists, clinical psychology and others, including the Colombian College of Psychologists (COLPSIC) and the Colombian Association of Psychology Faculties (ASCOFAPSI), the ones that have the greatest impact due to their role as representatives of the law at the training and professional level.

In addition to these, private professional associations, which bring together psychologists for theoretical dissemination or work models, carry out nonformal education and consulting activities in various fields. Nonformal education is offered to complement, update, and supplement knowledge and training in academic or labor aspects without being subject to the system of levels and grades established for formal education and is regulated by Law 115 of 1994 and Decrees 114 of 1996 and 3011 of 1997. To date, none of them explicitly offers or promotes qualification in supervision; although some of them, which train therapists in specific techniques, include hours of clinical practice supervised by professionals certified in them (examples are: ACBS Colombia, Socolpsi, Fundaterapia, Foro Colombia, among others). The truth is that there are no reports of cases or supervision models, which makes it impossible to establish the orientation, modalities or scope of the role of the clinical supervisor.

At the postgraduate level, in formal terms and with recognition from the Ministry of Education, there are specializations and master's degrees in clinical psychology and psychotherapy, which include, as a requirement, several hours of supervised clinical practice, as required for programs at the professional level. Such programs offer training in clinical psychology, which includes clinical practicum hours that require students to perform under clinical supervision as part of their training, allowing them to gain experience from other senior clinical psychologists.

It is important to note that the COVID-19 pandemic had a significant impact on clinical practice in general, including clinical supervision. Many clinical psychologists had to adapt their practices to the constraints of social distancing, which has increased the use of telepsychology and other forms of virtual care. This has also affected clinical supervision, which has had to adapt to new forms of clinical practice. At a practical level, they are visible in the proposed guidelines for the care of the population through telepsychology in the context of telehealth that has emerged as a result of the COVID-19 pandemic (Acero et al., 2020; Ministry of Health and Social Protection, 2020).

Supervisor Training

In most countries, including Colombia, experience in clinical practice, teaching skills, and training are required to be a clinical supervisor in psychology, but since there is no stable or decentralized offer for specialized training in clinical supervision in specific terms that promotes and guarantees the fulfillment of such requirements, the certification of the supervisor's competencies is not regulated and therefore the criteria on which higher education institutions rely to certify these requirements is quite lax.

This training or the development of these skills can be acquired through courses offered by some graduate programs in clinical psychology, but especially through participation in continuing education programs and workshops specialized in clinical supervision offered by some universities.

As of March 2023, only two clinical supervisor training programs have been offered (F. Universitaria Konrad Lorenz and Universidad de los Andes), under the perspective of the evidence-based supervision model (Milne & Reiser, 2017) that was developed based on teaching and learning strategies similar to those suggested for supervision and provides a supervision model that can be implemented systematically and can be evaluated in a specific way. The growing interest of professionals to improve their clinical supervision competencies is a factor that increases the demand for training and drives universities and higher education institutions to include them in their program offerings. These extension courses have had some graduates who are beginning to spread the importance of training for the practice of supervision. These programs are part of the continuing education courses for professionals (extension seminars and diploma courses). Undoubtedly, there will be an impulse to think about the constitution of an accreditation body to supervise the quality of these training programs.

It is important to emphasize that in the framework of this limited offer of qualification to clinical supervisors, very few of the mental health professionals who today are dedicated to the work of training clinical practitioners have received specific training in the subject, as say (Ballesteros de Valderrama et al., 2019).

Supervisors, Current Situation

A study conducted by Novoa-Gómez et al. (2019a, 2019b) characterized the state of clinical supervision in the country, following a mixed methodology, which used a multi-method-multi-source system and combined descriptive and functional levels of analysis. Sixty-four clinical practice supervisors in psychology were evaluated, in 25 undergraduate and graduate programs, linked to universities in different regions of Colombia.

The purpose of this study was to analyze clinical supervision practices in some categories: objectives, methodologies, elements of the relationship between supervisor and supervisee, competencies of the supervisee, evaluation, training, knowledge of the supervisees, and to discuss the relevance of training for clinical supervision according to what is described by evidence-based training models.

Relevance of Supervisory Training

The supervisors were asked about the training they have received for this work and their perception of the need for it. Fifty percent of the respondents reported that they had received training; in contrast to this statement, 90.3% of the participants said that they were unaware of training resources or programs. This implies that at least 40% of the supervisors contradict themselves, since they report having the training to supervise, but have not been trained to do so. In addition, it was found that of the supervisors surveyed, only 48.9% are aware of how Colombian law governs, controls, and limits supervision and clinical practice. This points to the need for dissemination and appropriation of supervision as an independent professional competence since training as a psychologist is not synonymous with competencies in supervision (Falender, 2014a, 2014b).

Supervision Objectives

The development of clinical skills in the supervisee (X = 1.96) was the most important of all those listed by the supervisors, followed by the development of the ability to identify the competencies one has and which ones should be learned for clinical work (meta-competence) (X = 2.36), by the protection of the client (X = 2.38), and, finally, providing feedback to the supervisee on his/her performance in the therapeutic process and on his/her performance in the supervision process (X = 3.23).

Supervision Methodologies

Group supervision is the second in use, with similar percentages between occasional use or as the main supervision strategy (see Table 1). Before COVID-19, the most used type was asynchronous individual supervision and the least used was virtual supervision; but with the changes faced after the requirements of virtual education and care, updating the current methodology is a task to be developed.

There are different modalities for delivering supervision: direct and synchronous, such as co-therapy which is an ideal form of supervision (Falke et al., 2015). There is the direct and asynchronous when it is done without the supervisor being physically present in the supervisee's therapeutic session, but is available (Whalen & Wendel, 2011) and through video or audio recordings. Finally, indirect and asynchronous when supervision does not occur at the same time as the session and is based on verbal or written reporting of what happened in session or written reports of what was done in session (Borders et al., 2014; Callaghan, 2006a, 2006b; Falender, 2014b; Martino et al., 2016; Newman, 2010; Reiser & Milne, 2012).

The most commonly used is indirect and asynchronous supervision, in which supervisors rely on written records of the session and the supervisee's oral report, which involves indirect knowledge of the session. The least employed is the reliance

Table 1 Percentage of frequency of use of monitoring modalities

Type of supervision	All sessions	Monthly	Semiannual	Never
Individual supervision	43.3	20.0	10.0	3.3
Group supervision	35.0	23.3	10.0	8.3
Virtual supervision	3.3	31.6	18.3	23.3

on video records of the therapeutic session and there is no trend in the use of direct and synchronous supervision. This contrasts with the suggestions of Borders et al. (2014) and Falender (2014a, 2014b) that involve the use of audio records, video, and live observation (Gesell Chamber).

In undergraduate programs, group supervision is more frequently used, while in postgraduate programs, supervision is typically based on videos, records, and case formulation. Finally, when comparing the methodologies used by supervisors by region, it is observed that the central region most frequently uses supervision based on video and audio recordings (see Table 2).

The above is complemented by the study of Ballesteros de Valderrama et al. (2019) who established the techniques most used by supervisors from the behavioral perspective to achieve training objectives: formulation of clinical cases, theoretical discussion, feedback, modeling, and shaping.

Relationship Elements

Regarding the elements of the supervisor-supervisee relationship, greater agreement was found with supervision as a space between colleagues where there is an exchange of knowledge for learning (X = 4.35), than on the opinion that there should be a directive and obedience relationship (X = 2.09), which is consistent with the literature. It has been posited that there is a parallel between the supervisory relationship and the therapeutic relationship (Bell et al., 2016; Hess, 1987).

These findings regarding the practice of supervision in Colombia are encouraging, as the central role of the working relationship in supervision has been highlighted by several authors.

Table 2 Percentage of frequency of use of monitoring strategies

Supervision strategy	All sessions	Monthly	Semiannual	Never
Direct and synchronous	10.0	18.3	15.0	35.0
Indirect and asynchronous	53.3	13.3	5.0	5.0
Based on video records	0	5.0	13.3	58.3
Based on written records and session protocols	48.3	16.6	8.3	3.3
Based on the supervisee's oral report	66.6	6.6	1.6	0
Based on case formulations	36.6	30.0	8.3	1.6
Through the use of specific therapeutic protocols	25.0	21.6	10.0	20.0

Competencies Developed by Supervisees

The Friedman test was used and significant differences were found (x = 93.8, gl = 12, p = .00, n = 46), when performing a bootstrap analysis, no skill was identified as being different from the others (95% confidence). This is consistent with what is reported in the literature, which does not make an assessment or hierarchy of the competencies to be transmitted, however, it does offer a logical framework of organization in the training and acquisition of competencies to optimize the training process and ensure the optimal development of the supervisee at the various levels of training (Borders et al., 2014; Falender, 2014a, 2014b; Hatcher et al., 2013).

The level of importance given by supervisors to these competencies was compared according to the level and using the chi-square test it was found that more supervisors at the postgraduate level consider it important to transmit efficient information management (x = 6109, gl = 1, p = .01, n = 46) and intervention skills (x = 6972, gl = 1, p = .01, n = 46). These findings may account for the needs that supervisors have at this level of training, focusing on practical practice as a therapist and implying less emphasis on the training of basic framework acquisition skills that should be acquired at earlier levels of training (e.g., undergraduate) (Rodolfa et al., 2005, 2012).

Supervision Evaluation

Regarding the evaluation of supervision, 60% of supervisors use some instrument to evaluate the supervision process, 78% use verbal feedback, while 38.2% use the institution's evaluation; finally, only 36.4% of the participants report that the evaluation is qualitatively carried out through a written document. In addition, there are no differences between the use of instruments and evaluation criteria. Ideally, this evaluation should not be unidirectional but should include the supervisee's evaluation of the supervisor's performance and the effect of the supervisor's behavior on the supervisee and the case. The fact that there are no significant differences in the use of any evaluation method is consistent with the literature, which does not report a hierarchy in evaluation methods.

Functional Analysis of the Supervisory Relationship

The strategies for measuring and training therapists are based on the interaction of the supervisor with the supervisee, which is natural since this is considered the vehicle through which the teaching variables are conducted (Cheon et al., 2009).

In a study conducted by Novoa-Gómez et al. (2019a, 2019b), a description of the types of responses that occur between the supervisor and the supervisee during the supervision process was sought for the formation of competencies of the supervisee. For this purpose, the same strategy was used as in the FASIT to organize the competencies suggested by the APA for therapist training. Subsequently, an observation of several interactions between supervisors and supervisees during their supervision was conducted to determine the frequency of occurrence of these kinds of responses. The study shows that the skills related to the psychologist's work in therapy are those that have a higher percentage of occurrence when the supervisor initiates the interaction, among them are the interactions aimed at training skills for assessment, intervention, and for conceptual management.

Skills Related to the Work of the Clinician

Assessment and intervention skills were presented in a higher percentage than the others, which coincides with the results of Rodolfa et al. (2013), in which it was evidenced that clusters related to assessment and intervention were considered essential for professional practice. On the other hand, a very low percentage of self-evaluation was presented in the supervision session, a fundamental competence (Karel et al., 2014), In addition, it is identified that both supervisees and supervisors initiate few interactions that lead to the formation of autonomy in the supervisee.

Fundamental Knowledge for Therapy

It is evident that the theoretical and conceptual knowledge required by supervisees occupies a fundamental place within supervision, this is consistent with Callaghan (2006a), Rodolfa et al. (2013), and Milne et al. (2011a, 2011b) who suggest that such competence should be integrated with the clinical skills developed during the supervision process, complemented with the supervisor's knowledge and methodology.

Cultural and Diversity Issues that Are Particularly Salient in Your Country

However, other related competencies, such as knowledge of legal aspects ethical case management and diversity skills occupy a small space in supervision. Hatcher et al. (2013) postulate that ethics—as a transversal competence to all the psychologist's work should have ample space within the process and exercises and activities should be carried out in which ethical and legal dilemmas are identified and resolved.

Regarding diversity training and taking into account that in Bogota immigration from other regions of the country is frequent, this aspect must be taken into account.

Interpersonal Relationship Skills

In general, a low dedication to the training of interpersonal skills of supervisees is identified. For example, skills such as conflict management, bidirectional communication, and interpersonal closeness are found in occurrences below 5%. This is striking because they are an important part of establishing adherence and therapeutic bonding (Duff & Shahin, 2010).

The skill in this set that occurs most often, in the case of supervisor-initiated interactions, is two-way communication. Interactions centered on bidirectional communication seek the training of the supervisee's discrimination or efficient response to the impact it has on others, which facilitates the formation of the therapeutic relationship with the consultant or the professional relationship with the supervisor (Callaghan, 2006c) and in this sense seems incompatible with an authoritarian relationship with the supervisee. This may be positive since according to several authors, authoritarian styles of supervision are considered a negative event in supervision, hindering the progress and learning of the supervisee (Grant et al., 2012; Herschell et al., 2010; Ramos-Sánchez et al., 2002). Despite this, it is an interaction with low occurrence, which implies that probably, more attention should be paid to the formation and use of these competencies.

An Appropriate Monitoring Approach for Colombia

It has been described that the Colombian regulation contemplates very general guidelines on supervision, applicable to the health professions and that for this reason, the training for the formation of supervisors that is offered is not mandatory and lacks specifications that standardize them, being the proposals very different from each other and resulting in the absence of an evaluation of competencies in the supervisory processes. The results of this review show the need for supervisors to receive formal training in the development of clinical supervision competencies.

The need for clinical supervision that ensures the protection of society and the development of competencies of the therapist-in-training is pressing. First, in Colombia, the Ministry of Health and Social Protection (2006), according to Law 1090 (Congress of the Republic, 2006), authorizes all psychologists with an undergraduate degree to practice any activity of teaching, application, and indication of psychological knowledge and its specific techniques. This fact diminishes the possibility of guaranteeing the clinical competencies required by professionals in this field. Secondly, the training of professionals in clinical and health areas requires compliance with supervision standards.

The absence of training programs and the need for training on the part of supervisors, however, is not very different from what is happening in the rest of the world. Globally, there seem to be no programs that train and evaluate the exercise of supervision outside a long number of recommendations, even when there is proliferative research on the methodological and theoretical level content of supervision (Falender & Shafranske, 2017; Milne et al., 2011a, 2011b). In such a program supervisory knowledge, skills, and attitudes must be systematically developed and monitored to ensure the development of supervisory competencies in the supervisor, positive impact on the supervisory relationship, and improvement in therapy outcomes and supervisee competencies (Falender & Shafranske, 2017).

The need for training programs is evident from a variety of sources. For example, in "the USA, the importance of research on defining what skills a supervisor should have, measuring and training them was seen" (Fleming et al., 1996, p. 6). In Australia, Spence et al. (2001) conducted a study with four mental health professionals that brought to their attention the paucity of information on the most effective ways to train supervisors. In a follow-up by Milne and James (2002) of a supervisor with expertise in cognitive behavioral therapy, they found deficiencies in his competence, even though he had accreditation from two professional organizations. Falender and Shafranske (2004) state, as a result of a summary of surveys, that formal training in supervision is not available to most psychologists in the USA. Fleming (cited in Milne, 2009a) notes that, in the UK, a survey found that most supervisors had some training and coaching, but there was variation in the design of the training received. The above data, from studies on the reality of supervision in different countries, shows the need to work on the training of clinical supervisors, as expressed by Milne (2009a).

Given the need to offer supervision that allows the development of the functions that have been attributed to it, concern has arisen about the competencies of the supervisor to exercise this function (Acosta et al. 2018) because it ignores the particularity of the training of psychologists and pretends to equate it with the traditional professions in the health sector (Botero-García et al., 2022). Studies such as those of González et al. (2021) point out that psychologists with more years of experience who have not had a clinical supervision process do not develop an effective experience in comparison with younger therapists who have received supervision in the field; since according to Ericsson (2006) cited in González et al. (2021) in the last periods of competency acquisition, there is a tendency to mechanize the activity so that making changes is an important task and more so being willing to improve performance, which is why researchers such as Goodyear et al. (2017) mention the importance of making improvements and actualization in therapists, being one of the priority tasks since currently many of the professionals dedicated to the clinic as their main means of support, according to the study conducted by Jiménez-Pérez et al. (2022), approximately 54.6% of the participants recognize the term evidence-based practices, however, when it comes to applying a strategy, they use methods not by evidence-based psychology, which may be derived from the lack of knowledge from their training processes among other factors that may be immersed.

References

Acero, P., Cabas, K., Caycedo, C., Figueroa, P., Patrick, G., & Rudas, M. M. (2020). *Telepsicología: Sugerencias para la formación y el desempeño profesional responsable*. Ascofapsi y Colpsic. https://ascofapsi.org.co/pdf/Libros/Telepsicologia_web.pdf

Acosta, M. R., Agudelo, D., Alarcón, A., Caycedo, C., Moncada, L., Novoa, M., & Utría, O. (2018). *Condiciones de calidad de las prácticas profesionales en psicología clínica, neuropsicología y psicología de la salud*. Ascofapsi. https://www.ascofapsi.org.co/observatorio/wp-content/uploads/2020/08/CONDICIONES-DE-CALIDAD-DE-LAS-PR%C3%81CTICAS-PROFESIONALES-EN-PSICOLOGIA-CL%C3%8DNICA-Y-PSICOLOG%C3%8DA-DE-LA-SALUD-2018.pdf

American Psychological Association. (2015). Guidelines for clinical supervision in health service psychology. *The American Psychologist, 70*, 33–46. https://doi.org/10.1037/a0038112

Ballesteros de Valderrama, B. P., Muñoz-Martínez, A. M., Novoa-Gómez, M., Bazzani-Orrego, D., Brandwayn-Briceño, N. E., Lasso-Báez, R. A., Pachón-Basallo, M., & Restrepo-Vélez, D. (2019). Características de la supervisión clínica en las terapias conductuales: un análisis del proceso de supervisión clínica. *Universitas Psychologica, 18*(4), 1–14. https://doi.org/10.11144/Javeriana.upsy18-4.csct

Bastidas-Bilbao, H., & Velásquez, A. M. (2016). Modelo lógico de la supervisión como actividad educativa para la formación en psicología clínica: Conceptions of Clinical Supervisors. *Avances en Psicología Latinoamericana, 34*(2), 293–314. https://doi.org/10.12804/apl34.2.2016.06

Bautista, A. M. (2014). Movilización de los aprendizajes de terapeutas en formación que surgen de las conversaciones reflexivas a partir de la emergencia del observador en el contexto de supervisión. *Quaestiones Disputatae: temas en debate, 7*(14), 67–80.

Benatuil, D., & Laurito, J. (2015). The role of supervised practicums in a sample of Psychology students from a private university in Argentina. PSIENCIA. *Revista Latinoamericana de Ciencia Psicológica, 7*(2). https://doi.org/10.5872/psiencia/7.2.141

Bernard, J. M., & Goodyear, R. J. (2014). *Fundamentals of clinical supervision* (5th ed.). Pearson.

Borders, L. D., Glosoff, H. L., Welfare, L. E., Hays, D. G., DeKruyf, L., Fernando, D. M., & Page, B. (2014). Best practices in clinical supervision: Evolution of a counseling specialty. *The Clinical Supervisor, 33*(1), 26–44. https://doi.org/10.1080/07325223.2014.905225

Botero-García, C., Giovanni, I., & Arias, C. M. (2022). Supervisión en psicología clínica: Una revisión sobre estudios empíricos 2012–2021. *Universitas Psychologica, 21*, 1–19.

Corlett, L. (2015). Future models of supervision: supporting practice and promoting professional growth and well-being in educational psychology through Collaborative Peer Support (CPS). *Educational and Child Psychology, 32*(3), 90–104.

Callaghan, G. (2006b). Functional Analytic Psychotherapy and Supervision. *International Journal of Behavioral and Consultation Therapy, 3*(2), 416–431. https://doi.org/10.1037/h0100794

Callaghan, G. M. (2006a). The Functional Idiographic Assessment Template (FIAT) system: For use with interpersonally-based interventions including Functional Analytic Psychotherapy (FAP) and FAP-enhanced treatments. *The Behavior Analyst Today, 7*(3), 357. https://doi.org/10.1037/h0100160

Callahan, J. L., Neumann, C. S., Cox, R. J., & Ruggero, C. J. (2017). The Supervisor Trainee Quarterly Evaluation (STQE): Psychometric support for use as a measure of competency. *Training and Education in Professional Psychology*. https://doi.org/10.1037/tep0000140

Carmel, A., Villatte, J. L., Rosenthal, M. Z., Chalker, S., & Comtois, K. A. (2016). Applying technological approaches to clinical supervision in dialectical behavior therapy: A randomized feasibility trial of the bug-in-the-eye (BITE) model. *Cognitive and Behavioral Practice, 23*(2), 221–229. https://doi.org/10.1016/j.cbpra.2015.08.001

Castañeda-Quirama, L. T., & Velásquez-Castrillón, J. A. (2021). Supervisión clínica en las prácticas profesionales de psicología. *Catálogo Editorial, 1*(145), 133–142. https://doi.org/10.15765/poli.v1i145.2826

Echeverri Gallo, C. (2018). Significados y contribuciones de las prácticas profesionales a la formación de pregrado en psicología. *Avances En Psicología Latinoamericana, 36*(3), 569–584. https://doi.org/10.12804/revistas.urosario.edu.co/apl/a.5490

Ericsson, K. A. (2006). The influence of experience and deliberate practice on the development of superior expert performance. In: *The Cambridge handbook of expertise and expert performance* (Vol. 38, pp. 685–705). http://doi.org/dc78

Falender, C. A. (2014a). Supervision outcomes: Beginning the journey beyond the emperor's new clothes. *Training and Education in Professional Psychology, 8*(3), 143–148. https://doi.org/10.1037/tep0000066

Falender, C. A. (2014b). Clinical supervision in a competency-based era. *South African Journal of Psychology, 44*(1), 6–17. https://doi.org/10.1177/0081246313516260

Falender, C. A., Cornish, J. A. E., Goodyear, R., Hatcher, R., Kaslow, N. J., Leventhal, G., Shafranske, E., Sigmon, S., Stoltenberg, C., & Grus, C. (2004). Defining competencies in psychology supervision: A consensus statement. *Journal of Clinical Psychology, 60*(7), 771–785. https://doi.org/10.1002/jclp.20013

Falender, C. A., & Shafranske, E. P. (2017). Competency-based clinical supervision: Status, opportunities, tensions, and the future. *Australian Psychologist, 52*(2), 86–93. https://doi.org/10.1111/ap.12265

Falke, S. I., Lawson, L., Pandit, M. L., & Patrick, E. A. (2015). Participant supervision: Supervisor and supervisee experiences of therapy. *Journal of Marital and Family Therapy, 41*(2), 150–162. https://doi.org/10.1111/jmft.12039

Fleming, R. K., Oliver, J. R., & Bolton, D. M. (1996). Training supervisors to train staff: A case study in a human service organization. *Journal of Organizational Behaviour Management, 16*, 3–25.

González, A. L., Elvira, A. C., & Escagedo, M. C. G. (2021). El efecto de la experiencia y la supervisión clínica sobre el éxito terapéutico en la Clínica Universitaria de la Universidad Autónoma de Madrid (CPA-UAM). *Análisis y Modificación de Conducta, 47*(175).

Hernández, P. (2008). The cultural context model in clinical supervision. *Training and Education in Professional Psychology, 2*(1), 10–17. https://doi.org/10.1037/1931-3918.2.1.10

Jalil, B. G., & Gómez, R. D. (2016). Modelo de acompañamiento del proceso de práctica profesional en Psicología: una experiencia pedagógica. En *VII Coloquio Internacional de Educación.* Universidad del Cauca, Colombia.

Jiménez-Pérez, A. L., Vargas-Contreras, E., Estrada-Vergara, N. Y., & Arreola-Sánchez, I. A. (2022). Práctica Basada en Evidencia en Adicciones: Conocimientos y Habilidades de Psicoterapeutas del Noroeste de México. *Acta de Investigación Psicológica, 12*(1).

LLEWELYN, S. (2004). Psychotherapy Relationships that Work J. Norcross (Ed.) Oxford: Oxford University Press, 2002. pp. 452. 49.50 (hardback). ISBN: 0-19-514346-9. *Behavioural and Cognitive Psychotherapy, 32*(2), 255–256. https://doi.org/10.1017/s1352465804241339.

Loubat, T. (2005). Supervisión en psicoterapia: Una posición sustentada en la experiencia clínica. *Terapia psicológica, 23*(2), 75–84.

Martino, S., Paris, M., Añez, L., Nich, C., Canning-Ball, M., Hunkele, K., & Carroll, K. M. (2016). The effectiveness and cost of clinical supervision for motivational interviewing: A randomized controlled trial. *Journal of Substance Abuse Treatment, 68*, 11–23. https://doi.org/10.1016/j.jsat.2016.04.005

Milne, D. L. (2009a). Can we enhance the training of clinical supervisors? A national pilot study of an evidence-based approach. *Clinical Psychology and Psychotherapy, 17*, 321–328. https://doi.org/10.1002/cpp.657

Milne, D. L. (2009b). *Evidence-Based Clinical Supervision: Principles and practice*. The British Psychological Society and Blackwell Publishing Ltd.

Milne, D. L., & James, I. A. (2002). The observed impact of training on competence in clinical supervision. *British Journal of Clinical Psychology, 41*, 55–72. https://doi.org/10.1348/014466502163796

Milne, D. L., & Reiser, R. (2017). *A manual for Evidence-Based CBT Supervision*. Wiley – Blackwell.

Milne, D. L., Reiser, R. P., Cliffe, T., & Raine, R. (2011a). SAGE: Preliminary evaluation of an instrument for observing competence in CBT supervision. *The Cognitive Behavior Therapist, 4*, 123–138.

Milne, D. L., Sheikh, A. I., Pattison, S., & Wilkinson, A. (2011b). Evidence-based training for clinical supervisors: A systematic review of 11 controlled studies. *The Clinical Supervisor, 30*(1), 53–71. https://doi.org/10.1080/07325223.2011.564955

Narváez, A. A. (2016). Realización de las Prácticas en Psicología Clínica en el Hospital Universitario del Valle "Evaristo García" E.S.E durante la crisis del 2015-2016. *Revista de Psicología GEPU, 7*(2), 194-ss.

Newman, C. F. (2010). Competency in conducting cognitive–behavioral therapy: Foundational, functional, and supervisory aspects. *Psychotherapy: Theory, Research, Practice, Training, 47*(1), 12. https://doi.org/10.1037/a0018849

Novoa-Gómez, M., & Córdoba, Ó. A. (2019). Pertinencia de la formación para la supervisión clínica. *Diálogos sobre investigación*. Fundación Universitaria Konrad Lorez.

Novoa-Gómez, M., & Córdoba-Salgado, O. (inédito). Revisión Sistemática de la Producción Científica en Supervisión Clínica (1982-2017). Repositorio universitario FUKL.

Novoa-Gómez, M., Córdoba-Salgado, O., Rojas, N., Sosa, L., & Cifuentes, D. (2019a). A descriptive analysis of the interactions during clinical supervision. *Frontiers in Psychology, 10*, 669.

Novoa-Gómez, M., Córdoba-Salgado, O., Rojas, N., Sosa, L., Cifuentes, D. A., Robayo, S., & Pardo, N. (2019b). *Competencias profesionales en Psicología clínica: Pertinencia de la formación para la supervisión clínica*. Fundación Universitaria Konrad Lorenz. Repositorio Universitario FUKL.

Reiser, R. P., & Milne, D. (2012). Supervising cognitive-behavioral psychotherapy: Pressing needs, impressing possibilities. *Journal of Contemporary Psychotherapy, 42*(3), 161–171. https://doi.org/10.1007/s10879-011-9200-6

Rodolfa, E., Bent, R., Eisman, E., Nelson, P., Rehm, L., & Ritchie, P. (2005). A cube model for competency development: Implications for psychology educators and regulators. *Professional Psychology: Research and Practice, 36*(4), 347–354. https://doi.org/10.1037/0735-7028.36.4.347

Rodolfa, E., Greenberg, S., Hunsley, J., Smith-Zoeller, M., Cox, D., Sammons, M., Caro, C., & Spivak, H. (2013). A competency model for the practice of psychology. *Training and Education in Professional Psychology, 7*(2), 71–83. https://doi.org/10.1037/a0032415

Rodríguez, B. y Fernández, A. (2014). La supervisión. En A. Moreno (Ed.), Manual de terapia sistémica (pp. 555-ss). Desclée de Brouwer. Recuperado de https://www.edesclee.com/img/cms/pdfs/9788433027375.pdf

Rodriguez, D., & Niño, J. A. (2006). Marco comprensivo para el estudio de los procesos de formación de terapeutas. *Diversitas, 2*(1), 42–54. https://doi.org/10.15332/s1794-9998.2006.0001.03

Rosenbluth, A., Cruzat-Mandich, C. V., & Ugarte, M. L. (2016). Metodología para validar un instrumento de evaluación por competencias en estudiantes de Psicología. *Universitas Psychologica, 15*(1), 303–314.

Spence, S. H., Wilson, J., Cavanag, D., Strong, J., & Worrall, L. (2001). Clinical Supervision in four mental health professions: A review of the evidence. *Behavior Change, 18*, 135–155.

Tomlin, A. M., Weatherston, D. J., & Pavkov, T. (2014). Critical components of reflective supervision: Responses from expert supervisors in the field. *Infant Mental Health Journal, 35*, 70–80. https://doi.org/10.1002/imhj.21420

Watkins, E., & Scaturo, D. (2013). Toward an integrative, learning-based model of psychotherapy supervision: Supervisory alliance, educational interventions, and supervisee learning/relearning. *Journal of Psychotherapy Integration, 23*, 75–95. https://doi.org/10.1037/a0031330

Whalen, T., & Wendel, G. (2011). New supervision standards: Discussion and justification. In I. Philibert & S. Amis Jr (Eds.), *The ACGME 2011 duty hour standards: Enhancing quality of care, supervision, and resident professional development* (pp. 39–45). ACGME.

Wielenska, R. C., & Oshiro, C. K. B. (2012). FAP group supervision: Reporting educational experiences at the University of São Paulo, Brazil. *International Journal of Behavioral Consultation and Therapy, 7*(2–3), 177–181. https://doi.org/10.1037/h0100953

Mónica Novoa Gómez holds a PhD in Psychology and a master's degree in psychology with an emphasis on behavior analysis. She also has a Diploma in Advanced Studies in Functional Analysis of Clinical and Health Contexts. Dr. Novo Gomez is an associate professor and senior researcher at Colciencias, focusing on clinical and health issues, clinical intervention, and mental health in contexts of psychosocial vulnerability and cultures of peace. She is also a trainer in clinical competencies, with a special emphasis on clinical supervision and the training of trainers/supervisors. She serves as a consultant for non-governmental organizations and the state, and she is a peer evaluator for the National Accreditation Council attached to the Ministry of National Education. Additionally, she is the Coordinator of the Permanent Committee on Mental Health Policies of COLPSIC. Email: mnovoagomez@gmail.com.

Part V
Reflections and Future Horizons

Demystifying Clinical Supervision: Essential Concepts and Practices

Rodney K. Goodyear and Carol A. Falender

Clinical supervision shares common origins with psychotherapy. In fact, the first written record of supervision had it occurring with Freud meeting with a small group of his followers in his living room (Freud, 1914/1986). Subsequently, for many of the following decades, mental health professionals assumed that if they were good therapists, they would be good supervisors or that they simply would "learn by osmosis" as they viewed supervision from their perspective as supervisees (Falender, 2018). But exceptional athletes do not necessarily make effective coaches and the same is true about mental health professionals who transition to the role of supervisor (Bernard & Goodyear, 2019). It is important, of course, to "know the game." But both coaching and supervising require additional competencies related to teaching and monitoring. Our point is that supervision is a distinct area of professional competence for which its practitioners should receive specific, systematic preparation (Falender & Shafranske, 2021).

As the field's embrace of this perspective has grown, so too has the literature on clinical supervision. In fact, it now has become quite robust in quality and quantity. That literature initially was dominated by Western (and Northern tier) scholars, although that has begun to change as supervision becomes increasingly international. This attention to supervision internationally has, in turn, spurred attempts to differentiate aspects of supervision that are universal versus that those which are unique to particular countries or regions (see Falender et al., 2021). Part II of this book examined how supervision is practiced differently across various countries,

R. K. Goodyear (✉)
School of Education, University of Redlands, Redlands, CA, USA

Department of Psychology, Pepperdine University, Los Angeles, CA, USA

C. A. Falender
Pepperdine University, Malibu, CA, USA

University of California, Los Angeles, Los Angeles, CA, USA

M. P. Grazioso et al. (eds.), *Clinical Supervision in Latin America*,
https://doi.org/10.1007/978-3-031-82373-2_12

highlighting the unique approaches and contexts specific to each nation. Differences are important to acknowledge. But the purpose of this chapter is focus on what we believe are universally important supervision practices and concepts.

We advocate a competency-based approach (Falender & Shafranske, 2021), which assumes that supervisor should be competent in two domains: (1) the professional practice they will be overseeing and (2) the competencies that are required to supervise. In what follows we will elaborate more on essential elements of a competency-based approach.

What Is Clinical Supervision

It is useful to begin with a definition of clinical supervision that will inform what we cover and then to use it to frame this chapter as we unpack each of its elements. We developed this definition in collaboration with supervision experts from eight countries that were geographically and culturally quite different from one another. Our goal was a definition that applies in any country.

> Clinical supervision is a distinct professional practice employing a collaborative relationship that extends over time, is facilitative, and has the goals of enhancing the professional competence and science-informed practice of the supervisee, monitoring the quality of services provided, and protecting the public. (Falender et al., 2021, p. 188)

We already have made the case the supervision is a distinct professional practice. This first portion of this chapter will unpack the remaining elements of this definition.

Supervision Relies on a Collaborative Relationship

Kilminster and Jolly (2000) concluded from their review of empirical studies of supervision that the supervisory relationship is more important than the specific techniques that supervisors use. But the "collaborative" aspect mentioned in our definition is key. Bordin (1979) is the theorist who formulated the current, dominant conception of the working alliance, which he described as a "collaboration for change" between client and therapist. He retained that concept of collaboration in his later extension of his working alliance model to supervision (Bordin, 1983). Collaboration means that the supervisor and supervisee are working toward goals that they share, using agreed-upon tasks and procedures. Engaging in that work provides the supervisor and supervisee the opportunity to develop a bond and mutual trust as a platform for their work together.

That trust is essential as we require supervisees to be make themselves vulnerable as they share their work and then we ask them to reflect on it. There are at least three practical implications of this emphasis on collaboration.

The Supervision Contract The supervision contract is an agreement about the goals of the work supervisor and supervisee will be doing together and how they will accomplish that work together. It also spells out the expectations that each person has for the other. Supervisors have an ethical obligation to engage in contracting with supervisees because it provides informed consent. But, as important, contracting us an important first step in developing an effective working alliance. There are a number of elements that go into a contract but in the interest of space, we simply will share some examples (http://www.cfalender.com/supervision-contracts.html).

In a competence-based approach, the goals of training are clearly specified and there will be an agreed-upon point at which the full range of expected competencies are evaluated. Therefore, in this contracting process, the supervisor and supervisee should agree on when formal evaluation will occur. The supervisor also should review with the supervisee the expected competencies and discuss the form that will be used for that evaluation. Appendix is an example of one such form that supervisors might consider. It specifies competencies supervisees are expected to meet and defines what each means. It differs from other such forms in that it also provides guidance on how the supervision might best use the form with supervisees.

Some supervisors treat contracting in a pro forma, legal manner ("read this and if you have no questions, sign it"). But this does not set the stage for the collaboration that will be so necessary for effective supervision. They are not discussing the goals and tasks that will be unique to the work of each supervisor and supervisee. As well, the supervisor and supervisee miss the chance to have important conversations about issues that are key to an effective working relationship. This means, for example, to acknowledge differences (race, gender, culture, age, country of origin, and so on) and to give each other permission to discuss how those differences may affect work together.

This contracting conversation is also a chance to acknowledge that in any relationship there will be times when the parties misunderstand each other, disagree, or find themselves in actual conflict—situations that, in themselves, are not necessarily a problem if the parties have the opportunity to discuss and resolve those differences. In fact, these can be opportunities to deepen the supervisor-supervisee relationship. Because of the power differences between supervisor and supervisee, supervisees are less likely to draw attention to those issues unless there has been an explicit invitation from the supervisor to do so.

Surprises in any aspect of treatment or supervision are counterproductive and interfere with client care. Of course, there are untoward events that may occur, but it is incumbent on the supervisor to inform the supervisee in as timely a manner as possible and arrange for alternatives. The supervisory contract is an important mechanism for minimizing the chance of surprises.

The Power of Humility In the past few years, advocates of a Multicultural Orientation approach to psychotherapy and supervision (Davis et al., 2018; Zhang et al., 2022) have emphasized the role of cultural humility. This is a constellation of attitudes and behaviors, including particularly being curious about and respectful of others, being considerate, open to different perspectives, and of not making assumptions. But the evidence supports a more pervasive value of humility in supervision that also includes relational humility (see Watkins Jr, 2020). For example, Nissen-Lie and colleagues have focused on one form of humility, professional self-doubt, and found that in therapists, it predicted better client outcomes Nissen-Lie et al. (2013) and directly to the point of the current topic, predicted better client ratings of the therapy relationship.

There are a number of factors in supervision to elicit and expert, teaching role in supervisors. For example, the relationship is inherently hierarchical and supervisors have more power in the relationship than supervisees; supervisees often look up to their supervisors and try to elicit expert behavior; and supervisors sometimes feel the need to show how much they know.

But it is possible to retain the necessary level of responsibility for supervision and oversight of the supervisee's work and still to retain the characteristics of humility, especially curiosity, respect and being careful about making assumptions. The effect is greater "felt-safety" by supervisees who in turn are more willing to reflective about their work and themselves. As well, Taylor and Ellis (2023) recently reported that supervisors' relational humility was inversely related to the extent to which supervisees withheld important information from their supervisors.

Supervision Extends over Time

In all forms of supervision—and especially in a competency-based approach—the supervisor assesses the supervisee's level of performance with the client(s) and in supervision, works with the supervisee to improve that performance, and then later assesses the extent to which the supervisee's performance has changed as a result of supervision. This means that they are working together over time.

Therapists and trainees often bring an issue with which they are struggling to a colleague or expert to use them as a sounding board and for advice. This, though, is consultation and not supervision.

Enhancing the Professional Competence and Science-Informed Practice of the Supervisee

This goal will strike many readers as obvious: This is what motivates supervisees to seek supervision and training programs to require that their trainees obtain it. What is more important in this section, then, is to speak to the pathways to that goal, in particular, exposure to evidence- based models, and movement towards science-informed practice. What is most important in addressing this stated goal, then, is the chance to articulate some essentials about science- informed practice, what supervisors focus on as they enhance supervisee development, and how they do this.

Science-Informed Practice Our definition of supervision speaks of science-informed practice, which we believe has two implications. The first of those concerns the integration of research findings into practice. And that, in turn requires that supervisors are at least conversant with that evolving literature (1) about professional practice in the area the person is supervising, and (2) about the practice of supervision. Most supervisors are practitioners who are short on time to read the literature or who may not have access to that literature. But there are other ways to remain current, including participating in professional development workshops, participating in peer consultation groups, and attending professional conference.

The second implication of science-informed practice concerns clinicians who function as what Stricker and Trierweiler (2006) referred to as "local clinical scientists": clinicians who bring the mindset and tools of the scientist to bear on their practices. Doing this does not require formal training in science! But it is a way of approaching problems systematically and, often, with data. And one important way to do that is to employ routine outcome monitoring (ROM) with clients. This means continually assessing client progress and clients' perception of their relationship with the therapist by administering established measures, session-by-session. The data related to using ROM are so compelling with respect to reducing dropouts and increasing client outcomes (de Jong et al., 2021) that this has become an accepted best practice in psychotherapy. Indeed, Muir et al. (2019) have raised the issue of whether *not* using ROM raises ethical questions.

There are many such measures available, including the Partners in Change Client Outcome Management System (PCOMS) and the Clinical Outcomes in Routine Evaluation (CORE) systems. PCOMS is free in the paper-pencil version (https://scott-d-miller-ph-d.myshopify.com/) and CORE is free to use both in paper-pencil and electronic versions (https://www.coresystemtrust.org.uk/). Both are available in multiple languages, including Spanish.

These and other measures can be important to use in supervision. To illustrate, consider the graphing of client progress depicted in Fig. 1. If this were a supervisee's client, it would be important to work with the that supervisee to address what might be happening to account for the negative change that occurred after session 5 in both the client's perception of the therapy relationship (the top line) and their own functioning (the bottom line). Grossl et al. (2014) and Swift et al. (2015) are among those who have discussed the use and value of ROM in supervision.

What Supervisors Focus on to Enhance Professional Competence Epstein and Hundert (2002) defined professional competence as "the habitual and judicious use of communication, knowledge, technical skills, clinical reasoning, emotions, values, and reflection" (p. 226). U.S. psychologists have articulated a range of competence targets for trainees (Fouad et al., 2009) and later in this document we will discuss the use of competence evaluation form that can be used in routine supervision practice (see Appendix).

Bernard's (1997) Discrimination Model was developed before competencies had become central in psychology training, but it provides a simple heuristic for

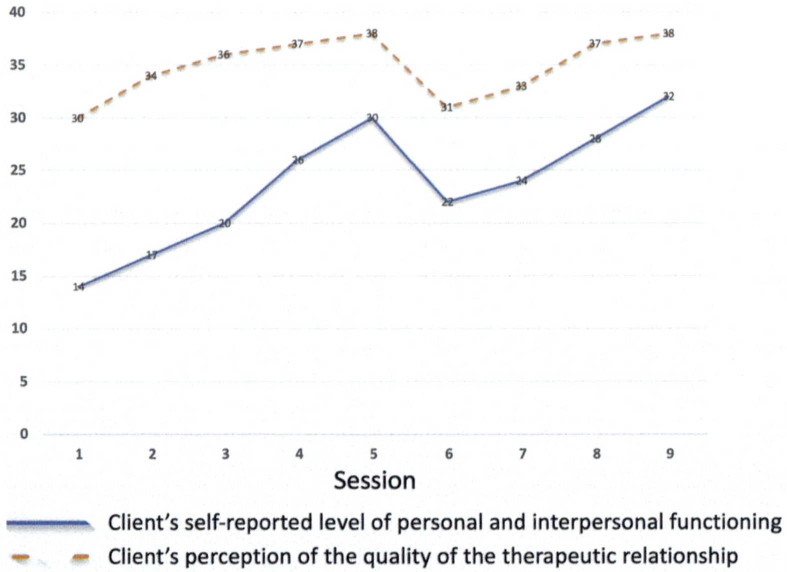

Fig. 1 Illustration of what client feedback might look like

supervisors and is largely compatible with the Epstein and Hundert definition of competencies as it focuses on:

- *Intervention skills*: These are the technical skills alluded to in Epstein and Hundert but also allude to the relational skills that are so important to effective therapy.
- *Conceptualization skills*: This attends to the clinical reasoning and reflection that Epstein and Hundert alluded to: how supervisees are understanding the client, the therapist-client treatment processes, and how to apply technical skills.
- *Personalization (self-awareness) skills*: This concerns trainees' emotions and values and is especially important in addressing countertransference.

As well, McKibben et al. (2019) added a fourth category that is important: *professional behaviors*, which concerns ethics and professionalism. The supervisor who uses this model can think of having a spotlight that at any given moment in supervision shines on one of these four areas. The extent to which a supervisor attends to particular areas of focus is determined by both supervisee's developmental level (e.g., very beginning supervisees are more concerned with technical skills) and theoretical model (e.g., CBT supervisors will tend to give relatively more attention to technical skills whereas humanistic and psychodynamic supervisors are likely to focus relatively more on personalization skills).

When McKibben et al. (2019) asked supervisees to report critical feedback from their supervisors, almost half of the reported instances of feedback concerned intervention skills (46.79%), followed in frequency by personalization skills (25%), professional behaviors (12.82%), and conceptualization skills (10.89%). The important message is that all four of these were being addressed. All are key to the development of competence and therefore, the effective supervisor will ensure that supervision attend to all four areas of focus.

The Pedagogy of Supervision: Developing Supervisees' Professional Competence

There are many techniques and strategies supervisors can employ to help facilitate their supervisees' development. It is parsimonious, though, to cluster those teaching methods as modeling, feedback and instruction, and the facilitation of reflection (see, e.g., Branch Jr & Paranjape, 2002; Goodyear, 2014).

Modeling We emulate those we look up to or to whom we perceive to be similar to us on some important dimension (Bandura, 1969). Supervisors fit both categories, which puts makes them an important source of vicarious learning. That modeling can become internalized to the extent that the supervisor lives on in the supervisee's mind (Geller et al., 2010). Rønnestad and Skovholt (2003) provided a vivid example from their qualitative study of therapist development:

> One of our informants, for example, talked about John, his supervisor twenty years ago: 'I have been running around in my mind words, phrases, quotes that I periodically pull back to … and sometimes I say to myself, how would John handle this situation?' (p. 25).

Supervisors can intentionally teach through modeling. For example, they might share videos of their own work with clients or work as co-therapists their supervisees who then can watch them in action. Supervisors also can "think aloud about clients, thereby teaching conceptualization skills." Goodyear and Sera (2024) also have found that supervisors can model handling of countertransference by self-disclosing responses that they themselves have had to particular clients. There are many more such examples of supervisors intentionally teaching through modeling.

Importantly, though, supervisees are learning from watching their supervisors, even when the supervisors are not intending to teach. As Watzlawick et al. (1967) famously asserted, "you can't not communicate." Supervisees always are observing their supervisors for messages about their relationship with the supervisor and about what is expected behavior of someone who is entering their field. This can be problematic, for example, when the supervisor behaves unprofessionally or unethically.

Facilitating Critical Reflection A great deal of supervisee learning occurs through critical reflection. That is, to engage in focused thinking about a specific situation or relationship with the supervisor's direction in order to understand it in a different way. But there are important developmental considerations that bear both on supervisees' readiness to engage in critical reflection and on the end goals of that process. These are suggested in Fig. 2, which is our adaption of a framework first suggested by De Philli et al. (1960).

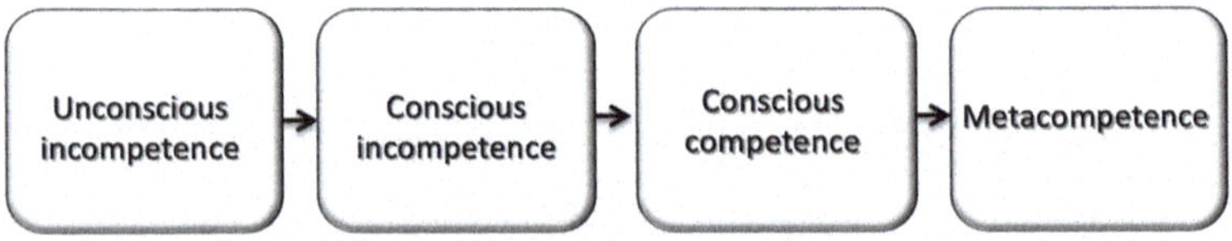

Fig. 2 A competence framework for depicting supervisee development

It suggests that the end goal of training is that supervisees will be able to self-supervise. That is, that they will have meta-competence (Falender & Shafranske, 2021), or the ability to self-assess and determine what one knows and what they do not know. And the mechanism for this is critical reflection. When supervisors facilitate supervisees' reflections on their work, they not only are addressing an issue of immediate importance in supervision but are simultaneously teaching them the habits and skills of critical reflection.

It also suggests why reflective practice is less useful for complete beginners (i.e., someone those who are unconsciously incompetent) than for those with more experience: To be able to reflect on performance, a person needs first to be able to recognize expected or desirable behavior. And to be able to observe their own reactions to the client and situation. The importance of reflection grows steadily as supervisees gain knowledge and experience, with correspondingly less attention given to feedback and instruction.

Interpersonal Process Recall (Kagan & Kagan, 1991) is a structured way of facilitating supervisee reflection. So too is the use of Socratic (Overholser, 1991), or at least open-ended questions. To illustrate how this might look using the framework we introduced earlier:

- *Intervention skills*: Example question—"based on how the client responded to that interchange, how would you respond differently next time?"
- *Conceptualizaation skills*: Example question—"how are you understanding how the neglect the client experienced growing up is affecting her current behavior?"
- *Personhood skills*: Example question—"when your client said that to you, what were you feeling?"
- *Professionalism*: Example question—"your client just asked you to write a letter of reference for him. What are the issues involved that will affect your decision?"

Those are the kinds of questions that can invite reflection. But unless the supervisee believes his or her responses will be received without criticism or judgment, the supervisee is unlikely to be completely forthright about his or her thoughts and feelings. This speaks, again, to the importance of a trusting and effective supervisory alliance.

Feedback Feedback is a critical component of supervision. It can be understood as information provided to a person about some aspect of his or her performance, delivered with the intention of reducing discrepancies between (a) that performance and (b) what would be desirable for that person to have done instead. But in naturalistic studies, supervisors have been shown to deliver feedback relatively infrequently (Friedlander et al., 1989; Milne & Westerman, 2001), despite what supervisors might believe they actually are doing. And yet supervisees highly value it when it occurs. For example, Li et al. (2016) found that when given a list of ten supervision interventions, supervisees ranked "feedback and correction" first in importance, whereas supervisors ranked it sixth (supervisor's first ranked intervention was "validating supervisees' feelings," which supervisees ranked ninth).

There are several factors that affect feedback quality. Each is important to acknowledge.

Factor One: Quality of Information about Performance Feedback is only as good as the information the supervisor has about the supervisee's performance. Notably, most supervision relies on supervisees' reports of their work. The value of feedback based on self- report is constrained by:

- What supervisees are able to report: even supervisees who are trying their very best to report accurately will have difficulty capturing the complexity of therapy interactions in a verbal report. For example, when Wynne et al. (1994) asked a group of licensed psychologists to recall the molar (main) and molecular (supporting) ideas from specific segments of actual therapy sessions. They had recall rates of 42% and 30%, respectively.
- What supervisees are willing to report: virtually all supervisees withhold information from their supervisors (Ladany et al., 1996). There are several reasons for this, including supervisees' levels of trust of their supervisors and the desire to present themselves as competent.

For these reasons, it has become expected practice now for supervisors to directly observe at least some of their supervisees' work with clients (e.g., APA, 2015). There are several ways this can occur, including conducting co-therapy with the supervisee, observing sessions as they are occurring (e.g., one-way glass or video feed) or video recordings. All of these have value, though the particular value of video recordings is that the supervisor and supervisee can study therapy microsequences in detail to develop rich and specific understandings of what was occurring.

A challenge in obtaining direct observations, though, is that supervisees will feel completely exposed, which can be very anxiety producing. One consequence is that they often then project that anxiety onto clients, assuring their supervisors that the clients will not permit them to record. Yet Briggie et al. (2016) found that most clients in their clinic were willing to be allow their sessions to be recorded. One variable that affected their willingness was in how the therapist made the request to record. This suggests how important it is to prepare the supervisee to make that request. In fact, there is particular value in rehearsing it in a role-play.

Factor Two: Reluctance to Give Difficult Corrective Feedback Given supervisees positive feedback is something most supervisors look forward to doing. But the situation is different when the supervisee is having difficulty demonstrated expected performance. Few people enjoy giving difficult feedback to others. This is true as well for supervisors. After all, they are therapists and are especially attuned to feelings. In fact, Merker et al. (2010) confirmed the difficulty that psychologists have giving that feedback.

Hoffman et al. (2005) found that supervisors who had difficulty feedback to provide supervisees reported that their tendency was to become more vague and indirect. And yet the supervisees whose performance does not meet expectation are those who most need clear feedback! It is notable as well that Burkard et al. (2014) found that White supervisors were similarly cautious in giving critical feedback to supervisees of color, for fear of appearing racist. In their own study of cross-racial supervision, Constantine and Sue (2007) labeled this behavior as a form of microaggression: No matter how well-intentioned it was, the effect was to deprive the supervisee of feedback that she or he could use to improve performance.

Factor Three: Giving Feedback that Is Specific and Task Focused Psychotherapy is a field in which is the person of the therapist is an important as the techniques the therapist uses. The role is strongly associated with who we are as people. For that reason, supervisees are no doubt especially attuned to any feedback that could be construed as telling them they were flawed in any way. One risk is shame (Yourman, 2003), and therefore wanting to "hide," including by withholding information from their supervisors.

Significantly, then Beddoe (2017) observed that supervisees are at risk of feeling pathologized when evaluative feedback focused on their personalities rather than their behaviors. This personal observation echoed the finding in Wisniewski et al.'s (2020) meta-analytic study that feedback about someone's motivation was much less effective than feedback on measurable performance.

The best feedback, then, should be focus on specific behaviors (and not the person), be clear, and be as detailed as possible. It should provide not only information about what did not go as well as it could, but also about what the supervisee might do to improve that behavior. That feedback should, of course focus on performance that will help supervisees reach trainee-specific goals that the supervisor and supervisee agreed to during the contracting process at the outset of supervision. But it should be guided as well by the full range of expected competencies the supervisee is expected to attain and against which the supervisee eventually will be evaluated (see the supervisee competence assessment form in Appendix).

Monitoring the Quality of Services the Supervisee Provides and Protecting the Public

It can be useful to think of supervision as a stool that is supported by three legs. We addressed one of those legs—enhancing the professional development of supervisees—in the section immediately above. In this section we will discuss, in turn, each of the other two legs.

Monitoring the Quality of Services that the Supervisee Provides This leg of the stool speaks to supervisors' ethical obligation—and in some jurisdictions, legal obligation as well—to ensure that their supervisees are "doing no harm" and that their clients are receiving competent care. In fact, this is supervisors' foremost responsibility. In the prior section we addressed ways that supervisors can obtain quality information about their supervisees' performance in order to provide effective feedback. In so doing, though, supervisors also are obtaining the information that they need to monitor client services. In fact, the arguments we made in the earlier section about the importance of directly observing supervisees' work is strengthened further by this important obligation to clients.

When supervisors observe that the clients are receiving less-than-optimal treatment, they have a range of options available to them, depending on the circumstances. For example, the supervisor might judge that issues or problems can be addressed by closer monitoring of the supervisee. This might mean, for example, reviewing video recordings of each therapy session with that client. Or in more challenging situations it might mean reassigning the client (which is possible in training clinics) or in situations whether where that is not possible, asking the supervisee to refer the client to another person. Whatever the decision, it needs to be in the best interests of the client.

In some supervisory contexts, the supervisor has no control over which clients the supervisee is to see. But when supervisors do have that control, it is their responsibility to ensure that cases assigned to the supervisee are within their area of competence, with the input and support of the supervisor. That is, the supervisor assigns cases in which the supervisee can be reasonably expected to perform with competence, based on their prior training and experience.

Protecting the Public This leg of the stool concerns supervisors' longer-term obligation to protect the public; in particular, the future clients the supervisee might eventually treat. This obligation is met if supervisors are successful in helping supervisees to become sufficiently competent to practice independently. That is, that they have developed the necessary meta-competence (Falender & Shafranske, 2021).

But some supervisees do not attain that level of competence and the supervisors' responsibility to protect the public becomes more challenging. In some contexts, supervisors can serve as gatekeepers. For example, a supervisor is working in the context of a university program is part of a training team that can work together to ensure that only competent trainees graduate from that program. Or, in some jurisdictions, supervisors who are working with supervisees who have received their degrees but have not received their licenses can refuse to attest to the licensure board or credentialing entity that the person is ready to be credentialed.

We do want to acknowledge that there are situations where monitoring quality of services and protecting the public can be especially challenging. This can occur, for example in jurisdictions where there is no licensure or in which the supervisees are hiring their supervisors to supervise them. In these cases, the supervisor is unlikely to be able to engage in any gatekeeping and may be hesitant to give corrective feedback or hesitant to insist that a supervisee transfer a client when it is in the client's best interest. Our advice to supervisors who are working in those situations and who have a supervisee who is experiencing problems of competence is to consult with their own supervisors or at least with trusted peers to think through a solution that will best protect current and future clients.

Ethics in Supervision

In the adaptation of Bernard's (1997) Discrimination Model that we presented above, we had added professional behavior (including ethical conduct) as the fourth area of supervisee development to which supervisors should attend. This is important enough that we end this chapter by focusing specifically on it.

Ethics is a professional competence that is internationally recognized. Ethics in Latin and South America are a central topic for the disciplines but have received less attention than that devoted to North American colleagues (Consoli et al., 2021). Ethics codes reflect countries' culture including history, customs, and practices (Oakland et al., 2012).

Supervisory ethical responsibilities include conducting respectful practice, with integrity, doing no harm, maintaining competence, ensuring confidentiality and clarifying its limits, and not entering into multiple relationships that may do harm. The supervisor must be competent to supervise the population and presentations that the supervisee is treating under supervision, use informed consent to provide clarity from the onset of clinical practice and supervision to ensure the client and supervisee are informed and agree to the treatment and to its supervision, responsibilities, and obligations implicit in the process. Other ethical standards include attending to perspectives and issues of diversity and multicultural competence, establishing boundaries and being mindful to avoid entering into multiple or dual relationships both in supervision and in psychotherapy that might do harm, providing informed consent and using a supervision contract, ensuring accurate documentation and record keeping by both supervisor and supervisee, ensuring evaluation and feedback are given, promoting and modeling self-care and wellness, providing emergency coverage, and providing a planful termination for both the clinical and supervisory relationships (Barnett & Molzon, 2014; Falender & Shafranske, 2021). Some of these may be culturally dissonant, requiring specific attention to cultural context, mores, and intent. For example, multiple relationships are generally approached with care, mindful of prohibitions in some cultures, while in other cultures, relationship and cultural mores may view these as relationships as strengths and of high value. Similarly, confidentiality may be more complex when extended family members and elders may have a significant role in decision making which may not be understood by the therapist from a different cultural milieu.

Historically, there have been multiple influences on development of ethics codes in the regions. The Mercosur countries (Argentina, Brazil, Chile, Paraguay, Venezuela, and Uruguay) developed an economic agreement to increase trade followed by a regional declaration of ethical principles for psychologists in 1997. Called the Ethics Framework for Professional Practice of Psychology in the Mercosur and Associated Countries (Leach & Leong, 2010), it was principle- based, with five ethical principles: respect for people's rights and dignity, professional competence, professional and scientific commitment, integrity, and social responsibility, all of which are explicitly or implicitly included in regional ethics codes and represent a shift to principle-based ethics.

The Universal Declaration of Ethical Principles for Psychologists (Gauthier et al., 2010), a generic set of morally based *principles* for use when developing or revising ethics codes, was instrumental in the development of the Guatemalan Ethics code (Jurado, 2021) and is a model for ethics codes revisions and updates.

Consoli et al. (2021) concluded that all Latin American countries have developed a national code of ethics applicable to psychologists in their countries, ethics committees to address complaints against professionals, and share a similar structure with principles and codes of conduct with emphasis on welfare of the peoples and communities being served. Clinical supervision is the mechanism of transmitting the profession to future generations. Rather than viewing ethics simply as a remedy for dilemmas, supervisees and supervisors alike should view ethics as a pillar of their profession and an invaluable tool for guidance and excellent practice.

Ensuring recognition of clinical supervision in all its complexity strengthens the profession of psychology and the ethical standards it entails to protect the public, supervisees in training, and the profession.

Appendix: Supervisee Competence Form

Using This Form in Supervision

As supervision begins:

- During contracting, discuss supervision goals and expectations that you and the supervisee have for each other , discuss the form and the competencies it describes. These will serve as goals for training and then be the basic for evaluation.
- Identify competencies the supervisee believes will need the most attention as you work together.
- Agree on when the formal evaluation will occur (in a university practicum usually at the end of the term; in other settings, the supervisor and supervisee discuss the scheduling of that assessment).

As supervision progresses:

- Periodically review the form to determine whether there is enough information to understand how well the supervisee is meeting each competency
- If there are competencies for which there is not enough information:What are ways that information might be obtained (e.g., direct observation of some kind?)

When it is time for formal evaluation:

- Supervisor and supervisee should come to that session with each having made their own ratings of the supervisee's proficiency level for each competency.
- Discuss those competencies for which their ratings, first, agree; and then, disagree. Use concrete examples of supervisee behavior in those discussions.
- Conclude by establishing next professional development goals for the supervisee (if continuing together, these goals will be useful in determining at least some of the goals for supervision)

Supervisee Name ___________	Supervisor Name ___________

How many clients serve as the basis for this conversation about this supervisee's competency attainment? _____

How many supervision sessions have you had together prior to this evaluation? _____

In how many of those sessions was the supervisee's work directly observed? _____

Was this supervision based on a supervision contract? Yes _____ No _____

Instructions: For each competency, indicate how characteristic of the trainee s behavior this competency description is. If you have had no opportunity to observe behavior related to that competency, check the ○ in the far right column.

		How characteristic of the trainee's behavior is this competency?					
		Not at all/ slightly		Moderately		Very	No opportunity to observe
Professionalism: behavior and conduct that reflects the values and attitudes of counseling and psychology							
1	**Deportment**	1☐	2☐	3☐	4☐	5☐	○
Is consistently professional and appropriate in how she or he communicates and behaves (behavior includes attire)							
2	**Accountability**	1☐	2☐	3☐	4☐	5☐	○
Accepts responsibility (that is, is willing to be answerable for) for own behavior. This includes acknowledging mistakes and being willing to use those mistakes as a chance to grow professionally							
3	**Professional identity**	1☐	2☐	3☐	4☐	5☐	○
Joins professional associations and actively participates in professional events, including but not limited to seminars, conferences and workshops							
4	**Use of professional and scientific literature**	1☐	2☐	3☐	4☐	5☐	○
Consults and refers to counseling professional and scientific journals and books to learn							
Ethical and legal competencies: In conducting professional activities demonstrates an understanding of legal issues and the application of ethical concepts							
5	**Awareness of legal implications of actions**	1☐	2☐	3☐	4☐	5☐	○
Demonstrates knowledge of therapy-relevant Chinese mental health laws and applies them to practice							

6	**Awareness of ethical implication of actions**	1 □	2□	3□	4□	5□	○
Understands and applies the Chinese Psychological Society's Code of Ethics for Counseling and Clinical Practice.							
7	**Ethical and legal decision-making**	1 □	2□	3□	4□	5□	○
(1) Identifies potential ethical concerns and legal issues and (2) uses a decision-making strategy to resolve them. As necessary, seeks consultation to help resolve those issues							
8	**Ethical decision-making: multiple relationships**	1 □	2□	3□	4□	5□	○
Recognizes multiple relationship situations and employs ethical decision-making processes to determine the most appropriate resolution							
9	**Client privacy**	1 □	2□	3□	4□	5□	○
Ensures client privacy in all situations, including the use of social media, recordings, and videoconferencing							
10	**Professional disclosures**	1 □	2□	3□	4□	5□	○
Appropriately informs the client about fees, confidentiality exceptions, the counselor's treatment model, the counselor's professional training (and that the counselor is being supervised), etc.							
Reflective practice and self-care: practice conducted with personal and professional self-awareness and reflection, with appropriate self-care							
11	**Reflective practice**	1 □	2□	3□	4□	5□	○
Demonstrates broad self-awareness; utilizes self-monitoring in interactions with clients and others							
12	**Within-session awareness and action**	1 □	2□	3□	4□	5□	○
Is attentive to in-session client responses and displays flexibility in adjusting own behavior accordingly							
13	**Attention to effects of personal issues on practice**	1 □	2□	3□	4□	5□	○
Recognizes and manages his or her own personal issues that could affect the therapy process							

14	**Self-care**	1☐	2☐	3☐	4☐	5☐	○
Pays attention to personal health and well-being to assure effective professional functioning							
Intervention and assessment: conceptualizes and responds effectively to issues and problems that clients present							
15	**Articulates a coherent model of treatment**	1☐	2☐	3☐	4☐	5☐	○
Can describe a model of how client problems develop and how they are addressed in therapy. That model can be either one of the formal, established model (e.g., CBT; psychodynamic; etc.) or a more personal, integrative approach							
16	**Intervention implementation**	1☐	2☐	3☐	4☐	5☐	○
Implements interventions that are consistent with an espoused model of treatment (see #1 immediately above)							
17	**Alliance development**	1☐	2☐	3☐	4☐	5☐	○
Develops effective therapeutic alliances with clients							
18	**Risk assessment and response**	1☐	2☐	3☐	4☐	5☐	○
Recognizes and responds appropriately to client risk situations (e.g., suicidality, homicidality, and any other safety issues)							
19	**Termination and referral competence**	1☐	2☐	3☐	4☐	5☐	○
Demonstrates ability to manage client termination of treatment effectively; this might include referral to other professionals		1☐	2☐	3☐	4☐	5☐	○
20	**Progress evaluation**	1☐	2☐	3☐	4☐	5☐	○
Utilizes session-by-session client outcome feedback measures to evaluate treatment progress		1☐	2☐	3☐	4☐	5☐	○
21	**Client assessment**	1☐	2☐	3☐	4☐	5☐	○
Selects, uses, and interprets appropriate methods to assess clients. These can include structured interviews, standardized tests and inventories, and so on.							
Interpersonal competence: the ability to effectively communicate, collaborate, and interact with others							

22	**Nonjudgmental stance**	1 ☐	2☐	3☐	4☐	5☐	○
Establishes a safe and nonjudgmental atmosphere with clients though open-mindedness, tolerance, respectful communication, and non-reactivity		1 ☐	2☐	3☐	4☐	5☐	○
23	**Comfort with client feelings and issues**	1 ☐	2☐	3☐	4☐	5☐	○
Appears comfortable with a variety of feelings and issues that clients share							
24	**Client attunement**	1 ☐	2☐	3☐	4☐	5☐	○
Actively and empathically attends to client's emotional experience, thoughts, and behaviors							
25	**Monitors and maintains relationships**	1 ☐	2☐	3☐	4☐	5☐	○
Recognizes relationship strains with clients when they occur and responds constructively							
26	**Countertransference management**	1 ☐	2☐	3☐	4☐	5☐	○
Is able to identify and manage reactions to clients							
Multicultural competence: recognizing the impact of cultural factors and having a commitment to addressing issues of diversity, equity, and inclusion to ensure therapy is effective and culturally sensitive							
27	**Self as shaped by individual and cultural diversity**	1 ☐	2☐	3☐	4☐	5☐	○
Recognizes ways in which culture, race, gender (or other forms of diversity) shape his or her identity, behavior and objectivity							
28	**Others as shaped by individual and cultural diversity and context**	1 ☐	2☐	3☐	4☐	5☐	○
Applies knowledge of others as cultural beings in assessment and treatment							
29	**Cultural humility**	1 ☐	2☐	3☐	4☐	5☐	○
Is open to other cultures, beliefs, and perspectives; is committed to challenging his or her own biases and assumptions; and, shows respect for others and motivation to learn from them							
Supervision: utilization of supervision as a trainee and recognition of the role of supervision in enhancing and monitoring the professional functioning of others							

30	**Commitment to the supervision process**	1 ☐	2☐	3☐	4☐	5☐	○
Contributes positively to the formation of the supervisory alliance; attends supervision regularly and on time							
31	**Actively participates**	1 ☐	2☐	3☐	4☐	5☐	○
Comes prepared for sessions; provides supervisor with recordings, case notes, and other concrete information from which the supervisor can assess his/her work							
32	**Feedback utilization**	1 ☐	2☐	3☐	4☐	5☐	○
Seeks and uses feedback from the supervisor; responds nondefensively to that feedback							

If there were particular competencies that were unclear and need to be discussed, list them here, by the number that was given that competency on this form: ______________
____

Domains of competence for

which the supervisee's ratings are highest:

Areas that should be the focus of the supervisee's next stage of professional development

- If supervisor and supervisee are continuing to work together, these areas for growth can be used in the revised contract as goals for the next phase of their work together

_______________________________ _______________________________

Supervisee signature and date Supervisor signature and date

References

American Psychological Association. (2015). Guidelines for clinical supervision in health service psychology. *The American Psychologist, 70*(1), 33–46.

Bandura, A. (1969). Social-learning theory of identificatory processes. In D. Goslin (Ed.), *Handbook of socialization theory and research* (pp. 213–262). Rand McNally.

Barnett, J. E., & Molzon, C. H. (2014). Clinical supervision of psychotherapy: Essential ethics issues for supervisors and supervisees. *Journal of Clinical Psychology: In Session, 70*(1), 1051–1061. https://doi.org/10.1002/jclp.22126

Beddoe, L. (2017). Harmful supervision: A commentary. *The Clinical Supervisor, 36*(1), 88–101.

Bernard, J. M. (1997). The discrimination model. In C. E. Watkins (Ed.), *Handbook of psychotherapy supervision* (pp. 310–327). Wiley.

Bernard, J. M., & Goodyear, R. K. (2019). *Fundamentals of clinical supervision* (6th ed.). Merrill.

Bordin, E. S. (1979). The generalizability of the psychoanalytic concept of the working alliance. *Psychotherapy: Theory, Research & Practice, 16*(3), 252.

Bordin, E. S. (1983). A working alliance based model of supervision. *The Counseling Psychologist, 11*(1), 35–42.

Branch, W. T., Jr., & Paranjape, A. (2002). Feedback and reflection: Teaching methods for clinical settings. *Academic Medicine, 77*(12 Part 1), 1185–1188.

Briggie, A. M., Hilsenroth, M. J., Conway, F., Muran, J. C., & Jackson, J. M. (2016). Patient comfort with audio or video recording of their psychotherapy sessions: Relation to symptomatology, treatment refusal, duration, and outcome. *Professional Psychology: Research and Practice, 47*(1), 66–76. https://doi.org/10.1037/a0040063

Burkard, A. W., Knox, S., Clarke, R. D., Phelps, D. L., & Inman, A. G. (2014). Supervisors' experiences of providing difficult feedback in cross-ethnic/racial supervision. *The Counseling Psychologist, 42*(3), 314–344.

Consoli, A., Flores, I., Sharma, H., Sheltzer, A., Gallegos, M., & Perez-Accosta, A. (2021). Psychology in Latin America: A qualitative study of commonalities and singularities. *Revista Interamericana de Psicologia Interamerican Journal of Psychology, 55*, 1627.

Constantine, M. G., & Sue, D. W. (2007). Perceptions of racial microaggressions among black supervisees in cross-racial dyads. *Journal of Counseling Psychology, 54*(2), 142–153. https://doi.org/10.1037/0022-0167.54.2.142

Davis, D. E., DeBlaere, C., Owen, J., Hook, J. N., Rivera, D. P., Choe, E., Van Tongeren, D. R., Worthington, E. L., Jr., & Placeres, V. (2018). The multicultural orientation framework: A narrative review. *Psychotherapy, 55*(1), 89–100. https://doi.org/10.1037/pst0000160

de Jong, K., Conijn, J. M., Gallagher, R. A., Reshetnikova, A. S., Heij, M., & Lutz, M. C. (2021). Using progress feedback to improve outcomes and reduce drop-out, treatment duration, and deterioration: A multilevel meta-analysis. *Clinical Psychology Review, 85*, 102002.

De Phillips, F. A., Berliner, W. M., & Cribbin, J. J. (1960). *Management of training programs*. Richard D. Irwin.

Epstein, R. M., & Hundert, E. M. (2002). Defining and assessing professional competence. *JAMA, 287*(2), 226–235.

Falender, C., Goodyear, R., Duan, C., Al-Darmaki, F., Bang, K., Çiftçi, A., González, V. R., del Pilar Grazioso, M., Humeidan, M., Jia, X., Kağnıcı, D. Y., & Partridge, S. (2021). Lens on international clinical supervision: Lessons learned from a cross-national comparison of supervision. *Journal of Contemporary Psychotherapy, 51*, 181–189.

Falender, C. A. (2018). Clinical supervision—The missing ingredient. *American Psychologist, 73*(9), 1240–1250. https://doi.org/10.1037/amp0000385

Falender, C. A., & Shafranske, E. P. (2021). *Clinical supervision: A competency-based approach* (2nd ed.). American Psychological Association.

Fouad, N. A., Grus, C. L., Hatcher, R. L., Kaslow, N. J., Hutchings, P. S., Madson, M. B., Collins, F. L., & Crossman, R. E. (2009). Competency benchmarks: A model for understanding and measuring competence in professional psychology across training levels. *Training and Education in Professional Psychology, 3*(4S), S5.

Freud, S. (1986). On the history of the psychoanalytic movement. In *Historical and expository works on psychoanalysis*. Penguin. (Original work published 1914.)

Friedlander, M. L., Siegel, S. M., & Brenock, K. (1989). Parallel processes in counseling and supervision: A case study. *Journal of Counseling Psychology, 36*(2), 149–157. https://doi.org/10.1037/0022-0167.36.2.149

Gauthier, J., Pettifor, J., & Ferrero, A. (2010). The universal declaration of ethical principles for psychologists: A culture-sensitive model for creating and reviewing a code of ethics. *Ethics & Behavior, 20*(3–4), 179–196. https://doi.org/10.1080/10508421003798885

Geller, J. D., Farber, B. A., & Schaffer, C. E. (2010). Representations of the supervisory dialogue and the development of psychotherapists. *Psychotherapy: Theory, Research, Practice, Training, 47*(2), 211–220. https://doi.org/10.1037/a0019785

Goodyear, R. K. (2014). Supervision as pedagogy: Attending to its essential instructional and learning processes. *The Clinical Supervisor, 33*(1), 82–99.

Goodyear, R. K., & Sera, H. (2024). Supervisees' perspectives on countertransference-focused practices and processes in clinical supervision: An exploratory study. *The Clinical Supervisor, 43*(2), 1–22.

Grossl, A. B., Reese, R. J., Norsworthy, L. A., & Hopkins, N. B. (2014). Client feedback data in supervision: Effects on supervision and outcome. *Training and Education in Professional Psychology, 8*(3), 182–188. https://doi.org/10.1037/tep0000025

Hoffman, M. A., Hill, C. E., Holmes, S. E., & Freitas, G. F. (2005). Supervisor perspective on the process and outcome of giving easy, difficult, or no feedback to supervisees. *Journal of Counseling Psychology, 52*(1), 3–13. https://doi.org/10.1037/0022-0167.52.1.3

Jurado, A. M. (2021). The history of the development of the code of ethics of Guatemala. In K. L. Parsonson (Ed.), *Handbook of international psychology ethics* (pp. 218–225). Routledge.

Kagan, N. I., & Kagan, H. (1991). *Interpersonal process recall*. Wiley.

Kilminster, S. M., & Jolly, B. C. (2000). Effective supervision in clinical practice settings: A literature review. *Medical Education, 34*(10), 827–840.

Ladany, N., Hill, C. E., Corbett, M. M., & Nutt, E. A. (1996). Nature, extent, and importance of what psychotherapy trainees do not disclose to their supervisors. *Journal of Counseling Psychology, 43*(1), 10–24.

Leach, M. M., & Leong, K. T. L. (2010). International dimensions of psychological ethics. *Ethics and Behavior, 20*, 1–4. https://doi.org/10.1080/10508421003798851

Li, C. I., Fairhurst, S., Chege, C., Jenks, E. H., Tsong, Y., Golden, D., White, L., Andreassen, A., Scott, S., Souris, M. J., Schmitt, S. S., & Schmitt, S. S. (2016). Card-sorting as a tool for communicating the relative importance of supervisor interventions. *The Clinical Supervisor, 35*(1), 80–97.

McKibben, W. B., Borders, L. D., & Wahesh, E. (2019). Factors influencing supervisee perceptions of critical feedback validity. *Counselor Education and Supervision, 58*(4), 242–256.

Merker, B. M., Hanson, W. E., & Poston, J. M. (2010). National survey of psychologists' training and practice in breaking bad news: A mixed methods study of the MUM effect. *Journal of Clinical Psychology in Medical Settings, 17*, 211–219.

Milne, D., & Westerman, C. (2001). Evidence-based clinical supervision: Rationale and illustration. *Clinical Psychology & Psychotherapy: An International Journal of Theory & Practice, 8*(6), 444–457.

Muir, H. J., Coyne, A. E., Morrison, N. R., Boswell, J. F., & Constantino, M. J. (2019). Ethical implications of routine outcomes monitoring for patients, psychotherapists, and mental health care systems. *Psychotherapy, 56*(4), 459–469. https://doi.org/10.1037/pst0000246

Nissen-Lie, H. A., Monsen, J. T., Ulleberg, P., & Rønnestad, M. H. (2013). Psychotherapists' self-reports of their interpersonal functioning and difficulties in practice as predictors of patient outcome. *Psychotherapy Research, 23*(1), 86–104.

Oakland, T., Leach, M. M., Bartram, D., Lindsay, G., Smedler, A., & Zhang, H. (2012). An international perspective on ethics codes for psychology: A focus on test development and use. In M. M. Leach, M. J. Stevens, G. Lindsay, A. Ferrero, & Y. Korkut (Eds.), *Oxford library of psychology. The Oxford handbook of international psychological ethics* (pp. 19–27). Oxford University Press.

Overholser, J. C. (1991). The Socratic method as a technique in psychotherapy supervision. *Professional Psychology: Research and Practice, 22*(1), 68–74.

Rønnestad, M. H., & Skovholt, T. M. (2003). The journey of the counselor and therapist: Research findings and perspectives on professional development. *Journal of Career Development, 30*, 5–44.

Stricker, G., & Trierweiler, S. J. (2006). The local clinical scientist: A bridge between science and practice. *Training and Education in Professional Psychology, S*(1), 37–46. https://doi.org/10.1037/1931-3918.S.1.37

Swift, J. K., Callahan, J. L., Rousmaniere, T. G., Whipple, J. L., Dexter, K., & Wrape, E. R. (2015). Using client outcome monitoring as a tool for supervision. *Psychotherapy, 52*(2), 180–184. https://doi.org/10.1037/a0037659

Taylor, E. J., & Ellis, M. V. (2023). Supervisee nondisclosure: Does relational humility matter? *The Counseling Psychologist, 51*(5), 756–779.

Watkins, C. E., Jr. (2020). Relational humility and clinical supervision: On hypotheses, method, and measurement. *The Clinical Supervisor, 39*(2), 148–167.

Watzlawick, P., Beavin, J., & Jackson, D. (1967). *Pragmatics of human communication*. Norton.

Wisniewski, B., Zierer, K., & Hattie, J. (2020). The power of feedback revisited: A meta-analysis of educational feedback research. *Frontiers in Psychology, 10*, 3087.

Wynne, M. E., Susman, M., Ries, S., Birringer, J., & Katz, L. (1994). A method for assessing therapists' recall of in-session events. *Journal of Counseling Psychology, 41*(1), 53–57. https://doi.org/10.1037/0022-0167.41.1.53

Yourman, D. B. (2003). Trainee disclosure in psychotherapy supervision: The impact of shame. *Journal of Clinical Psychology, 59*(5), 601–609.

Zhang, H., Watkins, C. E., Jr., Hook, J. N., Hodge, A. S., Davis, C. W., Norton, J., Wilcox, M. M., Davis, D. E., DeBlaere, C., & Owen, J. (2022). Cultural humility in psychotherapy and clinical supervision: A research review. *Counselling and Psychotherapy Research, 22*(3), 548–557.

Rodney K. Goodyear is a professor emeritus at the University of Southern California, where he directed the APA-accredited doctoral program in counseling psychology for two decades, and at the University of Redlands. He has been a member of the American Psychological Association's Commission on Accreditation, past president of the Society for the Advancement of Psychotherapy, APA Division 29, and served on the APA's Board of Educational Affairs (BEA) Oversight Guidelines Working Group. In 2015 he received the APA Distinguished Professional Contributions to Psychology Education and Training Award, and in 2018 the Distinguished Award for the International Advancement of Psychotherapy, Society for the Advancement of Psychotherapy, APA Division 29. He is co-author of Fundamentals of Clinical Supervision (2019), now in its sixth edition, and author of numerous chapters and articles on supervision. His work is increasingly focused on the international arena. Email: rodk.goodyear@gmail.com

Carol A. Falender has co-authored/edited seven books on clinical supervision and consultation and has presented workshops on clinical supervision, consultation, multicultural supervision, and decolonizing supervision. She led APA-accredited internship programs for more than 20 years and was chair of the American Psychological Association's (APA) Supervisory Guidelines Working Group. She received an APA Presidential Citation for his groundbreaking contributions to the theory and practice of clinical supervision, nationally and internationally, and received the APA's 2018 Distinguished Professional Contributions to Psychology Education and Training Award, and in 2023, the 29 Division Distinguished Award, Society for the Advancement of Psychotherapy, the Distinguished Award for the International Advancement of Psychotherapy. Dr. Falender is an adjunct professor at Pepperdine University; Clinical Professor, University of California, Los Angeles, Department of Psychology. Email: cfalender@gmail.com

Towards a More Differentiated Understanding of Supervision in Latin America

Maritza Gallardo-Cooper, Hector Fernandez-Alvarez, Ana Alicia Cobar, Rodney K. Goodyear, Carol A. Falender, and Maria del Pilar Grazioso

Introduction

The global study of clinical supervision enriches our multicultural understanding, offers solutions to professional challenges, and promotes new models of practice. Bernard and Goodyear (2019) underscore the value of the universal and unique aspects of this pedagogical intervention at the international level. Falender and colleagues (2021) further emphasize the importance of international collaboration to establish universal concepts and processes of supervision that incorporate diversity, multicultural sensitivity, and reciprocity. Similar conclusions were drawn from the contributions of clinical supervisors across several continents (Creaner & Timulak, 2016; Falender et al., 2021; Forrest, 2010; Watkins & Milne, 2014).

M. Gallardo-Cooper
Department of Clinical and School Psychology, Nova Southeastern University, Ft Lauderdale, FL, USA
e-mail: mg1011@nova.edu

H. Fernandez-Alvarez
Fundación Aiglé Argentina, Buenos Aires, Argentina

A. A. Cobar · M. P. Grazioso (✉)
Asociación Proyecto Aigle Guatemala, Universidad del Valle de Guatemala, Guatemala City, Guatemala
e-mail: aacoma@proyectoaigle.com.gt; aacobar@uvg.edu.gt; mpgrazioso@proyectoaigle.org.gt; mpgdero@uvg.edu.gt

R. K. Goodyear
University of Southern California, Los Angeles, CA, USA

School of Education, University of Redlands, Redlands, CA, USA

C. A. Falender
Pepperdine University, Malibu, CA, USA

University of California, Los Angeles, CA, USA

M. P. Grazioso et al. (eds.), *Clinical Supervision in Latin America*,
https://doi.org/10.1007/978-3-031-82373-2_13

From these perspectives, our book with its focus on Latin American policies, models, and practices represents a unique and significant advancement in the field of clinical supervision. This is an innovative proposal because, as we know, there is a marked tendency in academia to disseminate developments primarily from North America or Europe. These regions represent higher socioeconomic levels and specific cultural characteristics that are not necessarily transferable to the diverse contexts of our region.

Historically, these publications have been used to initiate the development of Latin American clinical supervision, transferring what are considered best practices or standards in the pedagogy of clinical supervision at both academic and professional levels. Narrative and systematic reviews that contribute to academic production often include studies primarily from English-speaking publications, making work conducted in other regions invisible and relegated. This issue is particularly critical for Latin American production, which has evolved slowly and is often dependent on non-Western countries. This phenomenon is prevalent across various areas of clinical psychology and supervision. However, in recent decades, we have witnessed significant development in these fields.

The dependence on Western and Northern hemisphere supervision scholarship has manifested in various ways: through the theoretical models used as references, the passive adoption of evaluation techniques, the application of methodologies, and the reliance on available literature. Consequently, Latin American contributions were scarcely known, even among professionals within the region.

In recent years, this has gradually changed with the emergence of new journals and the enhancement of existing, more sustainable publications for Spanish and Portuguese language readers. Periodicals such as *Avances de la Psicología Clínica en Latinoamérica*—Colombia (*Advances in Latin American Clinical Psychology*—Colombia), *Salud Mental*—Mexico (*Mental Health*—Mexico), *Revista Argentina de Clínica Psicológica* (*Argentinian Journal of Clinical Psychology*), *Revista Psicólogos*—Guatemala (*Journal of Psychologists*—Guatemala), *Revista Brasileira de Psicoterapia* (*Journal of Brazilian Psychotherapy*), *Terapia Psicológica*—Chile, (*Psychological Therapy*—Chile), *Revista Puertorriqueña de Psicología* (*Puerto Rican Journal of Psychology*), and *Revista Interamericana de Psicología* (*Interamerican Journal of Psychology*—from the professional organization, Sociedad Interamericana de Psicología) are some examples of publications that help disseminate the work of Latin American experts in the field.

The process of change, however, is slow. In the realm of supervision, the most widely used textbooks are written in English and primarily feature work from the most developed countries. Only recently have these texts begun to include multicultural and international perspectives from outside the Western context. When reviewing the references in these valuable texts, it becomes evident that contributions from Latin America are largely absent.

Noteworthy, this situation sharply contrasts with the realities of the region. Developments in Latin America are rich and often exhibit a strong, unique character. Experts in supervision across Latin America form a large and diverse group. Like the field of psychotherapy, clinical supervision in Latin America has produced extremely fertile work. For example, the special edition on clinical supervision in the Guatemalan journal *Revista Psicólogos* (*Journal of Psychologists*) published in 2017 and Tena's edited book (2021) are highly valuable. Yet, much of this work remains unknown internationally. This text aims to fill that gap.

Analysis

After exploring the current state of clinical supervision in various countries and regions of Latin America, as well as perspectives from the United States, we reach the culmination of our book. Each chapter uniquely provides rich details and examples of how clinical supervision is practiced, following a common structure. This approach allows for an analysis of clinical supervision in Latin America that was previously unavailable. In this section, we analyze these chapters through four common themes: similarities, differences, challenges, and contributions.

Similarities

Despite the vast distances and diverse contextual realities, the examples in the chapters of this book reflect shared areas of training, professional concerns, theoretical conceptualizations, and practices of clinical supervision in eight Latin American countries and in the care of the large and diverse Latino population in the United States. Consequently, the authors of this volume support the international trend reported a decade ago, where non-Latin American countries recognized the importance of supervision as an indispensable component of professional training in mental health (Watkins & Milne, 2014). Several keys support the vision of clinical supervision as an essential intervention in professional training: (a) the use of ethical codes based on universal concepts and aspirations, (b) the recognized need for formalized supervision training, (c) the importance of supporting supervisees, (d) the attention to social issues as modulating factors, (e) the challenges experienced with limited regulatory and certification structures, and (f) the evolution of theoretical frameworks guiding supervision.

Each country reviewed also supports the core goal of clinical supervision: to develop professional competencies that ensure client protection and community well-being. The commitment to professional psychological service training is evident in all chapters based on humanistic values and universal ethics, striving for best practices, and upholding psychological knowledge. The essence of supervision is, therefore, consistent across international borders (Bernard & Goodyear, 2014, 2019; Consoli et al., 2017; Falender et al., 2021; Falender & Shafranske, 2020; Fernández-Álvarez, 2017; Fernández-Álvarez & Grazioso, 2023; Goodyear & Falender, 2017; Watkins & Milne, 2014). The consensus is that supervision is fundamental in developing the clinical competencies of the mental health professional.

Given the distinct levels of educational preparation common in Latin America, such as *licenciatura* (license) and doctoral degree, more attention is given to supervising students at all levels of preparation for graduation. Additionally, increasingly relevant areas that need further progress include supervisory self-care, grassroots research, and development of culturally relevant evidence-based practices.

Furthermore, the Latin American perspective promotes the standing of supervision at the international level (Creaner & Timulak, 2016; Falender et al., 2021; Forrest, 2010; Watkins & Milne, 2014). These views support psychology's universal training concepts, impacting goals and processes in clinical supervision. However, the authors emphasize the need to consider differences arising from historical, cultural, and linguistic factors, as well as the state of development, preparation, and advancement of the profession in each country. Both perspectives reflect the necessity to recognize a universal vision while considering each country's unique context (Castañeda & Cóbar, 2017). As the authors from Mexico aptly state, "We believe that Mexico and Latin American countries have much to contribute to the dialogue of clinical supervision with characteristics that unite us as Latinos and those that make us unique as countries."

The methods, processes, and formats of supervision are also similar. Goodyear and Falender describe in the previous chapter essential concepts and tools of clinical supervision that support the practice of supervision in the global professional community. Latin American supervisors as indicated in the text also describe the use of several tools that enhance the process of supervision, such as:

(a) Conceptual formulation of the case.
(b) Self-reflection.
(c) Feedback.
(d) Interpersonal skills that facilitate dynamics of change in clinical work.
(e) Parallel processes such as transference and countertransference.
(f) The hierarchy of power.
(g) Reference to a theoretical framework of psychotherapy.
(h) The guiding force of ethical standards.
(i) The value of the alliance between the supervisee and the supervisor.

The prominent formats reported are individual and group supervision, with an increasing use of virtual supervision. On the latter point, we are witnessing the impact of the COVID-19 pandemic as a decisive event legitimizing tele-psychology as a standard practice and influencing the development of this discipline. Despite the opportunities offered by virtual technologies, we adopt a scientific stance on the need to further investigate the advantages and disadvantages of this mode of supervision in our countries (Fernández-Álvarez et al., 2019) and the risks of overlooking contextual variables and available local resources with distant supervision (Thomas, 2014).

Differences

All authors are candid in sharing their professional concerns while highlighting contributions unique to their contexts and experiences. The major differences across the chapters are found in several areas: pedagogical structure, the sequence of applied training processes, professional regulations, evaluation methods, the rate of research and scientific advances, and the idiosyncratic characteristics of diverse countries and regions.

Trends and patterns also emerge. When educational institutions formalize a curriculum with a required supervision course, there seems to be an increased interest in evaluation methods and empirical research. Several chapters refer to the need for assessment tools for supervisees. These evaluation methods contribute to research and the advancement of supervisory models aligned to different contexts. For example, in Guatemala, after completing the clinical supervision course, a team of female supervisors at the Universidad del Valle de Guatemala began collecting data on experiences during supervised practice. Research results led to actions and adaptations in supervision methods that are reflected in current practice (Cóbar et al., 2019).

The spectrum is broad in terms of professional training and supervision requirements, such as hours of supervised practice, allocation of time for supervision, required courses, educational sequences, and advances in training methods. These are closely related to the stage of development of psychology and psychotherapy in each country and region. One interesting factor is the emphasis on supervision in the early stages of training with students and trainees. A few countries, however, address the continued relevance of clinical supervision post-graduation and licensure as a lifelong professional endeavor to strengthen clinical competencies (e.g., Chile, Guatemala, and United States).

Examples of the differences in educational structures are clear. In Cuba, scholastic preparation has historically been the main source of psychological training, focusing on teaching specific therapy techniques for a career in "psychological guidance." Based on 10 years of research, new Cuban perspectives on professional development now favor the establishment of spaces to prepare clinical supervisors. In Colombia, training emphasizes a solid academic curriculum at the advanced and graduate levels, combined with an educational program that includes highly competent clinical supervisors. Chilean psychology educators provide group supervision at the undergraduate level, which shifts to individual supervision at the graduate level. In Guatemala, building clinical competencies through supervision is integrated into the undergraduate specialized 5-year program or *licenciatura* (license), continuing with graduate studies and a required supervision course. Training programs differ between the United States and Puerto Rico. Although both follow the doctoral curriculum requirements set by the American Psychological Association (APA), in Puerto Rico a psychology license is also attainable with a master's degree in psychology.

Differences are also found in methods of evaluation during supervision. Several authors support an indirect and asynchronous supervision style, while others use both direct and indirect supervision methods. However, most in both groups agree that supervision is based on what the supervisee reports to the supervisor.

Challenges and Contributions

The opportunities described and the commitment to high standards of practice shared in the chapters inspire colleagues and educators to create new pathways for professional training. This volume demonstrates that the historical landscape of clinical supervision evolves and responds to the specific contexts of each country, leading to creative and effective solutions that support clinical training. These processes identify common factors shared across different international contexts and specify inherent variables that represent the contextual relevance for each country. In the chapter on Cuba, for example, Zas emphasizes the importance of developing an autochthonous model of supervision that aligns with the country's service delivery model, which is crucial due to the differing socioeconomic and political structures.

In professional preparation, however, there are also challenges that drive the advancement of the profession and advocacy for optimal client/patient care. Below, we discuss examples from the chapters that address these challenges, and the contributions made, transforming clinical supervision in several areas: (a) supervision models, (b) supervisor competencies, (c) supervision formats, (d) multicultural factors, and (e) regulation.

Supervision Models There is a growing interest in applying theoretical and developmental frameworks to supervision while integrating psychotherapy theories. Using a model based on evidence, competencies, and professional development offers consistency and uniformity in the training process. An open theoretical application in case conceptualization, combined with developing clinical skills and a transtheoretical framework in the process of supervision, establishes a solid foundation for professional preparation.

Like the evolution of supervision in several Western regions, most of the countries included in the book are moving beyond the early practice of applying psychotherapy models to supervision, especially those rooted in psychodynamic theories. There is a growing shift towards focusing on professional competencies and related interpersonal supervision interventions through a developmental theory approach. For example, in Argentina, modifications to the supervisory approach include Fernández-Álvarez's (2016) integrative model, which aims at (a) education and training, (b) therapeutic guidance, and (c) institutional counseling.

We also observe how community needs, professional inventiveness, and focused scientific curiosity drive the creation of new models of professional development tailored to each country's realities. Examples of new models include the Psychological Supervision Operational Model (Cuba), frameworks developed in clinical training centers (Brazil, Chile), and evidence-based models (Colombia). In

Mexico, pragmatic models that address the evolution of professionalism, problem-solving skills, and analysis of inconsistencies are popular.

Authors also recognize the influence of personality and psychotherapy theories in supervision. Fernández-Álvarez and Grazioso, in the chapter "Landscape of Clinical Supervision in Latin America," clearly explain the historical evolution of supervision in Latin America, analyzing past and current barriers, the integration of frameworks, and new practice approaches. The theory of supervision based on psychotherapy has adapted well in clinical training in Latin America. For instance, supervision may heavily rely on specific therapeutic models such as cognitive behavioral therapy in some Brazilian training centers or family/systemic therapy in Chilean institutions. In Argentina, the influence of psychotherapeutic models, especially the psychoanalytic approach, has led to methods that strengthen the supervisee's idiosyncratic style, such as the Therapist's Personal Style model. Similarly, the influence of systems therapy in Latin America generates effective methods for refining live monitoring and supervision. In countries with high linguistic and cultural diversity, the multicultural model significantly enhances the supervision process (e.g., Guatemala, United States).

Experts in clinical supervision (Bernard & Goodyear, 2014, 2019; Falender & Shafranske, 2020; Fernández-Álvarez, 2016, 2017; Grazioso et al., 2021; Tena, 2021) emphasize the multiple roles held by the supervisor, such as mentor, evaluator, teacher, counselor, and consultant. Similarly, the book's authors describe the supervisor's multi-roles, which vary by function: *asesoría* (advisory), *guía* (guidance), *mentoría* (mentorship), *enseñanza* (teaching), *entrenación* (training), *orientación* (counseling), and *acompañamiento* (accompaniment).

This latter role has unique implications in Latinx interactions. The term *acompañamiento*, referred to in the Colombian and Guatemalan chapters and used in other Spanish-speaking contexts, holds a special significance in supervision and reflects cultural nuances. Similar to the value of *respeto* (respect), *acompañamiento* is a powerful construct that transcends a literal translation. It embodies broader codes of conduct and behavior among Latinx individuals. *a Acompañamiento* conveys the message from the supervisor to the supervisee, "I am with you" The term carries connotations at various interpersonal levels, highlighting the characteristics of the supervisor-supervisee relationship that supports the "supervisory alliance". It is also understood as approach ability, continuous presence, socio-affective intimacy, tolerance, respect, and transparency with an open mind - processes reflected in what we call "having trust" with equity. Describing clinical supervision as *acompañamiento* thus offers a valuable culturally responsive framework for clinical supervision that warrants empirical exploration and consideration in clinical training.

Frías Villanueva (2021) quotes Cabarrús (2000) in Spanish: "El que acompaña, camina junto al acompañado" ("The one who accompanies walks alongside the accompanied"), while reflecting on the relationship between pedagogical supervision and accompaniment. Borrowing from the pedagogical field, these authors describe how the educator relates to the student trainee in a way that parallels the clinical supervision relationship. The application of this term emphasizes equity and social justice, as well as minimizes the power differential in the supervisor-supervisee dyad (Boroel Cervantes et al., 2018; Frías Villanueva, 2021;

García-Pérez & Mendía, 2015). In clinical supervision, an *acompañamiento* approach can promote openness and receptiveness to feedback among supervisees by reducing anxiety, fears of evaluation and the sense of isolation often embedded in the hierarchical dynamics of supervision.

The process of *acompañamiento* is also linked to cultural humility, an element that strengthens the alliance between the supervisor and supervisee, increases the supervisor's effectiveness, and develops multicultural competencies in the supervisee (Fernández-Álvarez & Grazioso, 2023; Goodyear & Falender, 2017; Watkins, 2023; Watkins & Wang, 2014; Zhang et al., 2021). Cultural humility creates space in supervision discourse to broach cultural characteristics of the supervisor and supervisee (Jones & Branco, 2020), and to explore social justice experiences linked to biases, oppression, and discrimination (Watkins & Wang, 2014) while promoting continuous support, mentoring, and collaboration. The earlier chapter by Goodyear and Falender in this book expands on this essential supervision concept.

Supervision Competencies Except for Argentina, with its high ratio of mental health professionals to residents, the disparity between the limited number of psychologists in the countries discussed and the widespread need for mental health services negatively impacts access to competent supervisors. This issue is also evident in the United States, where there is a shortage of Spanish-speaking service providers and supervisors for the Latinx population (López & Torres Fernández, 2019).

How then are the limitations of competent supervisors addressed? Several chapters elaborate on academic training as the main source of strengthening professional competencies. Notably, in Guatemala, Puerto Rico (doctoral degree), and the United States, a graduate course in clinical supervision is required. Additionally, in Puerto Rico, supervisors must complete mandatory continuing education in clinical supervision each time they renew their psychology license. In Chile, the frequent use of group supervision helps address the shortage of competent supervisors.

An innovative example from Brazil involves students learning about supervision through a systematic process of exposure and modeling, tailored to their educational level. In the early stages of academic preparation, students take on an "observer supervisor" role, followed by an "assistant supervisor" role. After obtaining a bachelor's degree with a specialty in psychology, novice professionals can pursue advanced studies (master's and doctoral degrees). At this level, students assume the role of "supervisory monitors" under the oversight of a "titular supervisor" (professor or site supervisor). This model also includes peer supervision opportunities, a training method used in several countries featured in the book.

What structures support the preparation and competencies of supervisors? Fernández-Álvarez and Grazioso (2023) in their literature review on the trajectory of clinical supervision, report that psychotherapy skills developed without a training structure for supervisors. This gap has contributed to misconceptions about clinical supervision for many years. They emphasize the need to establish clinical supervision competencies as a specific area of specialization, distinct from clinical psychology and psychotherapy competencies. Several authors in this volume report a series of supervision skills not synonymous with psychotherapy skills and structure.

In this context, the Novoa-Gómez study in Colombia highlights the concept of "meta-competence," delineating a series of supervisor skills needed in the supervision process. Chile presents an interesting model for the evolution of supervisors' competencies based on: (a) self-paced training, (b) tutorial training (e.g., modeling, observation, participation, bibliographic information), and (c) informal training (supervision-specific learning structure that includes theories, practice, and integration of ethical standards).

A significant contribution with international implications, native to Latin America, is the creation of the first Higher University Diploma in Clinical Supervision by Héctor Fernández Álvarez of the Fundación Aiglé in Argentina. This board accreditation program requires a systematic and extensive educational approach to develop clinical supervision competencies. Initially begun as psychotherapy training at Fundación Aiglé, Argentina (Fernández-Álvarez, Grazioso, & Kirszman, 2019), this successful professional program has reached the international arena by incorporating virtual and in vivo training modules, benefiting participants from countries such as El Salvador, Guatemala, Paraguay, Spain, and Uruguay. In the United States, supervisory accreditation is only offered for marriage and family therapists and counselors through their respective national organizations, the American Association of Marriage and Family Therapy (AAMFT) and the American Counseling Association (ACA). In Brazil and Chile, supervision certification programs can be earned through psychotherapy training institutes.

Supervision Formats To respond to the needs of their professional communities and the preparation of new professionals, successful format solutions are reported. These are some examples, (a) group supervision that offers a cost effective format and responds to shortage of competent supervisors, (b) the use of a scaffolding or ladder system where supervision is first introduced with modeling followed by peer assistance that advances to more intense supervision involvement at the graduate level (Brazil), (c) professional collaboration with organizations that infuses new support systems to prepare novice students and professionals (Brazil, Mexico), (d) the use of technology as a practical option to increase access to supervision in inaccessible regions, (e) the use of the "supervision of the supervisor" formats (Borders, 2014) to strengthen the competencies of supervisors, especially those who do not have formalized training (Guatemala, United States), and (f) the access to informal supervision formats for practitioner growth and client care (e.g., Guatemala's, "team" and "follow-up of cases" meetings). This last example presents a model outside the traditional context of supervision that is recognized as innovative and enriching (Fernández-Álvarez, 2016).

Multicultural Factors Authors address multiculturalism and social justice factors with nuances. Some describe in detail the multicultural challenges experienced due to the geography of the country (Brazil, Chile), the diversity of the Latino population and the needs for bilingual supervision (United States), the prevalent stigmatization experienced in regions (Chile), the unmet needs of indigenous communities with a wide scope of characteristics (Guatemala, Mexico), the relevance of decolonization in conceptualizations (Puerto Rico), and the socioeconomic, cultural, and historical factors that need careful consideration in supervision (Argentina, Brazil, Chile, Cuba, Colombia, Guatemala, Mexico, Puerto Rico, and United States).

All authors, therefore, acknowledge the historical, sociopolitical, cultural, and geographical panorama of the country as elements that modulate the implementation and practice of supervision. These perspectives reflect what Tsui et al. (2014) describe as the factors that affect multicultural supervision such as the political context, the cultural context, and the organizational context, in addition to the methods of practice and the characteristics of the supervisory trio (e.g., supervisor, supervisee, and client/patient). In the content of the book, greater attention is paid to the three contexts cited with an emphasis on geography, economics, plurality, social inequality, training, and monitoring institutions.

The challenges faced with the underutilization of mental health services are intensified by a lack of uniformity in the expectations of regulation and professional monitoring in countries with distant rural regions. Given the vast geography and great diversity in countries such as Argentina, Brazil, Chile, Colombia, and Mexico, it is postulated that it is exceedingly difficult to set up a standard of supervised practice that responds to all the subcultures that exist in these communities. Oversight described in some countries adopts a cultural sensitivity compensatory framework that encapsulates the cultural contexts of these disenfranchised communities by emphasizing an awareness of social unrest, poverty, prejudice, and oppression in supervision. Competent clinical supervision is, therefore, considered by many in Latin America as an indirect weapon to combat social injustice, discrimination, and inequity of services evident in medical, mental health, and educational systems.

Several practices are contributing to cultural adaptations in this vast territory. Brazilian cultural values guide psychotherapy models and shape the structure and goals of clinical supervision. Therefore, the values of kindness, malleability, and empathy that govern therapeutic processes, also guide supervision practices. These person-centered values, reflecting cultural traits like personalism, contrast with more structured models that focus on supervision tasks and are guided by formal documents, such as supervision contracts and repeated assessments. Although several chapters mention the use of contracts, there is a greater emphasis on personal growth dynamics in supervision. In the United States, where professional malpractice litigation is common, a comprehensive approach to documentation is recommended to reflect continuous formative and summative assessments.

From a research point of view, Chilean supervisors highlight how grassroots scientific exploration advances the understanding of supervision processes native to their country, combining cultural context, clinical theories of psychotherapy, and supervision management. This tailor-made, integrative approach fosters innovative clinical training models (e.g., Multilevel Model, IPM) with a community orientation.

In the context of the supervisor-supervisee-client triad, more understanding is needed on how indigenous languages, social justice experiences, power dynamics, client characteristics, communication style, regulatory practices, and contextual variables intersect in supervision. The vibrant tapestry of cultural differences in Latin America offers opportunities to expand our practical and scientific knowledge of the impact of multicultural competencies in clinical supervision.

Regulation To address the lack of formal supervisor training and the absence of a certification and regulation system, several countries support the advancement of competencies through professional organizations that reinforce codes of ethics (Mexico) and train practitioners in clinical supervision (Brazil). An example from the Brazil chapter is the Federacao Brasileira Organization of Cognitive Therapies, which provides the first certification of specialized clinical supervision in the country.

The lack of a formalized regulatory body complicates the role of supervisors as guardians of the profession. In Puerto Rico and the United States, the judicial system and licensing boards provide systems of checks and balances to ensure adequate client/patient care, clinician competencies, and effective supervision. Given these realities, it is recommended that supervisors maintain professional malpractice insurance coverage.

Conclusions and Implications

The contributors to this volume eloquently testify to the development of clinical supervision in the included countries and regions. Latin America is a vast area with much cultural diversity. We selected countries from the regions that make up the continent: South America, Central America, Insular America (the Caribbean), and North America. We focused on work originally conducted in Spanish, except for Brazil, whose original language is Portuguese, due to their significant contributions to the field. We also included a chapter addressing the large and diverse Latino population in the United States. Lastly, we recognized that professional developments in Latin America are linked to different contextual realities, priorities, theoretical models, and areas of interest.

The work in supervision is associated with various theoretical approaches and structured according to idiosyncratic issues and particular modalities in different countries. Our readers will access a variety of examples from countries as diverse as Mexico and Chile, Colombia and Guatemala, Argentina and Brazil, the United States and Cuba. It is important to note that the selected examples are not exhaustive and do not cover all regions.

Although empirical studies are present, there is a predominance of studies prioritizing experiential aspects of the clinical supervision process. In Latin America, supervision is strongly focused on personal transformation. The available literature shows a strong dedication to qualitative studies, alongside a growing concern for evidence-based supervision. There is increasing interest in developing new assessment tools that respond more closely to regional phenomena and in adapting existing tools to support these contexts.

Multiculturalism continues to be a significant focus in Latin America, a continent rich in diverse roots and nuances. This diversity offers a privileged area for studying supervision processes, providing sustainable contributions for other population groups worldwide. Latin American cultural diversity, while not unique, allows for strong actions of transfer to other latitudes. Future stages of development will include attention to supervisors' self-care, attrition prevention, ethical dilemmas involving dual roles, and advanced education and training to extend supervision services at both educational and professional levels.

The team who prepared this volume themselves reflected the diversity of the region. This enriched the team's meetings, ensuring that the final product adequately represents varied perspectives. We aim for readers to understand that supervision in Latin America is not a mere replica of practices from other regions but is a genuine and original contribution from which we can all learn.

Among the most positive aspects in this area is the active movement taking place lately, aimed at developing systematic supervisor training programs. The cases of the programs under way in Argentina Chile, and Mexico, are very encouraging spearheads. Among the weaknesses, it is worth highlighting the relative delay in the work to develop specific assessment tools (including the correct adaptation of imported instruments) that are extensively used. Another weak point is the lack of regulation and accreditation in the competencies and entrepreneurship of the work of those who practice supervision. Even today, this role is usually fulfilled without adequate mechanisms to guarantee the legitimacy of the practice. So, it puts in a weak place the observance of many ethical issues that, as we know, are a priority in this territory.

We recognize the dynamic quality of human development embedded in clinical supervision and the progress made in the field. Dissonance, exploration, self-reflection, adaptations, and practice strengthen professional growth and service delivery. Latin American scholars and supervisors are advancing knowledge through conscientious work (Consoli et al., 2017; Fernández-Álvarez, 2017). The contributions in this book attest to the struggles and accomplishments of highly committed professionals and scholars of Latin American heritage who are making a difference. We close with the hope that this volume will be a link to continue opening paths of professional growth, empirical curiosity, and collaboration with our Latin American colleagues while transcending geographical, paradigmatic, theoretical, and methodological borders.

References

Bernard, J. M., & Goodyear, R. (2014). *Fundamentals of clinical supervision* (5th ed.). Pearson.

Bernard, J. M., & Goodyear, R. (2019). *Fundamentals of clinical supervision* (6th ed.). Pearson.

Borders, L. D. (2014). Best practices in clinical supervision: Another step delineating effective supervision practices. *American Journal of Psychotherapy, 68*(2), 141–272. https://doi.org/10.1176/appi.psychotherapy.2014.68.2.151

Boroel Cervantes, B., Sánchez Santamaría, J., Morales Gutiérrez, K. D., & Henríquez Ritchie, P. S. (2018). Successful education for all: Tutoring as a process of accompaniment school from the perspective of educational equity. *Revista Fuentes, 20*(2), 91–10. https://doi.org/10.12795/revistafuentes.2018.v20.i2.06

Cabarrús, C. R. (2000). *Cuaderno de bitácoras para acompañar caminantes* (5 edición). Desclée de Brouwer.

Castañeda, T., & Cóbar, A. A. (2017). Nuances of power and authority in clinical supervision in Guatemala. *Revista Psicólogos, II*(20a), 20–28.

Cóbar, A., Cazali, L., Erdemenger de Staebler, I., Gallardo-Cooper, M., & Grazioso, M. (2019). Integrative supervision model: Building a professional identity in the field of psychological counseling in Guatemala. *Brazilian Journal of Psychotherapy, 21*(2), 1–20. https://doi.org/10.5935/2318-0404.20190018

Consoli, A. J., Grazioso, M. P., Musso, A., Seshel, L. A., & Figueroa Briseño, M. (2017). Carta editorial. La supervisión: Perspectivas y horizontes nacionales e internacionales (Editorial letter. Supervision: National and international perspectives and horizons). *Revista Psicólogos, VII*(20a), 4–6.

Creaner, M., & Timulak, L. (2016). Clinical supervision and counseling psychology in the Republic of Ireland. *The Clinical Supervisor, 35*(2), 192–209. https://doi.org/10.1080/07325223.2016.1218812

Falender, C., Goodyear, R., Duan, C., Al-Daramki, F., Bang, K., Cifti, A., Ruiz González, V., Grazioso, M. P., Humeidan, M., Jia, X., Kagnici, D. Y., & Partridge, S. (2021). Lens on international supervision: Lessons learned from a cross-national comparison of supervision. *Journal of Contemporary Psychotherapy, 51*(1), 181–189. https://doi.org/10.1007/s10879-09497-5

Falender, C., & Shafranske, E. (2020). *Basic foundations for the clinical practice of competency-based supervision*. American Psychological Association.

Fernández-Álvarez, H. (2016). Reflections on supervision in psychotherapy. *Psychotherapy Research, 26*(1), 1–10. https://doi.org/10.1080/10503307.2015.1014009

Fernández-Álvarez, H. (2017). El futuro de la supervisión (The future of supervision). *Revista Psicólogos, VII*(20a), 97–108.

Fernández-Álvarez, H., & Grazioso, M. P. (2023). Challenges of supervision in psychotherapy [editorial]. *Journal of Psychotherapy, 34*(126), 1–8. https://doi.org/10.5944/rdp.v34i126.38692

Fernández-Álvarez, H., Grazioso, M. P., & Kirszman, D. (2019). Distant supervision in the Aiglé Foundation's Latin American Psychotherapy Training Program. *Journal of Clinical Psychology, 75*, 282–291. https://doi.org/10.1002/jclp.22721

Forrest, L. (2010). Linking international psychology, professional competence, and leadership: Counseling psychologists as learning partners. *The Counseling Psychologist, 38*(1), 96–120. https://doi.org/10.1177/0011000009350585

Frías Villanueva, G. J. (2021). Supervision versus acompañamiento (Supervision versus accompaniment). https://es.scribd.com/document/52365733472-Supervision-Versus-Acompañamiento

García-Pérez, A., & Mendía, R. (2015). Acompañamiento educativo: El rol del educador en aprendizaje y servicio solidario (Educational accompaniment: The role of the educator in solidarity learning and service). *Profesorado: Revista de Currículum y Formación de Profesorado, 19*(1), 42–58.

Goodyear, R., & Falender, C. (2017). Cómo pueden psicólogos/as maximizar su efectividad como supervisores/as? Ocho condiciones esenciales (How can psychologists maximize their effectiveness as supervisors? Eight essential conditions). *Revista Psicólogos, VII*(20a), 83–96.

Grazioso, M. P., Lubina, M., & Cóbar, A. A. (2021). Perspectivas sobre el desarrollo de la supervisión clínica en Guatemala. In A. Tena Suck (Ed.), *Supervisión clínica en psicoterapia: una guía con las mejores prácticas* (pp. 85–102). Vesalius.

Jones, C. T., & Branco, S. F. (2020). The interconnectedness between cultural humility and broaching in clinical supervision: Working from the multicultural orientation framework. *The Clinical Supervisor, 39*, 198–209. https://doi.org/10.1080/07325223.2020.1830327

López, A., & Torres Fernández, I. (2019). Exploring the experiences of supervisors and supervisees who engage in bilingual supervision. *Journal of Counselor Preparation and Supervision, 12*(1). https://digitalcommons.sacredheart.edu/jcps/vol12/iss1/10

Tena, A. (2021). *Supervisión clínica en psicoterapia: una guía con las mejores prácticas*. Vesalius.

Thomas, J. T. (2014). International ethics for psychotherapy supervisors: Principles, practices, and future directions. In C. E. Watkins & D. L. Milne (Eds.), *The Wiley international handbook of clinical supervision* (pp. 131–154). Wiley.

Tsui, M., O'Donoghue, K., & Ng, A. K. T. (2014). Culturally competent and diversity-sensitive clinical supervision: An international perspective. In C. E. Watkins & D. L. Milne (Eds.), *The Wiley international handbook of clinical supervision* (pp. 238–254). Wiley.

Watkins, C. E. (2023). Incorporating cultural humility and humbling guidelines into the psychotherapy supervised relationship: A commitment and a promise. *Journal of Psychotherapy, 34*(126), 9–18.

Watkins, C. E., & Milne, D. I. (2014). Clinical supervision at the international crossroads: Current status and future directions. In C. E. Watkins & D. L. Milne (Eds.), *The Wiley international handbook of clinical supervision* (pp. 673–696). Wiley.

Watkins, C. E., & Wang, C. D. C. (2014). On the education of clinical supervisors. In C. E. Watkins & D. L. Milne (Eds.), *The Wiley international handbook of clinical supervision* (pp. 171–203). Wiley.

Zhang, H., Watkins, E., Hook, J. N., Hodge, A. S., Davis, C. W., Norton, J., Wilcox, M. M., Davis, D. E., DeBlaere, C., & Owen, J. (2021). Cultural humility in psychotherapy and clinical supervision: A research review. *Counseling and Psychotherapy Research, 22*(3), 548–557. https://doi.org/10.1002/capr.12481

Maritza Gallardo-Cooper is a faculty member in the Department of Clinical and School Psychology at Nova Southeastern University, Florida. She has an extensive professional career working in the public and private sectors as a practitioner, supervisor, and administrator. Her professional experience includes the development of outpatient and residential clinics, school psychological services, prevention programs, clinical supervision, and internship programs. She has published several articles/chapters as well as co-authored two books on counseling Latinx populations in the USA. She has received recognition from the professional community for her leadership, innovation, and clinical performance. Dr. Gallardo-Cooper is a graduate from the University of Puerto Rico, received her master's degree from the University of Houston and her doctorate from the University of Florida. Her professional interests include therapeutic assessments, psychocultural factors in prevention and intervention, crisis intervention in schools, and bilingual practice and supervision. Email: mg1011@nova.edu

Hector Fernandez-Alvarez (1944–2023) obtained a PhD in Psychology, and was a psychotherapist, founder, and president of the Aiglé Foundation; since 1977 dedicated his work on education and training, research, and mental health assistance programs. He directed the Foundation's Center for Research in Psychotherapy and developed a Supervision Program based on his experience as a therapist and supervisor, the Specialization Career in Cognitive Psychotherapy of the Aiglé Foundation and at the National University of Mar del Plata and was a postgraduate professor at Argentine and foreign universities. He wrote, among others, the books Fundamentals of an Integrative Model in Psychotherapy; Intervention Guide in Personality Disorders; Integration in psychotherapy and social anxiety, conceptualization, and treatment. Among the many recognitions, he received the 2022 Distinguished Award for the International Advancement of Psychotherapy from Division 29 of the American Psychological Association (APA) and the International Sigmund Freud Award for Psychotherapy 2002 of the City of Vienna from the World Council for Psychotherapy (WCP). He chaired the Inter-American Society of Psychology (IAPA) and the Latin American chapter of the Society for Psychotherapy Research (SPR).

Ana Alicia Cobar holds a PhD in Applied Psychology, a master's degree in Psychological Counseling and Mental Health, and a bachelor's degree in psychology from the Universidad del Valle de Guatemala. Specialization in Family and Couple Psychotherapy with Cognitive Behavioral Orientation from Fundación Aiglé, Argentina and Universidad de Maimonides, Argentina. Internships at the Ackerman Family Institute in New York. Director, teacher, and supervisor in the Department of Psychological Counseling and Mental Health. Professor in the Department of Applied Neuropsychology and in the master's degree in Community Counseling at the Universidad del Valle de Guatemala. She is a member of the Aiglé Guatemala Project Association where she conducts her private practice as a psychotherapist and counselor for adults, couples, families, as well as providing clinical supervision. Areas of interest in research and publication are counseling, well-being and quality of life, self-management competencies, clinical supervision, crisis care, and expressive arts interventions. Member of the College of Psychologists of Guatemala, Inter-American Society of Psychology, Guatemala Chapter and American Psychological Association. Emails: aacoma@proyectoaigle.org.gt; aacobar@uvg.edu.gt

Rodney K. Goodyear is a professor emeritus at the University of Southern California, where he directed the APA-accredited doctoral program in counseling psychology for two decades, and at the University of Redlands. He has been a member of the American Psychological Association's Commission on Accreditation, past president of the Society for the Advancement of Psychotherapy, APA Division 29, and served on the APA's Board of Educational Affairs (BEA) Oversight Guidelines Working Group. In 2015 he received the APA Distinguished Professional Contributions to Psychology Education and Training Award, and in 2018 the Distinguished Award for the International Advancement of Psychotherapy, Society for the Advancement of Psychotherapy, APA Division 29. He is co-author of Fundamentals of Clinical Supervision (2019), now in its sixth edition, and author of numerous chapters and articles on supervision. His work is increasingly focused on the international arena. Email: rodk.goodyear@gmail.com

Carol A. Falender has co-authored/edited seven books on clinical supervision and consultation and has presented workshops on clinical supervision, consultation, multicultural supervision, and decolonizing supervision. She led APA-accredited internship programs for more than 20 years and was chair of the American Psychological Association's (APA) Supervisory Guidelines Working Group. She received an APA Presidential Citation for his groundbreaking contributions to the theory and practice of clinical supervision, nationally and internationally, and received the APA's 2018 Distinguished Professional Contributions to Psychology Education and Training Award, and in 2023, the 29 Division Distinguished Award, Society for the Advancement of Psychotherapy, the Distinguished Award for the International Advancement of Psychotherapy. Dr. Falender is an adjunct professor at Pepperdine University; Clinical Professor, University of California, Los Angeles, Department of Psychology. Email: cfalender@gmail.com

Maria del Pilar Grazioso has expertise in pediatric development and learning, community mental health, prevention, gender, multiculturalism, higher education, psychotherapy, counseling, and supervision. She has held administrative, research, teaching, and clinical positions, as well as professional duties in higher education and private practice. She developed graduate programs and began formal training in supervision at the university level in Guatemala. She has publications and recognition for her leadership and contributions to the development of Psychology having leadership positions at the international level. She is currently co-coordinator of the Aiglé Guatemala Project Association and is a researcher affiliated with the Universidad del Valle de Guatemala and Maya Health Alliance/Wuqukawoc. Email: mpgrazioso@proyectoaigle.org.gt

Correction to: Clinical Supervision in Latin America

Maria del Pilar Grazioso, Rodney K. Goodyear, Maritza Gallardo-Cooper, Hector Fernandez-Alvarez, Carol A. Falender, and Ana Alicia Cobar

Correction to:
M. P. Grazioso et al. (eds.), *Clinical Supervision in Latin America*, https://doi.org/10.1007/978-3-031-82373-2

The name of the author "Maritza Gallardo-Cooper" was misspelled in the initially published version and has been corrected throughout the book.

The updated version of this book can be found at
https://doi.org/10.1007/978-3-031-82373-2

M. P. Grazioso et al. (eds.), *Clinical Supervision in Latin America*,
https://doi.org/10.1007/978-3-031-82373-2_14

Index

M. P. Grazioso et al. (eds.), *Clinical Supervision in Latin America*,
https://doi.org/10.1007/978-3-031-82373-2

The manufacturer's authorised representative in the EU is Springer Nature Customer Service Centre GmbH, Europaplatz 3, 69115 Heidelberg, Germany. If you have any concerns regarding our products, please contact ProductSafety@springernature.com

Printed and bound by CPI Group (UK) Ltd, Croydon, CR0 4YY
30/09/2026
02225302-0006